Japan's Economic D

The Japanese economy, after decades of seemingly unsurpassable competitiveness, experienced a major crisis in the 1990s. The depth of the crisis has been as remarkable as Japan's renowned meteoric success. Economies rise and fall, to be sure; but the magnitude of the Japanese economy's swing within such a short time, and in the absence of major wars, is unprecedented. Observers of Japan are faced with a challenging question: How can one explain Japan's seemingly abrupt reversal from stunning prosperity to dismal stagnation?

Bai Gao, in this most illuminating and broadly comprehensive analysis of Japan's economic story, not only explains the reversion but also goes beyond other analyses to demonstrate how the same economic institutions could produce both stunning international economic success *and* the subsequent, intractable slump of the 1990s.

As with several recent studies of Japan's economic reversal, Gao finds seeds of the dilemma in Japan's failure to adjust the emphases of its postwar economic policy-making to changing world market conditions in the 1970s. But that account alone fails to explain why the path of Japanese economic growth has not been one long decline since the 1970s. Unlike other analyses, Gao's institutional explanation accommodates the inconvenient fact of Japan's spectacular growth spurt in the 1980s. By comparing the internal and external factors that sustained miracle growth in Japan in the 1960s and 1970s with the factors that led to the bubble economy of the late 1980s, Gao sheds new light on the long-term internal tensions in the Japanese economic system and describes how and why they came to create problems and finally to "burst the bubble" in the 1990s.

Scholars and students of the Japanese economy and politics, economic sociologists, economic analysts, and observers of globalization will find much useful and important information in this book. Those who have been following the lively debate over "What became of the Japanese miracle?" will be rewarded by Gao's richly detailed, historically informed, and multilayered contribution. More generally, his explanation of the ways in which Japan's internal economic policies and structures have clashed and merged with global economic developments enriches our understanding of the recent history of capitalism.

Bai Gao is Associate Professor in the Department of Sociology at Duke University. He is the author of *Economic Ideology and Japanese Industrial Policy: Developmentalism from 1931 to 1965* (Cambridge University Press, 1997), which received the 1998 Hiromi Arisawa Memorial Award for Best Book in Japanese Studies from the Association of American University Presses.

JAPAN'S
ECONOMIC
DILEMMA

THE INSTITUTIONAL ORIGINS OF
PROSPERITY AND STAGNATION

BAI GAO

Duke University

CAMBRIDGE
UNIVERSITY PRESS

PUBLISHED BY THE PRESS SYNDICATE OF THE UNIVERSITY OF CAMBRIDGE
The Pitt Building, Trumpington Street, Cambridge, United Kingdom

CAMBRIDGE UNIVERSITY PRESS
The Edinburgh Building, Cambridge CB2 2RU, UK
40 West 20th Street, New York, NY 10011-4211, USA
10 Stamford Road, Oakleigh, VIC 3166, Australia
Ruiz de Alarcón 13, 28014 Madrid, Spain
Dock House, The Waterfront, Cape Town 8001, South Africa

http://www.cambridge.org

First published 2001

Printed in the United States of America

Typeface Garamond 3 11/13 pt.   *System* QuarkXPress [BTS]

A catalog record for this book is available from the British Library.

Library of Congress Cataloging in Publication Data

Gao, Bai, 1955–
Japan's economic dilemma : the institutional origins of prosperity and stagnation / Bai Gao.
p.   cm.
Includes bibliographical references and index.
ISBN 0-521-79025-5 – ISBN 0-521-79373-4 (pb.)
1. Japan – Economic conditions – 1989–   2. Financial crises – Japan.   I. Title.
HC462.95 .G36 2001
330.952–dc21

2001025592

ISBN   0 521 79025 5   hardback
ISBN   0 521 79373 4   paperback

To the Memory of Marius B. Jansen (1922–2000)

CONTENTS

ACKNOWLEDGMENTS

During the process of this study, I received help and advice from many people. Without them, this book would have been a different one.

I owe special thanks to John C. Campbell, Rogers Hollingsworth, Richard Katz, and T. J. Pempel, who flew to Durham only several hours after Hurricane Floyd hit North Carolina in September 1999 to attend a workshop to critique this manuscript. Their tough criticism and constructive suggestions have helped me in many ways in the final revision. To be specific, John Campbell reminded me of the complicated dimensions in the studies on the welfare state, and as a result I decided to limit my discussion of social protection to the issue of unemployment. Rogers Hollingsworth encouraged me to take the fate of capitalism as the major issue in organizing the analytical framework for this book. Richard Katz reminded me of Robert Mundell's position on the floating exchange rate. T. J. Pempel suggested that I change the structure of the book from chronological to one tightly organized around a comparison between the high growth and the period following. I also thank the others who attended the workshop and gave me various helpful comments, including Raphael Allen, Ravi Bansal, Mary Child, John Coleman, Miles Fletcher, Martin Seeleib-Kaiser, Rob Sikorski, Masahiko Tatebayashi, and Edward Tiryakin.

I also received valuable comments from Frank Dobbin, Harry First, Roger Haydon, Peter Lange, Calvin Morris, Alvin So, and Edward Tiryakin on various versions of chapters or papers related to this study.

My biggest debt is to Bob Keohane. When I first talked to him about the dilemma of strong coordination and weak control and monitoring in the Japanese economy in the fall of 1998, he immediately encouraged me to place the focus of my framework on this dilemma and invited me to join the Duke Initiative on Globalization and Democratic Governance, which he headed. Throughout 1999, we had numerous meetings to discuss this project. I benefited greatly from his broad knowledge about the international political economy. Bob provided a generous grant, which enabled me to organize a special workshop on this project to which I was lucky to invite four outside experts and many Duke colleagues to comment on an earlier draft of the manuscript. In addition, he chaired the workshop on my behalf.

The fieldwork in Japan on this project was supported financially by two research grants: one from the Japan Foundation, and the other from the Social Science Research Council. Duke University also paid half of my salary during my leave in the spring of 1995. The School of International Business and Law at the Yokohama National University, the Faculty of Economics at Hitotsubashi University, and the Faculty of Law at Tokyo Keizai University hosted me as a visiting scholar and provided access to their libraries and housing arrangements. I want to thank Amakawa Akira, Nakamura Masanori, and Takemae Eiji for making these arrangements. Glen Fukushima, Kazuyuki Funabashi, Edward Lincoln, and Kisugi Shin spent their valuable time on interviews with me, and Chalmers Johnson and Sakai Tatsu helped arrange these meetings.

I presented the research for this project on various occasions, including several annual meetings of the American Sociological Association between 1994 and 2000, the 1998 annual meeting of the Law and Society Association at Aspen, Colorado, the University of California at Los Angeles, Harvard University, the University of Kentucky, and Yale University. I thank these audiences for their comments. I also thank Andrew Gordon and Steve Vogel for first inviting me to try out some of the basic ideas presented in this book at Harvard in 1997.

I owe special thanks to Mary Child, the social science editor at Cambridge University Press. I really appreciate her great confidence in this project and her effort of attending the workshop when the town in which she lived in New Jersey was still flooded as a result of Hurricane Floyd. Her detailed organizational and editorial advice was the key factor in the publication of this book. Copy editor Betsy Hardinger enormously improved my expression of ideas, and it was a pleasure to work with her. Production editor Camilla Knapp ensured that the whole production process went smoothly.

This book is dedicated to Marius B. Jansen, a great teacher of mine at Princeton University, who passed away on December 10, 2000.

Finally, I want to thank my family members. My father-in-law, Yongdeng Yang, my mother-in-law, Nongsheng Wang, and my wife's aunt Yufeng Liu came at different times to help us take care of our children. During the six years I spent on this project, my wife, Hongqiu, not only traveled to Japan twice with me and gave birth to both our son Michael and our daughter Julia, but also finished her own Ph.D. dissertation and started her own career after staying at home with our children for two years. Only she and our children can tell how much more time I was able to spend with them after the completion of this project.

Figure 4.1 (this volume) is a reprint of Figure 4.8, "Japan Invests Much More than Others," from *Japan, The System that Soured* by Richard Katz, © 1998 by M.E. Sharpe. Used by permission of the publisher M.E. Sharpe.

Table 6.1 (this volume) is reprinted from Michael Loriaux et al., *Capital Ungoverned: Liberalizing Finance in Interventionist States*. Copyright © 1997 by Cornell University. Used by permission of the publisher, Cornell University Press.

CHAPTER 1

INTRODUCTION

After demonstrating seemingly unsurpassable competitiveness for several decades, the Japanese economy experienced a major reversion from prosperity to stagnation in the 1990s. Observers confront a daunting question: How do we explain this reversion?

Some comparative statistics will illustrate the extent of the crisis. In the period following World War II, Japanese economic growth was astounding, occurring at an average annual rate of 9.3 percent in 1956–1973 and 4.1 percent in 1975–1991. From 1946 to 1976, the Japanese economy increased 55-fold (Johnson 1982, 6). Between 1955 and 1973, Japan quadrupled its gross domestic product (GDP) per worker from $3,500 to $13,500. This sustained record of growth is reflected in the conclusion drawn by Richard Katz (1998, 55): "No other major country, before or since, has managed this all-important development task in such a short time."

In the last decade of the twentieth century, however, the bubble of the Japanese economy burst. The depth of the crisis was as astonishing as the extent of the preceding success. In the 1990s, the Japanese economy grew at a mere 1 percent per year on average. In 1997 and 1998, it even experienced negative growth. According to one estimate, Japan lost 800 trillion yen in the stock and real estate markets between 1989 and 1992; this loss was equivalent to 11.3 percent of the country's national wealth. Both markets continued to slump after 1992, sinking to (or below) levels perhaps comparable to those in World War II, during which Japan lost 14 percent of its national wealth (Kikkawa 1998, 6–7).[1,2]

---

1 In the text, Japanese names appear according to Japanese custom, with the surname preceding the personal name. In the references, Japanese authors use surname-first order for Japanese-language publications and surname-last order for English publications.
2 This comparison may be an exaggeration. According to another source, Japan lost more than 25 percent, instead of merely 14 percent, of its national wealth during World War II. See Arisawa Hiromi (1976, 241).

I

Although the rise and fall of an economy is nothing unusual in history, the magnitude of the Japanese economy's swing within such a short period of time, in the absence of major wars, is unprecedented. The fall of the Japanese economy from glory to chaos presents a serious challenge for students of Japanese capitalism. Before the crisis of the 1990s, observers were engaged in constant debates attempting to explain the economy's high growth rate. With the advent of the recent crisis, a new explanation is needed as to why this highly successful model of capitalism suddenly reversed its course.[3] And as if each of these two spectacular processes weren't enough, students of Japanese political economy confront the most challenging task of all: to explain Japan's past success and its recent failure and to discover a coherent link between them.

THREE THEORIES

Several studies in the English-language literature have tried to explain the reversion of the Japanese economy by comparing its past prosperity and its present stagnation.

Robert Brenner emphasizes "the capital accumulation and profitability of the system as a whole" (1998, 23). Through an analysis of the American, Japanese, and German economies, Brenner provides a structural account of what he calls the long downturn of not only these three economies but also the global capitalist system as a whole in the second half of the twentieth century. Brenner argues that capitalist production is unplanned, uncoordinated, and competitive. Furthermore, competition in manufacturing involves large, fixed-capital investments in facilities and equipment. These facilities, however, tend to become outdated. In the 1950s and 1960s, sustained by a set of institutions that enabled the state, the banks, and the manufacturing industry to coordinate with each other, Japan and Germany enjoyed the advantages of unencumbered modernization through fixed-capital investment. This strong coordination not only protected Japan's domestic markets but also channeled its investments into new technologies. Then, when Japanese and German products penetrated the American market on a massive scale, rival fixed-capital physical plants were locked in confrontation, with no easy escape

---

3 Many studies have offered explanations of the recent crisis of the Japanese economy. Some studies focus on international factors. They argue that its causes include Reaganomics, the liberalization of finance, the coordination of multinational monetary policy, and rules promulgated by the Bank of International Settlements (Johnson 1998; Kikkawa 1998; Konishi 1999; McKinnon and Ohno 1997; Krugman 1999a, 1999b; Shibata 1996; Wade 1999; Yamada Shinichi 1996). In contrast, others have emphasized domestic factors. They have traced the origin of the crisis to either individual institutions, such as the Ministry of Finance and the Bank of Japan, or individual policies such as fiscal policy or window guidance (Asher 1996; Grimes 1995; Murphy 1996; Posen 1998; Werner 1999). For a discussion of window guidance, see also Chapter 2 of this volume.

to alternative lines of production. As a result, profits fell dramatically and in tandem across the entire advanced capitalist world. Even after two decades, they had still not recovered. As lower-cost producers continued to enter global competition, the rate of return on the older capitalist enterprises in advanced industrialized countries was further depressed. As a result, there was intensified, horizontal intercapitalist competition for overbuilt production capacity, and this competition in turn led to the fall of profitability at the aggregate level. The result was the long downturn of capitalism (Brenner 1998).

Richard Katz (1998) explains the reversion of the Japanese economy using the theory of development stages. He holds that the "catch-up" effect may explain 70 percent to 80 percent of Japanese growth and that the role played by state-mandated industrial and trade policies was simply to accelerate a normal catch-up process. In the 1950s and 1960s, many industries in the Japanese economy were in their infancy. The state's protection of these industries and its promotion of exports helped to sustain a set of catch-up structural processes: the economies of scale increased, the whole economy was shifting toward higher-productivity industries, the country imported technologies aggressively, and productivity increased in the agricultural sector. Meanwhile, the promotion of exports through government subsidies, along with the protection of domestic markets, sustained industrial growth through the rapid development of manufacturing industries. As the Japanese economy matured in the early 1970s, however, exports were no longer able to keep the economy growing. Meanwhile, the system began to resist the transformation of economic structures. Increasingly, state policy was aimed at preserving existing industries in an effort to protect resources unwisely invested in capital-intensive sectors and thereby prevent unemployment and maintain wage equality. As market-conforming industrial policy was replaced by market-defying industrial policy, the economy was "cartelized" and the dynamics for further growth were dampened.

T. J. Pempel (1998) offers a broad political explanation based on what he calls "regime shift." A regime, according to Pempel, consists of socioeconomic alliances, political economic institutions, and a public policy profile. Pempel attributes the primary sources of change to three important factors: socioeconomic alliances, the pattern of electoral politics, and the changes in international environments beginning in the early 1970s. During Japan's high growth period, conservatives dominated the electoral process. Public policies were adopted that strengthened the regime's socioeconomic base and increased overall public support. The regime also discredited the conservatives' political opponents, enhanced the conservatives' ability to control political offices, and minimized the need for compromise. However, as the economic structure shifted from agriculture to manufacturing industries, family businesses were increasingly replaced by corporations, and the tight labor market enhanced the bargaining power of labor unions. At the same time, the electoral pattern switched from two dominant political parties to multiple political parties. That began to threaten the conservatives' electoral hegemony. As a result of these changes, state economic policy-making became politicized, management had to compromise with labor unions, the government had to engage in deficit spending to enhance social infrastructure, and Japanese companies ceased being "embedded mercantilists" and became "international investors." All these factors eventually led to the Liberal Democratic Party's loss in the 1993 election.

These studies offer new insights that assist our understanding of Japanese political economy. First, they join a stream of recent social science studies that focus on the national economic system as the unit of analysis in the studies of comparative political economy.[4] As the distinctive patterns of national responses by the major industrialized countries to the First and Second Oil Shocks gave birth to the field of international and comparative political economy in the late 1970s, the ongoing debate on globalization has focused new attention on the national models of capitalist economies. This approach emphasizes "the systematic analysis of advanced capitalist economies," and it defines the institutional framework primarily at the national level, casting light on "how differences across economies in the con-figurations of these institutions might explain differences in micro behavior" (Soskice 1999, 101–102). This model is concerned not only with "identify-ing the various institutional mechanisms by which economic activity is co-ordinated" but also with "understanding the circumstances under which these various mechanisms are chosen, and with comprehending the logic inherent in different coordinating mechanisms" (Hollingsworth and Boyer 1997b, 1).

Second, these recent studies treat the early 1970s as the turning point at which a highly successful model of economic growth began to reverse its course. This is a major revision of the conventional wisdom of the past two decades, which interprets Japan's adaptation to the two oil shocks in the 1970s as highly successful, especially compared with that of other advanced industrialized countries. These studies show that although the macro-economic performance of the Japanese economy demonstrated no sign of approaching a major crisis until the early 1990s, an ex post analysis indicates

---

4 Several recent edited volumes represent this new trend. See Berger and Dore (1997), Kitschelt et al. (1999), and Hollingsworth and Boyer (1997a). In Japanese studies, the tradition of taking the Japanese economic system as the unit of analysis with clear comparative implications is reflected in the works of Johnson (1982), Dore (1973, 1987), Samuels (1987), and Vogel (1979). For recent studies on Japan that have attempted to adopt the national economic system as the unit of analysis, see Aoki and Okuno (1997 [1996]), Gao (1997), Noguchi (1995), Okazaki and Okuno (1993); Pempel (1998), and Vogel (1996).

that serious internal problems had begun to grow, masked by the rapid expansion of Japanese economic power in the international markets in the 1970s and 1980s. In global capitalist production, the success of Japan and Germany in exporting their products to the international markets not only went hand in hand with the failing competitiveness of the United States in 1971–1989 but also contributed to overproduction and to the decline of profitability of global capitalism as a whole. That triggered a long downturn of capitalism in all advanced industrialized countries (Brenner 1998). From the early 1970s, the Japanese economy was losing its momentum in catch-up. As a result, Japan's early practice of protecting domestic markets through heavy government regulation and cartels caused a serious problem of inefficiency (Katz 1998). Reflecting this structural change in the economy, both socioeconomic alliances and electoral patterns changed profoundly, leading to a politicized process of economic policy-making (Pempel 1998).

POINT OF DEPARTURE

My point of departure from these studies lies in the nature of the changes after the early 1970s that caused the reversion of the Japanese economy.[5] Methodologically, I contend that the nature of such changes can be better understood by comparing the state of the Japanese economy during the period of high growth with that during the 1980s. The reversion of the Japanese economy did not appear in a straightforward fashion of stagnation beginning in the early 1970s and continuing along a linear direction. Rather, before the crisis of the 1990s, the Japanese economy witnessed a sudden spurt of energy in an extreme form – the astonishing economic prosperity known today as the bubble. Any explanation of the reversion that fails to make the bubble of the 1980s the central point of analysis will miss an important episode and its accompanying theoretical significance. In the English-language literature, the 1980s are marked as a decade in which studies on Japanese political economy were dominated by issues related to trade and industrial policy (but see Sassen 1991); these studies focused on the strength of the Japanese economic system in production. In Japanese economic history, however, the 1980s was also highlighted by financial and monetary issues. It was during the 1980s that Japan emerged as the largest creditor country in the world; Tokyo overtook New York, becoming the largest international financial market; the land price of the imperial palace in Tokyo was worth more than

---

5 Indeed, comparing the period of high growth with the crisis of the 1990s provides a sharp contrast. It does not, however, help us enough to reveal the theoretical significance of this difference. The reason is that as long as there is a bubble, the burst is inevitable. Therefore, what is important is not why the bubble bursts or how badly it bursts but rather why the bubble occurs in the first place.

that of the entire state of California; Japanese investments were often the focus of intense interest in the North American mass media; and, after all, the prices of both stocks and land rose sharply, leading directly to the bubble. Trade- and production-related issues attracted great international attention in the 1980s. However, the most profound changes in the 1980s – not only in the Japanese economy but also in the international economy – were the emer- gence of financial and monetary issues and their interweaving with trade and industrial policy issues (Arrighi 1994; Frieden 1987; Gilpin 1987, 2000; McKinnon and Ohno 1997; Murphy 1996; Strange 1986). As the 1985 Plaza Accord indicates, even the means of reducing the U.S. trade deficits with Japan were no longer limited to strengthening the competitiveness of Amer- ican corporations or opening Japan's domestic markets; fiscal and monetary policies began to play an important role.

This study of the reversion of the Japanese economy from prosperity to stagnation adopts a kind of reverse logic. The existing literature, influenced by the research paradigm of trade and production, tends to treat the Japanese economic system as a successful model in the high growth period, a system that soured only after it became mature or after its strong competitiveness resulted in overproduction by the world capitalist system; Japanese politics is perceived as successfully maintaining a national consensus to promote exports during the high growth period, an approach that failed only after the socioeconomic alliances changed the electoral pattern. In contrast, I take the rise and the burst of the bubble as the starting point of theoretical reasoning. Rather than beginning with how the Japanese model was success- ful in promoting trade and production and then examining how this success- ful model was made obsolete by the structural changes beginning in the early 1970s, I derive my analytical framework by focusing on the institutions and mechanisms that sustained the bubble of the 1980s and reexamining their conditions during the high growth period, asking these questions: Did these institutions and mechanisms exist before? If they did, why did they not cause any major problem to the Japanese economy during the high growth period? What environmental changes made these factors a problem in the 1980s?[6] By

---

6 Both Brenner (1998, 79–82) and Pempel (1998, 65–73) discussed the impact of Japanese economic institutions on the high growth period. However, they attributed the dynamics of the reversion to struc- tural changes in both international and domestic economies. In the main thrust of their arguments, they paid less attention to, or at least failed to theorize on, the impact of these economic institutions on the reversion of the Japanese economy. In contrast, Katz (1998, 218–223) touched on some of the institutional impact on the rise of the bubble but did not trace this impact on the period of high growth. Stated differently, these authors have made a structural argument with institutional compo- nents. In contrast, I make an institutional argument with structural components, suggesting that the structural changes were nurtured, developed, and triggered by the intrinsic dilemmas contained in the international economic order and the domestic economic system, and that the structural changes in turn led to further institutional changes, including both adaptation and crisis.

applying the logic of reverse thinking, we can arrive at a set of coherent variables that have contributed to both the high growth and the bubble, and in this way we avoid using different variables to explain different stages. As a result, we can not only reveal the causal mechanisms of the reversion but also shed light on how the high growth was really sustained.

Emphasizing the financial and monetary side of the Japanese economy does not mean rejecting the importance of issues related to trade and industrial policy. Rather, it means reexamining these issues from a new angle. My emphasis is on how the innovation in production technology was financed in the 1950s and 1960s, through what mechanisms the innovation triggered the high-speed economic growth, what role the state really played in the process of industrial finance, and, more importantly, what it was in the financial and monetary institutions' design that promoted high growth but also contained the seeds of the rise of the bubble. The existing literature highlights the causal relationships between strong coordination in the Japanese economic system and Japan's success in achieving economic growth, and between the nation's highly egalitarian system of distribution and the resilience of the welfare society. A reexamination of the trade and industrial policy issues from the standpoint of financial and monetary issues, however, implies three other possibilities. First, these relationships may have been more co-relational than causal; second, although these relationships were causal, what worked in the past may not have worked in a new environment; and third, although the relationships were causal, the institutional configuration of the Japanese economic system that sustained these relationships also might have involved major tradeoffs.

Comparing the high growth period with the bubble and reexamining the trade and industrial policy issues from an angle of financial and monetary issues help us to capture two profound changes in the long-term movement of capitalist economies since the early 1970s: the shift in the cycle of capital accumulation from the expansion of trade and production to the expansion of finance and monetary activity, and the shift in the major policy paradigms in advanced capitalist economies from social protection to the release of market forces.[7] Unlike the structural changes along a leaner direction conceptualized by the three studies discussed earlier, the two shifts I discuss here have taken place repeatedly in the long-term movement of capitalist economies.

To put these shifts into perspective, let us take a brief look backward. Historically, capitalist economies have experienced repeated cycles of capital

---

7 The discussion on social protection or welfare state throughout this book is limited to the issue of unemployment, although social protection also involves other issues such as pensions and health care.

accumulation under each hegemonic order. In each cycle, according to Giovanni Arrighi (1994, 300; see also Arrighi and Silver 1999, 31), after a major expansion of trade and production, over-accumulation of capital and intense interstate competition for mobile capital would lead to an expansion of finance and monetary activity. In the postwar expansion of trade and production in 1950–1971, corporations in advanced industrialized countries invested heavily in fixed capital, but they faced vigorous competition from the latecomer countries in industrialization, and that led to the decline of corporate profitability starting in the early 1970s (Arrighi 1994; Arrighi and Silver 1999; Brenner 1998). Driven by what John M. Keynes (1920, 25) calls "the law of diminishing return," the expansion of finance and monetary activity became an alternative means to pursue profits, leading to widespread bank lending to the Third World and the growth of the Eurodollar markets (Hirst and Thompson 1996, 5). Meanwhile, the need to create new financial instruments to help the private sector hedge the risks of foreign exchange strongly demanded the removal of the regulatory barriers that previously restrained the free flow of capital across national borders (Eatwell and Taylor 2000). This does not mean that the expansion of trade and production was completely replaced by the expansion of finance and monetary activity; in fact, trade-to-GDP ratios in the advanced countries continued to increase. Rather, it means that the national economic systems began to face a completely new environment. Because "money's fructifying, enabling power for good [is] matched by its terrible disruptive, destructive power for evil, [and] mismanagement of money and credit [is] more dangerous than protectionism in the trade policy" (Strange 1986, vi–vii), sooner or later the expansion of finance and monetary activity will lead to a major crisis of capitalist economies on the global scale, a crisis in which the old international economic order is destroyed and a new one is created. Such a cycle has happened under all three major hegemonies – the Dutch, the British, and the American – in the history of capitalism (Arrighi 1994, 300). In this sense, what we know today as the globalization of production and the globalization of finance represent two different stages in the cycle of capital accumulation, with the globalization of finance signaling an increasing instability in the international economic order. Seen in such a context, what happened in Japan during the past two decades would go far beyond an isolated case in which crony capitalism fell into a major crisis; a much larger process took center stage, one that shows that it was the increasing free flow of capital that produced great instabilities in the international economy. The rise and burst of the bubble in Japan was neither the first – inasmuch as it was preceded by Latin America's Southern Cone crisis of 1979–1980 and the developing country debt crisis of 1982 – nor the last, inasmuch as it was followed by the Mexican crisis of 1994–1995, the Asian crisis of 1997–1998, the Russian crisis of 1998, and the Brazilian crisis of 1999 (Eatwell and Taylor 2000, 5).

Another profound change after the early 1970s was the shift in the long-term movement of capitalist economies from social protection to the release of market forces. Karl Polanyi ([1944] 1957) pointed out a long time ago that capitalist economies were driven by two counter forces: efforts in support of social protection and efforts in support of releasing market forces. In *The Great Transformation*, Polanyi demonstrates how the efforts to free up market forces starting in the late nineteenth century eventually led to the Great Depression, and how the efforts in support of social protection led to the rise of fascism, the New Deal, and socialism in the 1930s. I argue that the Polanyi framework can be extended to the second half of the twentieth century. Indeed, the fate of the Japanese economy in the twentieth century was shaped by a cycle of the birth, development, and deterioration of what Paul Krugman (1999a, 1999b) calls "depression-preventing" mechanisms; these mechanisms were established following the Great Depression and World War II in both the international economic order and national economic systems. The deregulation efforts in the banking industry soon spread over many industries. The shift from the expansion of trade and production toward the expansion of finance and monetary activity provided the dynamics of the shift from social protection to the release of market forces, and the release of monetary controls directly enhanced the power of market forces, causing deterioration in institutions designed for social protection. From the Polanyian perspective, the significance of the early 1970s as the turning point in the Japanese economy runs much deeper. It is not simply a starting point for the yen's appreciation or the cartelization of the Japanese economy. Rather, the early 1970s reflect a great transformation in which the freeing up of market forces became a powerful counter movement to the postwar policy of social protection in advanced industrialized countries, leading to a conservative revolution represented by the widespread adoption of deregulation, liberalization, and privatization programs. These programs have produced a "global squeeze" in jobs and wages in advanced industrialized countries (Longworth 1998). As a result, inequality is rising and different social groups are "growing apart" (Fishlow and Parker 1999).

AN INSTITUTIONAL EXPLANATION

Why did these two shifts take place? Through what causal mechanisms did they cause the reversion of the Japanese economy from prosperity to stagnation?

In contrast to the authors of structural accounts, I offer an institutional explanation of the origins of these two major shifts in the long-term movement of capitalist economies, emphasizing an intrinsic dilemma in the postwar international economic order.

The existing literature on institutional change often highlights the effects of exogenous shocks, which are best exemplified by Stephen Krasner's (1984) metaphor, "punctuated equilibrium." Exogenous shocks can block the reproduction of the institutional patterns and thus induce change, but they alone cannot effectively explain the causal mechanism that leads to the institutional change. Institutional change does not take place overnight, and in many cases it takes a long time. The metaphor of punctuated equilibrium simply leaves unexplained the internal institutional process between the point of exogenous shocks and the point of institutional change. Moreover, exogenous shocks do not simply block the reproduction of the institutional pattern. Rather, they often cause maladaptation by inducing the institution to follow the old institutional logic in a completely new environment.

The concept of intrinsic dilemma aims at revealing the causal mechanism that links the exogenous shocks to the institutional change. By "intrinsic dilemma" I mean a built-in contradiction in the institutional logic. "Institutional logic" refers to "a set of material practices and symbolic construction . . . which constitutes its organizing principles" (Friedland and Alford 1991, 248), which "are symbolically grounded, organizationally structured, politically defended, and technically and materially constrained, and hence have special historical limits" (Friedland and Alford 1991, 248–249; see also Hollingsworth and Boyer 1997b, 2). The intrinsic dilemma is that because the specific historical environment during the period of institutional formation often highlights the importance of one single task among many faced by the institution, overdevelopment of strength in solving one problem in the institutional logic often results in a weakness in solving others (Kester 1997). This situation often creates a logical contradiction because during its lifetime an institution often faces changing task environments. When it does, any weakness in dealing with competing tasks can lead to the malfunction of the institutional logic. This intrinsic dilemma, moreover, tends to worsen over time because institutions tend to tackle new problems by relying on the established institutional logic. When they reproduce themselves along a single direction, their actions deepen the contradiction in the institutional logic.

This kind of intrinsic dilemma may lead to institutional change in two ways. First, over the long run the weakness of the institution in solving other problems can create structural conditions that further exacerbate the mismatch between the institution's strength and its task environment. When its weakness in solving other problems becomes critical to the institution's survival, it may break down, triggering further structural changes in the environment. Often, understanding the dynamics of institutional change requires an examination that extends beyond the period of crisis. If we use the metaphor of an earthquake to represent the relationship between the intrinsic dilemma in an institution's logic and the crisis of the institution, it is the earthquake that we see; but it is the geological movements of tectonic plates – the explanatory device – that have been causing the buildup of the pressures that led to the quake, often for a long time.[8] Second, when the environment in which a national economic system, as an aggregation of institutions, is configured remains unchanged, the system tends to be sustained by the complementarity of homogeneous institutions and mechanisms (Aoki and Okuno 1996; Hollingsworth and Boyer 1997a; Okuno 1993). When the environment changes drastically, however, the institutions and mechanisms may no longer complement each other. Under such circumstances, the institutional logic of the national economic system may begin to malfunction.[9] That can create a major crisis for the institution.

The two shifts – from the expansion of trade and production to the expansion of finance and monetary activity and from social protection to the release of market forces – were not automatic. Rather, they were triggered by major changes in the international monetary and trade regimes induced by their intrinsic dilemmas. In his analysis of the previous wave of globalization in the early twentieth century, John Keynes pointed out the serious neglect of the intrinsic contradiction in capitalist economies on the eve of a global crisis (1920, 3):

> Very few of us realize with conviction . . . the intensely unusual, unstable, complicated, unreliable, temporary nature of the economic organization. . . . We assume some of the most peculiar and temporary of our late advantages as natural, permanent, and to be depended on, and we lay out plans accordingly. On this sandy and false foundation we scheme for social improvement and dress our political platforms, pursue our animosities and particular ambitions, and feel ourselves with enough margin in hand to foster, not assuage, civil conflict in the European family.

After World War II, advanced industrialized countries, under the leadership of the United States, established the Bretton Woods system and the

---

8 Roger Haydon used this metaphor to express his understanding of my argument in his comments on this chapter. I want to thank him not only for this metaphor but also for other comments.

9 Roger Friedland and Robert R. Alford (1991, 256–259) use the term "institutional contradiction" to reflect a similar phenomenon, but they emphasize the political dimension by arguing that "the premise of institutional contradiction derives from class theory."

General Agreement on Trade and Tariffs (GATT) system to promote social protection and to sustain the expansion of trade and production. This international economic order, however, contained the Triffin dilemma: On the one hand, the Bretton Woods system and the GATT system provided the ally countries of the United States with great opportunities to export their products — sustained by the undervalued currencies relative to the dollar — and to increase their trade surplus with the United States. On the other hand, the United States, as the key currency country responsible for sustaining confidence in the dollar, could not take any action to adjust trade deficits through the exchange rate. The United States enjoyed the benefits of the dollar as reserve, transaction, and intervention currency, thereby extending its economic and political privileges and freeing itself from concern about its balance of payments in the conduct of its foreign policy or the management of its domestic economy; but any devaluation of the dollar to improve American competitiveness would immediately have been wiped out by parallel devaluation of other currencies. Sooner or later, Robert Triffin predicted, either the system would collapse or alternative ways would be found to address this issue (Gilpin 1987, 137; Triffin 1960, 1964). Disregarding this dilemma, unfortunately, advanced industrialized countries pushed the expansion of trade and production beyond the capacities of the postwar international economic order. The increasing holding of the dollar outside the United States eventually forced the U.S. government to unlink the dollar and gold. That action led to the collapse of the Bretton Woods system.

The collapse of the Bretton Woods system triggered the shift from the expansion of trade and production to the expansion of finance and monetary activity. When governments maintained fixed exchange rates, the private sector was free from foreign exchange risk. When the system collapsed, as John Eatwell and Lance Taylor (2000, 2) point out, "risk was privatized." Two needs created by the collapse of the Bretton Wood system provided the incentive for various interest groups in advanced industrialized countries to assert the need for deregulation of international capital flows: First, after risk was privatized, those who traded in foreign markets faced the overwhelming need to hedge against the costs imposed on them by fluctuating exchange rates. They "needed to be able to diversify their portfolios at will, changing the mix of currencies and financial assets both at present and in the future in line with the changing perception of foreign exchange risk." Second, "once Bretton Woods collapsed and significant fluctuations in exchange rates became commonplace, opportunities for profit proliferated, regulatory structures inhibiting flows of capital were challenged as 'inefficient' and 'against the national interest,' and the modern machinery of speculation was constructed" (Eatwell and Taylor 2000, 2).

The privatization of risk demanded the creation of new financial instruments, which in turn required removing many of the regulatory barriers that had been created after the Great Depression and World War II to prevent depression. The removal of the regulatory barriers triggered the shift of capitalist economies from the expansion of trade and production to the expansion of finance and monetary activity. Deregulation, liberalization, and privatization, however, were not limited to the financial industry. They became the leading topics of rhetoric in public policy discourse for the entire economy. When regulatory barriers were removed in many industries, the depression-preventing regime deteriorated. Capitalist economies began to change gears from social protection to the release of market forces. Reflecting these two profound changes, the United States, facing increasing trade deficits, was forced to end its policy of asymmetric cooperation with Japan in international trade, a policy whereby Japan was able to export its products to the international markets while keeping its own domestic markets closed. The United States demanded greater access to the Japanese markets.

In contrast to explanations of the reversion of the Japanese economy that are based on domestic policy, my explanation focuses on the major impact of the international economic order on the domestic policy environment. Moreover, in contrast to those studies in which the primary impact of the international environment on the Japanese economy during the high growth is thought to be the Cold War, I explore the direct causal mechanism that linked the international economic order and Japan's domestic economic institutions.[10]

In 1950–1971, under the Bretton Woods system, a fixed exchange rate and rigid control over the free flow of capital across national borders enabled Japan to promote its own economic growth without being influenced by the financial policies of other countries. Restrained by the Dodge plan, which emphasized the control of inflation, the Japanese state could not continue to practice its expansionary fiscal policy in the 1950s and 1960s. Instead, it adopted a very important policy mix of an expansionary monetary policy to promote economic growth and a deflationary fiscal policy to control inflation. To make the expansionary monetary policy work, the Japanese state not only tried to allocate resources strategically through its industrial policy (a strategy emphasized by the existing literature) but also performed an important

10 This does not mean that the Cold War is not important but rather that the Cold War alone is not sufficient to explain what happened in the 1970s and 1980s. The Cold War did not end until the very end of the 1980s. Yet the bilateral trade frictions between the United States and Japan started in the late 1960s and intensified in the 1970s and especially in the 1980s, well before the Cold War was over. As I discuss in Chapters 2 and 5, the United States practiced asymmetric cooperation with its allies not only to support its strategic interests during the Cold War but also to build a multilateral international trade regime.

insurance function by reducing investment risks for private banks and corporations. Three policies – the so-called convoy administration practiced by
the Ministry of Finance (see Chapter 4), the stable supply of credit by the
Bank of Japan to major city banks, and the egalitarian distribution of foreign
currency quotas by Ministry of International Trade and Industry (MITI)
to big corporations – significantly reduced investment risks and enabled big
corporations and banks to aggressively invest in production capacity and
technological transfers (Miyazaki 1963; Morozumi 1963a). In 1950–1971,
the policy mix adopted by the Japanese state also strongly influenced the
Japanese pattern of social protection. Because the Japanese state adopted
a deflationary fiscal policy to control inflation and sustain an expansionary
monetary policy and it emphasized capital accumulation and the maintenance
of a small government, it was impossible for Japan to develop a welfare state.
Asymmetric cooperation with the United States within the framework of
GATT, meanwhile, enabled Japan to export aggressively without opening its
own domestic markets. That allowed the Japanese state to sustain employment by relying on cartels to protect medium-size and small companies and
family-owned mini shops. Instead of developing a strong, government-
financed unemployment assistance program, Japan relied on government regulations to protect the weak sectors of the economy and the sunset industries
(those that were becoming obsolete).

After the collapse of the Bretton Woods system shifted the expansion
of trade and production to the expansion of finance and monetary activity, Japan's international financial policy began to confront the Mundell-
Flemming trilemma (see Krugman 1999a, 1999b; this phenomenon is also
discussed in detail in Chapter 2 of this book). Japan adopted the floating
exchange rate system and joined the liberalization of finance initiated by
Britain and the United States. As a result of increasing the free flow of capital,
Japan began to lose its autonomy in determining its fiscal and monetary policies and began to face conflicting policy objectives (McKinnon and Ohno
1997). In this new environment, the Japanese state often had trouble maintaining a good balance in the policy mix between fiscal and monetary policies. With a floating exchange rate and increasing free flow of capital, efforts
by the Bank of Japan to maintain stable exchange rates through its intervention in the foreign exchange market often led to an oversupply of money.
This in turn upset the balance of domestic demand and supply, while the
efforts by the Ministry of Finance to reduce the trade surplus by adopting an
expansionary fiscal policy often served to channel private investments to the
real estate and stock markets. That triggered the bubble.

Meanwhile, the United States was no longer willing to continue asymmetric cooperation. It began to use its monetary policy to address trade issues.

The sharp increase in Japan's trade surplus with the United States directly led to increasing U.S. pressures on Japan to open its domestic markets, liberalize its finance industry, appreciate the value of the yen, and create domestic demand by increasing public spending. Under international pressures, Japan began deregulation and privatization. After the shift from social protection toward the release of market forces, the Japanese state policy also faced competing objectives. On the one hand, domestic pressure for increased government protection rose drastically after the end of the high growth period. On the other hand, international pressure for liberalization, deregulation, and privatization also built up quickly. The Japanese state often struggled between these competing policy agendas, and that increased the cost of job creation and made it more difficult to achieve the goal of maintaining equality in distribution.

In contrast to exclusively macro-level explanations, I emphasize the micro-level institutions and mechanisms that sustained the reversion of the Japanese economy in the two structural shifts. I argue that although the macro-level structural changes are powerful in explaining the general trend shared by various capitalist economies, the variations in the same two structural shifts among different industrialized countries can be better understood at the micro level. Moreover, in contrast to those studies that either focus on the cartelization of the Japanese economy or interpret the economic growth as a purely market-driven phenomenon, this book demonstrates how the efforts of coordination ended up encouraging excessive competition and how this intrinsic dilemma was responsible for both the high growth and the bubble economy.

The dilemma in Japanese corporate governance between, on the one hand, strong coordination and, on the other hand, weak control and monitoring provided the causal mechanism that led to excessive competition, a phenomenon that was critical both to Japan's high growth and to the bubble. In 1950–1971, sustained by the insurance function performed by the state in a predictable international environment, the Japanese economic system was reconfigured to strengthen coordination – a principle of economic governance that had emerged in the Great Depression and World War II for the purpose of adapting to the expansion of trade and production. "Coordination" here refers to the establishment and maintenance of contractual exchange among separate enterprises. "Control" refers to the control of shareholders over management due to the separation between ownership and management (Kester 1997), and "monitoring" refers to the mechanisms established by banks for "assessing the credit-worthiness of proposed projects; tracking the use of funds; distinguishing misuse from temporary bad luck and correcting it; as well as credible commitment to penalizing misuse as a safeguard against future misuse" (Aoki 1994, 109). At a time when the country was still suffering from a shortage of capital, strong coordination enabled Japan to successfully mobilize the national savings that sustained high growth. Strong coordination was achieved, however, at the cost of deliberately weakening shareholder control over management and weakening banks' monitoring over corporations at the micro level (Kester 1997; Miyazaki 1963; Morozumi 1963a). Protected by the state, private corporations and banks reduced their transaction costs through indirect financing, through the use of the main bank system, and through business group and reciprocal shareholding. Sustained by the permanent employment system practiced by big corporations and by multidimensional integration within business groups, strong coordination led not to a socialist, planned economy but rather to excessive competition among Japanese corporations in investing in production capacity and technological transfers. This excessive competition, in turn, triggered the high growth.

After the First Oil Shock, in contrast, banks' monitoring further deteriorated as corporations began to build financial independence, separating themselves from the main banks. In the liberalization of finance, banks' leverage over corporations was weakened because corporations began to raise capital through equity finance and *zai'tech* (financial technology). After the Plaza Accord, moreover, the mishandling of international demand resulted in not only an oversupply of money but also the adoption of an expansionary fiscal policy that shifted the incentive structure of private investments from production to the stock and real estate markets. When the state policies served to significantly increase investment risks, the weak control and monitoring that characterized Japanese corporate governance contributed directly to the rise of the bubble.

After the long-term movement of capitalist economies shifted gears from social protection to the release of market forces, another causal mechanism that led to the stagnation of the Japanese economy was the dilemma between stability and the upgrading of the economic structure. "Stability" here refers to political stability in the process of economic development, which is sustained by the rise of employment opportunity and the fall of economic inequality. The "upgrading of the economic structure" could involve actions at three levels (not necessarily simultaneously): private companies lay off surplus workers; an industry or a sector eliminates inefficient companies through corporate bankruptcy as a result of market competition; and capital and labor in an economy leave the sunset industries and enter the sunrise industries. In 1950–1971, under the protection of asymmetric cooperation with the United States, the Japanese state relied on private institutions to perform the welfare function while it concentrated on capital accumulation.

Big corporations institutionalized a permanent employment system, providing job security for their employees. Medium-size and small companies organized various cartels in an effort to restrain competition and thereby avoid bankruptcy. Meanwhile, the weak sectors and sunset industries enjoyed the protection of various government regulations. Although the persistence of this dual economic structure created significant gaps in income distribution, Japanese women played an important role in mitigating the problem of inequality in distribution, resulting in a high level of equality in distribution measured by household income, instead of individual income, in the Gini index.[11] As a marginal labor force, women entered and left the labor market flexibly according to the economic situation (Nomura 1998). By tying various political interests to the existing economic structure, Japan was able to pursue "development without losers" and to concentrate its resources in promoting economic growth (Weiss 1998).

But when capitalist economies shifted gears from social protection to the release of market forces in the early 1970s, the contingent conditions that had sustained the Japanese model of the welfare society began to disappear. The First Oil Shock ended the high growth period, the rapid appreciation of the yen put great pressure on the Japanese economy to improve efficiency, and the United States began to put strong pressure on Japan to open its domestic markets. Because Japan did not have a good unemployment assistance program, labor unions strongly demanded job security, and companies in the weak sectors and industries demanded more government protection. These demands led to the cartelization of the economy and the politicization of economic policy-making (Katz 1998; Pempel 1998). In 1971–1989, Japan was able to maintain stability along with a low unemployment rate. The cost of doing so, however, became very high because the permanent employment system forced companies to keep surplus workers, the cartels forced industries to keep inefficient companies, and government regulations forced the economy to keep sunset sectors and industries. Meanwhile, market forces were released, resulting in increased inequality of distribution as a result of the different degrees of ownership of land and stocks during the bubble of the 1980s (Nomura 1998; Tachibanaki 1998).

In contrast to the studies of the reversion of the Japanese economy based on one individual institution or policy area, I offer a comprehensive account of this process.

11 The Gini index of income or resource inequality is a measure of the degree to which a population shares that resource unequally. It is based on the statistical notion known in the literature as the "mean difference" of a population. The index is scaled to vary from a minimum of zero to a maximum of 1, zero representing no inequality and 1 representing the maximum possible degree of inequality. See Robert Leslie, in "Exploring the Gini Index of Inequality with Derive," www.agnesscott.edu/aca/depts_prog/info/math/leslie/gini.htm.

As indicated in this high-level summary of the events and discussed in more detail in the chapters that follow, I argue that the reversion of the Japanese economy against the two structural shifts in the global capitalist system in the late twentieth century was a complicated process. This comprehensive approach cannot provide all the details concerning each individual institution. It does, however, present a bigger picture. When capitalist economies show significant cross-national variations in their responses to a common challenge, it is often not the individual institutions, but rather the configuration of these institutions in the economic system, that better explains the outcome.[12] The term *economic system*, as I use it in this study, consists of multiple institutions at the national, intermediate, and corporate levels. It defines the relationships between the state and private corporations, between the state and private citizens, between banks and manufacturers, between one company and its trading partners, between employers and employees, and between producers and consumers.[13] These relationships are an integrated entirety, and together they determine the national solution to the two major issues every economy must confront: how to organize production and how to distribute economic welfare. The pattern of the national solutions reflects the guiding principles underlying the economy. In the Japanese context, at the state level, it involved a policy mix that included balancing payments, the convoy administration practiced by the Ministry of Finance, the Bank of Japan's role in the supply of long-term capital, and MITI's support of competitive oligopolies. At the intermediate level, it involved the main bank system, indirect financing, reciprocal shareholding, and the multidimensional integration of business groups. At the corporate level, it involved a strong growth orientation sustained by the permanent employment system.

In the existing English-language literature, many of these institutions and mechanisms have been studied by others. In this study, my contributions seek to (1) bring these independent analyses of individual institutions together into a general picture and see how they have sustained excessive competition and total employment, the two causal mechanisms that have contributed to both the high growth and the rise of the bubble, and to (2) reexamine those

---

12 Recent literature on comparative capitalism has emphasized the cross-national variations of economic systems. See Berger and Dore (1997), Hollingsworth and Boyer (1997a), and Kitschelt et al. (1999).

13 Rogers Hollingsworth and Robert Boyer argue that a social system of production contains, on the one hand, the industrial relations system, the system of the training of workers and managers, the internal structure of corporate firms, and the structured relationships among firms in the same industry, and, on the other hand, the firms' relationships with their suppliers and customers, the financial markets of a society, the conceptions of fairness and justice held by capital and labor, the structure of the state and its policies, and a society's idiosyncratic customs and traditions as well as norms, moral principles, rules, laws, and recipes for action (1997b, 2). The term *economic system* as I use it in this book is somewhat narrower, focusing only on those institutions and mechanisms related to production and distribution.

issues that have been discussed under the research paradigm of "trade and production" with a new perspective of "finance and monetary activity" either by using new, original data or by revealing the Japanese debates on these issues at various points in history. As a result, I reveal the weak control and monitoring of corporations and the low capacity of the Japanese economy to make rapid structural adjustments, as the major tradeoffs both for strong economic coordination and for the stability of the Japanese economic system. For each institution and mechanism that has been perceived as contributing to strong coordination, I show that it has also weakened control and monitoring, sustaining excessive competition. For each institution and mechanism that has been portrayed as contributing to the low level of unemployment and high level of egalitarian distribution, I show that it has also weakened the system's capacity to upgrade its economic structure.

THE STRUCTURE OF THIS BOOK

The organization of the book is driven by my theoretical concerns. This introduction is followed by Chapter 2, which further discusses my three major propositions. The empirical analyses are divided into four distinctive stages according to the major changes in the long-term movement of capitalist economies.

Chapter 3 describes the stage of the crisis as it exists in the last cycle of the long-term movement of capitalist economies. This chapter covers the period of the Great Depression and World War II and offers a brief historical background to the postwar evolution of the Japanese economy. In this stage, the collapse of the gold standard also created competing objectives in the financial and monetary policies of the state. The mishandling of these policies also created a bubble after World War I and led to a decade-long stagnation before the Japanese economy was hit by a major financial crisis and the Great Depression. Japan, like its Western counterparts, shifted gears toward social protection, departing sharply from its own version of the liberal tradition. Influenced by fascism, the Japanese pattern of the great transformation distinguished itself from both the liberal response represented by the New Deal in the United States and the socialist response represented by the planned economy in the Soviet Union. To survive the unprecedented economic hard times and to mobilize the country to wage wars with other nations, the Japanese state promoted two guiding principles: coordination and stability. They emerged as the two guiding principles of the Japanese economic system, leading to the rise of a new set of institutions and mechanisms that later contributed to Japan's postwar economic development.

Chapters 4 and 5 cover the period of the postwar expansion of two structural movements of capitalist economies: trade and production on the one

hand, and social protection on the other hand. These two chapters deal separately with these two issues in the Japanese economic system during the
high growth period in 1950–1971. They show that the Bretton Woods
system and Japan's asymmetric cooperation with the United States sustained
the postwar development of coordination and stability that reconfigured the
Japanese economic system to adapt to the expansion of trade and production
and to extend social protection via changes in the Japanese pattern of social
welfare. Reexamining the literature that regards coordination and stability as
the key factors enabling Japan to become a big winner in the globalization
of production, I study the Japanese debates during the 1950s and 1960s on
the nature of the country's economic system, revealing another side of the
same institutions discussed in the existing literature. I show that the real
secret of Japanese high growth lay in excessive competition, a side effect of
the efforts to strengthen coordination at the cost of deliberately weakening
control and monitoring of corporations. The real secret of the welfare society
lay in the strategy of total employment, which traded off stability for the
capacity to make quick structural adjustments. I show that the existence of
both characteristics rested on contingent conditions in the historical environment – including international economic regimes such as the Bretton
Woods system and the asymmetric cooperation with the United States
under the GATT system – and two structural conditions: the bottleneck of
payments and the rapid expansion of both international and domestic
economies.

Chapters 6 and 7 discuss the shift from the expansion of trade and
production to the expansion of finance and monetary activity and the shift
from social protection to the release of market forces between the early 1970s
and the late 1980s. Chapters 6 and 7 also deal separately with these
two issues. These two chapters show that beginning in the early 1970s, all
the contingent conditions that sustained excessive competition and the
welfare society began to disappear. The Bretton Woods system collapsed; the
United States was no longer willing to continue asymmetric cooperation,
putting increasing pressure on Japan; the balance of current account turned
from trade deficits to trade surpluses; and the high growth period ended.
As the expansion of trade and production began to shift toward an expansion
of finance and monetary activity and as the long-term movement of
capitalism shifted gears from social protection to the release of market forces,
the Japanese economic system began to malfunction. The intrinsic dilemmas,
formerly under control, began to strike out at the system. The principles
of coordination and stability began to yield different outcomes in the
new external environment, leading the Japanese economy toward the
bubble.

Chapter 8 covers the crisis stage in the current cycle of the long-term movement of capitalist economies in the 1990s. This chapter shows that after the bubble burst, the persistence of the demand for stability in the first half of the 1990s and the sudden reversion of the institutional logic of coordination in 1996 led the Japanese economy not only into a long stagnation throughout the decade but also into a liquidity trap in 1997–1998. Driven by pressure to improve efficiency, many main banks refused to rescue their corporate borrowers, many corporations began to lay off workers, a number of financial institutions went bankrupt, the ban on holding companies was lifted, many manufacturers began to send their subcontracts overseas instead of to their domestic suppliers, cartels were threatened by price collapses, and both financial institutions and corporations were selling the stocks they had held. Even though the Japanese economic system began to address the issue of inefficiency, it did so neither in the fashion of a class-based political struggle nor in the zero-sum type of distributional politics. The lack of a strong government-sponsored unemployment assistance program has made a radical structural adjustment very difficult. In the meantime, inevitably, inequality has increased rapidly. Because the state had to readopt an expansionary fiscal policy to stimulate the economy, its budget deficits have reached an all-time high. The goal of avoiding deflation sharply conflicts with the goal of rebuilding the financing of governance. Because many uncertainties still exist in the international economic order, the question of whether the Japanese economic system can revitalize itself remains to be seen.

CHAPTER 2

THREE THEORETICAL ISSUES

In this chapter, I elaborate on the three theoretical issues presented in Chapter 1. I argue first that globalization is an institutional process. The two structural shifts described in Chapter 1 – the expansion of trade and production and the efforts for social protection in the 1950s and the 1960s, and the later shifts toward the expansion of finance and monetary activity and toward the release of market forces – were driven by the rise and fall of the Bretton Woods system in conjunction with important changes in the GATT. Second, I argue that changes in the international economic order led to the malfunction of the Japanese economic system, which had suffered from two dilemmas: the dilemma between strong coordination and weak control and monitoring of corporations, and the dilemma between the system's high stability and its low capacity for elevating the economic structure.

THE INSTITUTIONAL PROCESS OF GLOBALIZATION AND THE TWO STRUCTURAL SHIFTS

The process that has come to be called *globalization* is often measured by production factors, such as capital, goods, technology, and even the labor force (in the form of immigration). Both sides in the debate on globalization, moreover, often use the ratio of international trade against the world GDP to make their points: Those who favor globalization emphasize the rapid increase of this ratio, from 6 percent in 1953 to 9 percent in 1971 and 15 percent in the mid 1990s. In contrast, those who do not favor globalization focus on a comparison between the two peaks in the movement of the ratio between 1913 and 1995. They point out that in 1913, the last peak of globalization, international trade was about 14 percent of the world GDP. Through two world wars and the Great Depression, the ratio bottomed out at 6 percent in 1953. From that point on, it gradually recovered and reached 15 percent by the mid 1990s (see Figure 2.1; Fligstein 1998, 9). Inasmuch as it took almost 70 years for the ratio of trade against the world GDP to return to its pre-World War I level, the concept of globalization as something new may have been heavily exaggerated (Fligstein 1998; Wade 1997). The extreme view even holds that "globalization amounts to very little and is therefore of no consequence" (see the discussion by Rodrik 1998, 3).

Because globalization is sustained by institutions, however, it is not simply a structural process. The international economic order has played a crucial role in the rise and fall of the trade ratio against the world GDP in the twentieth century. Without highlighting the impact of international monetary and trade regimes on the process of globalization, we cannot fully explain why the postwar expansion of trade and production occurred in the first place, how capitalist economies sustained social protection in the 1950s and 1960s, why the expansion of trade and production shifted toward an expansion in finance and monetary activity, and why efforts directed toward social protection were replaced by efforts to release market forces.

The preceding peak of globalization, 1870–1913, was sustained by the international gold standard and various international treaties on tariffs. Both monetary and trade regimes were backed up by British hegemony. In the international gold standard system, the Bank of England used its discount rate to influence the movement of gold both domestically and internationally. The stability of the gold standard relied on two things: a hierarchical structure in which London was the most important financial center in the world, and confidence in the continued convertibility of sterling and other major currencies into gold at par value (Keohane and Nye 1977, 67–71). In the international trade regime, the Cobden-Chevallier Treaty of 1860 between Britain and France not only yielded reciprocal tariff cuts but also led France to sign tariff treaties with other European countries and the German customs union (Kenen 1989 [1985], 213).

The downturn in the ratio of trade against world GDP did not start naturally as a structural process. Rather, as Figure 2.1 indicates, it was triggered by the collapse of the international gold standard in 1914. In the same year, World War I broke out. These two events ended what John M. Keynes called an "extraordinary episode in the economic progress of man" (cited by Rodrik 1998). At the Genoa conference of 1922, the major powers agreed to establish a gold exchange standard in which currencies would be exchanged at fixed parities. Britain returned to gold in 1925, with an emphasis on sterling-dollar convertibility, but left gold again in 1931 during the Great Depression. Japan tried to follow the British lead, but the attempt quickly failed. Between 1931 and 1944, there was no comprehensive and agreed-on set of rules or norms governing international monetary arrangements

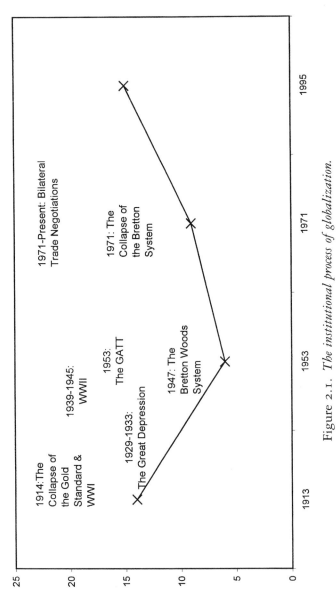

Figure 2.1. *The institutional process of globalization.*
Source: Based on the data in Fligstein, 1998, p. 9.

(Keohane and Nye 1977, 73–76). The First World War, the peace settlement, and shortsighted policies disrupted trade patterns in international trade, and protectionist pressures began to build up everywhere. As major industrialized countries adhered to the so-called lifeline theory, they fought over markets, materials, and resources and tried to establish their spheres of influence. These conflicts led to World War II.

Nor was the postwar upturn of the ratio of trade against world GDP simply a structural recovery. Rather, as Table 2.1 shows, it was sustained by the Bretton Woods system and the GATT. The core of the Bretton Woods system, created by the United States and Britain, was the provision that countries belonging to the International Monetary Fund would set and maintain official par values for their currencies, which were to be changed only to correct a fundamental disequilibrium in a country's balance of payments (Keohane and Nye 1977, 79). The core of the GATT was the most-favored-nation clause, under which each tariff bargain made at a GATT meeting was extended to all members. The GATT's rules discouraged withdrawals of concessions inasmuch as countries injured by an increase in a member's tariffs were entitled to retaliate by withdrawing concessions made to the offending member (Kenen 1989 [1985], 217). Both of these international economic regimes played important roles in sustaining the expansion of trade and production in capitalist economies in the 1950s and 1960s.

Sustained by these two international economic regimes, advanced industrialized countries focused on social protection in the 1950s and the 1960s. They deliberately established what Paul Krugman calls "the depression-preventing regimes" (1999a, 1999b). As Dani Rodrik points out (1997, 23),

> At the height of the gold standard, governments were not yet expected to perform social-welfare functions on a large scale. Ensuring adequate levels of employment, establishing social safety nets, providing medical and social insurance, and caring for the poor were not parts of the government agenda. Such demands multiplied during the period following the Second World War. Indeed, a key component of the implicit postwar social bargain in the advanced industrial countries has been the provision of social insurance and safety nets at home (unemployment compensation, severance payments, and adjustment assistance, for example) in exchange for the adoption of freer trade policies.

For two decades, the development of various institutions and mechanisms for social protection seemed to confirm Karl Polanyi's assertion that "the protective countermovement was not external; rather, it was essential for the vitality of a capitalist order" (see Block 1990, 39).

Table 2.1 *Changes in the International Economic Order (1950–Present)*

Period	Goals of the International Economic Order	The Institutionalized Practices	Implications to the Japanese Economy
Period 1 (1950–1971)	The Bretton Woods system aimed at promoting the expansion of trade and production, and it provided certainty.	Fixed exchange rate and rigid control of the free flow of capital.	Japan had the independence of a monetary policy promoting economic growth without being influenced by other countries' financial policies. The risks of foreign exchange were managed by the state and the central bank.
	The GATT, under the leadership of the United States, aimed at promoting a multilateral trade regime by first supporting Japan and Western Europe in their postwar economic recovery.	The United States practiced asymmetric cooperation with its ally countries within the framework of the GATT.	Japan could aggressively export to the United States while protecting its own domestic markets.
Period 2 (1971–Present)	The new monetary regime aimed at promoting the expansion of finance and monetary activity, and it created uncertainty.	The floating exchange rate system and liberalization of finance.	The financial policy of the United States could directly influence that of Japan. Risk management of foreign exchange was privatized.
	The United States began to push the equal market access agenda in the GATT.	Bilateral trade negotiations.	Increasing U.S. pressures to open domestic markets, appreciate the yen's value, and create domestic demand.

As the GATT and the Bretton Woods system sustained the expansion of trade and production, the structural conditions they created gradually grew beyond their institutional capacity for governance. The Bretton Woods system deteriorated over time, and it collapsed in the early 1970s. From the beginning, the Bretton Woods system was subject to the Triffin dilemma. This dilemma resulted in part from the incompatibility between the international trade regime, which promoted the free flow of goods, and the international monetary regime, which initially deliberately controlled, instead of encouraging, the free flow of capital, relying instead on a pegged exchange rate system (Gilpin 1987; Helleiner 1994). This incompatibility was a result of a political compromise between the United States and Britain, the two countries that designed the Bretton Woods system. The United States emphasized the principle of multilateralism, particularly in trade. Britain, in contrast, focused on its policy autonomy in order to "resolve the dilemma between internal and external financial stability" and "ensure that countries which conduct their affairs with prudence need not to be afraid that they will be prevented from meeting their international liabilities by causes outside their own control" (Gardner 1969 [1965], 78). Under this political compromise, industrialized countries were able to pursue the domestic policy objectives of full employment and economic growth without being undermined by speculative and disequilibrating international capital flows. In other words, the postwar liberal trade regime was sustained in part by a nonliberal monetary order (Gilpin 1987; Helleiner 1994; Ikenberry 1993; Keohane and Nye 1977; Ruggie 1982).

This intrinsic contradiction in the Bretton Woods system was aggravated by what Robert Keohane (1984) calls "the asymmetric cooperation" between the United States and its allies. Driven by its strategic interests, the United States adopted a foreign policy that emphasized the provision of economic benefits to its allies in exchange for their political, diplomatic, and strategic cooperation. In the international trade regime, whereas the U.S. government actively worked to reduce tariffs and took the lead in pressing for the removal of discriminatory restrictions, it also tolerated temporary Japanese and European regional discrimination and permitted them to maintain temporary postwar barriers during the period of the dollar shortage. As a result, Japan and other U.S. allies benefited greatly from the effects of the overvalued dollar on their own exports and easy access to the huge U.S. markets, but the United States could not depreciate the value of the dollar. This led to a rapid increase in U.S. trade deficits. In the late 1960s, the U.S. government demanded that its ally countries adjust their exchange rates. Driven by the established institutional logic, however, Japan refused to take action. As a result, the intrinsic contradiction created by the Triffin dilemma continued to weaken the Bretton Woods system and eventually led to its breakdown.

The collapse of the Bretton Woods system began in 1971 and triggered the two structural shifts referred to earlier. In 1971, the United States ended the convertibility between the dollar and gold. As a result, Japan shifted to a floating exchange rate system. In conjunction with the First Oil Shock, Japan, as well as other industrialized countries, was forced to fight economic hard times by expanding public spending, which led to huge government budget deficits. Then, beginning in the early 1980s, as Eric Helleiner (1994) points out, the U.S. government began to promote a liberalization of finance for three reasons. First, speculative capital movements served as an important tool in the U.S. strategy of encouraging foreigners to absorb the adjustment burden required to correct the country's large deficits in current accounts in the early 1970s. Second, a market-oriented system would strengthen the "structural power" of the United States in global finance because the dollar's position as a world currency would be preserved and reinforced, in turn because U.S. financial markets and the Eurodollar market would still be the most attractive international markets for both private and public investors, whereas no such markets existed to make either the yen or the deutsche mark as attractive a reserve currency. Third, international markets helped the United States retain policy autonomy in the face of large domestic and external economic imbalances (see also Pauly 1988; Strange 1986). Sustained by the combination of information technology and financial technology, the liberalization of finance broke down national borders and induced the free flow of capital.

The shift from social protection to the release of market forces was also triggered by the changes in international trade. After the United States successfully pushed the liberalization of trade through the Kennedy Round – in which the GATT members, especially the major industrialized countries, agreed to cut tariffs for manufactured goods by 50 percent – the U.S. Congress began to consider bills that would have put import quotas on many products. At first, the U.S. government tried to mollify the protectionists by negotiating voluntary restrictions on Japanese and other imports to the United States. The Nixon administration, however, adopted the strategy of calling for a new round of GATT negotiations in 1971. In the Tokyo Round between 1973 and 1979, the U.S. government began to single out trade practices "unfair" to the United States, and it began to adopt a bilateral approach to solving the trade disputes between the United States and other countries. In other words, asymmetric cooperation between the United States and its ally countries witnessed a profound change beginning in the 1970s. The United States began to strongly demand equal access to the markets of other countries, and especially to Japan's domestic markets. In the 1980s, the conservative revolution changed the leading agenda to liberalization, privatization, and deregulation. The entry of newly industrialized countries, developing countries, and former socialist countries intensified international competition; additionally, rapidly increasing oil prices put strong pressure on industrialized countries to improve efficiency. As a result, both the model of the welfare state and the model of the government-protected or cartel-based welfare society began to face a major challenge.

More importantly, with financial and monetary expansion, trade issues and monetary issues began to interact closely with each other in the international political economy. This interaction had direct implications for Japan. Beginning in the early 1970s, the United States was able to use the exchange rate to balance its payments when foreign dollar holdings increased through trade surpluses with the United States. In the 1980s, according to Jeffrey Frieden, it was recognized in the United States that "when monetary policy is associated with currency values, it has effects similar to a trade policy. Depreciation is functionally equivalent to an increase in trade protection or export subsidies, while appreciation has effects similar to a trade barrier reduction or export tax" (Frieden 1996, 112–113). In other words, "devaluing the dollar will, by itself, reduce the U.S. trade or current account deficit, and that exchange rate change can be treated as a rather clear and acceptable instrument of economic policy" (McKinnon and Ohno 1997, 12). By the early 1970s, when the dollar came under increasing attack, those who supported the free trade regime in the United States began to see a dollar devaluation as the lesser of two evils: "better a depreciated dollar than either trade protection or capital controls, or both" (Frieden 1996, 122–123). These observers recognized that "producers are more likely to be able to organize for product-specific trade protection than for an economy-wide devaluation. However, it may be easier to organize a broad pro-devaluation coalition than a protectionist logroll" (Frieden 1996, 112–113). Accordingly, these supporters of the free trade regime opposed direct protectionist measures but supported the effort to use monetary policy to solve trade frictions. As a strategy for dealing with Japan, the United States has pursued a policy of "coupling protectionist threats with demands, implicit or explicit, for yen appreciation" (McKinnon and Ohno 1997, 11). The interaction between trade issues and monetary issues served to mutually reinforce the two structural shifts, greatly accelerating the process of globalization.

COORDINATION VERSUS CONTROL AND MONITORING:
THE MECHANISM OF EXCESSIVE COMPETITION

The changes in the international economic order influenced the Japanese economic system in two distinctive ways. First, in 1950–1971, the Bretton Woods system and the GATT sustained the expansion of trade and production. Japan's adaptation to this specific international environment profoundly shaped the institutional reconfiguration of the Japanese economic system. Maintaining a fixed exchange rate and tight control over the free flow of capital enabled Japan to pursue high growth without being influenced by other countries' financial policies, and Japan's asymmetric cooperation with the United States also allowed Japan to export aggressively while keeping its own markets closed. When the Bretton Woods system collapsed, it not only triggered the shift from the expansion of trade and production to the expansion of finance and monetary activity – resulting in a new environment to which each national economic system had to adapt – but it also eliminated the enabling factors in the international economic order. The latter, in turn, directly restrained the adaptive capacity of the Japanese economic system. This worsened the intrinsic contradiction created by the dilemma between strong coordination and weak control and monitoring in the Japanese economic system, creating new structural conditions under which its institutional logic began to malfunction.

The dilemma of choosing between coordination and control in corporate governance has been studied separately in terms of transaction cost economics and the agency theory of industrial organization.[1] Carl Kester (1997), however, brings the two horns of the dilemma together in a competing relationship. Kester points out that all modern corporations must address two problems: the problem of coordination associated with the establishment and maintenance of contractual exchange among separate companies, and the problem of control associated with the separation of ownership and management. Having evolved under different historic circumstances, the corporate governance that is strong in coordination often has difficulties in exercising control, and vice versa. Coordination and control, then, are two intrinsically conflicting tasks of modern corporate governance. Measures taken to strengthen one often lead to the weakening of the other, both in a relative sense (Kester 1997). In this book, I historicize the Kester argument by demonstrating how the dilemma between strong coordination and weak control was created by a specific pattern of Japanese adaptation to the postwar expansion of trade and production in the 1950s and the 1960s.

Sustained by the Bretton Woods system, the Japanese state relied on an expansionary monetary policy to promote economic growth and a deflationary fiscal policy to control inflation in the 1950s and the 1960s. This expansionary monetary policy served not only to promote economic growth but also to balance Japan's payments. Until the late 1960s, the imbalance

---

1 On the issue of coordination, see Coase (1937, 386–405) and Williamson (1985). On the issue of corporate control, see Berle and Means (1932) and Jensen and Meckling (1976). For a good discussion on the relationship between these two issues, see Kester (1997).

of payments – in the form of trade deficits – had always been a bottleneck to the growth of the Japanese economy. As a result, Japan practiced its expansionary monetary policy in relation to the cycle of payments adjustment. In other words, monetary policy served a dual role of sustaining economic growth and balancing payments. The cycle started with an easy money policy to stimulate economic growth. As wholesale prices rose and as increased imports during the economic boom created large trade deficits, payment imbalances would worsen. The state then had to shift to a tight money policy. The stability of domestic prices, by itself, was never regarded as an independent policy objective, because the Japanese state gave a higher priority to economic growth.[2] The major parameter for exercising a tight money policy was the imbalance of payments. Because foreign exchange was under strict control and because private corporations strongly depended on bank loans, a tight money policy, in the form of reducing credits from the Bank of Japan, quickly cooled the economy, usually creating a recession. When wholesale prices and imports declined, exports increased, and Japan's payments situation was improved, the state would shift back toward an easy money policy, and the economy would begin to grow again (Ōkurashō 1991, Vol. 9, 35–36).

As Table 2.2 shows, a set of institutions and mechanisms was devised to strengthen coordination under this expansionary monetary policy so as to promote exports and economic growth. To maintain a stable supply of industrial capital, the Bank of Japan ensured access to its credit by major city banks (Miyazaki 1985). To sustain the stability of the banking industry, the Ministry of Finance practiced convoy administration (see Chapter 4), tightly controlling entry to the financial markets and preventing bank insolvency (Sakakibara and Noguchi 1977; Okazaki and Okuno 1993). To direct the limited capital to big banks and big corporations, the Ministry of Finance approved the opening of new branch offices according to the size of the city banks, and MITI distributed quotas of foreign currencies according to the size of the corporations (Miyazaki 1985).

To overcome the shortage of self-capital, corporations relied on indirect financing by borrowing from banks, in contrast to direct financing by issuing stocks and bonds (Gerlach 1992; Okumura 1975). To ensure a supply of capital to manufacturing companies, the main banks, which originated in the war mobilization of the early 1940s, not only provided the largest share of loans to these corporations but also held equity and were expected to monitor the companies, intervening when things went wrong (Aoki and Patrick 1994;

---

2 The Japanese had a major debate on this issue in the late 1940s, when the easy money policy adopted to stimulate economic reconstruction caused severe inflation. Eventually, the pro-growth approach dominated state policy-making. See Gao (1997).

Table 2.2 *Strong Coordination Seen from the Perspective of Production*

The International Economic Order	The Role of the State	Intermediate-Level Institutions	Corporate Governance
The Bretton Woods System Fixed exchange rates Control over free flow of capital	*Expansionary Monetary Policy* Maintained stable supply of credits to major city banks *The Convoy Administration* Maintained stability by rescuing the failing banks Concentrated resources by approving new branch offices of city banks according to their size *Promotion of Exports* Concentrated resources by distributing foreign currency quotas to big corporations according to their size	*Indirect Financing* Mobilized national saving *The Main Bank System* Ensured industrial capital *Reciprocal Shareholding* Strengthened coordination *Development of Keiretsu* Strengthened coordination	*Permanent Employment System* Stabilized labor relations and improved the quality of products *Strong Coordination with Banks and Trading Partners* Sustained innovation

Sheard 1989). To reduce transaction costs and prevent hostile takeovers, banks and corporations practiced reciprocal shareholding (Nishiyama 1975; Okumura 1975). To strengthen coordination both vertically and horizontally, the *keiretsu* (see Chapter 4) developed around a major bank and a trading company (Gerlach 1992; Okumura 1975). In addition, big banks and big corporations institutionalized the practice of permanent employment in an effort to stabilize labor relations and sustain quality control and innovation (Dore 1973, 1987; Vogel 1979).

This strong coordination, however, was achieved at the cost of weakening control and monitoring shown in Table 2.3, and that resulted in the phenomenon known as *excessive competition* among private banks and corporations. The ensured access to credit from the Bank of Japan encouraged city banks to overlend (Suzuki 1974). The Ministry of Finance's rescue of the failing banks from bankruptcy induced what is often referred to as "moral hazard," or the practice of aggressively lending money without regard to the risks. Size was used as the criterion for the Ministry of Finance's approval of new branch offices of city banks and MITI's distribution of foreign currency quotas, an approach that encouraged banks and corporations to grow still bigger to receive greater future benefits (Miyazaki 1963; Morozumi 1963a). Indirect financing made shareholders less important to the company and directly weakened their control over management. Reciprocal shareholding (the practice of mutually holding stock) between banks and corporations created a "hostage effect" (discussed later in the chapter) that counterbalanced the incentive of institutional shareholders to control management and banks' monitoring over corporate borrowers, and that led both to the banks' overlending and to the corporations' overborrowing (Nishiyama 1975). The main banks often failed to monitor their corporate borrowers closely because they had to compete vigorously in lending to big corporations (Miyazaki 1963, 1985; Morozumi 1963). In addition, the permanent employment system sustained the strong growth orientation of Japanese banks and corporations because a company's growth would create more opportunities for promotions and increase employee salaries and bonuses (Nishiyama 1975; Okazaki 1993; Okumura 1975, 1995a). Business groups adopted a one-set investment strategy, in which corporations were pushed to make aggressive investments to gain market share in various emerging industries (Miyazaki 1963; Morozumi 1963).

Indeed, strong coordination contributed to high growth, but it did so as much by its own direct action as through the mechanism of excessive competition, which resulted from weak control, the other side of the coordination coin. According to the Japanese distinction, in *normal* competition, private corporations make a business plan, supervise production, and make

Table 2.3 *Weak Control and Monitoring Seen from the Perspective of Finance*

The International Economic Order	The Role of the State	Intermediate Level Institutions and Mechanisms	Corporate Governance
The Bretton Woods System Fixed exchange rates Control over free flow of capital	*Expansionary Monetary Policy* Stable supply of credits to major city banks encouraged overlending	*Indirect Financing* Weakened the shareholders' control over management	*Permanent Employment System* Strong growth orientation Strong coordination, but weak control led to overborrowing and aggressive investments in production capacity and technological transfer
	The Convoy Administration Rescuing the failing banks induced moral hazard Approving new branch offices of city banks according to their size encouraged banks to grow bigger	*The Main Bank* Weakened the bank's monitoring over corporate finance	
	Promoting Exports Distributing the foreign currency quotas to big corporations according to their size encouraged them to grow bigger	*Reciprocal Shareholding* Hostage effect weakened both control and monitoring	
		Development of Keiretsu One-set investment strategy induced excessive competition	

investment decisions according to the profit principle. *Excessive* competition, in contrast, observes the market-share principle.[3] I argue that this distinction may not be adequate. As demonstrated by Japanese corporate investment behavior during the bubble, excessive competition also could have taken place for the purpose of making additional profits through financial speculation. Drawing on the perspective of organizational ecology, I argue that excessive competition really means that corporations compete vigorously, rushing toward a common investment target, disregarding the declining survival rate of the increasingly dense organizational population.[4] In theory, normal competition should lead to production concentration. Because competition produces both winners and losers, the winners should grow in size and realize economies of scale. The excessive competition among Japanese corporations, however, did not significantly reduce the number of companies in an organizational population, and it failed to achieve an increased concentration of production. Although the level of capital concentration certainly increased in the 1950s and early 1960s, the level of market shares held by each keiretsu, an indicator of production concentration, declined compared with that of the prewar period. In other words, an increasing level of capital concentration coexisted with a decreasing level of production concentration. Even though the Japanese financial institutions were able to channel the country's oversaved money to the manufacturers through various business networks, none of the private companies was able to build a dominant position in the market (Miyazaki 1963, 52–58).

The dilemma of the struggle between strong coordination and weak control, and its consequence of excessive competition, sheds light on two major issues related to the debate on the developmental state referred to in Chapter 1. First, it shows that while the industrial policy practiced by the developmental state emphasized strategic allocation of resources, its financial policy focused instead on maintaining a stable supply of capital and reducing investment risks. Second, it shows that although the developmental state focused on coordination, its efforts often created the unexpected outcome of encouraging excessive competition. Together, these two pairs of seemingly contradicting yet supplementary facets explain the difference in coordination between the developmental state in the Japanese economy

---

3 The term *excessive competition* in the Japanese context has two different implications. One is that numerous small businesses coexist and compete with one another. In many cases, they must cut the prices of their products below production cost. This kind of excessive competition has contributed both to companies' low profits and employees' low income. In discussing this issue, Japanese scholars often use the term *dual structure*. The other implication of the term *excessive competition* is that big corporations compete with one another rigorously in investing in production capacity and technological transfers (Miyazaki 1963, 1966; Morozumi 1963a).
4 See Hannan and Freeman (1989).

and a socialist state in a planned economy. Unlike the strong coordination that is typical in a planned economy dominated by direct bureaucratic control, the strong coordination in the Japanese economic system did not replace but in many cases unintentionally encouraged competition, especially in the export sector. This competition can be attributed in part to the state's role in maintaining a stable supply of industrial capital and reducing invest-ment risks. Without such a competition component, in contrast, the coordi-nation in the planned economies of the former socialist nations, which was much stronger than that of the Japanese economy, never yielded strong inter-national competitiveness.

The role of the Japanese developmental state in reducing investment risks was as important as the country's strategic resource allocation. Under the Bretton Woods system, the central bank bore the responsibility of holding the exchange rate fixed. That released the corporate financial managers from the need to worry about day-to-day changes (Strange 1986, 11). In contrast to the financial systems of Germany (credit-based but institution-dominated) and Britain and the United States (capital market-based), the system of Japan, like that of France, is credit-based and price-administered. Through such a financial system, the Japanese state exerted a great impact on economic growth (Zysman 1983). This, however, does not mean that "in Japan a ratio-nal banker *must* wish to follow the lead of the central bank. The government's industrial priorities of growth and exports *will be* met. The banks entangled with selected sectors *will not be* constrained by their ability to fund their loans, though banks in other sectors of the economy *will be*" (Zysman 1983, 248).[5] In contrast to France, where the Ministry of Finance was in charge of both financial and industrial policies, in Japan these two responsibilities were divided among MITI, the Bank of Japan, and the Ministry of Finance (Calder 1993). The Bank of Japan and the Ministry of Finance concentrated on ways to use macroeconomic policy to sustain economic growth. They cared much less than MITI about specific industrial policies. The Bank of Japan practiced *window guidance*, which focused on the amount of loans and various interest rates but did not involve direct control over the credit allocation of private banks. Instead, the bank ensured the credit of major city banks and then let these banks, which were the main banks of keiretsu companies, decide which company or which project to finance. Although the Japanese state did not control the credit allocation of private banks (Calder 1993), it nonetheless played an extremely important role in reducing investment risks. Without considering the insurance function performed by the state, one can hardly explain why Japanese banks were not afraid of bankruptcy when their loans

---

5 Italics added except on the word *must*.

greatly exceeded the deposits they had generated, no matter how strategically clever these private banks might be.

Why did excessive competition not result in a major crisis for the Japanese economic system during the expansion of trade and production in the 1950s and 1960s? The reason is that it was supported by the three contingent conditions. First, the Bretton Woods system allowed the Bank of Japan to use its monetary policy to simultaneously balance payments and promote economic growth. Second, the bottleneck of payments in the Japanese economy often forced the Bank of Japan to tighten the money supply, a policy that was enhanced by the shortage of capital along with the corporations' reliance on bank loans. Although private banks and corporations failed to control and monitor themselves, the Bank of Japan and the Ministry of Finance performed that role at the macro level. And third, the continuing expansion of trade, the easy access to international markets under asymmetric cooperation with the United States, and the high growth of the Japanese economy helped absorb overbuilt production capacity and overlapping investments in technological transfers.

Beginning in the early 1970s, however, these contingent conditions began to disappear. First, the reduction in investment risks through government control of banking and the ultimate monitoring of the entire economic system through the Bank of Japan's monetary policy were significantly weakened. When a floating exchange rate replaced the fixed exchange rate, the Bank of Japan could no longer bear the responsibility of keeping the exchange rate fixed. After Japan's payments turned from trade deficits to trade surpluses, the Bank of Japan lost another means of simultaneously balancing its payments and stimulating domestic growth. With the easing of the payments bottleneck, the Bank of Japan was not subjected to pressure from the periodic tightening of the money supply (Ōkurashō 1991). During the liberalization of finance, moreover, state control of the banking industry was weakened. Private corporations were allowed to raise capital in the overseas markets, and banks were allowed to compete with one another by offering low interest rates. As a result, the effectiveness of the ultimate control and monitoring functions formerly performed by the Bank of Japan declined.

Second, control and monitoring at the corporate level, already weak, became still weaker. When the Bank of Japan could no longer control investment risks for Japanese corporations, an alternative mechanism of self-control and monitoring was in order. What actually took place, however, was the opposite. After the First Oil Shock ended the high growth period, Japanese corporations were under strong pressure to improve efficiency. To save interest payments, they began to reduce the amounts of loans they borrowed from the banks (Miyazaki 1985). The liberalization of finance in the 1980s increased the corporations' freedom to raise capital through equity finance. As a result of these two changes in the relationship between banks and big corporations, the banks' monitoring of big corporations deteriorated further. Having lost their leverage over big corporations, banks could not monitor them closely even had they wanted to do so. With the increase in equity finance in the 1980s, shareholders' control over management should have been strengthened, but it was not, because the practice of reciprocal shareholding remained intact and many of the newly issued stocks were purchased by institutional investors. The resulting hostage effect of reciprocal shareholding served to increase managerial autonomy and weaken the institutional shareholders' control over management.

Third, investment risks increased substantially during the financial and monetary expansion of the 1980s. Not only was there an increasing free flow of capital across national borders, but also, after the high growth period ended, it took much longer for overbuilt production capacities to be absorbed. Corporations that had significantly overinvested began to face serious consequences. As manufacturing companies tried to avoid the danger of being caught by their own overinvestment in production capacity, they became more aggressive investing in the stock and real estate markets in an effort to make up profits, a practice called *zai'tech* (financial technology).

The factor that increased investment risks most, however, was the Mundell–Flemming trilemma faced by the state's international financial policy after the collapse of the Bretton Woods system. Under the conditions of a free flow of capital and a floating exchange rate, the goal of maintaining a stable exchange rate often conflicted with the two other goals: that of maintaining convertibility and that of promoting domestic economic growth. At most, a state can achieve two of these three goals simultaneously (Krugman 1999a, 1999b). In the 1970s, the dollar-based prices of tradable factors in the international markets increased rapidly. If Japan had chosen to appreciate the yen's value to reduce its trade surplus, it would have prevented increases in the prices of domestic goods because the appreciation of the yen would have strengthened Japan's purchasing power in international markets. Instead, the Japanese state chose an expansionary fiscal policy to balance its trade surplus amid the rapid increase of inflation in international markets. For Japan to shift its economy from being driven by exports to being driven by domestic demand, the relative prices of nontradable factors had to rise at a faster pace than those of tradable factors. As a result, the domestic prices of tradable factors were maintained at the same level as those of the international markets, but the prices of the nontradable factors increased at a faster pace. Making this choice, Japan inevitably suffered from hyperinflation (Ōkurashō 1991, Vol. 9, 417). Then, in the early 1980s, to finance its undersaved economy, the United States kept its interest rates high to attract international capital. The inflow of foreign money increased the demand for the dollar, and that kept the dollar strong in the first half of the 1980s. Because a strong dollar meant a weak yen, Japanese corporations were able to export massively to the U.S. markets, and that drastically increased U.S. trade deficits with Japan. To reduce the U.S. trade surplus with its ally countries, Japan joined with the United States to initiate a multilateral, cooperative monetary policy, known as the Plaza Accord, in 1985. When the Bank of Japan's intervention in the foreign exchange market created an economic slowdown in late 1986, the bank reversed its monetary policy in an effort to stimulate economic growth. This action led to an oversupply of money in both 1986 and 1987. On top of that, the Japanese state also adopted an expansionary fiscal policy, and the urban development plans it sponsored served to channel a flood of private investments into the real estate and stock markets, which in turn created a favorable environment for the bubble.

When the state and the central bank could no longer reduce investment risks but rather served to increase investment risks, and when the self-control and monitoring function declined further, Japanese corporations responded to the financial and monetary expansion by turning to zai'tech and equity finance, engaging actively in massive financial speculation in the real estate and stock markets. Ironically, even as the Western countries were speaking of Japan's long-term thinking as a cultural virtue, Japanese corporations were allowing themselves to be driven by short-term thinking in the form of short-term profits. This reveals another facet of the mechanism of excessive competition, namely, joining the competition driven by a common trend and disregarding the risks – created by the density of organizational ecology – that are involved in such competition.

STABILITY VERSUS ELEVATING THE ECONOMIC STRUCTURE: THE MECHANISM OF TOTAL EMPLOYMENT

Social protection in Japan during the 1950s and 1960s had been sustained by the international economic order. The Bretton Woods system and the asymmetric cooperation with the United States within the GATT had shaped the postwar settlement in Japan in significant ways. The Bretton Woods system allowed the Japanese state to use the policy mix of an expansionary monetary policy to promote economic growth and a deflationary fiscal policy to control inflation. The latter policy, together with the state's low taxation policy, however, seriously restrained the possibility of developing a welfare state in Japan. To maintain political stability with limited public resources, the Japanese state privatized its function of social protection, meanwhile relying on its growth policy to create new jobs and its cartel policy and regulations to maintain the existing jobs.

In discussions about the welfare state, measured by its ratio of welfare spending against GDP, Japan is often put in the same group with the United States. Based on the strong preference of the Japanese economic system for stability over radical adjustment, however, a label of liberalism is sometimes misleading. As far as the system's preference is concerned, Japan should belong to the same group with European countries instead of the United States. Because the mechanism of social protection practiced in the welfare state in Europe differs from that of the welfare society in Japan, we cannot apprehend the nature of the Japanese case simply based on public spending on social welfare. Japan relied on privatized social protection. Its cartel policy and government regulations played an important role in maintaining employment. As far as employment is concerned, these strategies were functionally similar to the macroeconomic policy adopted by the welfare state in European countries because both of them aimed at maintaining employment. Without a strong government-sponsored unemployment assistance program, the Japanese state emphasized not only job creation, often in the sunrise industries, but also job maintenance by cartels and government regulations in the sunset industries (Kume 1998; Tilton 1996; Upham 1993; Uriu 1996).

This strategy is called *total employment* (Nomura 1998). Total employment is different from the concept of full employment in Keynesian economics. *Full employment* means that at the present wage level, all those who want to be employed have a job, a situation that reflects the best allocation of human resources. By definition, however, the concept of full employment does not mean "no unemployment." Unemployment does exist among those who voluntarily withdraw from the labor market because of their dissatisfaction with present wage levels or those who, because of the difficulties of mobility among industries or geographical regions, cannot get a job. Total employment, in contrast, means that all those who want to work have some kind of job. It suggests neither that human resources are optimally allocated nor that everyone who works is satisfied with his or her wage (Nomura 1998, 36–38).

As Table 2.4 shows, the Japanese total employment strategy was sustained by three major cornerstones. First, the state promoted economic growth and favored the oligopolies in its competition policy, which in turn enabled big corporations to institutionalize the permanent employment system. This mixed both the production function and the distribution function in the same

Table 2.4 *The Mechanism of Total Employment and Egalitarian Distribution*

The International Economic Order	The Role of the State	Type of Business Organization and the Impact of State Policy on Employment	The Gender Role Played by the Wife in Egalitarian Distribution
The Bretton Woods system	Policy mix of expansionary monetary policy, deflationary fiscal policy, and low taxation (Both made the welfare state impossible and led to privatized social protection.)		
	Promoting oligopolies	Big corporations (permanent employment)	Full-time housewife (reducing household income)
Asymmetric cooperation between the United States and Japan (aggressively exporting while keeping domestic markets closed)	Tolerating cartels	Medium-size and small companies (nonpermanent but stable)	Part-time worker (increasing household income)
	Government regulations	Family-owned mini shops (nonpermanent but stable)	Work both at home and family business (increasing household income)

Note: This table has incorporated the argument made by Nomura Masami (1998) regarding the three employment patterns in Japan.

private corporations and ensured job security for their employees. Second, the state allowed the medium-size and small companies to organize cartels, especially during times of economic recession. This measure served to prevent bankruptcies of those companies that were keeping their workers employed. Third, the state enacted rigid regulations protecting the domestic sector, such as agriculture and retail industries. By restraining competition in these industries, these government regulations enabled numerous tiny family shops to survive.

In the existing literature, it is often the inefficiency that resulted from cartels and government regulations that attracts attention. Their important role in the general picture of Japanese employment tends to be obscured. Many analysts are quick to point out that the permanent employment system covers only about one-third of the Japanese labor force (which is true), but such statements tend to imply that the other two-thirds of the Japanese labor force have faced the same kind of job insecurity as their counterparts in the West. No one has explained why, if that is so, the other two-thirds of Japanese workers have not acted in the same way as their Western counterparts in protecting their jobs, either through confrontation with management or active participation in distributive politics at the national level. The truth is that because most of the other two-thirds of the Japanese labor force work for either medium-size and small companies or the family-owned mini shops, most of them are under several types of protection: cartels and other types of uncompetitive industrial practices defined by trade associations, or government regulations in the sunset industries and sectors. The overall level of job insecurity in Japan, comparatively speaking, was indeed much lower than that of their Western counterparts until the collapse of the bubble.

Although these three cornerstones helped sustain employment, they also created a sharp social hierarchy because of the large gaps in income among the three categories of family shops, small and medium-size companies, and big corporations. Given these well-known income gaps, how did Japan also achieve a high level of egalitarian distribution?[6] The secret of the coexistence of a sharp social hierarchy and egalitarian distribution was that Japanese women played an important role in providing supplementary *household income*, a major measurement of economic equality used by the Gini index (Nomura 1998). Women in the Japanese economy functioned as a *marginal labor force* whose entry into and exit from the labor market was flexible. Among the three categories, the wives of employees who worked for big corporations

---

6 Japan specialists tend to quickly point out that the permanent employment system covers only one-third of the Japanese labor force and that women and employees of the medium-size and small companies receive much lower wages. In contrast, comparatists, citing various statistical data, assert that Japan is one of the most egalitarian societies in the world.

tended to stay at home, playing the role of education mothers[7]; the wives of employees who worked for medium-size and small companies tended to work part-time to make a supplementary income for the household; and the wives of self-employed workers tended to help at work when the business was busy (Nomura 1998).[8] This employment pattern resulted in both a low unemployment rate, inasmuch as part-timers were not counted as unemployed, and a more egalitarian distribution of household income.

The total employment strategy has several merits. Most importantly, it helped Japan to maintain political stability. By keeping everyone in business, the state was under much less political pressure to provide unemployment assistance. This enabled Japan to keep a small government and to concentrate its limited national resources on production rather than on distribution, two important factors in explaining its high growth. In addition, permanent employment in big corporations tied innovation to its rewards. An agreement on how to distribute the gains generated from innovation using an institutional framework served to promote innovation, because the boundary of competing interests blurred when the same institution was responsible both for sustaining economic growth and for distributing economic welfare (Sabel 1994). The strategy of "development without losers" adopted by the Japanese state made the economic system very "encompassing" (Olson 1982), and that served to defuse domestic tensions and conflicts, creating a favorable political environment for high growth.

A major drawback of the total employment strategy is that it seriously weakens the system's capacity to elevate the economic structure in the long run. Because "the reorientation and reorganization of the economy inevitably entails social dislocations and political conflicts," a country must "displace powerful and entrenched industrial interests in order to accomplish the sectoral shifts and reorganization of production essential to continued growth" (Zysman 1983, 53). But Japan chose to avoid social dislocations and political conflicts by keeping everyone in business and accommodating the interests of the incumbent sectors and industries. As a result, the system indeed became encompassing, affecting the interests of all major players in national politics. This encompassment, however, was based on a political compromise among the major distributional coalitions. The encompassing organization and the distributional coalition often form a dichotomy in which the encompassing organization sustains economic growth while the distributional

---

7 As used in Japan, this phrase refers to women whose primary role is to stay at home full time and make sure that their children perform well at school and pass the examination for college.

8 Nomura admits that the three patterns of employment among Japanese women he has presented do not cover those women who work full-time, and thus his explanation is partial instead of complete. I share his position but still believe that his explanation, even partial, provides a powerful explanation of egalitarian distribution in Japan.

coalitions tend to be counterproductive. The encompassing Japanese economic system, however, may also contain the seeds for stagnation because as the interests of each major distributional coalition are locked into the present economic structure, the political system loses the dynamics to break the equilibrium in support of reform. As a result, "there [would] be less diversity of advocacy, opinion, and policy, and fewer checks to erroneous ideas and policies" (Olson 1982, 52). The more that egalitarian societies prosper economically, the more difficult it is for them to reorient their economic systems politically. When a well-developed unemployment assistance program does not exist and the interests of the major distributional coalitions are protected by the current economic structure, a nation faces only two alternatives: Either suffer from a stagnation if it prefers stability, or suffer from the pain of radical reform if it prefers a significant upgrading of its economic structure.

During the high growth period, the strategy of total employment, as the Japanese postwar settlement for social protection, worked well only under certain contingent conditions, especially the Bretton Woods system and the GATT.[9] First, sustained by asymmetric cooperation with the United States, the absence of international competition in Japan's domestic markets supported the creation of cartels and the government protection of the domestic sector or sunset industries. When the domestic markets were closed, cartels or government regulations basically served to assume the task of domestic distribution. As long as the major coalitions in Japanese distributional politics agreed, the disabling effect of cartels and government protections would be, in a political sense at least, under control. Second, the continuing high-speed economic growth during the international expansion of trade and production created major gains in productivity, which outweighed the loss of efficiency created by the total employment strategy, and the benefits generated by this solution for maintaining political stability were huge. Third, there existed many sunrise industries in the 1950s and 1960s. The huge gains in productivity in the rapid expansion of these industries made tolerable the inefficiency that resulted from keeping the sunset industries and sectors (Katz 1998). In this period, the Japanese strategy of upgrading its economic structure was simply to keep adding the sunrise industries on top of the sunset industries instead of shifting away from the latter to the former.

Starting in the 1970s, however, two competing forces began to challenge the strategy of total employment, significantly increasing the cost of maintaining political stability through privatized social protection. On the one

9 I thank Robert Keohane for reminding me that by encouraging the free flow of goods, the GATT was rather a destabilizing factor to social protection. I stress here that it was the asymmetric cooperation between the United States and its ally countries that sustained the theme of social protection by allowing these countries to keep their domestic markets closed.

hand, pressure to improve efficiency increased dramatically after the First Oil Shock ended the high growth. The liberalization, privatization, and deregulation programs released market forces that increased inequality in distribution. As the long-term movement of capitalist economies shifted gears toward the release of market forces, the United States was no longer willing to continue asymmetric cooperation, and it demanded greater access to Japan's domestic markets, fair competition, and a reexamination of the transparent rules of business transactions. These actions shook the political foundations of Japanese cartels and government protections. At the same time, the entry of newly industrialized countries, developing countries, and former socialist countries into international competition began to challenge the Japanese position in international trade. As the Japanese economy matured, there were not many sunrise industries any more and the Japanese could no longer rely on the old strategy of adding sunrise industries on top of sunset industries (Katz 1998). As a result of the bubble, egalitarian distribution (measured by the Gini index of household income) deteriorated substantially because there was a large gap in economic well-being between those who owned land and stocks and those who didn't. After the bubble collapsed in the early 1990s, Japan moved quickly toward an inegalitarian society. Driven by intense international competition and deregulation, increasing numbers of big corporations moved their production bases or parts supplies offshore, and their former medium-size and small suppliers lost their contracts and had a hard time surviving. Meanwhile, Japanese women became the first victims of layoffs, and they could no longer play the role of enhancing household-based distributive equality.

On the other hand, the state continued to protect inefficient domestic sectors and industries that were not only increasing inefficiency but also preventing Japan from elevating its economic structure. For two decades, Japan seemed to have outperformed other advanced industrialized countries in the structural adjustment after the First Oil Shock. In North America and Western Europe, the crisis of the 1970s had destroyed the compromise forged in the postwar period. Major distributional coalitions had an increasingly hard time managing the terms of their accommodation. As capitalist economies shifted away from social protection, "market considerations [were] pressing all of them in ways contrary to the patterns built up over several decades" (Gourevitch 1986, 30). In Japan, in contrast, rapid changes in the political landscape had not appeared. The Japanese model of the welfare society lacked a good government-sponsored unemployment assistance program. As a result, the political cost of a radical structural adjustment was very high. As the Japanese economy confronted the challenges of a rapidly appreciating yen and higher oil prices, the weak sectors and industries forced the state to provide additional government protections (Kume 1998; Pempel 1998; Tilton 1996). Under such circumstances, the efficient export-related sector had to pay the cost of the inefficient non–export-related sectors (Katz 1998; Vogel 1999a, 1999b). To subsidize a low-price strategy in overseas markets and to bear the financial burden of maintaining permanent employment and seniority-based wages, Japanese corporations maintained high prices in Japan's domestic markets. The high domestic prices resulting from the cartels and government protection became a serious political problem, not only internationally but also, increasingly, domestically.

This dilemma between maintaining stability and elevating the economic structure sheds light on the debate concerning social welfare in Japan. It shows that Japanese developmentalism not only focused on strategic resource allocations, promoting the exports sector and industries, but also paid great attention to maintaining political stability by relying on private institutions to perform the welfare function (Katz 1998; Murakami 1994). These two sides do not conflict but rather are mutually dependent and reinforce each other. The conventional Eurocentric measurement of the welfare state in terms of the state's formal welfare spending is not adequate to describe the mechanism of equal distribution in Japan because "there are more ways than one to distribute the fruits of growth and to 'socialize the costs of change' that might otherwise destabilize industrial order" (Weiss 1998, 157). At the same time, the dilemma also shows that the Japanese model of the welfare society has serious limits. The liberal model represented by the United States emphasizes equal opportunity in competition, whereas the European model of the welfare state focuses on equal rights in social entitlement. The Japanese model of the welfare society, in contrast to both models, highlights an equal outcome in distribution. (This statement neither suggests that Japan does not have an inequality problem nor rejects the existence and intensity of political conflicts regarding the distribution of economic welfare among different interest groups in Japan.) Moreover, the equal outcome in distribution (measured by household income) is achieved, not intentionally but rather as an unexpected outcome of women working as a marginal labor force and suffering gender-based discrimination. Rather than treat everyone as equal in competition, Japanese industrial and competition policies have a strong orientation in favor of big corporations.

The preference and institutional arrangement for social protection have important consequences to an economic system's performance in structural adjustment during the 1990s. Between stability and the elevation of the economic structure, one system tends to do well only in one of these two tasks. In terms of preference, both Japan and Europe prefer stability, whereas the United States prefers quick adjustment. Although both prefer stability,

Europe relies on the welfare state whereas Japan relies on the welfare society. In both the American and, to some extent, the European models, achieving efficiency is the primary goal of private corporations, and the role of providing unemployment assistance is designated primarily to the state. In the Japanese model of privatized social protection, in contrast, both the function of improving efficiency and the function of maintaining jobs are the responsibility of the same private institutions. The combination of a system's preference and its institutional arrangement for social protection has yielded three distinctive patterns in the response to the globalization in the 1990s. The United States has plenty of low-paying jobs but little job security. Europe has high unemployment but also high-paying jobs. Japan has both stability and stagnation (for discussion of the three patterns of the responses, see Longworth 1998).

CHAPTER 3

THE RISE OF THE PRINCIPLES OF COORDINATION AND STABILITY

Why does a study of the reversion of the Japanese economy in the 1990s have to start in the 1930s? The reason is that from the perspective of the long-term movement of capitalist economies discussed by either Giovanni Arrighi (1994) or Karl Polanyi (1957 [1944]), the postwar expansion of trade and production and the efforts to support social protection in the 1950s and 1960s must be considered as part of a larger process in this movement. In the previous wave of globalization, the collapse of the gold standard in 1914 triggered a series of crises for capitalist economies on a global scale; in response to the Great Depression and World War II, coordination and stability emerged as the two leading principles of the Japanese economic system, which have significantly influenced the postwar institutional evolution of the Japanese economy. The two structural shifts that took place after the early 1970s and the discussion of the so-called third way (discussed later in this chapter) in the ongoing debate on globalization have reopened two questions: whether the long-term movement of capitalist economies actually occurred as a cycle and what the contemporary implications are of the industrialized countries' responses to the crisis that followed the previous wave of globalization.

In this chapter, I briefly discuss how the collapse of the gold standard and Japan's maladaptation to the new environment led to a series of crises, both domestic and international, and how coordination and stability became the leading principles in the Japanese economy during these crises. During the Great Depression and World War II, strengthening coordination and maintaining stability became the top priorities of the Japanese economic system. Avoiding massive unemployment was the key in Japanese efforts to control the negative impact of the Depression. In 1931, the Japanese state enacted the Important Industry Control Law in an effort to rely on the mandatory cartels to battle unemployment by preventing bankruptcies. During the war mobilization, stability continued to be a major concern of the state.

When Japan started a full-scale invasion of China in 1937, the state began to prohibit both layoffs and labor strikes. Then, as the country prepared for a total war against the major Western powers, Japan made great efforts to strengthen coordination in order to optimize its resource allocation for the war mobilization. These efforts led to many drastic changes in Japanese economic institutions. The state began to exercise tight control over resource allocation by enacting various government regulations and practicing industrial licensing. To design and implement a war mobilization plan in a capitalist economy, the state organized compulsory trade associations, which played an important role in distributing production materials. Because individual as well as institutional investors were worried about the high risks associated with investments in munitions-related industries, indirect financing became the major source of industrial capital, and the main bank system emerged to ensure a continuing supply of capital to manufacturing companies. Meanwhile, subcontracting became an important component in wartime coordination between big corporations and the medium-size and small companies.

THE COLLAPSE OF THE GOLD STANDARD AND THE CRISIS OF THE LAST PEAK OF GLOBALIZATION

The fate of the Japanese economy in the period 1914–1931 shares many similarities with that of the period 1971–1989. Here are some examples. Recall that in 1914, Britain ceased its support of the convertibility between the pound and gold, and the gold standard collapsed. In the same year, World War I broke out. From the perspective of the Japanese economy, the first similarity between the two periods is that stagnation did not begin immediately in 1914 but instead took hold following a major economic boom. In 1914–1919, Japan's GNP increased at an average annual rate of more than 17.5 percent. Japan's trade deficit of some 65 million yen became a trade surplus of 352 million yen. Measured by the gold reserve, the Japanese national wealth ranked second among the five great powers, behind only that of the United States (Asher 1999, 9). Second, the money supply of the Bank of Japan increased rapidly, from 386 million yen at the end of 1914 to 1.14 billion yen at the end of 1918. Third, there was an economic recession. The end of World War I also ended the wartime economic boom. Taking wholesale prices in July 1914 as 100, they reached 225 in November 1918 when the war ended; but between November 1918 and March 1919, prices for many consumer goods declined sharply. Fourth, to counter this downturn, the Japanese state adopted an expansionary fiscal policy, shifting from, on the one hand, an orthodox policy of domestic monetary restriction to balance the trade deficits to, on the other hand, providing domestic industries with ample funds while discounting the debts of exporters (Asher 1999, 19).

This expansionary fiscal policy was created by Takahashi Korekiyo, known as "the Keynes of Japan," who became Japan's finance minister in September 1918. He held that inflation was inevitable in the expansion of trade and would not necessarily cause a rise in consumer prices. A tight money policy would lead the economy to a recession. Takahashi decided to increase public spending to strengthen national defense, improve the transportation and communication infrastructure, promote education, and encourage industrial development.

Fifth, this expansionary fiscal policy triggered a bubble in the Japanese economy. Taking wholesale prices in July 1914 as 100, between March 1918 and March 1919 they increased from 213 to 338. Retail prices increased 160 percent in March 1919 compared with the preceding year. The Tokyo stock exchange index more than doubled within one year, jumping from 239 yen in March 1919 to 549 yen in March 1920. In Osaka, land that formerly sold at 1,700 yen per *tsubo* (one tsubo is equivalent to 3.954 square yards) now jumped to 4,500 yen. In Tokyo, land that formerly sold at 1,000 yen now was selling at 3,000 yen. This inflation led to a further increase in public spending. In the 1918 and 1919 fiscal years, 20 percent of the public spending was caused by inflation (Gotō 1973, 47–48). On March 15, 1920, stock markets in both Tokyo and Osaka crashed. By May of that year, 74 banks had gone bankrupt. The country whose records in both wartime and postwar economic booms had prevailed over other industrialized countries now entered a postwar economic recession until it was hit by a major financial crisis in 1927.

In comparison with how the Japanese economy stands today, its situation was much worse in the late 1920s. The miscalculated timing in returning to the gold standard (Japan did not do so until 1929) further deepened the Japanese financial crisis in the late 1920s. The policy makers held that Japan's expansion in China would require hard currency. In addition, to lift the ban on gold exports, in place since 1917, Japan would have had to stabilize wartime inflation and obtain a stable value for the yen. Achieving both goals would require a deflationary fiscal policy. Accordingly, in 1922 the government shifted to a deflationary policy. Initially, this policy helped to reduce trade deficits and lower consumer prices. But in 1923, before the government made the decision to return to the gold standard, Japan suffered a major earthquake. The recovery efforts led to a rapid increase in trade deficits, and lifting the ban became impossible (Arisawa 1976, 41). When the state finally lifted the ban on gold exports in 1929, it adopted a deflationary policy aimed at lowering wages, stimulating corporate concentration, and improving corporate profits in the long run. It also reduced public spending on national defense and tightened fiscal spending. The lifting of the gold embargo, however, exerted a strong negative impact on the stock market. Stock and commodity prices declined rapidly. Only three months after Japan lifted the ban on gold exports, the New York stock market crashed, marking the beginning of the Great Depression. Because the lifting of the ban on gold exports strengthened the links between the Japanese economy and international markets, the Depression, which started in the United States, quickly reached Japan.

MAINTAINING STABILITY AND THE RISE OF THE MANDATORY CARTELS

When the Great Depression led to massive bankruptcies, maintaining employment became critical to political stability in Japan. Between 1929 and 1931, Japan's gross national product (GNP) declined 18 percent; exports, 47 percent; household consumption, 17 percent; and investment in plants and equipment, 31 percent. The stock market also crashed. If we set the January 1921 market average at 100, the average stock price in 1930 was only 44.6 (Arisawa 1976, 53–54). In addition, the economic hard times increased the incidence of labor disputes. In 1930, 195,805 Japanese workers were involved in 2,289 disputes, and 81,329 people took part in 906 strikes.

Until 1931, Japanese companies enjoyed the freedom not to join cartels and not to follow agreements made by cartels. That changed when the state enacted the Important Industry Control Law in 1931 to "battle the anarchy of Japanese industry and eliminate the root of economic instability" (Takahashi 1933, 63). To reduce the damage caused by reckless competition, the law established mandatory cartels (Rinji Sangyō Gōrikyoku 1932, 1–5). According to this law, when two-thirds of the companies in one industry joined a cartel, the state had the authority to ask the outsider companies to obey any agreement made by the cartel. When the state believed that the cartels' agreements violated the public interest, moreover, the state also had the power to change or dissolve them. This law led to a rapid development of mandatory cartels in Japan (see Figure 3.1). Among the 110 cartels existing in 1933, dates of establishment are available for 96. Among these 96 cartels, only 13 existed before 1920. Twenty-eight were established in the 1920s, and 55 were established between 1930 and 1933. Among the 110 cartels in 1933, 33 were in heavy industry, 30 in the chemical industry, and 11 in the textile industry (Takahashi 1933).

The rise of mandatory cartels was driven by the changing role of the state in economic governance. In the past, the state had acted more or less as a

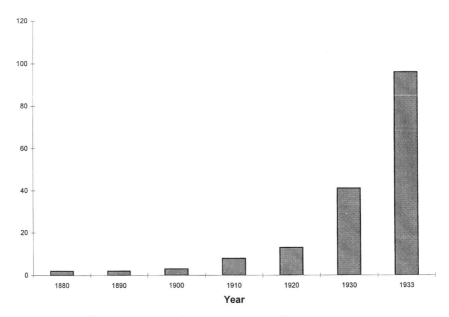

Figure 3.1. *Number of Japanese cartels: 1880–1933.*
Source: Takahashi, 1933, pp. 121–126.

"night watchman." It emphasized the release of market forces constrained by mercantilism and medieval guilds by establishing and enforcing property rights. The state enforced both civil and business laws to regulate and adjust relationships among private individuals and legal persons. The responsibility for maintaining stability was left to either the market or private planning.

Although cartels maintained stability, however, they soon became the subject of public policy because they raised the issue of monopoly. In the late nineteenth century and the early twentieth century, two schools emerged regarding state policy on competition. One school, represented by the United States, asserted that cartels monopolized markets and obtained huge profits at the cost of consumers and wage earners and that cartels were major barriers to efficiency and economic equality. To restrain cartels, the United States enacted the Sherman Antitrust Act in 1890. Canada, New Zealand, and Australia, all of which shared the common law tradition, were influenced by this school of thinking. Another school, represented by Germany, maintained that in a market economy, recession took place in the form of an economic cycle. To avoid this waste of an enormous amount of wealth, cartels could be used to organize the national economy and establish a balance between production and consumption. Consequently, cartels were encouraged rather than discouraged in Germany and in those countries that followed the German tradition (Kunihiro 1941). Japan belonged to the German school.

While cartels had been formed in large numbers in Japan, they existed mainly in the textile industry and their self-regulation had not changed the atomistic structure of small businesses. Their major function in the early years was to reach agreements to postpone production for a certain number of days. Between the Sino-Japanese war in 1894–1895 and World War I, some voluntary cartels emerged, generally among small-scale exporters; most were short-lived. Cartels in heavy industries developed rapidly after the Russo-Japanese war of 1904–1905, mainly to control sales and seldom to control production. Only after World War I did cartels begin to control production and sales simultaneously. Even then, however, they were still few in number (Haley 1991, 146; Inotani 1937; Takahashi 1933, 138–139). After World War I, the *zaibatsu,* or financial combines, became conglomerates. Unlike cartels that were confined to one industry and were organized by similar types of organizations, zaibatsu conglomerates included membership of all sorts of business organizations, and they coordinated businesses of their member companies in multiple industries (Kunihiro 1941, 7–9). Nevertheless, private ordering was dominant in the Japanese economy before the Great Depression.

The creation of mandatory cartels by the 1931 law was intended to maintain stability by preventing bankruptcies and unemployment. These cartels enacted quotas for production and sales, determined minimum prices, and organized joint marketing and distribution channels. Although some private companies did not join the cartels, the economy in general became more organized in comparison with the pre-1930 period. Mandatory cartels represented a new stage of associational order; they differed from the traditional cartels based on private initiative. In this new associational order, the property rights of private companies, including those of the zaibatsu conglomerates, were seriously restrained (Arisawa 1937b; Inotani 1937; Shimizu 1940). Private ordering by the zaibatsu in the past had transformed atomized production into an integrated process. It had enabled private companies to coordinate pricing policy, marketing channels, and the amount of production. In the final analysis, however, the coordination by the zaibatsu had served to promote the interests of each business group rather than to maintain stability of the economy as a whole. When the economy confronted the Great Depression, the state assumed leadership in restoring economic order (see Johnson 1982, 109).

Driven by its need to control resource allocation during war, the Japanese state further increased its emphasis on the stability principle. That led to the rise of an early pattern of total employment in the form of state control over both layoffs and strikes. After the China War broke out in 1937, the mobilization of human resources became an important policy priority. To ensure its war mobilization, the Japanese state began to control labor relations. It not only prohibited job transfers for individual workers but also controlled starting salaries. From then on, all salaries were raised together once a year (Otaka 1993; Noguchi 1995; Kobayashi et al. 1995). In October 1941, all Japanese males aged 16 to 40, and all unmarried females aged 16 to 25, were required to register their "occupational ability" with the state. Because of the shortage of skilled workers, the state sponsored various training programs.

The needs of the war mobilization forced the Japanese state to address the issue of distribution. Indeed, World War II marked an important new stage of state-building in the history of capitalism in many industrialized countries. Whereas state-building in the eighteenth and nineteenth centuries had achieved enormous success in establishing democratic political institutions, underprivileged social groups still existed. Now the existence of these groups and the inequality they had suffered became the greatest political barriers to the wartime mobilization of human resources. Many industrialized countries tried to compel these social groups to assume wartime political responsibility by enforcing compulsory equalization (Yamanouchi 1995). For its part, the Japanese state began to control wages and employment through the National General Mobilization Law of 1938, which was aimed at preventing any disturbance in controlling the labor market for the war mobilization. This law led to the institutionalization of earlier patterns of permanent employment: a seniority-based wage system and company-based labor unions. In the past, private companies had often laid off workers to reduce production costs during recessions, a practice that had led to instability. Under this law, the property rights of private companies were restrained.

In 1940, the Japanese state began to reorganize industrial patriotic associations, an action that had a profound impact on labor relationships. In the war mobilization, the ability-based wage was rejected; wages were not directly linked to workers' performance. Rather, they were interpreted as ensuring a certain standard of living. The logic was that workers worked for the state, whose duty was to ensure a certain standard of living. To control inflation and the production costs of munitions industries, the state began to adopt the so-called livelihood wage, "which in theory would meet the basic material needs of a worker and his family by rising automatically with age, seniority, and greater family responsibility" (Gordon 1985, 275). The central mission of the industrial patriotic associations after the Pacific War broke out was to promote productivity. In contrast to pre-1937 labor relations, when white-collar and blue-collar workers belonged to different unions, these new industrial patriotic associations included both groups as members.

These changes in labor relations were sustained ideologically by the combination of a version of the Marxist theory of production force and the fascist ideology that subscribed to what was called "compulsory equality." This version of the Marxist theory of the production force argued that to promote a nation's production power, it was crucial to rationalize the social structure in a reform. To mobilize Japanese workers into the state program of a managed economy, the working conditions of labor would have to be improved. Without a social policy to protect and train the labor force, the capital would not have been able to sustain the cycle of reproduction of the labor force.[1] The profit principle of private companies was regarded as the major barrier to war mobilization because it suggested that companies paid workers as little as possible to reduce production costs. Production in the wartime economy would need to be sustained, not by individuals' pursuit of profits but rather by their motivation to fight for the interests of the nation. Individuals would assume this motivation as a social function; they were integral parts of the body of the managed economy, which operated under the control of the state. Under such circumstances, social policy was important to the Japanese economy, not only because it was in the interest of the working class but also because it was in the interest of "aggregated capital." Without a proper social policy, aggregated capital would not have been able to "sustain the order of reproduction." Such a social policy was "a capitalist effort to eliminate the contradictions contained in the capitalist system." Because individual capitalists always acted in their own interests and did not support the adoption of a social policy, the state would have to take action on behalf of aggregated capital.

When the maximization of munitions production and the maintenance of political stability were the top policy agendas, the state did not allow any move by market forces to interfere with the program of war mobilization. In this special historical environment, efficiency and equality were no longer two competing agendas. Rather, they were perceived as supplementing each other. If the state had not addressed the issue of equality, it would have been impossible to generate wider public support for its military endeavor. Put

---

1 In the Marxist literature, *reproduction* means that production does not stop after one cycle. The profits earned in the process of production may be reinvested in the next cycle of production. This repeated next cycle of production is called "reproduction" in the literature on political economy.

differently, equality became a means of promoting efficiency. As then Japanese Minister of Commerce and Industry Kishi Nobusuke pointed out in 1942, during the war the state needed to ensure not only munitions production but also political stability. In a total war, the survival of the nation-state was at stake. The state had no choice except to mobilize the entire country. To achieve these goals, the state needed a type of governing structure fundamentally different from that of private interest groups, a structure that could carry out the national policy through cooperation between the state and the private sector and between management and labor (Kishi 1942).

DIRECT STATE CONTROL OF RESOURCE ALLOCATION

As part of war mobilization by the Japanese state, the early pattern of coordination for production relied heavily on the coercive measures of the state as it tried hard to control the allocation of resources. Many tools derived for strengthening coordination in war mobilization were used again in the postwar period to promote the high growth. To control entry into defense-related industries, the state began licensing business operations in these fields. In addition, it enacted many regulations that directly controlled the distribution of materials used in the production of both defense-related and civilian goods (Arisawa 1937a, 1937b, 1937c; Inotani 1937).

The state had always needed resources to build infrastructure, to maintain national security, and to redistribute economic welfare among citizens. Before the twentieth century, however, the scope of direct state control over resource allocation had been limited. But the national mobilization for the two world wars, especially World War II, forced the state in major industrialized countries to control resource allocation to an unprecedented level. The German theory of total war maintained that modern war involved not only military forces but also the entire economy, and victory would be determined not only by the superiority of weapons but also by the strength of a nation's economic institutions (for detailed discussion, see Gao 1994 and Gao 1997, Chapter 3). By extension, the theory argued that "the state [was] becoming increasingly important. It [had] to plan and organize the comprehensive employment of national resources even in peacetime" (Matsui 1938, 35). The state had to restrain the freedom of private companies because the pursuit of profits could jeopardize national mobilization. When the production of civilian goods conflicted with the interests of national security, the former was strongly repressed by the state (Yomiuri Shinbunsha 1972).

Licensing was the first form of state control over resource allocation. In 1940, 80 percent of Japanese firms employed five or fewer persons and contributed only 7.4 percent of the total industrial production; 97 percent of the firms employed fewer than 30 persons and contributed 27.1 percent of the total production (see Ueda Hirofumi 1987, 200). Between 1937 and 1941, the Japanese state enacted a series of laws governing the following industries: artificial gasoline, iron-steel, machine tools, shipbuilding, aircraft, light metal, and organic chemistry. To allocate the limited resources more effectively for war mobilization, the state not only forced inefficient medium-size and small firms out of business but also used its power of bureaucratic licensing to prevent them from entering munitions-related industries. The state typically would identify certain companies in these industries that deserved government support according to their significance to national defense rather than their profitability. Then the state would assist those who had encountered a deficit, faced the danger of bankruptcy, or confronted foreign competition. By preventing the entry of medium-size and small companies into these industries, the state was able to avoid competition for limited resources (Arisawa 1937a; Inotani 1937; Tsūsanshō 1964). These industry laws went into effect together with a set of practices that later became the mechanisms and policy tools in Japan's postwar industrial policy.

According to these industry laws, private companies needed government permission to operate businesses in these industries, and those that obtained permission had to submit their business plans to the government. Foreign companies were prohibited from entering into these industries in Japan. Meanwhile, the government would provide various means of assistance, in the form of land, tax breaks, tariff exemptions on imported equipment, grants for research and development, government subsidies for production, special treatment of corporate debts, and enforced reduction of business equipment (Minemura 1940; Shimizu 1940). The companies that received these benefits were responsible for executing their business plans. Government approval was required for any stock transactions to other parties, plans to begin or cease operations, mergers, and bankruptcies. These companies were obligated to make standardized products. The state had the authority to examine their businesses without advance notice and also tightly controlled the production and sale of products. The state also had the authority to demand that these companies buy, increase, or improve equipment, adopt new production procedures, change business plans, research special products, preserve raw materials and production materials, and merge with other companies. In exchange, the state also made a commitment to provide financial compensation to these companies when they encountered any losses (Tsūsanshō 1964). Any violation of the law would lead to the removal of a company's business license and its chief executive officer.

The National Mobilization Law of 1938 directly controlled the distribution of capital, labor, production, and daily materials through its annual national mobilization plans. This comprehensive law delegated to the executive office of the Japanese state unprecedented power in lawmaking and enforcement. To exercise its control over the economy, the Ministry of Commerce and Industry alone issued more than 80 ordinances in two years (Nihon Keizai Renmeikai 1940, 305–308). Under the National Mobilization Law of 1938, the Japanese state relied heavily on punishment at the discretion of the executive branch to enforce its policy objectives. Among the 50 articles of this law, 18 concerned penalties. Those people who violated the state's rules concerning labor, trade, production, and use of resources were subject to a prison term of up to three years and a fine of up to 5,000 yen. An Economic Security Division was established in each prefecture's police department; the overall force totaled more than 1,200 specialized officers. By 1940, the number of economic police stood at more than 4,000. According to statistics of the Economic Security Division of the Police Bureau of the Ministry of Home Affairs, by October 1939 more than 225,000 individuals had been charged with violating the state's economic regulations. By the end of 1938, a Council on Economic Police had been established in every prefecture; the councils became the center of coordination between the state and the private sector in enforcing government economic regulations (Ogino 1988, 351–355).

This expansion of power held by the executive branch was a common characteristic in many industrialized countries during the war (Arisawa 1937b; Miyazawa 1940; Wagatsuma 1948). Delegating legislative authority to the executive became a characteristic shared in different degrees by all industrialized countries. Not only did a new type of economic governance emerge, with increasing state constraints on the freedom of individuals in economic activities, but also the legal system witnessed a shift of legislative power from the parliament to the administration. During this process, however, countries fell into two groups depending on their constitutional structures. In Japan, Germany. and Italy, which adhered to the continental legal tradition and were influenced by fascism, this trend took place as a radical change of political institutions toward totalitarian regimes. The executive branch of the state obtained legislative power without any consultation with the legislative branch (Miyazawa 1940). As Tanaka Jirō (1942, 796) pointed out,

> In the past, laws emphasized legal stability and restrained the state intervention in the economy, aiming at nothing more than ensuring the intrinsic order of the economy. At present, laws reflect the will of the state on the economy, exemplify the detailed standards for the economy and establish an order for

the economy. The transition of the mission of the legal system brought about changes in not only the content of laws, but also the form of laws. It is under this context the increase of delegated legislation, elastic definitions or comprehensive articles can be properly explained.

In contrast, in the common law countries such as the United States and Britain, this shift appeared as a reform that maintained the previous general principles. Accordingly, the polity in these countries remained democratic, and the legislative bodies maintained their supervisory power even with the great expansion of executive power (Miyazawa 1940; Wagatsuma 1948, 7).

THE DEVELOPMENT OF INDIRECT FINANCING AND THE MAIN BANK SYSTEM

As Japan mobilized for war, financing of the munitions industry was a top priority. Indirect financing and the main bank system – two practices that played a very important role in the postwar coordination of the Japanese economy – became institutionalized in the war mobilization. Before the mid 1920s, stock markets had been the major channel for raising capital, and the proportion of indirect financing in the total capital supply was quite small. One reason for the dominance of direct financing was that the corporation had been the primary form of Japanese business organization since 1872. It had first begun to dominate the railway, textile, and banking industries in the 1890s and then had spread to all kinds of sectors of the economy. When the total number of Japanese companies increased from 8,994 to 34,345 between 1905 and 1925, the percentage of corporations increased from 46.9 to 51.3. Corporations had been predominant in this period, and their share of the total paid-up capital in Japan was always higher than 84 percent in the five-year intervals (Okazaki 1993, 101). Meanwhile, stocks and bonds on average constituted more than half the total financial assets of Japanese companies in the nonfinancial sectors. Before 1925, more than 50 percent of the capital of Japanese corporations was generated through stocks and bonds. Then in 1937, the major source of industrial capital for private companies shifted quickly from direct financing in the form of stocks and bonds to indirect financing in the form of bank loans. The percentage of stocks in the total supply of capital declined from 35.5 percent in 1937 to 6.1 percent by 1944, whereas that of bank loans increased from 31.9 percent in 1937 to 90.9 percent in 1944 (Teranishi 1993, 79).

When the traditional pattern of direct corporate financing could no longer sustain the military demands in an increasingly risky business environment, the main bank system was developed to ensure the supply of capital for munitions production. In the Japanese context, the term *main bank system* refers to two different relationships between manufacturers and banks. The first is the structure of corporate debts. Although every company took out loans from several banks, the largest lender, or main bank, was the relatively stable one. The second dimension was the services provided by the largest lender to its borrowers. The main bank not only took care of the company's settlements, its issuing of corporate bonds, and its information services, but also acted as the representative of the company's other lenders, providing detailed information and help in emergencies. The first relationship was a direct outcome of the war mobilization; the second relationship also emerged at that time but developed more fully in the postwar period (Itō 1995, 94).

Two factors that contributed to the rise of indirect financing and the main bank system were the state's control of dividends and the high risks involved in investments in the munitions industry. State control was initiated in September 1937, following the outbreak of the China War, when the Japanese state enacted the Law Concerning Temporary Capital Adjustment. The Ordinance Regarding Company Dividend and Finance was enacted in 1939, and the Ordinance Regarding Banks Capital was enacted in 1940. Any company whose total capital was greater than 200,000 yen was subject to regulation by the 1939 law, which established the dividend rate that prevailed between December 1937 and November 1938 as the standard rate. To pay a higher dividend rate, companies had to apply for government approval. Between April 1939 and October 1940, 130 such applications were filed but only 50 were granted. When shareholders no longer received the expected dividend, they sold their stocks, leading to a sharp decline in stock prices in 1940–1941 (Okazaki 1993, 110–111).

Reducing the investment risks in the wartime financing of munitions industries also was a major driving force behind the development of the main bank system. To disperse the risk, in 1937–1941 the banking industry created a 130-member "loan syndication," a collective investment by multiple financial institutions in a single project. This group comprised the ten largest commercial banks, the Industrial Bank, and the five largest trust funds. In August 1941, the state changed the name of the group to Cooperative Investment Group, changing it yet again, in May 1942, to the National Finance Control Association. The syndication's loans in 1937–1941 constituted only 14 percent of the total financing by those banks. In contrast, after the National Finance Control Association was created, it controlled most of the supply of capital. After the Munitions Industry Law was enacted in October 1943, the operation of munitions companies, which numbered 600, no longer needed shareholders' approval if the company received a production order from the state; companies could even refuse to make management information available 'o shareholders. As a result, banks were no longer able to monitor their corporate borrowers, and managers obtained great autonomy. In other words, the dilemma between strong coordination and weak control-monitoring had existed since day one after the birth of the main bank system. Driven by the urgent needs for national survival during World War II, however, no one really paid serious attention to the long-term negative impact of weak control and monitoring on the Japanese economy.

Beginning in early 1944, the state began, through three designations, to assign a particular bank to each munitions company as its chief capital provider, or main bank. This designation was based on the bank's lending record, the nature of the business transaction, the relationships between the bank and the manufacturer in terms of capital supply and corporate bonds, personnel exchange, the bank's capacity to provide capital, and the number of its institutional borrowers. City banks competed vigorously for the main bank designation. They feared that if they failed to be so designated, they would fall into the status of local banks and would lose good corporate customers. Mitsubishi Bank, for example, became the sole financier for 12 companies in the first designation and for 38 companies in the second one. Yasuda Bank was the sole financier for only 2 companies in the first round and 47 in the second round. In February 1945, the Japanese state enacted the Munitions Finance Special Measure Law. It not only legalized the system of designation of main banks but also expanded it to companies outside the munitions industry (Itō 1995, 83–84).

THE CONTROL ASSOCIATIONS

The control association was an important form of coordination in the Japanese economic system during World War II (Kunihiro 1941; Sanekata 1944). As discussed earlier, the creation of the control association was driven by the need to control resource allocation for war mobilization; another factor was strong resistance to direct state control. By the eve of the Pacific War, the Japanese state had not intervened directly in the production process of private corporations but relied instead on the mandatory cartels for coordination. With Japan facing the challenge of waging a war with a major world power, however, the cartels' control over prices was no longer sufficient to ensure munitions production. After all, the cartels' primary goal was to serve their own interests. The state might control the cartels' pricing policy and determine the quota for the supply of capital, material, and labor, but as long as these measures remained exogenous constraints, private companies still had the freedom to pursue their own goals, and the state was unable to ensure munitions production. Because war with the United States was imminent, the Japanese state took steps to strengthen its control over the economy.

Thus, the control associations became important instruments of the state in the war mobilization. As Minister of Commerce and Industry Kishi Nobusuke pointed out at the time, "The state expected the control associations not only to participate in drafting important policy because their knowledge about the industries was essential for any pragmatic policy, but also to play a major role in helping the state carry out its policy" (Kishi 1942). The state placed 22 industries under the rule of control associations and thereby remedied the chief weakness of cartels from the standpoint of effective state control: voluntary membership. Control associations were industrywide compulsory trade associations of which every company in the industry had to be a member. In contrast to cartels, which could make their own decisions within the constraints established by the state, control associations not only participated in government planning by collecting various data but also supervised the implementation of the annual national mobilization of resources in each industry (Kunihiro 1941). The Japan Steel Association, for example, directly controlled steel distribution in the industry. Working closely with the state, the association named designated agents, designated wholesalers, and secondary wholesalers for each specific major product in the industry. These agents and wholesalers made sure that raw materials and products were not distributed for any business purposes that conflicted with the state's policy objective (Tsūsanshō 1964). In early 1943, the state bureaucracy further empowered control associations to determine production quotas, ration production materials and equipment, and distribute products.

Despite these steps, the Japanese state failed to achieve the expected degree of control over the control associations. The daily operation of Japanese control associations was in private hands, and in attempting to restrain the property rights of private companies, the state encountered strong resistance from the private sector. State proposals to give managers official status and to control the profits of private companies were seen as not only communist-oriented but also violating the Constitution. In December 1940, eight important business associations issued a statement opposing these government proposals. By mobilizing right-wing conservatives and drawing on the anticommunist orientation of fascism, the private sector was able to force the arrest of the bureaucrats who had drafted the policy proposal (Gao 1994). Although private companies had failed to protect their interests through the written law, they succeeded in doing so through the politics of law enforcement.

Thus, the actual operation of control associations reflected a political compromise. It enabled the private sector to resist direct bureaucratic control of the internal affairs of private companies. It also enabled the state to prevent market forces from disturbing its policy objective. In this new structure of governance, private companies worked closely with the state under the condition that they maintain a certain degree of autonomy for running the daily operation of control associations.

THE WEAKENING CONTROL OF MANAGEMENT BY SHAREHOLDERS AND BANKS' MONITORING OF CORPORATIONS

As a result of strengthening coordination in war mobilization, Japanese corporate governance witnessed profound changes. The most important change was the decline in shareholders' control over corporate management. Before World War II, sustained by direct financing, shareholders exercised effective control. The exercise of this control varied between zaibatsu companies and non-zaibatsu companies. In the latter, large shareholders constituted about 20 percent of the members of boards of directors. Big shareholders could automatically join the board of directors and supervise managers from the shareholders' perspective. In zaibatsu companies, in contrast, few big shareholders became senior managers. Even if we count the managers who represented the holding companies, the percentage of big shareholders was much smaller than in non-zaibatsu companies. Instead, the zaibatsu companies were controlled by the holding company in each zaibatsu group. All board agenda items had to be submitted to the board of trustees at the holding company and had to be approved by that board as well as the managers who were in charge of that part of the business operation at the holding company (Okazaki 1993, 103).

Because the holding company was the major supplier of capital to the zaibatsu companies within the group, the holding company functioned as an internal capital market. Various departments at the holding company closely examined the business plans and monitored the business operation of zaibatsu companies. Although the business planning and operations were handled by the managers, the holding company closely controlled personnel and made all important decisions about the assignments of senior managers. In this system, Japanese companies, especially zaibatsu companies, established an incentive system to mobilize managers to act in the interests of shareholders, and the bonuses paid to managers were closely tied to profits.

Managers, in return, demonstrated a strong orientation toward profits. This was particularly visible in non-zaibatsu companies, because the holding companies of zaibatsu companies were able to take a long-term perspective and did not press their subordinates very hard for short-term profits (Okazaki 1993, 105).

As corporate financing shifted from direct to indirect mode in the war mobilization and as each corporation was assigned to a main bank, the banks' monitoring of corporate borrowers was weakened. Banks faced a dilemma: whether to choose (a) the traditional managerial principle that emphasized the corporate financial health of borrowers or (b) the new environment, in which banks would make no money without heavy involvement in financing the munitions industry. In a memorandum to branch offices, the director of the Department of Munitions Finance at Mitsubishi Bank pointed out that compared with the past, after the implementation of the main bank system these branch offices were paying much less attention to the efficient use of capital and the company's management. Yasuda Bank complained that banks had fallen into the status of the company's accounting division (Itō 1995, 86).

Many banks, moreover, did not remain passive in this situation. Rather, their attitude about lending shifted from cautious to aggressive. When the China War started, they still perceived munitions financing as highly risky. During the Pacific War, however, they aggressively made loans to munitions companies, not because they no longer feared the risk but because they now feared the loss of corporate customers in competition with their rivals. The Ministry of Finance attempted to insert an article in the Munitions Finance Special Measure Law of 1945 that would allow a public agency to audit the munitions companies. Because of strong opposition from the military and the Ministry of Munitions, however, it had to withdraw this proposal. At the end of World War II, the Ministry of Finance, which had previously been regarded as rigid on the question of the health of companies' finances, tended to "trust the self-discipline of the companies and enforce the regulations concerning the managed economy in a more flexible manner" (cited in Itō 1995, 86). In the end, the managed economy became very inefficient, with companies often emphasizing the promotion of production regardless of cost.

Although these phenomena occurred in a war context, the mechanisms by which these problems were created were similar to those that prevailed in postwar Japan: The increase in indirect financing led to the decline of shareholders' control over management. The establishment of the main bank system led to the weakening of the banks' monitoring of corporate borrowers. Less attention to the profit principle in turn led to practices that often created inefficiency.

THE DEVELOPMENT OF SUBCONTRACTING

Another important outcome of Japan's wartime efforts to strengthen coordination was the rapid development of subcontracting. During this period, subcontracting became a popular form of coordination between big corporations and medium-size and small companies to control the uncertainty of transaction in the wartime environment. Although subcontracting existed in the prewar period, contractors and their subcontractors had not developed a stable relationship. Big companies frequently changed subcontractors as well as the amount and content of subcontracted production. When a recession came, they often ceased employing their subcontractors. In contrast, as soon as demand increased in the marketplace, subcontractors would stop their subcontracted production and turn to their own production of high-profit finished goods. In the absence of a stable subcontracting relationship, subcontractors did not attempt to improve their use of technology; as a result, big companies had major problems in dealing with subcontractors. The opportunistic behaviors of both sides were driven by the motive of profit (Ueda 1995, 220).

Because big companies and their subcontractors had not been able to nurture mutual trust, the state stepped in to play the role of enforcer, sanctioning opportunistic behavior. On December 21, 1940, the Japanese state approved the Outline of the Reorganization of Machinery and Iron-Steel Product Industries. This law was aimed at establishing exclusive and stable relationships between big companies and their subcontractors and at promoting the specialization of production among medium-size and small companies. According to this document, the Machinery Control Association would clearly define the production field for its member companies, and big companies would not be allowed to enter the production fields of their subcontractors. A public subcontractor designation system was established. In principle, designated subcontractors were allowed to fill only subcontracted production orders, and big corporations could not issue business contracts to nondesignated subcontractors. Subcontractors were pushed to specialize in production and to develop exclusive relationships with their contractors. The state held the contractor companies responsible for cooperating with their subcontractors in improving management, providing technical consultation and financial support, and helping subcontractors continue business operations after their contracts ended. Contractor companies were also responsible for providing production materials to their subcontractors (Ueda 1995, 218).

After the public subcontractor designation system was established in 1941, 3,480 factories became designated subcontractors. Among them, 1,312 factories received contracts exclusively from a single contractor, and 2,168 of them received contracts from multiple contractors; 473 factories received contracts directly from the military, and 750 also produced their own finished products in addition to their subcontracted production. After the outbreak of the Pacific War, big corporations were not able to meet the demands of the military. And despite the state's efforts to achieve strong coordination, transaction costs remained high in wartime. However, the solution to this problem – forging exclusive relationships between big companies and small companies – was not easy. According to several surveys conducted in the Tokyo and Osaka areas, subcontractors tended to receive their contracts from two to four big companies. Only the very small workshops, which often became the target of reorganization, had only one contractor. It was difficult for those that had multiple contractors to commit to only one contractor. In addition, both big companies and their subcontractors were reluctant to apply for the designation because after they were designated, they would no longer be able to respond to business situations flexibly. To big companies, increasing the number of their subcontractors meant increasing responsibilities and decreasing sources for alternative subcontractors. To medium-size and small companies, establishing an exclusive relationship with one major contractor meant decreasing business opportunities and increasing risks (Ueda 1995, 226–227).

Responding to these problems, the Japanese state increased the flexibility of the rules on exclusive subcontracting relationships. Big companies, through certain bureaucratic procedures, were allowed to subcontract their production to nondesignated companies. Two companies that had already entered into an exclusive subcontracting relationship could apply to terminate it. When the control associations were established in 1942, previously established business organizations, such as the Machinery Association, were dissolved and the control associations began to play a supervisory role. From that point on, subcontracting expanded and the application procedure was simplified. The number of designated subcontractors was doubled. In many cases, subcontractors could still receive contracts from companies other than their designated contractors, but subcontracting was nevertheless widely institutionalized. In many instances, exclusive subcontracting relationships began to emerge.

In sum, the Japanese state played an important role in the development of subcontracting. To support war mobilization, the state sanctioned opportunistic behaviors of both contractor companies and their subcontractors. Because private companies had difficulties in forging mutual trust, the state acted as the enforcer of cooperation between big companies and their subcontractors. To promote a stable relationship between them, the state forced contractor companies to take care of their subcontractors. Meanwhile, it also forced subcontractors to establish an exclusive relationship with their contractors.

CONCLUSION

This chapter shows that after the collapse of the gold standard in 1914 and after World War I, 1914–1918, capitalist economies entered a chaotic stage. In Japan, the competing policy objectives of the state's financial and monetary policies created a bubble that subsequently burst. As a result, the Japanese economy fell into stagnation and encountered a major financial crisis in 1927. The ill-timed return to the gold standard in 1929 further worsened the economic situation.

During the Great Depression and World War II, the Japanese response was characterized by two leading principles: coordination and stability. Both principles represented a movement that countered the earlier trend of globalization. In this movement, many of the most important institutions that sustained the postwar economic growth took shape. The efforts to strengthen coordination and maintain stability, however, created considerable tension and conflict in the Japanese economic system. Influenced by fascist ideologies, the Japanese pattern of coordination and stability in 1931–1945 differed greatly from the pattern that evolved after the war. It placed greater emphasis on direct state control and tight restraints on private property rights.

Nevertheless, the institutions and mechanisms devised for strengthening coordination and maintaining stability laid an important foundation for the postwar period. Although the democratic reforms during the postwar occupation had a great impact on these institutions and mechanisms in one way or another, from the perspective of the long-term movement of capitalist economies, the 1931–1945 period can still be regarded as the early stage of the Japanese economic system moving toward coordination and stability.

CHAPTER 4

COORDINATION, EXCESSIVE COMPETITION, AND HIGH-SPEED ECONOMIC GROWTH

In 1950–1971, the Japanese economic system was reconfigured to cope with the new international economic order sustained by the Bretton Woods system and the GATT system. Because the purpose of coordination changed from, on the one hand, restoring economic order after the Great Depression and mobilizing resources for national survival during World War II to, on the other hand, promoting economic growth, the means of coordination also changed significantly. Unlike the situation in wartime, after 1952 the state no longer directly controlled the distribution of production materials and consumer products. Although the state still applied various policy tools to affect the behavior of private corporations, it could no longer use coercive power to achieve its goal. Sustained by the Bretton Woods system, the state was able to rely on an expansionary monetary policy to promote economic growth and meanwhile maintain a stable exchange rate with the dollar. Engaged in asymmetric cooperation with the United States, the state aimed at maximizing Japan's gains in international trade by promoting exports.

To coordinate national efforts to achieve economic growth, both the state and the private sector devised a number of important institutions and mechanisms. The Ministry of Finance practiced convoy administration, which was aimed at maintaining stability in the banking industry by restraining market entry and competition. To support aggressive lending by major city banks to manufacturers, the Bank of Japan supplied money, directly offering the banks credit and ensuring a minimum supply of credit. MITI not only adopted a pro–export development strategy, emphasizing the strategic allocation of foreign currencies to the heavy-chemical industries, but it also nurtured Japanese corporations in international competition by encouraging competitive oligopolies. Japanese corporations continued to rely heavily on indirect financing and the main bank system for their capital. To prevent hostile takeovers, they also adopted reciprocal shareholding. After the occupation ended in the early 1950s, former zaibatsu companies reorganized themselves into a new type of business groups, called *keiretsu*, centered on major city banks and trading companies. To promote productivity and innovation, big Japanese corporations improved labor relations by institutionalizing permanent employment.

However, these institutions and mechanisms, designed to strengthen co-ordination, also weakened shareholders' control over management and banks' monitoring of corporate finance. They also encouraged moral hazard: Banks lent money aggressively without close scrutiny of their corporate borrowers, and corporations borrowed and invested money aggressively at a level far beyond their capital worth. Excessive competition for market share led both to the banks' overlending and to the corporations' overborrowing. Although MITI regarded the resulting excessive competition as a major threat to Japa-nese corporations' economies of scale and to Japan's international competi-tiveness, the vested political interest was too strong for any possible reform. The close relationship between coordination and excessive competition is the key to understanding not only how the high growth was institutionally sus-tained but also the contingent dependence of the Japanese economic system on the international economic order and state policy mix. The implication is that when the contingent conditions that had tolerated excessive competi-tion began to change after the collapse of the Bretton Woods system and the end of high growth in the early 1970s, the Japanese economic system was destined to malfunction. In this sense, the adoption of the reverse logic, tracing the roles played by the institutions and mechanisms that triggered the bubble economy in the 1980s back in the process of the high growth, has yielded a new explanation of how the high growth of the Japanese economy was really triggered and sustained in the 1950s and the 1960s.

HIGH GROWTH AND EXCESSIVE COMPETITION

How was high growth sustained in Japan in 1950–1973? In the past two decades, the academic debate among Western scholars has focused on the issue of whether or to what extent the industrial policy practiced by the Japanese state allocated resources to strategic industries. Both sides in this debate treat the state as an actor, and they are divided by the issue of whether the state was autonomous in policy-making or was also influenced by the private sector or other societal forces. The Japanese economic stagnation in the 1990s, however, has significantly changed the context of the academic debate, and the new situation demands a coherent explanation of Japan's past success as well as its recent failure. In the 1990s, neither the state nor the private sector seemed to be taking the lead in badly needed reform. The pressing question

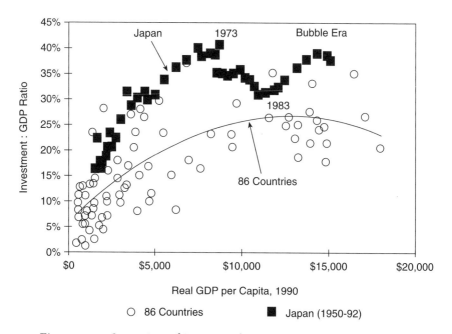

Figure 4.1. *Comparison of investment between Japan and 86 countries.*
Source: Katz, 1998, p. 67. Permission located on p. xi, this volume.

is no longer who was the most important player in Japan's high growth but
rather what kind of major tradeoffs contained in the institutions and mechanisms that sustained high growth now served to lead the Japanese economy
into the crisis of the 1990s.

Reexamining the high growth of 1950–1973 with the later concern about
the origin of the bubble in the 1980s, my investigation starts by looking
at the identical pattern of corporate investments in both periods. I argue that
the same investment pattern – in the form of excessive competition – resulted
in very different outcomes, and that is the key to understanding how globalization has profoundly changed the environment in which the national
models of capitalist economies operate.

Investment is a crucial factor in economic growth. A high speed of economic growth necessitates a huge input of production factors. Without a
rapidly increased input of labor and capital, high growth cannot be sustained.
During the high growth period 1950–1973, as Figure 4.1 shows, the
Japanese investment ratio was far above the average of the other 86 countries. To a large extent, the high growth of the Japanese economy was a function of aggressive investment by Japanese corporations. To comprehend the

dynamics, we must examine the nature of the institutions and mechanisms that induced and sustained these investments through excessive competition. To understand why the Japanese economic system malfunctioned in the 1980s and 1990s, we must reveal the contingent conditions, both international and domestic, that allowed these institutions and mechanisms to sustain excessive competition without creating any major crisis. At the state level, the high growth was sustained by both Japan's industrial policy and its macroeconomic policy. These two policies, however, not only were practiced by different state bureaucracies but also differed significantly in their goals and implementations. To test Japan's macroeconomic policy, one should not formulate a hypothesis based on the goal and the means of implementation of Japanese industrial policy. Although both policies served to promote economic growth, they focused on different facets of the same process.

The aggressive investments that triggered high growth were sustained by the Japanese banks' overlending (also called "overloan") and Japanese corporations' overborrowing. A bank's balance sheet consists of both assets and debts. Assets include cash; short-term bonds and commercial papers that can be exchanged for cash at the money market; loans; and investments in securities. Debts include money borrowed from the central bank and the money market, and deposits and capital the bank has generated. The bank's business is to make profits by using the deposits and capital it has generated to issue loans and invest in securities. By *overlending* we mean that the total of a bank's loans and investments exceed the deposits and capital it has generated, and the bank's balance sheet registers a negative worth (Suzuki 1974, 3–5). Suzuki Yoshio further points out that in the Japanese context, overlending is not a microphenomenon, limited to individual banks, but rather is a macrophenomenon. This means that Japanese banks as a whole lent and invested more money than they had generated (1974, 5). Overborrowing, the other side of this coin, refers to the high percentage of bank loans in Japanese corporate finance. Driven by the excessive competition, Japanese corporations invested aggressively in production capacity and technological transfers, investments that went far beyond the corporations' capital worth (Suzuki 1974, 12–13).

During the high growth period, overlending and overborrowing were driven by Japanese corporations' excessive competition in investing in production capacity and technological transfers. Recall that excessive competition in the Japanese context contrasts with normal competition, in which managers of private companies plan their business operations, supervise production, and make investment decisions according to the principle of allocative efficiency; profits are their top concern. Excessive competition, in contrast, is driven by the motive of increasing a company's market share

(Miyazaki 1963; Morozumi 1963a). Thus, to increase market share, Japanese corporations always borrowed more capital than they could return, and Japanese banks always lent more money than allowed by the deposits they had generated (Suzuki 1974).

Here, it is necessary to make a distinction between Richard Katz's development stage argument and my institutional argument. Katz's structural argument is partially right, in that the aggressive investments by Japanese corporations during the high growth were related to the fact that many infant industries were then created by the technological revolution. The main thrust of such a structural argument, however, cannot explain the rise of the bubble in the 1980s. In contrast, I make an institutional argument. I argue that structural conditions come and go, but institutions have an enduring impact on the economy. What mattered most in the reversion of the Japanese economy was not that the economy entered a new stage beginning in the early 1970s. Instead, what mattered was that the institutions derived in the 1950s and 1960s to strengthen coordination in corporate investments and cope with the rise of numerous infant industries sustained both excessive competition and the same aggressive corporate investment; but when the expansion of trade and production was replaced by the expansion of finance and monetary activity in the early 1970s, these actions led to completely different outcomes because this time the investment targets became real estate and stock markets.

What institutions in the Japanese economy enabled Japanese corporations to invest so much more than their counterparts in other countries? Did Japanese banks not worry about the high risks associated with overinvesting? Why did the shareholders allow Japanese corporations to invest so aggressively without exercising control over management? Does knowledge about the institutions that sustained these aggressive investments also shed light on the mechanism of the bubble economy? To answer these questions, we must analyze how the Japanese economic system was configured and understand how the structural power of the state shaped the incentive structure and formulated the insurance function that induced the aggressive investing.

AN IMPORTANT POLICY MIX

To cope with the international economic order that existed from the 1950s to the early 1970s, the Japanese state adopted a mixed policy comprising an expansionary monetary policy to promote economic growth and a deflationary fiscal policy to control inflation. This policy mix was an extremely important mechanism that linked the international economic order and Japan's domestic economic institutions. As I show in this chapter, many Japanese economic institutions that are often considered to be determined by Japanese culture or social structure in fact are also an outcome of institutional reconfiguration undertaken to adapt to a new international environment.

Japanese monetary policy in this period served both to promote economic growth and to balance payments. Until the late 1960s, an imbalance of payments in terms of trade deficits had always been a hindrance to the growth of the Japanese economy. As a result, the state adopted an expansionary monetary policy in relation to the cycle of payments adjustment. This adjustment usually started with the adoption of an easy money policy to stimulate economic growth. As wholesale prices rose and as an increase in imports during the economic boom created big trade deficits, payment imbalances increased because Japan used its foreign reserve to maintain a stable exchange rate. It was at that point that the state shifted from an easy money policy to a tight money policy. The stability of domestic prices alone, however, was never regarded as an independent policy objective, because the Japanese state gave a higher priority to economic growth.[1] The major parameter for exercising a tight money policy was the imbalance of payments. Because foreign exchange was under strict control and because private corporations strongly depended on bank loans, a tight money policy, in the form of reducing credit extended by the Bank of Japan, cooled the economy quickly and usually created a recession. When wholesale prices and imports declined, exports increased and Japan's payments situation improved; then the state would return to an easy money policy, and the economy would again begin to grow (Ōkurashō 1991, Vol. 9, 35–36). Rather than the main banks using delegated monitoring (discussed later in this chapter), the Bank of Japan, driven by concern for balancing payments, performed the ultimate monitoring function: the use of a tight money policy.

To adjust the deficits in the balance of payments, a state has three major policy tools: an exchange rate policy, a fiscal policy, and a monetary policy.[2] Because the Japanese regarded the promotion of exports as their top priority, the exchange rate was politically untouchable. Why did the Japanese state not use an expansionary fiscal policy to adjust trade deficits while using a deflationary monetary policy to control inflation? Part of the reason was historic. As I discussed in Chapter 3, when Japan adopted an expansionary

1 The Japanese debated this issue in the late 1940s, when an easy money policy, adopted to stimulate economic reconstruction, caused severe inflation. Eventually, the pro-growth approach dominated in state policy-making. See Gao (1997, Chapter 4).
2 Yoshiko Kojo (1993) discussed four opinions, including using foreign reserves or international borrowing, trade control, exchange rate, and financial policy. Using both foreign reserves and international borrowing works only for short-term adjustment, and trade control is not desirable. To see the Japanese policy mix in comparison with the European experience, I differentiate two aspects of financial policy: fiscal policy and monetary policy.

fiscal policy to counter the recession after World War I, the action created a bubble; it subsequently burst, driving Japan into a long recession in the 1920s. To counter the Great Depression, the state again adopted an expansionary fiscal policy in the 1930s. This time, however, this choice resulted in a rapid increase in public spending on national defense, spending that led Japan to its Asian aggressions, its war with the United States, and its defeat in World War II (Arisawa 1976; Gotō 1973). More important, if the Japanese state had relied on an expansionary fiscal policy to adjust the payment imbalances and on a deflationary monetary policy to control inflation, there would have been a negative impact on the capital accumulation of private corporations, and national resources would have been shifted away from manufacturing industries to real estate and construction industries closely related to public spending. This result would have defeated the state's policy objective of generating economic growth by promoting exports (Ōkurashō 1991, Vol, 9, 38–39).

The policy mix in force from the 1950s to the early 1970s was not a choice but rather was forced on Japan by the occupation authority. In the late 1940s, the Japanese economy had been sustained by deficit government budgets, which the United States supported with economic aid. The state strongly preferred economic recovery over its own financial health (see Gao 1994; Gao 1997, Chapter 4). At the end of 1948, the GHQ (General Headquarters) carried out a financial stabilization policy package, known as the Dodge plan, that was intended to eliminate inflation by balancing government budgets. As a result, the Japanese economy faced the danger of a deflationary spiral. To counter the shock effect of the Dodge plan, the Bank of Japan adopted a "disinflation policy," actively coordinating lending by private banks to corporations. The Bank of Japan supplied a huge amount of capital, totaling 53.9 billion yen, between June 1949 and April 1950. Because the Dodge plan strongly restrained the expansion of fiscal spending and government subsidies, the Japanese state later had no choice except to rely on an expansionary monetary policy to promote economic growth. Started as a measure to ensure a soft landing for the Japanese economy, the expansionary monetary policy later became a powerful instrument for sustaining economic growth. The Ministry of Finance adhered strictly to the balanced budget principle until 1965 (Johnson 1982, 202–204; Ōkurashō 1991, Vol. 9, 61–63).

In the debate about the Japanese political economy, one issue of contention has been the question of whether the monetary policy practiced by the Bank of Japan directly supported the industrial policy practiced by MITI (Calder 1993; Johnson 1982; Zysman 1983). I take a different approach here. I separate the high growth experienced by the economy from the development of strategic industries. In the Japanese context, "high growth" refers to the astonishing macroeconomic performance measured in terms of the annual growth rate of the economy. As the Japanese bubble economy of the 1980s indicates, the high growth rate need not rely solely on the development of strategic industries. As long as investment capital was pouring in, as Paul Krugman (1994) pointed out on the eve of the 1997 Asian financial crisis, there could be high-speed economic growth. Thus, the key to understanding Japan's high growth is to determine what sustained the high level of capital investment. To explain that, we must understand how a country's savings are mobilized and how investment risks are reduced or dispersed.

Between the late 1940s and the early 1960s, the Fiscal Investment and Loan Program practiced by the state, often called "the second budget," played an important role in providing industrial capital to finance heavy-chemical industries (Johnson 1982; Noguchi 1995; Tsuruta 1982). A strong case for direct government allocation of capital to strategic industries is also evident in the "special banks" (*tokubetsu ginkō*), such as the Industrial Bank of Japan (IBJ). Legally speaking, special banks were not public institutions, but they were established explicitly with a public function. In the 1950s, the IBJ provided between 20 percent and 30 percent of the total capital for long-term industrial finance. Between 1951 and 1955, 23.5 percent of the total capital provided to strategic industries such as iron-steel, coal, ship-building, and electricity came from the IBJ. At the end of 1955, 58.3 percent of the IBJ's production capacity finance went to these four industries (Ueda 1993). After the mid-1960s, the major allocation of government funding shifted to infrastructure-related fields and agriculture (Tsuruta 1982).

The responsibility for implementing industrial and macroeconomic policies was divided among the Bank of Japan, the Ministry of Finance, and MITI. The agency in charge of finance was not in charge of industrial policy, and each agency had its own institutional priority. In contrast to MITI's strong orientation toward strategic allocation of resources, the Ministry of Finance and the Bank of Japan placed more emphasis on a stable supply of industrial capital (Calder 1988, 1993; Campbell 1977; Itō 1995; Miyazaki 1963, 1966, 1985). The Bank of Japan and the Ministry of Finance were concerned more with the high growth. In contrast, MITI emphasized the development of specific strategic industries. Restrained by its institutional logic – which focused on the stability of macroeconomic performance rather than strategic resource allocation – the Bank of Japan did not use its leverage to force private banks to invest in certain industries. Rather, it concentrated a major portion of its credit to the major city banks, and it allowed these banks – the main banks of keiretsu companies that had already been investing aggressively in the exports-related sector – to decide which company to finance.

The policy mix of an expansionary monetary policy to promote economic growth and a deflationary fiscal policy to control inflation had profound implications for production and distribution in the Japanese economic system. In this chapter, I explain how the institutions and mechanisms devised by the state to strengthen coordination of production served to stimulate excessive competition. I argue that it was excessive competition in corporate investments and bank lending – a side effect that was quite contrary to the goal of coordination – that triggered the high growth of the Japanese economy. This argument was initially explored by Miyazaki Yoshikazu (1963) in a study of the Japanese case and by Michael Loriaux (1991) in a study of the French case. I hold that the pattern of aggressive investment and lending by Japanese corporations and banks was shaped to a great extent by the institutions and mechanisms devised by the Japanese state to strengthen coordination. The impact of the Japanese state on growth can be clearly reflected by a study of how it created a favorable environment for private banks to lend money aggressively and for private corporations to borrow and invest money aggressively in production capacity and techno-logical transfers. I do not reject the importance of technological innovation to Japan's high growth, but I stress that the Japanese way of financing innovation involved major tradeoffs.

A STABLE SUPPLY OF INDUSTRIAL CAPITAL

Japan has a credit-based and price-administered financial system, in contrast to the credit-based but institution-dominated system in Germany, and the capital market–based financial systems in Britain and the United States (Zysman 1983). If the Bank of Japan had chosen to purchase corporate notes or bonds in the money market as a way of supplying money, instead of offer-ing credit directly to Japanese banks, banks would have had to sell their assets to get the currencies issued by the Bank of Japan. When banks' assets declined, they would have had to reduce their loans and investments in securities. Under such circumstances, overlending would have disappeared. Thus, by supplying money through providing credit to major city banks, the Bank of Japan served to support the banks' aggressive lending (Suzuki 1974, 6). The pro-growth macroeconomic policy practiced by the Bank of Japan was different from the pro-export industrial policy practiced by MITI. In the former, the major goals were to mobilize national saving into aggressive investments and to maintain a stable supply of capital. In the latter, the major goal was to allocate resources

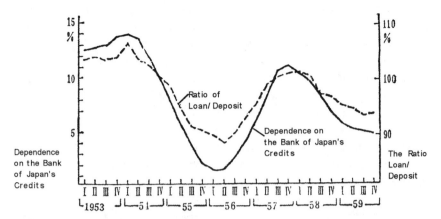

Figure 4.2. *The correlation between the credits from the Bank of Japan and the ratio of loan/ deposit (all banks).*

Source: Miyazaki, 1985, p. 64.

to certain strategic industries. Although the two policies are mutually dependent, each operates according to its own unique logic.

Miyazaki Yoshikazu (1963) argues that the Bank of Japan's adoption of an expansionary monetary policy was directly responsible for excessive competition, first because it provided major city banks with overly easy access to credits. Miyazaki finds a strong correlation between the overlending of commercial banks and their dependence on credit from the Bank of Japan. When the city banks' loans to manufacturers exceeded their deposits, the banks simply applied for and received more credits from the Bank of Japan (see Figure 4.2). Thus, Japanese city banks did not need to maintain an adequate deposit-loan ratio, and they lent money aggressively to big corporations. Because big corporations could easily obtain industrial capital from the banks, they tended to borrow more and invest more. (I discuss later how aggressive investment by Japanese corporations was also sustained by weak control of shareholders over management.)

Second, the Bank of Japan also sustained its overlending to private banks by adopting the so-called *sōbana shugi* ("please everybody") approach in the distribution of credit to major private banks (Miyazaki 1963, 1966). In theory, the Bank of Japan should have lent money to private banks according to their capacities of capital mobilization (see Calder 1993, 87–90). In reality, however, the Bank of Japan tended to ensure a certain minimum amount of credit, almost equally, to each of the major city banks. Miyazaki writes that in 1960 and the first half of 1961, each of the major Japanese city banks, with the exception of Mitsui and Daiichi, received a similar amount of credits from the Bank of Japan. In September 1960, most banks obtained credit amounting to 30 billion yen. In March 1961, each bank got around 50 billion yen. In September 1961, each got 90 billion yen. Miyazaki (1963, 55–56) concludes that "the pattern of the Bank of Japan's capital supply aimed not simply at promoting domestic productivity with low interest rates. Rather, it aimed at promoting domestic productivity by actively sustaining the one-set investment strategy of the keiretsu." This meant that as long as the Bank of Japan backed the keiretsu banks, they would aggressively lend money to big corporations that competed vigorously in investing in every frontier industry.

During the high growth period, the Bank of Japan's egalitarian distribution of credit among major city banks served to weaken the banks' monitoring of corporate finance and to weaken the corporations' self-discipline (Miyazaki 1963, 1966). In 1961, the Financial Institution Investigation Committee of the Ministry of Finance conducted a series of studies on overlending. Its 1963 report points out that the institutionalized practice of overlending had numbed the banks' sense of rational lending and caused them to fail to take action even when their capital positions deteriorated. It also discouraged the corporations from making cautious investment decisions and enabled them to continue making large-scale investments even when their financial condition deteriorated. Finally, overlending also exerted restraints on the state's ability to adopt a tight money policy. Because banks and corporations had borrowed too much, any tight money policy might have caused a stabilization panic. Even when the state had to take action, it tended to take an incomplete one (Itō 1995, 229).

During the high growth period, the Japanese economic system might have relied less on the city banks for monitoring than on the Bank of Japan. The city banks followed the practice of so-called delegated monitoring, which I discuss later in this chapter. When Japan's payments reached their limit, the Bank of Japan monitored corporate finance at the macro level through its tightening of the money supply and providing *window guidance,* a policy whereby the bank aimed to quantitatively adjust the total amount of loans made by private banks. Window guidance originated in July 1947 after the establishment of the Capital Division in the Operation Bureau of the Bank of Japan. Until 1952, window guidance was basically a tool of industrial policy and was used to control the distribution of capital for the priority production program. Beginning in September 1953, window guidance became the tool of macroeconomic policy, and throughout the high growth period was the Bank of Japan's most important policy tool. Unlike the interest rate policy, window guidance involved direct intervention by the Bank of Japan. The Japanese state held that indirect control of banks' lending, by raises in interest rates or call rates, could not achieve the policy goal in a timely way. Although the Bank of Japan could adjust the amount of capital supply by increasing its credit to private banks or selling the bonds it owned, the core of the money floating in the market was the cash held by private banks. The demand for cash depended on the production activity generated by past loans; this demand was not elastic, at least in the short run. Under such circumstances, if the Bank of Japan tried to control its supply of money, it might cause major disturbances in the short-term capital market. It was not enough for the Bank of Japan to act merely as a last resort, rescuing banks when they were in trouble; rather, it needed to prevent the trouble in the first place (Ōkurashō 1991, Vol. 9, 72).

The Bank of Japan had played two conflicting roles. On the one hand, it had to support economic growth by supplying industrial capital. On the other hand, in its role as a last resort, it also was required to discipline the private banks' lending behavior. To promote economic growth, it would have been desirable for the Bank of Japan to supply money in a passive manner, whenever private banks needed credit. Private banks' too-easy access to credit, however, had weakened the ability of the Bank of Japan to exert its disciplinary authority. An example of the problem is that in the high growth period, when the Bank of Japan tightened its money supply and required private banks to reduce their loans, the banks nonetheless kept increasing their loans. By June, such loans totaled more than 100 billion yen. It took six months for the total to be brought back to the level permitted by the quotas.

A major weakness in the procedure encouraged Japanese banks to over-lend. On the loan-return deadline date, private banks would collect their loans from corporations in the form of drafts. The trick was that the actual transaction of the draft would not take place until the next day. At that time, banks simply made new loans to the corporations, which in turn used these new loans to pay the drafts they had submitted to the banks the day before. To cope with this dilemma, the Bank of Japan exercised window guidance (Ōkurashō 1991, Vol. 9, 35–36), which was designed as an ultimate restraining mechanism on the private banks' lending behavior. However, window guidance applied only to city banks and long-term trust banks, whose lending behaviors were under relative control; it was the lending by other banks – those serving medium-size and small companies – that was not under control. Therefore, the effect of window guidance as a macroeconomic policy tool was often counterbalanced (Ōkurashō 1991, Vol. 9, 73).

CONVOY ADMINISTRATION AND THE REDUCTION
OF INVESTMENT RISKS

Whereas the Bank of Japan contributed to excessive competition by making capital too easily available to major city banks, the Ministry of Finance did so by providing an insurance service and an incentive structure to private banks through a practice known as *convoy administration*. The insurance function enabled banks to lend money aggressively, and the incentive structure implemented rewards for banks that lent aggressively. These kinds of policies contrast with those in a country such as the United States. The American model of government intervention in financial matters emphasizes ex post measures. For example, the U.S. federal government insures saving deposits up to $100,000 per account and avoids intervention in the details of banks' operations. The Japanese model, in contrast, focuses on ex ante measures, and the state is heavy-handed in its approach to overseeing bank operations. It not only restrains competition but also regulates various aspects of the banking industry. The convoy administration of the Japanese Ministry of Finance involved not only macro-level monetary policy (which is very important) but also state intervention at the micro level, defining the governing mechanisms and rules of financial transactions.

One area in which the convoy administration exercised tight control concerned entry by new banks into the finance industry; new entry was, in principle, prohibited. As a result, the number of Japanese financial institutions remained stable in the postwar period, with 13 city banks, 3 long-term credit banks, and 7 trust banks. In addition, mergers and changes in business direction fell under strong government regulation. Because mergers among city banks might reduce the degree of excessive competition, they were encouraged by the Japanese state; but mergers between city banks and local banks were prohibited because they tended to escalate such competition. The Japanese state played an active role in identifying merger partners for troubled banks. In the 1950s, there was tight control over the number of new branch offices. Between 1950 and 1955, each city bank on average lost one branch office. Between 1955 and 1960, each city bank on average lost fewer than one (0.6) office. The Japanese state also provided administrative guidance to the banking industry regarding budgets, rates of dividends, ratios of real estate in assets, rates of loans, rates of self-capital, ratios of capital flow, loans for huge projects, and distributions of capital (Itō 1995, 177–195). In short, during the high growth period the Japanese state provided a safety net for the banking industry.

How did the convoy administration sustain excessive competition? The answer is that the convoy administration provided an insurance service to private banks. The rationale was that economic growth sustained by techno-logical innovation would require huge amounts of investments involving high risks. The uncertainty of the finance industry was caused not only by changing economic structures and technological innovation but also by com-petition in the financial market. The convoy administration was aimed at maintaining stability and providing a predictable business environment for economic growth, both to protect consumers and to maintain the credibility of financial institutions. Financial transactions depended heavily on deposi-tors' confidence in individual banks and in the banking industry as a whole. Depositors' confidence was a precondition for the credibility of the financial institutions as well as the operation of financial settlements. When banks failed to settle, they might create a snowball effect: The loss of depositors' confidence would lead to the collapse of the banking system (Itō 1995, 218). However, when private banks, protected against bankruptcy by the con-voy administration, engaged in moral hazard, they did not have to seriously scrutinize the financial health of corporate borrowers. Thus, ironically, the practice that aimed at restraining competition ended up encouraging competition.

In many ways, Japanese industrial finance in the high growth period resembles the portrayal by Michael Loriaux of the French overdraft economy and moral hazard. Unlike John Zysman (1983), who notes a strategic allo-cation of bank credits by the French state, Loriaux (1991, 10) sees an over-draft economy, meaning that companies depending heavily on institutional lenders' credit allocation take the assured borrowing power for granted. Con-trary to Zysman's perception of a strong state control, Loriaux describes what he sees as moral hazard by French banks and corporations. Private companies became less concerned about their own financial viability because they were assured the power of borrowing.

Thus, Zysman's portrayal of the credit-based and price-administrated financial system did indeed contribute to the Japanese high growth. The state role in this system, however, was not reflected primarily in its control of credit allocation in strategic industries. Rather, it is reflected in its emphasis on the stable supply of industrial capital and reduction of investment risks. Both policies created a predictable business environment, significantly reducing marketplace uncertainty and lowering transaction costs. The state enabled banks to lend aggressively to corporations. As the chief capital suppliers to private corporations, banks clearly knew that exports-related sectors would be the major area for business activities and that those activities would be the major source of profits. Even in the early 1960s, when the state attempted to restrain private banks' overlending to the exports-related sector, banks refused to listen. The high growth was as much an intentionally created outcome as it was the unexpected consequence of self-accelerating mechanisms of excessive competition.

MITI AND COMPETITIVE OLIGOPOLIES

In the early 1980s, the strategic image of Japanese industrial policy began to attract major attention. This attention, however, often emphasized that the state favored certain industries or corporations. MITI's competition policy, which encouraged competitive oligopolies, was often neglected in the analyses. Whereas MITI tended to discriminate against medium-size and small companies in its distribution of foreign currency, keeping them from entry into strategic industries, it adopted a rather egalitarian approach toward big corporations, often basing quotas on current production capacities. This approach encouraged the expansion of production capacity (Morozumi 1966, 63). Foreign reserves had been under tight state control in postwar Japan. Although Japanese companies had the freedom to export their products, the foreign currencies generated from exports had to be sold to the bank in charge of foreign currency control within 10 days after the transaction. The Japanese government established a budget quota system for foreign currencies. It tightly controlled any imports of manufactured goods, especially those that threatened domestic industries. Meanwhile, it devoted the greater part of foreign currencies to the importation of technologies, needed raw materials, and important production equipment that Japan could not make domestically.

The goal of MITI's egalitarian distribution of foreign currency quotas among big corporations was to nurture competitive oligopolies. Conventional critics assume that, driven by the strategic consideration of upgrading Japanese industries, MITI would have given all the foreign currency to a select one or two firms. However, MITI's competition policy was aimed at improving Japanese companies' competitiveness in international markets, and in the distribution of foreign currencies MITI tended to treat major Japanese producers equally. In the petrochemical industry, for example, MITI supported Sumitomi Chemical, Mitsi Petro-Chemical, Mitsubishi Petro-Chemical, Nippon Petro-Chemical, Furukawa Chemical, Showa Petro-Chemical, and Nippon Synthetic Gum (Miyazaki 1990 [1985]).

The Japanese strategy of nurturing competitive oligopolies draws a clear distinction between a socialist state and a developmental state. Although both kinds of states practiced strategic planning, they differed sharply in defining how to achieve the desired goals. In Japan, after MITI identified a strategic industry, it would channel foreign currency quotas to that industry. The state would also encourage private banks to provide industrial capital to the big corporations in these industries through the banks' connections with the main banks in their business groups. Neither of these measures, however, was limited to one to two companies, and they were applied to multiple companies competing with one another in both domestic and international markets. From this competition, some companies would become the leading producers. In a socialist economy, in contrast, the state would channel all resources to one or two companies, thereby creating a national champion. By doing so, however, the national champion companies often did not have the competitiveness in international markets.

THE DEVELOPMENT OF THE KEIRETSU

Mediating between, on the one hand, the state and, on the other hand, corporations and banks, were the keiretsu. However, as I have argued, the institutions and mechanisms created to strengthen coordination within the keiretsu – indirect financing, the main bank system, and reciprocal shareholding – instead induced excessive competition. These coordinating mechanisms in the keiretsu transformed the strong growth orientation of Japanese corporations into the one-set investment strategy, which was a direct cause of excessive competition.

The development of the keiretsu was aimed at strengthening coordination in international competition. At the end of the 1940s, when Japan reconnected with the international market, coordination emerged as a major goal in the Japanese competition policy. In prewar Japan, excessive competition among private companies had resulted in dumping and low-quality products. As a result, the Japanese state enacted the Exports Association Law and the Trade Association Law, urging private companies to reach agreement and organize cartels. This governing mechanism, however, was destroyed by postwar democratic reforms. Under the Antimonopoly Law of 1947, any type of joint action was prohibited. When the promotion of exports became the national goal in the 1950s, the Japanese state twice amended the Antimonopoly Law, encouraging the reorganization of former zaibatsu companies. Coordination efforts first took the form of reviving Mitsui and Mitsubishi, two former zaibatsu trading companies and major players in international trade. During the occupation, Mitsui and Mitsubishi had been dissolved into more than 130 companies each. In July 1954, the standing capital of a revived Mitsubishi Trading Company was worth 650 million yen. By the end of the same year, its total capital had increased to 2.5 billion yen. The Mitsui Trading Company followed a similar path (Okumura 1975, 38–39).

When the liberalization of trade began in the early 1960s, economies of scale became critical to Japan's international competitiveness. In comparison with their Western competitors, the leading Japanese corporations seemed to be too small, and company officials were urged to increase their size through mergers. However, a MITI survey among 68 companies that had merged between 1955 and 1961 reported that major barriers existed to mergers: 33.8 percent of the companies reported that differing salary levels between the two companies was problematic; 17.6 percent cited concerns about the future arrangement of CEOs and managers; 11.8 percent attributed problems to differing levels of strength; 5.9 percent considered labor unions' strong opposition to job transfers and layoffs to be a problem; and 4.4 percent saw as barriers their differing positions regarding the terms of the mergers (Morozumi 1962e, 228). As an alternative, many Japanese companies tried to cooperate in the form of joint ventures or further development of business groups, of which a major example were the keiretsu.

By increasing the economies of scale when the prospects of growth were no longer encouraging, the development of the keiretsu in the late 1960s became a major survival strategy for Japanese corporations. In the 1950s, the centrifugal power of the keiretsu was not as strong as it became in the late 1960s. When new industries, such as petrochemicals and atomic power, emerged in the 1950s, the keiretsu often entered these industries by sustaining multiple companies in each industry. Mitsubishi and Mitsui, for example, each had two companies in the petrochemical industry. At the end of the 1960s, the automobile industry was expected to enter a stagnation period after 1973, the home electronics industry was predicted to offer fewer new products in the future, and it was projected that the iron-steel industry would not be able to grow after 1975. To deal with such predictions, the keiretsu began to pursue further growth by exploiting the advantages of business grouping. They began to emphasize the adjustment of internal resource allocation, a focus on the machinery and electronics industries (which still had high growth potential), a movement toward knowledge-intensive and high-value-added durable goods, and investments in overseas markets (Okumura et al. 1970, 9).

By the end of the 1960s, Mitsubishi had transformed itself from a former zaibatsu to a giant keiretsu, following a two-decade reorganization with 26 member companies' presidents participating in its Thursday meetings. The Mitsubishi group was organized around three major companies: the Mitsubishi Bank, the Mitsubishi Trading Company, and the Mitsubishi Heavy Industry. At that time, the deposits held by the Mitsubishi Bank were ranked third, trailing only the Fuji Bank and the Sumitomo Bank. The Mitsubishi Trading Company, which had been divided into more than 130 companies during the zaibatsu dissolution, reunited in the 1950s. In 1964, the Mitsubishi Trading Company, together with the Mitsui Trading Company, became the first two "one trillion yen annual sales companies" in Japan. During this process, the Mitsubishi Trading Company had changed itself from a "commissioned merchant" to an "information producer" and a "system organizer" (*Shūkan Tōyō Keizai* 1970, 17) becoming the center of the Mitsubishi group. After reunification of the three companies, the mammoth Mitsubishi Heavy Industry emerged as the largest enterprise in Japan.

By the end of the 1960s, Mitsubishi envisioned a new strategy for the future. In the 1950s, when the growth potential of the petrochemical industry was high, Mitsubishi had supported the entry of two of the group's companies into this industry. As a result, coordination between these two became difficult. Consequently, Mitsubishi began to focus on external expansions, encouraging its member companies to form strategic alliances with outsiders, with the goal of building a "Greater Mitsubishi." "Internationalization" and "popularization" became two major Mitsubishi slogans, and Mitsubishi paid close attention to the defense industry, its traditional strength. To build an infrastructure for the entire group of its member companies, Mitsubishi established the Mitsubishi Comprehensive Research Institute. The member companies also made many joint investments, establishing new companies that forged new partnerships with outsiders, both domestic and international.

In the high growth period, the American ideal of antitrust – reflected in the original 1947 version of Japan's Antimonopoly Law – was strongly contested in Japan. It was argued that a Japanese competition policy had to fit the market structures and historical background of the Japanese economy. There were basic differences in market structure between Japan and the Western countries. In the latter, a field of small companies typically would be reduced to a smaller number of monopolies through competition. As a result, big companies as well as medium-size and small companies could find a niche in the markets. In Japan, in contrast, big companies were not an outgrowth of competition. Rather, they had been created and supported by the state for the purpose of industrialization. Big corporations in light industries might have experienced competition, but those in heavy-chemical industries were monopolies from the very beginning. The Japanese state had protected these industries in domestic markets from international competition and had sustained a self-sufficient system of production in World War II. During this process, civilian markets for these products had not fully developed, and free competition had not existed (Itō 1959, 114–117).

Big Japanese corporations constituted the foundation of the entire Japanese economy and were the major actors in promoting industrialization and productivity. An antimonopoly policy needed to consider not only the issues of fair competition and economic equality but also the issue of international competitiveness, of which the major issue was the gap in production costs. The Japanese believed that the antimonopoly policy would hurt Japan's international competitiveness (Itō 1959, 114–117).

INDIRECT FINANCING

Indirect financing as the major source of industrial capital for Japanese corporations is distinctively different from the sources of industrial capital for corporations in other major industrialized countries. American, Italian, and German corporations emphasized internal capital, whose main source was either the depreciation of previous investment or the preservation of profits. External sources were accessed when additional capital was needed. In the United States, bank loans represented only 5.8 percent of the total capital supply; in Britain, 4.3 percent; in West Germany, 18.8 percent; in Italy, 12.4 percent. In contrast, Japanese corporations relied heavily on an external supply of capital (Morozumi 1963a, 29). As Table 4.1 shows, between 1957 and 1974 the ratio of bank loans in the total capital supply ranged from 65.2 percent to 83.3 percent. Most individual savings were deposited in banks, which became the major suppliers of capital. The proportion of bank loans in the total capital supply was very high. In the 1950s, about 70 percent of Japanese personal financial assets took the form of savings in banks. Stocks and bonds occupied only 20 to 30 percent. According to another statistic, between 1953 and 1960 the percentage of loans from banks in the total capital supply ranged from 74.9 percent to 83.7 percent. In contrast, the percentage of stocks and bonds together ranged from 16.3 percent to 25.1

Table 4.1 *Distribution of Sources of External Corporate Finance (percent)*

Period	Equity	Bonds	Loans
1957–59	20.5	11.1	68.3
1960–64	21.2	13.6	65.2
1965–69	8.0	12.1	79.9
1970–74	6.4	10.3	83.3
1975–79	19.6	25.3	55.1
1980–84	30.0	25.1	45.0
1985–88	38.6	51.4	10.0

Source: Ueda, 1994, p. 105.

percent. Only in the French corporate financial setting was there a bank loan imbalance similar to that of the Japanese (Morozumi 1963a, 29–30).

Indirect financing was aimed at strengthening coordination in three important ways. First, it bridged the gap between corporations' strong need for capital and households' oversaving through the mediation of banks. To compete in technological innovation, Japanese companies aggressively invested in production capacity and technological transfers. Although they accumulated huge amounts of capital during the high growth period, the amount of their investments was far beyond what they could afford. Consequently, they borrowed heavily from banks. In 1961, for example, the total investment of Japanese companies was 4.8 trillion yen. The internal capital raised through reservation of profits and depreciation provided 2.5 trillion yen, and they needed an additional 2.3 trillion yen. In the same year, personal savings in Japan were 2 trillion yen and, for the most part, were absorbed by financial institutions. Japanese banks played a crucial role in bridging the gap between overinvested corporations and oversaved households (Morozumi 1963a, 27–28).

Second, indirect financing sustained and even enhanced the Bank of Japan's expansionary monetary policy. The money supply could be increased through three channels: an increase in the Bank of Japan's credit to private banks; an increase in public spending through fiscal stimulus packages; and an increase in the trade surplus. Between 1955 and 1961, whenever the trade surplus appeared, it was soon counterbalanced by government taxes. Most of the increases in the money supply reflected increases in the Bank of Japan's credit to private banks (Katamatsu 1995, 316). To promote economic growth, the Bank of Japan maintained low interest rates. State taxation policy also favored indirect financing over raising capital in the stock and bond markets. With the support of the Bank of Japan, Japanese city banks mobilized not only their certificate deposits but also their short-term deposits in order to issue more loans. In theory, the Bank of Japan should have exercised certain controls over its outflow of credit. But by the time the overlending problem of private banks was brought to the attention of the Bank of Japan, it was often too late for the bank to control the situation because the projects financed by these private companies were already too far in debt. The Bank of Japan often had no choice except to issue credit (Morozumi 1963a, 36).

Third, indirect financing also served to tie the keiretsu together. During World War II, as I demonstrate in Chapter 3, Japanese corporate finances shifted from direct to indirect. After Japan's defeat, Japanese companies suffered from a shortage of capital, relying heavily on loans from commercial banks. Given the frequent tightness and uncertainty of the financial market, Japanese corporations preferred to keep close ties with their banks. Even when they could get money elsewhere, they continued to borrow from banks because such sustained transactions would further strengthen their ties with banks (Morozumi 1963a, 29, 34–35). In the 1950s, keiretsu banks were major suppliers of capital to their member companies. From 1953 to 1960, between 23.5 percent and 31.9 percent of the total loans issued by the Mitsubishi Bank went to companies in the Mitsubishi group. In the same period, the percentage of loans borrowed from the Mitsubishi Bank in the total loans companies in the Mitsubishi group ranged between 19.5 percent and 23.8 percent (Morozumi 1963a, 32).

Although indirect financing contributed to the coordination of various economic actors to promote high growth, I have argued that it also functioned to intensify excessive competition by weakening shareholders' control over management. The weight of individual shareholders kept declining while the weight of institutional shareholders kept rising. Institutional shareholders did not have strong incentives to control the managers. When private corporations relied heavily on bank loans for capital, shareholders became less important to the corporations. This strengthened the autonomy of corporate managers. As a result, Japanese corporations issued meager dividends, and shareholders' interests received little attention. Consequently, the stock market did not develop as an effective alternative source of capital.

The interaction between managers and shareholders became a vicious cycle: The more that corporations relied on indirect financing, the more autonomous managers became and the less leverage shareholders had. The fewer dividends that individual shareholders received, the less incentive they had to make investments. The smaller their investments, the less developed the stock market was. The less developed the stock market, the greater the dependence of corporations on indirect financing. Although indirect financing indeed greatly strengthened coordination among the state, private banks, and corporations in the national effort to promote economic growth, it achieved this goal at the cost of weakening shareholders' control over management.

In indirect financing, Japanese banks' overlending (lending more money than the bank had on deposit) also weakened the banks' monitoring of corporate finance. When banks made too many loans, it lowered the mobility of their money, and they became dependent on credit from the central bank. The increase in the proportion of the Bank of Japan's credit indicates the deterioration of the banks' financial health. As this practice continued over a long time, city banks lost the sense that they needed to maintain capital mobility and simply rushed into making loans. Overlending also weakened the Bank of Japan's last-resort function. When private banks were provided with ensured access to central bank credits, they assumed a casual attitude toward making loans. Because overlending also meant easy access of corporations to capital, it served to delay the development of both long-term and short-term capital markets. In addition, overlending weakened the function of interest rates in adjusting the money supply at the macro level (Katamatsu 1995, 318).

THE MAIN BANK SYSTEM

The main bank system emerged with the transformation of Japanese corporate finance from direct financing to indirect financing in the national mobilization during World War II. Although many wartime institutions became targets of postwar democratic reforms, the main bank system survived. Initially, the GHQ thought seriously about reforming Japan's financial institutions. The Antitrust and Cartels Division included financial institutions in its proposal for deconcentration. The Economic Reconstruction and Reorganization Standard Law also covered the banking industry. However, resistance from a united front – including the Japanese government, officials at the Finance Division of the GHQ, and even some officials in the U.S. government – defeated this effort. As Eleanor Hadley (1970, 164) points out, "Throughout the combine-dissolution program, financial institutions were consistently treated preferentially. No bank became a designated holding company, though banks qualified for such designation a good deal more fully than certain other operating companies named." T. A. Bisson (1954, 154) also argues that "the failure to apply Law No. 207 [the Elimination of Excessive Concentrations of Economic Power Law] to financial institutions and notably to the big Zaibatsu commercial banks represented the most serious omission in the deconcentration program."

The main bank system established its central place in the Japanese economy in the reconstruction process. Because of the severe shortage of capital, loan coordination through the Bank of Japan became the institutional framework of corporate finance in the late 1940s. The Reconstruction Bank, established in 1947, became an important public source of capital, supplying about one-fourth of the total capital supply by the end of the 1940s. The Bank of Japan coordinated loans or organized a loan syndicate according to applications from the company's main bank. In July 1948, the Loan Coordination Committee was established, consisting of the chief lenders from 19 major city banks and directors of related bureaus at the Bank of Japan. This committee was to establish the principles of lending, examine important cases, and report the progress of corporate finance, creating a list of priorities for industrial financing and identifying companies that might need help. Not only were the main banks indispensable in the companies' applications for loans, but they were also responsible for supervising companies' situations after the loans were issued and for reporting to the Bank of Japan and other banks that participated in the syndicate. The Bank of Japan performed the same function of coordinating corporate finances as did the wartime national financial control association (Okazaki 1993, 124). After implementation of the Dodge plan in 1949, loans from the Reconstruction Bank were no longer available and private banks became the manufacturers' sole financiers. The relationship between the main banks and corporations that had formed during the war continued to function without any major interruption (Itō 1995, 117).

By definition, a main bank provides the largest share of loans to a given corporation. As a result, other lenders do not monitor the company with the same intensity. Rather, they rely on the judgment of the main bank. Some economists point to this phenomenon, known as *delegated monitoring*, as evidence that the main bank system provided monitoring of Japanese corporations. Delegated monitoring by the main bank can be exercised in three stages. *Ex ante* monitoring involves screening corporate investment proposals and checking the corporations' capacity to implement them. *Interim* monitoring refers to the gathering of information on the ongoing businesses of the borrowing companies. *Ex post* monitoring verifies the outcome of investment projects and disciplines managers of a failing company. Masahiko Aoki (1994, 128) argues that delegated monitoring provides effective discipline of Japanese corporations and reduces the transaction cost of duplicating ex ante and interim monitoring. Unlike Miyazaki, who maintains that the government-industry-bank framework for coordinating the investment decisions leads to excessive competition, Aoki holds that such a framework nurtured the ex ante monitoring capacity of Japanese city banks (1994, 131). Contrary to the Miyazaki argument that the convoy administration led to excessive competition, Aoki writes that the convoy administration sustained delegated monitoring. In Aoki's interpretation, excessive competition during the bubble of the 1980s reflected the decline of the delegated function caused by the gradual removal of regulations on interest rates and bond issue requirements. During the high growth period, he asserts, the delegated monitoring function was rather effective (1994, 135).

However, a recent study on the Japanese steel and chemical industries (Hidaka and Kikkawa 1998) strongly questions the delegated monitoring argument. In his study of six major Japanese steel makers, Hidaka finds that the main banks played an active role, not in monitoring corporate investment but rather in encouraging excessive competition. Between 1955 and 1960, the World Bank financed between 40 percent and 50 percent of 11 projects for these six Japanese steel makers. As a condition of the loans, the World

Bank demanded that these Japanese steel makers reach a 1 : 1 debt/capital ratio. It held that healthy corporate finance would enable Japanese steel makers to raise capital in the overseas financial markets. All these Japanese steel makers, through the Japan Development Bank, applied for an extension of the deadline for the improvement of corporate finances. The World Bank sent several delegations to Japan, urging these Japanese companies to be cautious about the danger of building surplus production capacity. The World Bank's advice caused a strong reaction. Japanese managers insisted on the importance of gaining market share, arguing that this principle justified surplus production capacity in a high growth period. The World Bank was surprised to find that its view of corporate financial health was not shared by the Japanese at all. Nevertheless, in 1962, the World Bank extended to 1967 the deadline for reaching the 1 : 1 debt/capital ratio. In 1965, the Japanese applied for a second extension, offering a compromise of a 2 : 1 debt/capital ratio, and the World Bank agreed. As a result, by 1975, the production capacity of these Japanese steel makers increased several times. Meanwhile, their debt ratio also increased substantially, creating a heavy interest burden. In his study of the Japanese chemical industry, Kikkawa tells the same story (Hidaka and Kikkawa 1998, 4–14).

Even during the high growth period, many Japanese economists argued that main banks could not effectively monitor their corporate borrowers, for several reasons. First, although the main bank provided the largest share of bank loans to manufacturers, the bank's influence on the borrower was not necessarily strong, especially among big companies. The reason was that as big corporations increased the total amount of their loans, the share of the total debt held by the main bank became less important. In 1962, among 25 companies that borrowed more than 30 billion yen, the loans from their main banks averaged only 15 percent. Because companies borrowed from many banks and the share by the main bank was relatively small, the function of delegated monitoring was weakened significantly (Tsuruta 1962, 39).

What about the interim monitoring option – was it effective? Most main banks held stock in their corporate customers. Although good short-term performance could bring the main banks some profits, the banks' stakes in the corporations' long-term development were much greater. Concern for the former could easily be counterbalanced by expectations for the latter. In the high growth period, when Japanese corporations competed vigorously in investing in production capacity and technological transfer, the main banks were under strong pressure to lend money to big corporations. To retain customers who had high growth potential, banks made strong efforts to bring them into their business groups. Banks not only expected to make money through these loans, but they also benefited from attracting more businesses because the subcontractors and trading partners of big corporations tended to do business with the branch offices of the same commercial banks. This kind of keiretsu financing, however, weakened the banks' monitoring over their corporate borrowers. In Western countries, if a company's performance declines, it becomes more difficult for it to issue corporate bonds or stocks. A weak company could not borrow money from banks at favorable terms. Not so in Japan. There, the banks wanted to keep their favored customers. If they refused a loan to companies, they might lose them in the battle with their rival banks. As a result, the banks failed to monitor the companies that borrowed money from them (Miyazaki 1963a).

Concerning the ex post monitoring option, the convoy administration changed the incentive structure for Japanese banks. As Hidaka pointed out, the convoy administration tightly controlled not only the banks' interest rates but also the expansion of their branch offices. When the only way to generate more profits was to make loans but banks could not generate more deposits by expanding the network of their branch offices, it was rational for the main banks to support their corporate borrowers' business expansions; in this way, the expansion of the business would lead to additional corporate deposits. When the total size of the bank deposit increased, it would be easier for the banks to get approval for their expansion of branch offices from the Ministry of Finance (Hidaka and Kikkawa 1998, 16–17).

This suggests that the impact of Japanese industrial policy on the behavior of private banks materialized rather indirectly via the keiretsu: MITI had a strong impact on big corporations in the exports-related sector through both its stated policy preference and its distribution of foreign currency. In addition, the big corporations were closely associated with the keiretsu banks, which lent money aggressively to big corporations in the exports-related sector without direct control by the Bank of Japan. As a result, industrial financing in Japan was not always rational. In fact, it often "lost its way" during the high growth period, and overlending by private banks led to excessive competition. If the Bank of Japan had actually controlled the banks' lending behavior, the massive speculation by Japanese corporations during the bubble in the 1980s would not have happened at the same level.

RECIPROCAL SHAREHOLDING

Another practice aimed at strengthening coordination was the practice of reciprocal shareholding. This practice, however, ended up weakening shareholders' control over management and weakening banks' monitoring over corporate borrowers' financial health, thus serving to sustain excessive competition.

Reciprocal shareholding emerged as a corporate strategy to prevent hostile takeovers in the stock market. It started with the Yōwa Real Estate Company, which had been established in 1891 by the founder of the Mitsubishi group. This company owned land in the Marunouchi area, a central place (in terms both of location and importance) in Tokyo. In 1952, an individual speculator purchased 35 percent of the Yōwa Real Estate's standing stocks through the stock market. The Mitsubishi group regarded this purchase as a major threat. After a meeting of the CEOs, the Mitsubishi group decided to buy back the Yōwa Real Estate Company, regardless of the cost. The shares were divided among 11 companies in the group, and the transaction was financed by the Mitsubishi Bank. Usabi Jungen, president of the Mitsubishi Bank and the person who handled the transaction, recalled that it was a major event for companies in the former Mitsubishi group. It meant that these companies would have to cooperate again after having been dissolved into numerous small companies and even having been denied the use of the Mitsubishi trademark. Although the event did not revive the zaibatsu of the past, the spirit of cooperation was reborn (Okumura 1975, 37–38). After the Antimonopoly Law was relaxed in 1953, the exchange of personnel and reciprocal shareholding became legal again. The companies in the Mitsubishi group formerly held 11.7 percent of the shares of Mitsubishi Corporation (the trading company in the group) before it was divided by the occupation authority. After it was reorganized in 1954, the shares owned by the companies within the Mitsubishi group jumped to 33.5 percent (Okumura 1975, 38–39). Hostile takeovers also took place in the Mitsui Real Estate and Taishō Marine and Fire Insurance companies. Companies within the group responded in the same way as had the Mitsubishi group. To prevent this kind of hostile takeover, these companies began to hold each other's shares. This stimulated the development of reciprocal shareholding. Meanwhile, CEOs from various businesses began gathering and forming into groups.

Table 4.2 shows the reciprocal shareholding relationships between the Mitsubishi Bank, on the one hand, and Mitsubishi Heavy Industry, New Japan Steel, Mitsubishi Trading Company, Asahi Hyaline, Tokyo Marine and Fire Insurance, and Mitsubishi Motors on the other.

After the 1953 amendment of the Antimonopoly Law, reciprocal shareholding appeared within former zaibatsu groups as well as within non-zaibatsu groups. In the 1950s, reciprocal shareholding was used by Japanese corporations as a strategy for maintaining close relationships with banks to secure capital. According to a survey, in 1949 only one-fourth of the 473 companies owned more than 5 percent of stock in other companies. By the end of 1960, that figure had jumped to 78.4 percent. This change indicates

Table 4.2 *Reciprocal Shareholding of Mitsubishi Bank (1974)*

Top Ten Companies Owned by Mitsubishi Bank	Shares (thousand)	%	Standing
Mitsubishi Heavy Industry	122,395	5.7	1
New Japan Steel	68,636	1.4	10
Mitsubishi Trading Company	52,592	7.8	1
Asahi Hyaline	44,310	7.6	1
Mitsubishi Chemical	43,875	5.6	3
Mitsubishi Motors	39,600	3.3	4
Mitsubishi Real Estate	36,013	3.9	2
Tokyo Marine and Fire Insurance	34,746	5.7	2
Kikki Japan Railway	26,732	3.5	2
Japan Vessel	26,221	4.3	2
Top Ten Owners of Mitsubishi Bank			
Meiji Life Insurance	77,584	5.9	1
Tokyo Marine and Fire Insurance	61,475	4.7	2
Daiichi Life Insurance	46,874	3.6	3
Mitsubishi Heavy Industry	43,215	3.2	4
Japan Life Insurance	41,701	3.2	5
Asahi Hyaline	26,309	2	6
Mitsubishi Trading Company	18,200	2	7
Mitsubishi Motors	18,200	1.4	8
New Japan Steel	17,472	1.3	9
Mitsubishi Trust Bank	17,452	1.3	10

Source: Okumura, 1975, p. 91.

the rapid development of reciprocal shareholding (*Kōsei Torihiki Iinkai* 1977, 135).

The second wave in the development of reciprocal shareholding came in the late 1960s amid the liberalization of foreign investment. Toyota was the first company to use this strategy to prevent a potential hostile takeover by foreign companies. Toyota's management asserted, "It would not be threatening at all if the big three automobile makers from the United States simply entered the Japanese markets by opening their own factories. Toyota has enough competitiveness against them. What is threatening is that Toyota's stocks can be bought or taken over by foreign companies. Toyota cannot compete with this strategy" (Okumura 1975, 62). To avoid this dangerous

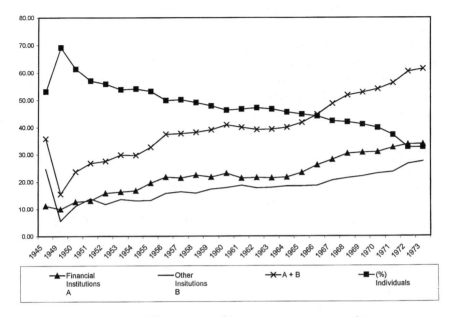

Figure 4.3. *The structure of Japanese corporate ownership.*
Source: Based on the data from Okumura, 1975, p. 45.

situation, Toyota first stabilized 50 percent of its stocks with big banks in
1967; then it added another 10 percent by bringing in the steel makers and
Toyota's subcontractors. Following Toyota, automakers such as Nissan, Isuzu,
Ninno, and Daihatsu all adopted the same strategy. Nissan, for example,
achieved 65 percent of mutual shareholding with big banks and its major
trading partners.

Figure 4.3 indicates that throughout the 1950s and 1960s, the proportion
of institutional shareholders in the structure of corporate ownership continued to increase, driven in part by the strategy of stabilizing shareholders.
In 1950, individuals held 61.30 percent, and institutions held 23.66 percent.
By 1973, the share of individuals declined to 32.7 percent (less than one-
third). In contrast, the shares of institutions increased to 60.40 percent.
There was a rapid change during the liberalization of foreign investment.
In the eight years between 1965 and 1973, the proportion of institutional
shareholders increased by almost half, from 41.75 percent to 61.40 percent.
In addition, the proportion of financial institutions (excluding mutual
funds) as institutional shareholders increased more rapidly than that of
other institutions. In 1950, the gap in shareholding between financial
institutions and other institutions was only about 1.6 percent of the total

standing stocks. By 1973, this gap had enlarged to 3.6 percent of the total standing stocks.

The Japanese government strongly supported the private initiative of stabilizing shareholders as a countermeasure to the liberalization of foreign investment. In February 1970, when General Motors decided to buy Isuzu stock, Miyazawa Kiichi, then Minister of MITI, stated at the Diet hearing that

> On automobile industry's cooperation with foreign capital, the Japanese government would approve Japanese automakers' establishing a joint capital-venture with the big three automakers of the United States if such an endeavor fits the principle of the Japanese government. In the joint-venture, it is extremely important that the Japanese side protects its autonomy in management. It is necessary to have Japanese shareholders and create stabilizing forces that are strong enough to compete effectively with foreign capital in order to prevent the management's being taken over. (Okumura 1975, 64)

In comparison with March 1946 – the eve of the zaibatsu dissolution – the total shares held by financial institutions in March 1957, both within and outside the group, increased 50.7 times in the Mitsubishi group, 56.4 times in the Mitsui group, and 51.9 times in the Sumitomo group. The number of companies belonging to these three new groups increased 7.4, 6.1, and 3.4 times, respectively. The reciprocal shareholding within the Mitsui group recovered to 11.4 percent in comparison with 53.5 percent before the dissolution. The reciprocal shareholding of Mitsubishi and Sumitomo reached 16.4 percent and 21.2 percent, in comparison with 29.9 percent and 26.2 percent, respectively. Among the total internal reciprocal shareholding within these groups, 67.7 percent, 77.8 percent, and 68.4 percent, respectively, were held by financial institutions and major manufacturers. In the prewar zaibatsu groups, the institutional shareholding went in one direction: from financial institutions to major manufacturers and then to nonmainstream companies. In the keiretsu, in contrast, shareholding became reciprocal. Major manufacturers held shares of financial institutions and also held shares among themselves.

Reciprocal shareholding apparently achieved the goal of preventing hostile takeovers and strengthening the ties among banks and private corporations in Japan. This practice, however, has had strong side effects in weakening the shareholders' control over management. If a Japanese corporation does not practice reciprocal shareholding, it is not difficult to imagine that its managers have less autonomy than managers of companies that follow this practice. As mentioned earlier, reciprocal shareholding has a hostage effect

(Nishiyama 1975). When the shareholders' control over management becomes mutual, managers in both companies that share each other's stocks will be worse off. They will both be better off if they do not exercise shareholders' control over each other at all.

THE ONE-SET INVESTMENT STRATEGY OF THE KEIRETSU

Supported by the state's expansionary monetary policy, indirect financing, reciprocal shareholding, and the main bank system, the Japanese keiretsu, especially the former zaibatsu groups, developed a so-called one-set investment strategy. This strategy, an extreme form of multidimensional integration, was characterized by aggressive investments in production capacity and technological transfer in all frontier industries. Most studies of the high growth period done by Japanese scholars emphasized the phenomenon of "aggressive investments in production capacity and technological transfer." In other words, they argue that the rapid increase in the production factor, in the form of capital, triggered the high growth. As Figure 4.1 shows, Japanese corporations invested much more than their Western counterparts in the 1950s and 1960s. Big corporations were the major players in these investments, and, moreover, these investments were made by the business groups in competition in all new industries.

The one-set investment strategy was a direct cause of excessive competition, as reflected in three different patterns. The first pattern was in sales. Companies competed with one another by cutting the prices of their products below production costs. In the camera industry, for example, the price declined 30 percent in the two years between 1957 and 1959. The profit and sales ratio changed from 7.6 percent to −2.2 percent. Of 35 companies, 15 went into bankruptcy. To increase subscriptions, newspapers spent a total of 200 million yen for gifts. Nevertheless, what increased was neither the total number of subscriptions nor the subscriptions of individual newspapers, but rather companies' production costs. Juice producers ran lotteries for passenger cars, houses, and world tours; whiskey producers ran lotteries for a trip to Hawaii (Morozumi 1963a, 17–23).

A second way that companies engaged in aggressive competition was in aggressive product differentiation. In the automobile industry, 10 makers produced 12 kinds of sedans, 5 kinds of compact cars, and 11 kinds of minicars. In the home electronics industry, the top 5 producers brought out 54 brands of refrigerators, 36 brands of TVs, and 83 brands of electronic fans. As models of products changed constantly, there was a shortage of parts to repair the older models, and production costs rose (Morozumi 1963a, 17–23).

The third pattern of excessive competition was in the promotion of production capacity and technological transfer. In the steel industry, for example, each major producer prepared more than 2,480 acres of land for new factories. They competed to build factories whose annual production was 600 million tons. As a result, the amount of underused production capacity continued to increase. In the petrochemical industry, Japan already had 5 refinery centers. Another 5 were under construction, and 20 more were in the planning stage. Competition for technological transfer was most intensive in cameras, motorcycles, and home electronics (Morozumi 1963a, 17–23).

Why did Japanese keiretsu adopt the one-set investment strategy? There were some structural reasons. As Miyazaki Yoshikazu (1963, 54) points out, the deconcentration of excessive economic power by the occupation authority made market entry easier than before. In addition, technological innovation was widely perceived as the only way to build Japan's international competitiveness in the 1950s. Enlightened by Joseph Schumpeter's idea of innovation, Japanese keiretsu invested aggressively in the petrochemical, synthetic fiber, resins, automobile, and home electronics industries in an effort to close the 10-year gap between Japan and the West created by World War II (see Gao 1997, Chapter 5). Facing intensive competition in technological transfer in the frontier industries, leading manufacturers in each keiretsu group pursued both a backward integration (aimed at a stable supply of raw materials) and a forward integration (aimed at obtaining markets for the company's product), with an eye toward keeping the entire production process within the business group. They also adopted multidimensional integration, extending their business operations into various related industries. In this way, they hoped to tide themselves over during fluctuations in the economic cycle by balancing products in declining markets and products in upward markets and by balancing high-profit, seasonal products and lower-profit products having sustained sales (Miyazaki 1963).

Nevertheless, an important institutional reason for the one-set investment strategy was changes in the governance structures of the Japanese economy. Compared with prewar zaibatsu, the function of coordination in postwar keiretsu was strengthened, but that of control was weakened.

Let's look first at the postwar change in coordination. In the prewar zaibatsu, relationships between organizations were largely reflected in the vertical control of capital. Member companies within one zaibatsu often lacked a horizontal relationship in production technology. In other words, the relationships were reflected more in the shared distribution channel of the trading company and thus were remote and indirect. Faced with the new technological environment of the 1950s, that type of business organization would lose most of the benefits of business grouping. Unless they combined the strength of technological know-how in related production fields, business groups were no longer economically feasible. Thus, even as the formal zaibatsu groups were reorganized, the status of the companies in sunset industries – often the major players in the prewar period – declined, and companies in petrochemical, synthetic fibers, and electrical engineering became the new center. Some formal zaibatsu groups even brought in manufacturers in oil refinery and electrical engineering, which had not previously belonged to the zaibatsu. The rise of the new postwar business groups, such as the Daiichi Bank group and the Fuji Bank group, reflected not only the efforts of new actors to compete with formal zaibatsu groups but also the strategic response of capital to the postwar structural changes and the increasing linkages among production technologies.

Meanwhile, however, the control function of the keiretsu declined. During the zaibatsu dissolution in the late 1940s, the stocks of the holding company in each zaibatsu were sold, and zaibatsu family members were purged from managerial posts. In comparison with the zaibatsu, the postwar keiretsu had some new characteristics. First, although reciprocal shareholding became a common practice among former zaibatsu companies after the 1950s, no longer did any company control 50 percent or more of its subordinates' stock. In addition, individual shareholders also functioned to further diversify the concentration of capital. In terms of ownership, Japanese corporations were under no exclusive control by other corporations in the postwar period (Minosō 1963, 83–84).

Second, sustained by such nonexclusive reciprocal shareholding, the interorganizational control through exchange of personnel also changed. In the prewar zaibatsu, control was one-way: from the holding company to subordinates. In the postwar keiretsu, in contrast, there was no center of control, although the bank and the trading company were often regarded as the center of each keiretsu. Similarly, the nature of personnel exchange in the postwar horizontal integration of keiretsu must be understood as at best mutual control, rather than dominant control by one particular company. For this reason, informal gatherings of company presidents became a common practice in postwar keiretsu. Although the power of each individual president within the same keiretsu varied, in the end the gathering was a place of coordination (Minosō 1963, 83–84).

Third, whereas the prewar zaibatsu was characterized by the vertical yet concentrated dominance of Mitsui, Mitsubishi, Sumitomo, and Yasuda, in the postwar era several business groups, in addition to the former zaibatsu groups, emerged and competed for power. Moreover, unlike formal zaibatsu groups, many of whose member companies were in the sunset industries such as coal, chemical, and natural fiber; all the new business groups were organized around the frontier industries and thus were more dynamic (Minosō 1963, 83–84).

PERMANENT EMPLOYMENT AND THE STRONG GROWTH ORIENTATION OF JAPANESE COMPANIES

In the English-language literature on Japanese corporations, permanent employment has generated considerable attention. Although most of the attention has centered on employee loyalty, morale, and job satisfaction or company control over employees, less attention is given to the impact of this practice on Japanese corporate governance and investment patterns. A review of the debate on excessive competition in the early 1960s shows that the practice of permanent employment directly contributes to a strong growth orientation in Japanese companies, an orientation that often materializes through aggressive corporate investments and bank loans. Permanent employment was the micro-level foundation of the causal chain of mechanisms that led to excessive competition which triggered the high growth (Itō 1968).

The impact of permanent employment on Japanese corporate governance, sustained by other mechanisms discussed in this chapter, is that it changes the priority of management from generating more profits for shareholders to the collective survival of all employees, including both managers and employees. Because there was no mobile labor market in postwar Japan, employees were not able to move easily to other companies to obtain more economic benefits. They had to compete in an internal labor market. Because permanent employment tended to create tension and conflict within the company, Japanese employees often reported lower levels of job satisfaction compared with their Western peers. To reduce internal tension and conflict, Japanese companies pursued strong growth, measured by market share, in the hope that it would lead to increases in salary, bonuses, and managerial positions. The prestige of a company depended more on its size than on its solid financial basis, and medium-size and small companies were at a significant disadvantage in the public eye. Because the power of individual shareholders in Japanese corporate ownership kept declining and because institutional shareholders usually did not directly intervene in the management of the company they owned, company managers were under less pressure to generate short-term profits, and they were eager to promote the status of their companies. The interests of both managers and employees were tied closely to their company's market presence (Itō 1968).

In Japan, a company whose shareholders or managers are willing to sell the company whenever an opportunity arises has a difficult time attracting any employees. Such people would be criticized as betraying employee expectations, which go far beyond the provisions of the employment contract and the labor contract. These kinds of expectations become a centrifugal force, reflected in group orientation and loyalty. Neither property rights nor economic rationality can change this expectation. When these principles are pursued at the expense of employees' expectations, the company will cease functioning well. Employees' expectations play a large role in mergers; within the permanent employment system it is difficult for employees to leave the company, and, as a result, employees form close ties in various human communities within the company. Thus, the Japanese view of accounting is quite different from that of American and European companies that focus on either shareholders' interests or employees' own interests. Japanese businesses pay more attention to achieving the minimum profit that can sustain the survival of the community of employees. Profits, in the Japanese context, are the necessary condition for sustaining the community of human beings, instead of the purpose of business per se (Itō 1968, 142–143).

THE LIBERALIZATION OF TRADE AND FOREIGN INVESTMENT

The Japanese liberalization of trade started in 1959. From the end of World War II, the Japanese government had restricted imports and foreign exchange because of economic instability and the shortage of dollars. This practice was allowed by Article 14 of the International Monetary Fund. The liberalization process started in Western Europe when the Organization for Economic Cooperation Development (OECD) was established in 1949 to carry out the Marshall Plan for Europe's postwar economic reconstruction. The resolution that established the OECD stated that a united European market would be built by establishing a multinational trade system and an international payment system, and by eliminating restrictions on trade; the OECD required member countries to be responsible for liberalizing trade in Europe by at least 90 percent by the end of June 1959.

This goal was largely achieved by 1955, but the liberalization of trade with the dollar areas was much slower. Countries such as West Germany and Switzerland, whose currencies were strong against the dollar, took the initiative; countries such as France, Italy, and Britain, which had a shortage of dollars or whose competitiveness with the United States was weak, did not reach the same level until 1958. Under strong pressure from the United States, these countries rescinded their restrictions on imports of American products. By 1958, they resumed convertibility between the U.S. dollar and their own currencies (Keizai Kikakuchō 1976). By doing so, these countries moved toward Article 8 status in the International Monetary Fund (IMF), which prohibited any restriction on foreign currency to balance international payments. At the end of the 1950s, a free trade regime, sustained by the Pax Americana, began emerging in the international economy. At that time, Japan's domestic markets were tightly protected. At the end of August 1959, 74 percent of Japanese imports faced government-imposed restrictions (Economic Planning Agency 1990, 102).

The stimulus of change was extrainstitutional inasmuch as international agencies and foreign pressures set new rules for the games played domestically in Japan. In mid-1959, Japan became a target of criticism from Western countries on the issue of liberalization. When Prime Minister Kishi Nobusuke visited the United States to renew the security treaty between the two countries, the U.S. government demanded that Japan proceed with the liberalization of trade. At the annual meetings of both the IMF and the GATT, the U.S. representatives strongly criticized Japan for its restrictions on imports, warning that if Japan did not quickly rescind restrictions on imports from the dollar areas, the United States might restrict imports of Japanese products (Masamura 1985). Under these strong international pressures, the Japanese government began liberalizing trade in 1960. The import liberalization ratio was raised to 70 percent by the end of 1961, to 88 percent by October 1962, to 92 percent by August 1963, and to 94 percent by February 1970. The number of import-controlled items decreased from 492 at the end of 1961 to 123 at the end of 1964. In 1964, yielding to pressure by the IMF and the OECD, Japan also withdrew its restrictions on its foreign currency exchange.

The Japanese liberalization of capital investment started in the mid-1960s. When Japan became a formal member of the OECD, it had to accept 18 reservations, a number trailing only Portugal's 28 and Spain's 19. Japan was forced to liberalize its capital transactions, which at the time referred to the liberalization of direct foreign investments. The OECD reviewed the reservations of its member countries every 18 months. In the OECD's first review in October 1965, it urged Japan to speed up its liberalization of foreign investments and was harshly critical in the second review in January 1967. In 1966, the Business and Industry Advisory Committee (BIAC), an advisory organ of major economic organizations of the OECD member countries, demanded that Japan fulfill its obligations to the OECD and IMF as well as its bilateral commercial treaties with the United States and Britain, and that it draft a schedule for the final elimination of restrictions on direct foreign investments. Beginning in 1965, Japan's major trading partner, the United States, initiated several talks, at both the government and civilian levels, that pushed Japan to withdraw its restrictions on foreign investments.

In response to strong international pressure, Japan's liberalization of foreign investments underwent several stages between 1966 and 1973. Each later stage of progress was also a response to foreign pressure. In the beginning, in industries in which Japanese companies had already built strong international competitiveness, the Japanese government allowed foreign capital to own 100 percent of a company. In contrast, in industries where Japanese companies were competitive in international markets but there was still a gap in comprehensive competitiveness (measured by technology, capital, equipment, and raw materials), foreign investors were allowed to own no more than 50 percent of a company's total stock. Meanwhile, in the industries related to national security and energy, infant industries, and industries that were undergoing structural improvement, restrictions were maintained. In 1970, most industries moved to the 50 percent level. In 1973, 100 percent of foreign capital shareholding in a company was achieved (Tsuruta 1982, 145).

THE IMPACT OF EXCESSIVE COMPETITION ON ECONOMIES OF SCALE

The challenge imposed by the liberalization of trade and foreign investments forced the Japanese in the 1960s to recognize the negative impact of excessive competition on their economy. In the new, more open economy, economies of scale became critical because big corporations could afford to offer lower prices to remain competitive in the market. At the time, the Japanese were deeply concerned about the size of Japanese companies because even as large as they were, Japanese companies had to be regarded as medium-size compared with other international businesses. According to statistics published in 1961 by *Fortune,* widely cited in the Japanese debate on the liberalization of trade, only four Japanese companies were ranked among the world's top 150 companies, with Hitachi ranked 77th, Yamato Steel 92nd, Toshiba 101st, and Fuji Steel 140th. Among the 150 world's largest companies, American companies occupied 99 positions; German, 17; British, 14; Canadian, 5; French and Italian, 3 each; and Swiss and Belgian, 2 each (Morozumi 1963a).

The disadvantage of the lack of economies of scale was obvious in the iron-steel, automobile, electrical machinery and appliances, chemical, and oil industries. Yamato Steel, the largest Japanese iron-steel maker, achieved only 15 percent as much in sales, owned only 16 percent as much in assets, and earned only 12.5 percent as much after-tax profits compared with U.S. Steel, the largest iron-steel maker in the world; the comparable figures for Toyota, the largest Japanese automobile maker, were 2.7 percent, 2.2 percent, and 3.2 percent, respectively, compared with General Motors, the largest automobile maker in the world; for Hitachi, the largest Japanese electrical machinery and appliances maker, the figures were 14.9 percent, 29.2 percent, and 25.5 percent, respectively, compared with General Electric, the largest company in that industry in the world; for Sumitomo Chemical, the largest Japanese chemical company, the figures were 6.3 percent, 6.6 percent, and 2.4 percent, respectively, compared with Du Pont, the largest chemical company in the world; and for Nippon Oil, the largest Japanese oil company, the figures were 3.7 percent, 1.6 percent, and 2.1 percent, respectively, compared with Standard Oil, the largest oil company in the world (Morozumi 1963a). When the liberalization of trade and foreign investments lowered many formal trade barriers imposed by state regulations, these giant international companies were able to enter Japanese markets with a great advantage in the economies of scale.

Why did Japanese companies not become bigger through merger? In the 1950s, there were about 400 mergers each year. These mergers, however, usually aimed at multidimensional business integration and occurred among companies that belonged to the same business group and had held long-term relationships in capital and personnel. Only a few mergers within one industry had increased the concentration of production. As a result, these mergers tended to produce an economy of scope rather than an economy of scale, and they tended to occur either between a big company and a medium-size company or between medium-size companies. In general, they were minimized because when companies engaged in aggressive investments in technological innovation, mergers often meant taking over old equipment; and no economy of scale or increase in market share in the frontier industries could be expected. The gap in wages between big companies and medium-size and small companies made subcontracting more attractive than mergers (Tsūsanshō 1989, Vol. 5, 315–316).

In theory, competition should lead to concentration of production resources. Because competition produces winners and losers, the winners should have grown in size and increased their economy of scale. Even though competition among Japanese companies in investment in production capacity had been "excessive," it had not significantly reduced the number of companies in the organizational population, and it had failed to promote concentration of production. The level of capital concentration certainly increased; meanwhile, however, the market share of each keiretsu, an indicator of production concentration, declined compared with those of the prewar period. In other words, the increasing level of concentration of capital was accompanied by a decreasing level of concentration of production. Although Japanese financial institutions were able to channel the country's excessively saved money to the manufacturers through various business networks, none of the private companies was able to build a dominant position in the market (Miyazaki 1963, 52–58). As Figure 4.4 indicates, in comparison with the 1950 level, production concentration in 1960 developed rapidly only in the food industry but declined in the metal, fiber, paper pulp, machinery, chemical, oil, and pottery industries (Tsuji 1969).

According to organizational ecology, with the same amount of resources, the existence of an increasing number of firms should have reduced the rate of survival for each individual firm, because when more firms compete for the same amount of resources, their chance of obtaining more resources or even maintaining the same level of resources declines (Hannan and Freeman 1989). In the Japanese case, however, even when more companies entered the market to compete for the same amount of resources, most of them survived. This meant that each individual Japanese company received a relatively smaller share of resources, accounting for the low level of concentration of production capacity. The inefficient allocation of resources led to an increasing burden for business operation. To compete for scarce capital, Japanese companies had to pay more interest. Taking the production cost of Japanese manufacturing industry as 100, the cost of corporate finance in 1936 was about 6.2, but it jumped to 24.6 in 1961. In the same period, the burden of taxes also rose from 8.7 to 17.4. Interest and taxes combined, as a percentage of production cost, was 14.9 percent in 1936 but rose to 42 percent in 1961 (Kodō 1963, 110–111).

In the 1950s, even companies within the same business group competed with one another in the same industry. In the petrochemical industry, for example, two subgroups emerged to compete with each other within the Mitsui group. In the construction machinery and automobile industries, three companies that had been divided from the former Mitsubishi Heavy Industry during the zaibatsu dissolution competed intensively. When each of these big manufacturers developed its own supplier network, that action launched the trend of vertical integration. In the Mitsui group, some companies even disconnected themselves from the keiretsu, becoming independent giant producers (Okumura 1975, 51).

In short, excessive competition in the high growth period had the following characteristics. First, it was driven not by quality considerations but by price reduction. Companies did not need to have a niche in technology, and entry to market was easy. The enlargement of production capacity increased interest costs for loans and labor but reduced capital accumulation.

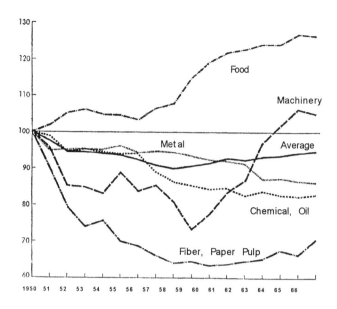

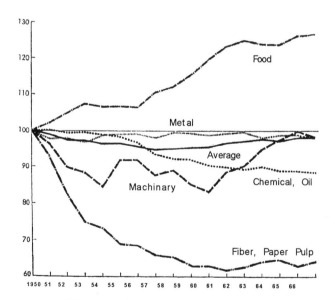

Figure 4.4. (*1*) *The index of production concentration (top three in 1950 as 100). (2) The index of production concentration (top ten in 1950 as 100).*
Source: Tsuji, 1969, p. 102.

The power to set product prices, moreover, was in the hands of the salesmen; rather than rely on techniques of sales engineering, they simply competed with one another in reducing prices (Itō 1968).

Second, competition in Japan was aimed at increasing market share rather than profits. Companies feared that if they failed to occupy the market during the period of rapid growth, they would not be able to gain economies of scale and would eventually be driven out of the competition. Psychology and social pressures also played a role in this definition of business aims. Small companies, even when they had a solid business base, tended to be looked down on in Japanese society. Although it was difficult for employees to move to other companies, they had strong expectations for the growth of their own company. Even the internal evaluation of a manager's performance was not based on how much profits were made but on how much market share was obtained under his leadership (Itō 1968).

Third, excessive competition in the 1950s was driven not by the strategy of innovation but by the strategy of emulation, or what Paul DiMaggio and Walter Powell (1983) call "mimetic isomorphism." Emulation was a cost-efficient, low-risk strategy that allowed companies to accumulate technological know-how quickly. Being the forerunner in Japanese domestic markets involved a huge marketing cost, and such companies enjoyed only a short period of monopoly profits. In many cases, it was more beneficial to be the second or third company in the market. In addition, because the internal culture of Japanese companies emphasized consensus, it was difficult to achieve collective consensus about innovative ideas but easy to claim legitimacy for the practices of foreign companies or domestic competitors (Itō 1968, 144–145).

This analysis suggests that the mechanism that induced excessive competition in the Japanese economic system also enabled Japanese corporations to invest much more than their Western counterparts in technological innovation and to build strong international competitiveness. It shows that the astonishing achievement by Japanese corporations in innovation during the high growth period was financed through a special pattern of industrial finance whose effectiveness was heavily dependent on many contingent conditions. This analysis also sheds light on the discussion of the Japanese production system as a model of flexibility. It reveals that this widely praised production system was in fact a by-product of excessive competition. Excessive competition led to aggressive product differentiation. In the process of the liberalization of trade, the lack of economies of scale (a basic characteristic of mass production) was perceived by the Japanese as a problem, something that should disappear when Japan embraced the era of mass production represented by Fordism in the United States. The Japanese system indeed had an equivalent effect – that of flexible production. This was, however, more an unintentional default of excessive competition, a side effect of coordination, rather than the goal of coordination itself.

THE FAILURE OF THE NEW INDUSTRIAL SYSTEM

The support by MITI of the strategy of stabilizing shareholding reflected a major dilemma for the Japanese industrial policy concerning the issue of keiretsu financing. Although MITI and its think tanks regarded keiretsu financing as the major cause of excessive competition, they still supported the private sector initiative to rely on the holding of manufacturers' shares by commercial banks and insurance companies, a practice that simply strengthened the ties between banks and manufacturers and deepened the problems of keiretsu financing. By promoting the institution of the keiretsu, the strategy of stabilizing shareholders spread a fatal disease into the governance of the Japanese economy.

Why was keiretsu financing no longer regarded as a major cause of excessive competition and a serious threat to the economy? The answer is that excessive competition in investing in production capacity was a double-edged sword. The practice of keiretsu financing had two major implications for the Japanese economy; one was structural, and the other was institutional. Excessive competition as a structural outcome of keiretsu financing was the chief concern of policy makers and business leaders in the early 1960s. They were afraid that massive entries into the market might result in a low level of production concentration and might reduce the economies of scale, thus weakening the competitiveness of Japanese companies. It might also lower the profits of private companies, and this would mean that companies could not expect a normal return from their capital investment.

For a number of reasons, these concerns disappeared in the second half of the 1960s. The strong efforts by Japanese companies in technological innovation sustained by keiretsu financing had created a myth of high growth. In 1968, Japan became the second-largest economy, measured in GNP, in the capitalist world, and its shares in the international markets kept expanding. Under such circumstances, the excessive competition in investment in production capacity materially prepared Japanese companies for a long march toward the dominance of global markets; this dominance peaked in the late 1980s. When structural concerns disappeared, the other institutional implications of keiretsu financing, which had been recognized in the early 1960s, were neglected. The practice of keiretsu financing enhanced the ties between banks and manufacturers. Meanwhile, keiretsu financing also weakened the role of banks in monitoring the manufacturers. Although transaction costs became low, agency costs turned out to be very high.

THE PERSISTENCE OF THE DUAL ECONOMY

After the liberalization of foreign investment began in the mid-1960s, mergers became a major strategy for promoting economy of scale. The idea of promoting mergers had surfaced in the early 1960s, but neither MITI nor the private sector regarded it as a top priority. At the time, MITI put its support into the Special Measures Law for the Promotion of Designated Industries (SMLPDI). In contrast, the private sector held that the freedom of merger was no longer an issue after the FTC approved a number of mergers in the late 1950s; what was seen as more desirable was the freedom to organize cartels. In the recession between 1964 and 1965, the number of cartels increased rapidly, from 971 in March 1964 to 1,052 in December 1965. Meanwhile, the number of mergers declined, from 979 in 1963 to 864 in 1964, increasing slightly to 894 in 1965 (Maeta 1966, 51).

To the Japanese, the liberalization of foreign investment appeared more threatening than did the liberalization of trade. As pointed out in the report by the Comprehensive Policy Research Institute, after the liberalization of trade, foreign products still faced disadvantages in transportation costs and tariff barriers, whereas the prices of Japanese products reflected relatively low domestic wage costs. When foreign capital came to Japan to open its own factories, however, the previous disadvantages no longer applied. Foreign companies not only enjoyed the same advantages as Japanese companies, but they also enjoyed the additional advantage of huge, low-cost transactions (Arisawa and Tsuchiya 1967, 6). MITI bureaucrats as well as business leaders asserted that to enhance the economies of scale of Japanese companies, the state should encourage coordination through mergers among big companies rather than encourage competition by maintaining a tough antimonopoly policy. MITI was defeated by the private sector in the struggle concerning the SMLPDI, but it regarded big corporate mergers as the second-best strategy for realizing the same goals of enhancing economies of scale and reducing excessive competition.

According to FTC statistics, proposals for mergers among big corporations increased rapidly in the second half of the 1960s. In the 1950s, there had been no merger in which the combined capital after the merger was more than 10 billion yen. Between 1960 and 1965, the FTC processed 30 such merger proposals. The liberalization of foreign investment began in 1966; between 1966 and 1976, the FTC processed a total of 75 such mergers. The same trend appeared in mergers with a combined capital of between 5 billion and 10 billion yen. In the 1950s, only three cases fit this category. Between 1960 and 1965, this number increased to 18 cases. Between 1966 and 1976, there were 36 cases. Many of these mergers were horizontal mergers, and some of them were among companies that had been divided by the deconcentration program during the postwar occupation. In 1963, the three companies in heavy industries in the Mitsubishi group merged after having been divided for more than a decade. The proposed but aborted merger among three paper pulp companies in the Ōji group also belonged in this category. The merger between Yamato Steel and Fuji Steel is a major example of how Japanese business circles made a comeback from the post–World War II reforms.

According to an FTC survey, production concentration in Japanese manufacturing industries in the 1960s demonstrated a slow upward trend in the food, fiber, and paper pulp industries, and there was a halt in the declining trend in the chemical, oil, and pottery industries. The upward trend was most visible in the machinery industry. Taking the 1945 level of production concentration as the reference for comparison, most Japanese industries were still less concentrated in 1966. However, taking the 1960 level as the reference, it becomes clear that production concentration increased in the first six years of the 1960s. Measured by the levels of production concentration of both the top three companies and the top ten companies, the two figures show that a system of competitive oligopolies was emerging. On average, the share of the top three companies showed a slight decline, whereas that of the top ten companies demonstrated a slow upward tendency. The reason was that new players with high growth potential continued to enter the industries. These were often big corporations, inasmuch as the minimum size for survival in these industries increased rapidly. The entry by big corporations into these industries had a great impact on the existing major players, lowering the share of the top three companies in the industries (Tsuji 1969).

The same FTC survey identified five types of production concentration. The first pattern was a high concentration pattern: the share of the top 10 companies in the industry increased, but, more important, the share of the top 3 companies also increased, both relatively and absolutely. This pattern was demonstrated in 45 industries. They tended to be industries with low growth that had experienced mergers among big corporations. The second pattern was ordinary concentration. The share of the top 10 companies increased, but the share of the number 4 through number 10 companies in the industry increased more quickly. This pattern implies that the gaps among the top 10 companies were narrowed. Thirty-six industries showed this pattern of production concentration. They tended to be industries with a moderate level of growth and a moderate level of concentration. The third pattern was a concentration with two extremes. The shares by the top 3 companies and the companies beyond the top 10 increased, and the share of the number 4 through number 10 companies declined. This pattern appeared in 20 industries, primarily industries not related to exports. The fourth pattern was a stable concentration, which covered 32 industries. They tended to be non-export-related industries with a low rate of growth but a high level of concentration. The fifth pattern of movement in production concentration was one of low concentration, a pattern that was shared by 59 industries. In this pattern, the share by the top 10 companies was relatively small because the share by the companies beyond the top 10 increased, or the share by the number 4 through number 10 companies increased and that of the top 3 declined. This pattern was most obvious in frontier industries with an extremely high growth rate. The empirical data proved that excessive competition by big corporations in frontier industries had produced a low level of production concentration, a condition that continued for at least the first six years of the 1960s (Tsuji 1969). These data indicate that, as I have argued, the mechanisms and institutions established to strengthen coordination in an effort to promote exports ended up sustaining excessive competition, something that in turn reduced the economy of scale in these industries.

CONCLUSION

Throughout the high growth period, the Japanese economic system was reconfigured to strengthen coordination and promote economic growth. Coordination made sense in the postwar international economic order. Under the Bretton Woods system, the Japanese state, like its Western counterparts, was able to pursue its domestic policy objectives while maintaining a stable exchange rate. The United States allowed Japan to export its products to American markets while keeping Japan's domestic markets relatively closed. Under such a favorable international environment, the greatest challenge to Japan's economic growth was how to maximally mobilize its domestic resources. Shareholders' control over management and banks' monitoring of corporate finance served to keep the economy healthy but also reduced the speed of economic growth. Clearly, the Japanese recognized the advantages provided by the Bretton Woods system and the GATT system.

A set of institutions and mechanisms emerged that supported two major functions. One function was to establish an incentive structure that induced private corporations to borrow aggressively and private banks to lend capital aggressively; the other function was to sustain such investment and lending patterns by diversifying the high risks associated with investments in technologies. These two functions were mutually dependent: Without an insurance mechanism, no corporation would overborrow and no bank would overlend over a long period. Without the pattern of aggressive bank lending and corporate borrowing, insurance would become unnecessary.

The excessive competition in the postwar Japanese economic system, however, was not a result of strategic planning but rather was an unintended consequence. The Japanese economic system focused so much on coordination that it had to diversify risks. However, this also induced moral hazard by Japanese banks and corporations. When shareholders lost control over management and banks failed to monitor corporate borrowers, the institutions and mechanisms that were designed to strengthen coordination now weakened it because they encouraged excessive competition. Even MITI, which had a strong strategic orientation in its allocation of resources, was not able to control the situation because the excessive competition was sustained by many institutions and mechanisms that went beyond MITI's control.

The various economic policies adopted by the Japanese state – the ensured supply of credit to major city banks, the expansionary monetary policy, the approval of new bank branch offices, and the distribution of foreign currency quotas among corporations considered big according to then-current standards – did not aim directly at promoting any specific corporations or industries. However, these policies created an environment in which big corporations and banks had a strong incentive to grow bigger in order to receive more benefits in the future. Thus, the structural power of the state exerted a great impact on the outcome of excessive competition. Without the ensured supply of credit by the Bank of Japan, city banks would not have been able to overlend. Without the criterion of approving new bank branch offices and distributing foreign currency quotas according to the sizes of city banks and corporations, banks would have had less incentive to lend money aggressively and corporations would have had less incentive to borrow money aggressively. Without the convoy administration, Japanese banks would have been able to make profits by competing with one another by lowering their interest rates, instead of generating more corporate deposits by supporting big corporations' risky investments.

The practice of permanent employment and the lack of a mobile labor market led to a strong growth orientation at individual corporations and banks. The story becomes a series of "withouts." Without a mobile labor market, Japanese employees would not be able to have a lternative means of pursuing their economic welfare. This strong growth orientation of Japanese corporations was sustained by indirect financing, the main bank system, and reciprocal shareholding. Without indirect financing, Japanese corporations would have had to rely on the stock market to raise capital, and shareholders would have had greater leverage over management. Without the main bank system, the relationship between Japanese corporations and banks would have been less stable, and banks would have more closely monitored their corporate borrowers' financial health. Without reciprocal shareholding, institutional shareholders would have supervised the companies they owned, because the hostage effect would not have existed. Under the conditions that did exist, however, managers in the stockholding companies did not have to worry about losing their own autonomy because the company they owned was not able to exercise any control over them.

The success of this system in promoting economic growth depended heavily on certain contingent conditions. Without fixed exchange rates and rigid control over capital flow under the Bretton Woods system, the Japanese state would have had to worry about the stability of exchange rates when it adopted an expansionary monetary policy to promote economic growth. Without the asymmetric cooperation with the United States, the Japanese state would not have been able to promote exports aggressively while keeping Japan's domestic markets closed. The whole system had been configured when trade deficits were still the major problem in Japan's balance of payments. When trade deficits were the major form of payment imbalances, the expansionary monetary policy was under control because an oversupply of money would lead to an overheated economy and the increased imports would immediately cause the balance of the current accounts to deteriorate. That would force the central bank to change gears and tighten the money supply. Although shareholders' control over management and banks' monitoring of corporations were weak, they might not have created a major threat to the economy; after all, Japanese corporations had constantly experienced a shortage of capital because of the convoy administration, and they could not easily have raised capital in the stock markets, either international or domestic. Because the capital of most Japanese corporations came from banks, when the central bank tightened its monetary policy, the effect on Japanese corporations would have been felt immediately through banks' tightened lending policy. In addition, the state's industrial policy emphasized the promotion of exports and national competitiveness based on production technology. Although corporations borrowed and invested aggressively, most of the capital was channeled into the production field. When the economy grew very rapidly, it could easily have absorbed the overbuilt production capacity.

CHAPTER 5

STABILITY, TOTAL EMPLOYMENT, AND THE WELFARE SOCIETY

In 1950–1971, the international economic order helped the Japanese economic system to maintain stability by allowing it to develop its own model of a welfare society. In this system, the size of government was minimized and the social welfare function was performed by private institutions. As outlined in Chapter 2, the core of this model was a total employment strategy, which in turn was sustained by three pillars. First, big corporations institutionalized a permanent employment system, providing job security to their employees; second, medium-size and small companies, with support from the state, organized numerous cartels to avoid bankruptcy and keep everyone in business; and third, family-owned mini shops were protected by heavy government regulations. All these measures served to reduce pressure on public spending for unemployment assistance. Although these three categories were separated by significant differences in income distribution, Japan managed to achieve a high level of egalitarian distribution (measured by the Gini index) in terms of household income. The reason for this was that Japanese women played the role of a marginal labor force. Depending on the kind of company her husband worked in, a married Japanese woman became either a full-time housewife or a part-time worker. The incomes of part-time female workers supplemented their husbands' incomes, proportionately equalizing income distribution (Nomura 1998).

This social welfare system was not a strategic choice but rather was a by-product of Japan's developmental program of promoting exports, a program that was created under historical conditions defined by the Bretton Woods and GATT systems. This means that the Japanese pattern of social protection was shaped by the policy mix of an expansionary monetary policy and a deflationary fiscal policy and by the strong desire for capital accumulation. The deflationary fiscal policy and a low taxation policy, both adopted by the Japanese state for the purpose of accumulating capital and promoting economic growth through private investments, seriously constrained the country's ability to develop a European-style welfare state. Meanwhile, the asymmetric cooperation between Japan and the United States under GATT enabled Japan to protect its domestic markets while exporting aggressively. Heavy protection of domestic markets enabled the Japanese state to allow medium-size and small companies to organize cartels and enact regulations that restrained competition among medium-size and small companies and family-owned mini shops. Initially, the state's neglect of social welfare and its strong preference for capital accumulation resulted in serious political tension and conflict, which threatened the stability of Japan's economic growth. From the beginning, therefore, the total employment strategy was the outcome of political compromise.

Although the total employment strategy significantly reduced the state's burden of developing a social welfare program and enabled Japan to concentrate its limited resources on economic growth, it also seriously weakened the capacity of the economic system to make quick structural adjustments at three different levels. First, permanent employment led to the retention of surplus labor, something that increased the burden of big corporations. Second, cartels sheltered inefficient companies from the forces of market selection, something that reduced the overall level of Japanese companies' competitiveness in a given industry. Third, government protection prohibited companies in the weak sectors from exploiting potential economies of scale, something that increased the general level of inefficiency in the overall economy. Japan's international competitiveness was promoted by the addition of new industries rather than the elimination of the old ones. This approach created vested political interests and tied them tightly to the existing economic structure.

In relying on private institutions to perform the welfare function, moreover, the Japanese state had failed to develop an effective unemployment assistance program. Any major layoff or the introduction of competition faced immediate, strong political opposition and threatened the stability of the entire system. Under such circumstances, the only way to maintain political stability was to keep the inefficient sectors and industries untouched.

In addition, the success of this model of social protection in the high growth period relied on several contingent conditions, especially Japan's asymmetric cooperation with the United States, the existence of infant industries, and the constant expansion of the Japanese economy. Only under these conditions was the cost of the total employment strategy in creating inefficiency outweighed by the gain of political stability, which was indispensable to the high growth.

STABILITY AND TOTAL EMPLOYMENT

Political stability in the high growth period was sustained by the total employment strategy, which had three components: the permanent employment system, which was institutionalized in big corporations; cartels organized by the medium-size and small companies, which prevented them from bankruptcies and thus maintained employment; and government regulations, which protected weak domestic sectors, especially retail industry and agriculture, where many family-based businesses provided employment opportunities. The total employment strategy yielded two outcomes: low unemployment and egalitarian distribution. Both of these contributed to political stability.

The Japanese unemployment rate shows three characteristics. First, compared with those of the United States and Germany, Japan's unemployment rate has been low. Between 1948 and 1964, it never reached as high as 2 percent. In the 1960s and until the First Oil Shock, Germany's unemployment was even lower than Japan's, but after that, it rose rapidly, especially after unification. Even as the United States has been enjoying the new economy, its unemployment rate remains higher than Japan's. Second, even external crises, such as the two oil shocks in the 1970s, had little impact on Japanese unemployment. Third, beginning in the 1970s and excluding the late 1980s, when the bubble created a significant labor shortage, the Japanese unemployment rate in the long run showed a trend of increasing (Nomura 1998, 12–13, 31). Of course, there is a difference between the Japanese and U.S. statistical methods. The Japanese definition of the unemployed is narrower than that used in the United States. However, even taking this into account, the Japanese unemployment rate is still significantly lower than that of the United States (Nomura 1998, 14–16).[1] A low unemployment rate results in greater political stability. When people have jobs, they have the financial means to survive, and society is less likely to witness major political tension or conflict driven by the employment issue than when many people are out of work.

Another major outcome of the total employment strategy was egalitarian income distribution. Despite the big gaps in income between the

---

1 Taira Koji points out that the Japanese unemployment rate would be much higher if the statistics of the Japanese unemployment rate did two things: treated as unemployed those who temporarily leave the labor market, those who have a job but will start within a month, and those who apply for jobs but are not qualified as labor; and not treat as employed those who work fewer than 15 hours per month in family-owned shops. Critics, however, argue that layoffs in the United States are different from the practice of temporarily leaving the labor market in Japan. Those who temporarily leave the labor market cannot be considered unemployed. But even after adjusting the statistical method, the Japanese unemployment rate is still much lower than that of the United States. For details, see Nomura (1998, 14–16).

big corporations and the medium-size and small companies, Japan is one of the most egalitarian societies in the world. Among 18 OECD countries, not only was Japan ranked as the third most egalitarian in income distribution, but also it was the only one of the top 11 countries that had no social democratic or labor party participation in government from 1965 to 1981 (Cameron, cited by Pempel 1998, 8–9). As Figure 5.1 shows, in the high growth period of the 1960s, the equality in income distribution measured by the Gini index in Japan improved greatly (also see Imada Takatoshi, cited by Pempel 1998, 9; and Tachibanaki 1998, 65–67). Egalitarian income distribution resulted in the presence of fewer social tensions and conflicts.

Unlike the situation in many European countries, much of the job creation and egalitarian distribution in Japan was sustained by private institutions instead of the public sector. As Richard Samuels points out, "Japan is a singular case of public policy without public ownership" (1987, 2). According to Toshimitsu Shinkawa and T. J. Pempel (1996, 304), "Public welfare expenditure in Japan during the early 1960s accounted for only 7.0 percent of GDP, while the figure was 17.0 percent in France, 16.5 percent in Germany, 13.6 percent in Italy and Sweden, 12.6 percent in the UK, and 10.3 percent in the US, respectively."

As an alternative, the Japanese state relied in part on its competition policy to sustain its total employment strategy, and the significant political compromises induced by the total employment strategy in turn sustained political stability. Big corporations had long been favored by the state's industrial policy and received various kinds of special treatment in the national efforts to promote exports. In return, big corporations institutionalized the permanent employment system, providing job security to their employees. The medium-size and small companies, in contrast, were allowed by the state to organize cartels, helping them restrain competition and thus reduce the probability of bankruptcy. These companies collectively survived market competition by dividing market share through their cartels. Politically, big corporations could not complain about the inefficiency resulting from the practice of cartels because the big corporations themselves received many state-sponsored benefits; by the same token, the medium-size and small companies could not complain about the state's unequal distribution of national resources because they, too, received favorable treatment, being allowed to organize cartels and to transfer their burden to consumers. Consumers, in turn, did not complain very much because the total employment strategy had provided them with jobs and income. As a result, not only did the state privatize its social welfare function, but the total employment strategy also sustained political stability.

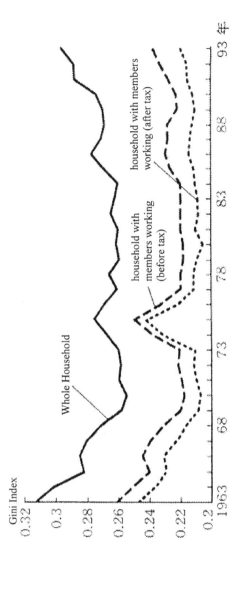

Figure 5.1. *Inequality in income distribution measured by the Gini Index.*

Note: The database includes only nonagricultural households with two or more members
Source: The Prime Minister Office's "Household Survey." Cited in: Tachibanaki 1998, p. 65.

Both low unemployment and egalitarian income distribution can be considered as having contributed greatly to Japan's political stability, but the ineffective Japanese response to the economic crisis of the 1990s has raised serious questions: If the total employment strategy played an important role in sustaining high growth, why has it not enabled Japan to recover quickly from the current crisis? Moreover, why did Japan choose to rely on private institutions, instead of a welfare state, for social protection in the postwar period? To answer these questions, we must understand the contingent nature of the success of the total employment strategy. In short, neither the Japanese pattern of social welfare nor the total employment strategy is a universally applicable, successful model that can operate without time and space constraints. Both were shaped by the special position of the Japanese economy in the postwar international economic order.

THE U.S. EFFORT TO BUILD A MULTILATERAL INTERNATIONAL TRADE REGIME, JAPAN'S STRONG DEVELOPMENTAL ORIENTATION, AND PRIVATIZED SOCIAL PROTECTION

The first set of important contingent historical conditions that shaped the Japanese pattern of privatized social protection comprised two elements: the state policy mix – an expansionary monetary policy to promote economic growth through private investments and a deflationary fiscal policy to control inflation – and the state's strong orientation toward capital accumulation, which led to low taxation. Both elements, moreover, resulted from the special position of the Japanese economy in the postwar international economic order.

In the state policy mix, the deflationary fiscal policy resulted from the implementation of the Dodge plan in 1949, whereas the expansionary monetary policy emerged as a counter measure to the adjustment recession created by the implementation of the Dodge plan. After this policy mix was formulated in the early 1950s, it continued to exist until the end of the 1960s.

In the existing literature, discussions on the Dodge plan and the Marshall plan have focused on their relation to the Cold War. Both Fred Block (1977) and William Borden (1984), however, highlight an extremely important but often neglected facet of the Dodge plan and the Marshall plan, namely, their roles as part of the U.S. effort to create a multilateral international economic order for the postwar world that favored free trade. According to Block and Borden, American leaders, having learned from the crisis that followed the previous wave of globalization, recognized the critical value of prosperity to peace. They were haunted by the U.S. failure in the interwar period to stimulate world trade and were convinced that "a multilateral world economy, based on durable institutions to regulate trade imbalances and outlaw extreme protectionism, was necessary to prevent destructive nationalistic political conflicts" (Borden 1984, 19). Block argues that at the time "American policy-makers were more concerned about national capitalism in Western Europe than they were with a possible invasion by the Red Army or successful socialist revolution. . . . It is necessary to place the Cold War in the context of the American effort to create a certain type of world economy" (Block 1977, 10).

In the late 1940s, the future of the free trade regime that had sustained the postwar prosperity of industrialized countries was rather unclear because there was a severe imbalance in the world economy. This imbalance, which had resulted from the economic supremacy of the United States after World War II, had created a major shortage of the dollar, or a dollar gap, in many ally countries of the United States. As Borden (1984, 24) points out,

> The postwar world economy was divided into "soft" and "hard" currency areas. Soft-currency nations protected their currency by not allowing it to be converted into dollars. Thus, they were forced to trade primarily within the soft-currency area, not with the United States. Inconvertibility forced foreign buyers to limit their dollar imports, regardless of price or quality, in order to reserve the few dollars they received from the sales of goods and services to the United States for their essential imports.

If this continued, American products would be frozen out of world markets and that would lead to a great contraction in the U.S. economy. Responding to this challenge, the U.S. government formulated the Marshall plan for Western Europe and the Dodge plan for Japan. In both plans, the U.S. government pressured these countries for stabilization of prices (for export competitiveness and sound currencies) as well as balanced government budgets.

Against this historical background, the Dodge plan ended the expansionary fiscal policy practiced by the Japanese state throughout the 1930s and the early 1940s as well as the period 1946–1949. In the early postwar period, the operation of the Japanese economy was sustained by aid of roughly $500 million annually from the United States. Joseph Dodge, the U.S. envoy who drafted this grand plan for bringing the Japanese economy back on track, held that "wealth is created by profitable capital investment and is dissipated by nonprofit social welfare and public improvement expenditure. The Japanese people had to consume less than they could afford . . . to accumulate the capital to enable the private banking system to finance industrial recovery"

(Borden 1984, 92). The essence of the Dodge plan was to establish a balanced budget and control the supply of currency in order to stabilize inflation. In the 1949 annual budgets of both central and local governments, "red" records were eliminated, and the standing government debts were repaid (Tsūsanshō 1957, 10). This means that the deflationary fiscal policy practiced by the Japanese state in the 1950s and 1960s, as an important part of the policy mix, initially resulted from the U.S. effort to build a multilateral international economic order via the Dodge plan.

The implementation of the Dodge plan, however, threatened political stability. When a fixed exchange rate (one dollar equal to 360 yen) was established by the Dodge plan in 1949, the production cost of Japanese minerals was 20 percent to 60 percent higher than the international standard. To cover the $500 million gap that had been filled previously by financial aid from the United States, Japan had to promote exports. To achieve that goal, lower production costs became the central issue in industrial policy (Kōsei Torihiki 1953a, 18–19). In response to this challenge, the focus of Japanese industrial policy shifted from ensuring production in the key industries at any cost to an efficient use of capital and resources. To lower the prices of Japanese products to the international level, Japanese corporations conducted massive layoffs. From February 1949 to May 1950, private companies fired 400,000 employees, and government and public agencies fired another 419,000 employees. Meanwhile, most companies froze the hiring of new workers and began to use temporary and unskilled workers. When many big corporations were forced to reduce production, medium-size and small companies no longer received production orders from their parent companies and went bankrupt (Nihon Seisansei Honbu 1985, 24–27). These actions led to a series of confrontations between management and labor.

To counter the recession created by the Dodge plan, the Japanese state began to practice an expansionary monetary policy, providing private corporations with bank credit. To make this policy work, the deflationary fiscal policy, which was forced upon the Japanese state by the Dodge plan, became useful in controlling inflation.

The key component of Japan's policy mix was its expansionary monetary policy. The second component, its deflationary fiscal policy, was adopted only to sustain the expansionary monetary policy. The reason? When both monetary and fiscal policies are expansionary, they create hyperinflation. When both policies are deflationary, they drive the economy into recession. Ideally, these two policies must be adopted in a countervailing manner. Because the Japanese state relied on a deflationary fiscal policy to control inflation and low taxes to encourage capital accumulation, it simply did not have many resources to create jobs by developing a big public sector or building government-sponsored social welfare programs.

The strong preference for capital accumulation and the strong opposition to higher taxes also contributed greatly to the formation of the Japanese pattern of privatized social protection. In contrast to Western European countries, in which the major focus of resource allocation by the welfare state was the equality in distribution, the developmental state in Japan tried to avoid any income supplement that was not tied to production because it held that "welfare payments to the unemployed have the effect of making the unemployed state permanent" (Murakami 1996, 196). Supported by a conservative political alliance among the Liberal Democratic Party (LDP), state bureaucrats, and business circles, Japan minimized public spending on social welfare (Shinkawa 1993, 16). In the 1950s, the entire country was overwhelmed by the tasks of capital accumulation and promoting exports by improving efficiency. The issue of social welfare was largely neglected. Meanwhile, the medium-size and small companies, farmers, and shopkeepers, all of them belonging to the voting constituency of the LDP, strongly opposed any initiative to increase taxes for a government-sponsored unemployment assistance program (Shinkawa and Pempel 1996, 299). Because the Japanese state could not adopt a heavy taxation policy, it lost another important source to finance a government-sponsored unemployment assistance program.

The lack of public financing of social welfare, however, does not mean that the Japanese economic system could operate smoothly without social welfare. Social protection had become very important when the Japanese state's efforts to encourage coordination led to excessive competition. Both within the same industries and among differing industries, the developmental programs and excessive competition often led to what Murakami Yasusuke (1996, 190) called "excessive disparities" characterized by frequent bankruptcies, unemployment, and the rise of monopolies. The great political discontent generated from this situation directly threatened economic growth. Without measures to address the distribution issues, "the industrial policy would probably always fail. [In this sense,] the industrial policy and the distributive policy needed to be seen as one" (Murakami 1996, 190).

With little public spending on social welfare, how did the Japanese economic system maintain stability and sustain employment? The Japanese state made great efforts to privatize its own social welfare function by encouraging private corporations to develop programs addressing the issue of income distribution and job security. The most notable government assistance to enterprise welfare was tax deductions. In 1952, the Japanese state amended its tax law, allowing employers to claim certain portions of retirement allowances as nontaxable business expenses (Shinkawa and Pempel 1996, 300). More importantly, as I discuss in the following sections, the Japanese state relied on its competition policy to support the total employment strategy. As Japanese economist Tōbata Shiichi, who envisioned the total employment strategy, argued, when everyone had a job, even if it was a part-time job that would not lead to a career, it was not a bad thing politically for public policy (Nomura 1998, 37). When people had a job, they had a means of survival and the state did not have to provide unemployment assistance. By keeping everyone "in business," Japan would be able to maintain a small government and concentrate all national resources on economic growth through private investments.

The Japanese model of welfare society significantly altered the pattern of distributional politics in Japan. Studies influenced by the framework of corporatism have often emphasized the weakness of the labor movement in Japan (Pempel and Tsunekawa 1979). The critics, in contrast, have tried to focus either on the strong participation of labor unions in management at the company level, or collective bargaining for wage increases in the form of a spring strike (Kume 1998; Weiss 1998). Recently, some scholars have tried to demonstrate the impact of labor unions on the policy-making process, especially in the period after the First Oil Shock (for a review of this debate, see Kume 1998). This study sheds light on the debate by highlighting the impact of the welfare society model on the characteristics of labor politics. It shows that the Eurocentric framework of the tripartite political structure, in which labor unions, businesses, and the state negotiate on public policy issues, is less useful for apprehending the Japanese case. The reason is that distributive politics is institutionally sustained. In the European model of the welfare state, the public sector is a major player in the economy. Thus, job security and workers' wage increases are directly sustained by public policy. Without organizing the peak organization and participating in the policy-making process, labor unions would have no alternative way to protect their interests.[2] In contrast, in the Japanese model of social welfare during the high growth period, it was the private institutions – such as permanent employment, the seniority-based wage system, and firm-based labor unions – rather than the public sector or government-sponsored social welfare programs, that directly influenced workers' economic interests. Thus, Japanese labor unions had less incentive to participate in the debate on macroeconomic policy at the national level because there were not many resources to fight for in the first place. When employment and wage-related issues were addressed more

2 *Peak organization* is a phrase used in the literature of comparative politics. In this context, it refers to a national labor union that would represent all industry-based labor unions. In the European context, such a peak organization often involves public policy making.

through private institutions than through public policy, "a focus on aggregate welfare expenditures may be completely misleading as a guide to the state's most important measures for distributing the costs of change more evenly throughout society" (Weiss 1998, 157).

ASYMMETRIC COOPERATION WITH THE UNITED STATES AND THE WELFARE SOCIETY IN JAPAN

If the U.S. effort in building a multilateral international economic order via the Dodge plan, by ending the expansionary fiscal policy practiced by the Japanese state, contributed to the Japanese choice of privatized social protection, the asymmetric cooperation between the United States and Japan in the GATT system made this choice possible by allowing Japan to keep its domestic markets closed, legalize cartels, and undertake heavy government protection, which were three cornerstones that sustained the total employment strategy.

The Cold War was a commonly recognized factor that led to the asymmetric cooperation. Driven by its strategic interests in fighting with the communist bloc, the United States was willing to absorb exports from Japan, South Korea, Taiwan, and a number of Southeast Asian countries, meanwhile allowing them to keep their own domestic markets closed. As a National Security Council document argued, "The economic strength of the free nations of the world, and their hope for economic progress, are among the strongest forces that can be brought to bear against Soviet Communist aggression. Our present economic policies are designed in the long run to build this strength and provide this hope" (Borden 1984, 39). In Asia, as George Kennan argued, "If we could retain effective control over these two archipelagoes [Japan and the Philippines], in the sense of assuring that they would remain in friendly hands, there could be no serious threat to our security from the east within our time" (cited by Fallows 1994, 135).

As Borden points out, however, the U.S. effort in building a multilateral international trade regime by helping its ally countries to balance their payments was as important as the Cold War in engaging the United States in asymmetric cooperation with its ally countries. The dollar gap was $7.8 billion in 1946, $11.6 billion in 1947, and $6.8 billion in 1948. If American products had continued to dominate the international markets and if the United States had not practiced asymmetric cooperation, its ally countries would have become insolvent vis-à-vis the United States and would not have been able to purchase American products (Borden 1984, 23). Restrained fundamentally by their imbalances of payments, Japan and European countries had to keep their domestic markets closed to accumulate the dollar, and the

United States had to adopt an incremental approach in its effort to build a multilateral free trade regime.

In fact, according to Robert Gilpin (2000), the U.S.-led international monetary and trade regimes and the American security umbrella were the two pillars of international political and economic order after World War II. The guarantee provided to Europe and Asia by the American military presence provided a national security rationale for Japan and the Western democracies to open their markets. Free trade helped cement the alliance, and in turn the alliance helped settle economic disputes. The dollar's reserve and transaction-currency role also solidified the open postwar system. In other words, to promote liberal economic integration in the world, the United States sought to create equilibrium by artificially reducing the dollar gap using two methods: first, through dollar grants in the form of the Marshall Plan in Europe and procurements to Japan during the Korean War; and second, by allowing its ally countries to keep their domestic markets closed to American products for the time being, meanwhile allowing them to export aggressively to the U.S. market.

The asymmetric cooperation between the United States and Japan sustained the total employment strategy in three distinct ways. First, it provided big corporations with great export opportunities, and increasing profits and continuing expansion made it possible for these big corporations to practice permanent employment. Second, by allowing Japan to keep its domestic markets closed, asymmetric cooperation turned the total employment strategy, which had serious implications for foreign competition, into an issue purely of domestic politics instead of an international one. Third, it provided a favorable political environment for the Japanese state to amend the original Antimonopoly Law in order to legalize cartels and other types of anticompetition measures. These measures were essential to the employment of medium-size and small companies.

The easy access of Japanese exports to the U.S. market and technology and the huge amount of procurements Japanese corporations received from the U.S. government during the Korean War were the major outcomes from Japan's asymmetric cooperation with the United States. When Japanese Prime Minister Yoshida Shigeru visited the United States in 1954, he proclaimed, "What Japan desires most is that the United States market be stabilized for Japan's export goods so that her export industries can depend on it over the long term" (Borden 1984, 182). In asymmetric cooperation with the United States, Japan not only obtained access to the huge U.S. market but also, with U.S. support, gained access to the markets of many other countries. To help Japan promote its exports and also share the burden of Japanese exports, "the United States signed fourteen trilateral agreements with

Asian and European countries, in which the United States granted tariff concessions to the third party in return for that nation's granting concessions to Japan" (Borden 1984, 187). As I have pointed out elsewhere, the United States was the biggest technological exporter to Japan in 1950–1966, selling 2,471 of the 4,135 patents imported by Japanese companies (Gao 1997, 181). During the Korean War, Japan received a total of more than $3.5 billion worth of procurements from the U.S. government, which boosted Japanese exports from $510 million in 1949 to $1.3 billion in 1951 (Gao 1997, 193). These factors helped the private sector, especially big corporations, to create job opportunities.

Asymmetric cooperation with the United States helped Japan to keep its domestic markets closed. At the end of August 1959, only 26 percent of Japanese imports were free of government-imposed restrictions (Economic Planning Agency 1990, 102). By 1959, the U.S. share in the world exports of industrial products had declined to 22 percent (from 38 percent in 1948). As the outflow of dollars worsened the international payments of the United States, however, the U.S. government urged western European countries and Japan to abolish their discriminatory restrictions on imports from the United States. Britain, France, and Italy rescinded many restrictions on the import of American products; meanwhile, in 1958, they resumed convertibility between the U.S. dollar and their own currencies (Keizai Kikakuchō 1976). Japan, as a member of the IMF and the GATT, was required to stay abreast of the liberalization of trade and foreign currency exchange. Although it started liberalizing trade in the early 1960s, its domestic markets were still organized by cartels and other types of nonmarket governing mechanisms, such as trade associations and business groups. The United States did not begin to question its asymmetric cooperation with Japan until 1968. In that year, for the first time in postwar history, the U.S. government, under the Johnson administration, demanded that Japan restrain its steel exports to the United States. This action was followed in 1969–1971 by a bitter dispute over synthetic textiles under the Nixon administration (Cohen 1998, 22). Thus, asymmetric cooperation with the United States helped Japan to keep its domestic markets closed throughout the 1950s and 1960s.

While it lasted, asymmetric cooperation between Japan and the United States had a direct impact on the resurgence of cartels in postwar Japan, an element in the total employment strategy that sustained the employment opportunities in medium-size and small companies. Driven by strategic considerations of the Cold War and building a multilateral international economic order, the U.S. government reversed course and changed its policy toward Japan in the late 1940s from one of democratization and demilitarization to one of supporting Japan's economic reconstruction. It was under such circumstances that the Japanese government amended the Antimonopoly Law in 1949, an action that opened the door for the cartels' revival. According to the 1947 version of the Antimonopoly Law, any type of participation in cartels was prohibited. In the late 1940s, however, international cartels were still commonplace. The Japanese argued that to facilitate business agreements between Japanese companies and foreign companies concerning the supply of materials, sales of manufactured goods, and technology licensing, Japanese companies needed the right to sign international contracts and join in international agreements (Kōsei Torihiki Iinkai 1977, 52). The Keidanren (Federation of Economic Organizations) proposed a radical amendment that would lift all restraints on common actions. In the Japanese perception, the Antimonopoly Law had been imposed on the nation by the occupation authority as a penalty for its loss in World War II. This law would only weaken the economy because it would harm Japan's international competitiveness as well as curtail Japan's domestic economic growth (*Kosei Torihiki* 1953a, 22).

Although asymmetric cooperation with the United States indeed enabled Japan to organize cartels, it would be wrong to argue that the impact of the United States on Japan was only one-way. Indeed, the United States tolerated the actions of its allies in slowing the process of trade liberalization. However, its ultimate goal was to build a liberal trade regime represented by the GATT which was sustained by multilateralism. Moreover, Japan may have been tolerated by the United States, but other Western countries would not allow Japan to go too far. This pressure was evident in the debate on the amendment of the Antimonopoly Law in 1953. At the time, MITI and the Economic Deliberation Agency asserted that the then-current procedure of obtaining advance approval from the FTC to organize cartels should be changed to de facto registration, and that measures to limit cartels and prevent trusts should also be softened. This proposal faced strong opposition from the Ministry of Foreign Affairs and the Ministry of Finance, which maintained that it would give the world the impression that Japan would promote exports by dumping. At the time, Japan was in the process of applying for membership in the GATT. Both Britain and Australia had asserted that the GATT should take a careful look at Japan's application. Japan was also negotiating with the U.S. government on the Japan-U.S. Trade and Transportation Treaty. During the Cold War, the Soviet Union asserted that modern capitalist economies were dominated by monopoly capital. As part of its Cold War policy, the United States not only practiced asymmetric cooperation with its allies but also tried to build an image of antimonopoly in the international economy. Thus, the U.S. government insisted that the treaty should have an article that would eliminate business customs that restrained competition. Eventually, the Ministry of Foreign Affairs and the Ministry of Finance won (Kōsei Torihiki Iinkai 1977).

THE PERMANENT EMPLOYMENT SYSTEM

The lack of public spending left Japan without a good government-sponsored social assistance program. The permanent employment system in big corporations had been a cornerstone of Japan's total employment strategy. This choice, however, was not easily made. The system evolved in the postwar period as a major political compromise between management and labor unions following decade-long confrontations. It was the need for innovation and the changing conditions in the labor market that forced both sides to abandon the confrontational strategy of dealing with each other and allowed them to reach this political compromise. For this very reason, the permanent employment system had vested interests and could not be easily changed.

In mobilizing for World War II, the Japanese state attempted to stabilize employment in an effort to prevent political unrest. Democratic reforms during the postwar occupation and the beginning of the Cold War, however, distorted the balance of power between management and labor. In the early occupation period, the GHQ regarded labor unions as the social foundation for democracy. Under its support, labor unions became powerful in Japanese politics. In the so-called reverse course, or changing of its occupation policy, however, the GHQ shifted its position from supporting labor unions to supporting management. After the implementation of the Dodge plan in 1949, management regained its control over companies. When the Korean War broke out, the Japanese state purged the labor leaders, and the power of the unions in national politics declined significantly.

The implementation of the Dodge plan led to layoffs. Concurrent with the weakening of labor unions, bank loans were increasingly relied on as the major source of industrial capital. The GHQ held that Japan should rely on the capital market for long-term capital and on financial institutions only for short-term corporate finance. To achieve this goal, Japanese companies were allowed to make secondary public offerings to raise additional capital. After the Japanese government failed to make war compensations to the munitions companies, it allowed them to depreciate their assets as much as 90 percent. However, although the demand for capital was strong, it was very difficult for Japanese corporations to raise capital by issuing new stocks or corporate bonds because stock prices were too low to attract investors. After the implementation of the Dodge plan, the risk of lending money to those companies that had surplus employees and poor performance increased rapidly. Thus, the main banks often insisted that a plan for reducing surplus employees be included in a company's reconstruction plan. Similarly, the loan syndicates organized by the Bank of Japan also often required a reduction in personnel as a precondition for continuing the supply of capital. At Toshiba, the loan syndicate even demanded a change of management. In the early 1950s, the main banks played an important role in monitoring companies and took actions that influenced managerial practice (Okazaki 1993, 132–134).

These two factors – strengthening of the monitoring function by the main banks and the managerial emphasis on allocation efficiency – often led to disputes between labor and management. At the time, the major players – including the GHQ, the Japanese state, big corporations, and labor unions – all took a confrontational strategy. The GHQ changed its pro-labor policy and began supporting management. In addition, the Japanese state revised the Labor Union Law to restrain the rights of labor unions. Supported by the state, management at big corporations aggressively reestablished its control. Labor unions responded by calling strikes. The major issues in Japanese labor relations during the first half of the 1950s were job security and low wages. In 1949, the Labor Union Law was amended to outlaw financial aid from companies to labor unions and to enforce the automatic extension of labor contracts. As a result, Japanese corporations no longer consulted the labor unions on decisions regarding personnel and general company management (Nishinarita 1994, 143–144).

The first change that provided an incentive for big corporations to institutionalize permanent employment was the perceived technological revolution in the second half of the 1950s. In 1955, the Japan Committee of Economic Development initiated the productivity movement. This movement was aimed at solving the dilemma between efficiency and the distribution of economic welfare by linking production and distribution in the Japanese corporate system. Supported by the state, this committee established a Headquarters of Productivity, in which representatives of management, labor unions, government officials, and academicians met to discuss how to improve productivity. Labor unions expressed concern about the impact of the productivity movement on job security and wages. The major players began to build consensus on three famous principles. First, the ultimate purpose of promoting productivity was to increase employment; government and business must make every effort to prevent unemployment. Second, management must consult with labor on how to promote productivity according to the conditions at each firm. Third, the benefits created by the promotion of productivity must be distributed fairly between the firm and labor (for details on this process, see Gao 1997, Chapter 5; Gao 1998a). "The productivity movement would not have any reason to be supported, unless it proved empirically that its achievement would fit not only the interest of managers and capitalists but also the interest of labor and the general public" (Nakayama [1956] 1972, 337–344). The principles of the productivity movement provided an important foundation for a systematic solution to the dilemma between efficiency and the distribution of economic welfare.

The strong preference for political stability after the national-level confrontation between management and labor during the Miike dispute in 1960 was the major driving force behind the increasing popularity of the practice of permanent employment in big corporations. The tension started when the Mitsui group announced that it intended to lay off 6,500 workers in the sunset coal industry. Both the labor union and management were backed by their supporters at the national level. Eventually, the labor union lost the battle. This political division took place in conjunction with a much bigger one concerning the renewal of the U.S.-Japan security treaty. As part of the overall transition in Japanese politics, the division resulted in a political compromise among the major players regarding job security. After Iketa Hayato became prime minister, he called for a shift by the nation from a political season to an economic season so that the conservative LDP could rebuild its political support and maintain political stability. Ishida Hiroo, the newly appointed minister of labor, began to emphasize the need for compromise between management and labor on the issue of job security. The shift was also sustained by the changing labor market situation. In 1963, for the first time in postwar Japan, the demand for labor was greater than the supply. Under such circumstances, finding ways to retain skilled workers became critical to big corporations. In response to these challenges, permanent employment became widely institutionalized in big corporations (see Gao 1997, Chapter 6). As discussed in Chapter 4, permanent employment became the norm in big corporations and began to assume the status of a powerful ideology.

The evolution of permanent employment in postwar Japan sheds light on the debate concerning the role of labor unions in policy-making. It shows that Japanese labor unions were very militant in the late 1940s. Even when the Cold War and the implementation of the Dodge plan led to the decline of the labor unions' power in national politics, the unions remained deeply involved in public policy domains such as national defense. "Corporatism without labor" (Pempel and Tsunekawa 1979) was more an outcome of a conservative strategy whose purpose was to shift employment and wage-related issues away from public policy to the arena of private institutions; this strategy deliberately aimed at reducing tensions and conflicts and maintaining political stability for sustaining high growth.

The impact of permanent employment on political stability could be found in the labor unions' position on issues related to antimonopoly policy. In the late 1960s, two major national labor unions – the General Council of Trade Unions (GCTU) and the Iron-Steel Labor Union (ISLU) – engaged each other in a policy debate on the Yamato and Fuji merger. The GCTU (sōhyō), which had 4.2 million members, neither supported nor strongly opposed the proposal. The major reason was that the ISLU, with 190,000 members, was one of the GCTU's major subunions. The ISLU supported the proposed merger because labor unions at the time wanted to further develop industry-based activities, and because it would lead to a merger between two labor unions. That would help the ISLU to realize its own goals. The General Federation of Labor, with 1.8 million members at the time, was a rival to the GCTU in labor politics. The ISLU stated that it did not oppose the idea of industrial reorganization and would take a more active position in the new industrial system through negotiations before the merger. Meanwhile, however, it asserted that the government should establish a supervisory agency to prevent the problems of monopoly prices (Shūkan Tōyō Keizai Henshūbu, July 3, 1968, 154–155).

Big corporations often used the labor unions' fear of layoffs to push mergers. Business leaders maintained that if foreign companies occupied a large share of the Japanese markets, Japanese companies would go bankrupt and unemployment would become a significant problem. But individual Japanese were not only domestic consumers but also international producers. Although monopolies might cause individual Japanese people to endure higher consumer prices, the businesses would also be able to attain the status of international producers and could assure their employees an income sufficient to pay the higher prices. This argument helped Japanese corporations claim legitimacy for mergers among big corporations, but it also established a criterion that de-legitimized those that would involve layoffs. An example was a proposed merger between two major textile producers. Because the merger plan proposed layoffs, it met with strong resistance, not only from labor unions but also from white collar workers and senior managers. In the end, the proposed merger did not take place (Ekonomisuto 1966, 16).

THE ROLE OF CARTELS

The role played by cartels in state policy regarding sunset industries has attracted wide attention (Katz 1998; Tilton 1996; Uriu 1996). My focus here, however, is the role played by cartels in sustaining the total employment strategy at the medium-size and small companies. I show that as an important cornerstone in the Japanese model of privatized unemployment protection, cartels should be treated more as a governing mechanism for distribution than as a governing mechanism for production.

To sustain total employment, the key was employment at the medium-size and small companies. The percentage of manufacturing employment absorbed by companies that hired fewer than 300 employees ranged from 70.9 percent in 1953 to 73.0 percent in 1955, 69.6 percent in 1960, 68.8 percent in 1965, and 67.5 percent in 1970 (Maotani 1978, 49). In other words, the medium-size and small companies provided more than two-thirds of Japanese employment opportunities in manufacturing industries during the high growth period. In many other industries, the share of these companies in total job creation was even higher: In 1975, it was 99.9 percent in construction, 99.5 percent in manufacturing, 99.6 percent in wholesale and retail, 100 percent in real estate, and 99.5 percent in transportation and communication. Medium-size and small companies employed 92.9 percent of the total labor force in construction, 70.7 percent in manufacturing, 86.8 percent in wholesale and retail, 97.6 percent in real estate, 85.6 percent in transportation and communication, and 71.1 percent in service (Maotani 1978, 39).

Cartels were prohibited in the 1947 version of the Japanese Antimonopoly Law. At the beginning of Japan's asymmetric cooperation with the United States, however, the Japanese state was able to amend the Antimonopoly Law twice: in 1949 and again in 1953. In the 1950s, it also enacted about 30 cartel exemption laws. The cartels thus exempted can be divided into five general categories (Kōsei Torihiki Iinkai 1977, 105–106):

· Those organized in industries, such as transportation and insurance, where competition might be harmful to public interest
· Those organized to encourage cooperation and organization among companies that operated on a small scale and tended to engage in excessive competition
· Those organized to prevent excessive competition in the exports-related sector
· Those organized during economic recession to adjust the balance between demand and supply
· Those organized to promote rationalization in manufacturing industries, including automobiles and electronic power.

Sustained by various antimonopoly law exemptions, cartels were organized in many industries during the high growth period (see Figure 5.2). In 1952, only 53 cartels were exempted by various pieces of legislation. That number grew to 79 in 1953, 162 in 1954, 348 in 1955, 312 in 1956, 401 in 1957, and 509 in 1958. By 1959, the number of cartels organized according to these exemption laws reached 595. Among these, 370 were exempted by the

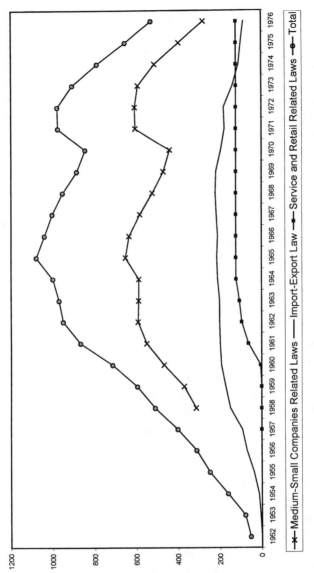

Figure 5.2. *Cartels exempted from the enforcement of the Antimonopoly Law.*
Source: Based on the data in Kōsei Torihiki Iinkai, 1977, pp. 767–769.

Medium and Small-Size Company Business Organization Law, and 172 were exempted by the Exports-Imports Transaction Law. Together, these two types of cartels constituted about 90 percent of the total (Kōsei Torihiki Iinkai 1977, 81). In the 1960s, the cartel exemption laws emphasized the medium-size and small companies and the sunset industries. During the liberalization of trade in 1960s, especially during the 1964 recession, the number of exempted cartels increased rapidly. In 1960, the total number was 714. It peaked at 1,079 in 1965 and stayed above 1,000 during 1966 and 1967. In 1970, Japan still had as many 976 cartels exempted from enforcement of the Antimonopoly Law (Kōsei Torihiki Iinkai 1977, 769).

How did cartels become so popular in postwar Japan? Because public spending on social welfare was limited, one of the cornerstones that sustained the total employment strategy was to rely on cartels to keep the medium-size and small companies from bankruptcy. In 1952, MITI enacted two new laws: the Temporary Measures Law Toward Specially Designated Medium and Small-Size Companies (which, after several amendments, became the Medium and Small-Size Companies Stabilization Law) and the Exports Promotion Law (which later became the Exports-Imports Promotion Law). These industry-specific exemption laws served as MITI's major weapons in overcoming the restraints of the Antimonopoly Law, and the FTC could not generate enough political support to stop such efforts.

The Medium and Small-Size Companies Stabilization Law enabled the Japanese state to designate 26 industries as subject to its rules. The Exports Promotion Law, in contrast, admitted cartels among producers and domestic distributors and also spread out among all important industries. Both laws gave MITI the power to approve the laws' applications and regulate outsiders' activities. In the beginning, the organization of these cartels required approval by the FTC. After 1955, however, *approval* by the FTC was changed to *consultation*. Registration was the only requirement to organize exports-promotion cartels. When MITI regulated outsiders' activities, the FTC merely received notice (Imamura [1956] 1970, Vol. 1, 165).

In 1953, MITI proposed the Important Industry Stabilization Law. This legislation would give MITI comprehensive authority to exempt cartels organized by big corporations from the enforcement of the Antimonopoly Law. To a large extent, this legislation was modeled on the Important Industry Contro Law of 1931. According to the bill, the state would have the power to designate "important industries." When the market failed to reach an equilibrium between demand and supply in these industries, the state would allow private companies to organize cartels – whereby they could agree to limit the amounts of production, sales, and production capacity – exempting these joint actions from enforcement of the antimonopoly law. The failure of the market was to be measured by (1) prices of Japanese products (in domestic and international markets) that were lower than production cost or (2) signs indicating a trend toward insufficiency of the company's management in these industries and the failure of rationalization measures to solve the problems. In a normal situation, many companies would be driven out of the market. To prevent bankruptcy, MITI attempted to organize *adjustment associations* to facilitate joint action. When a cartel was organized by companies whose production or sales constituted more than half of the total amount in an industry, the minister of MITI would have the power to order companies that were operating outside these adjustment associations to obey the agreements made by the cartel (Tsūsanshō 1989, Vol. 5, 273–274).

MITI's proposal, however, was strongly criticized by both the FTC and the Keidanren. The FTC argued that it was not a good idea to let the state designate important industries and intervene in their business operations by executive order. Contrary to MITI's expectation, the private sector also objected to this proposal. The Keidanren held that the government should thoroughly revise the Antimonopoly Law rather than make temporary legislation. Too much legislation would complicate the process of business operations and create excessive power among bureaucrats (Tsūsanshō 1989, Vol. 5, 273–274). Eventually, MITI's attempt failed.

Nevertheless, to prevent bankruptcy and sustain the strategy of total employment, the Japanese state often directly organized joint actions among private companies in the high growth period. A policy of *advised production reduction*, which started in 1952, served to restrain production by direct order from the state. It became the principal means adopted by MITI to reduce the oversupply of goods resulting from either declining demand or overinvestments in technological innovation. Despite strong criticism from the FTC, MITI practiced advised production reduction in 29 industries in the 1950s, especially in the late 1950s. With MITI's administrative guidance, a *purchasing agency* was established by private companies to buy oversupplied goods and hold them until market demand increased. This practice was used primarily in the textile industry. Holding the oversupplied goods served to reduce supply and reduce the likelihood of bankruptcy for the medium-size and small companies.

Freezing the stocks, which can also be regarded as part of the advised reduction of production, meant that during a recession, private companies, advised by MITI, would freeze their stocks of certain goods that were in oversupply and then "unfreeze" them when the market situation improved. The difference between the two methods was that, in the freezing method, it was individual producers, rather than the purchasing agency, that would hold the goods.

In the *public sales system*, applied mostly in the iron-steel industry, manufacturers were responsible for reporting to MITI their estimated amount of monthly sales. Then manufacturers would meet simultaneously with wholesalers, at which time a sales price was reported to MITI. After this price was reported, it could not be changed. Once the wholesalers determined the volume of product they wanted, the manufacturers again reported to MITI, disclosing the aggregated results and choosing their wholesalers. If manufacturers were not able to sell all their products, they could seek to sell to other wholesalers at a different price. Meanwhile, production would be reduced in the following month according to the amount of overproduction for the current month.

Manufacturers that violated the MITI-advised production amount and sales price would be punished. Every manufacturer had to submit a statement of commitment to MITI, with the signature of the president of the company (Kōsei Torihiki Iinkai 1977, 95–99). These measures continued in the 1960s, but the frequency of application and the number of affected industries declined (Kōsei Torihiki Iinkai 1977, 234–235).

Even the FTC, which refused to admit cartels on a comprehensive basis, agreed that cartels played an important role in governing the Japanese economy. As Sakane Tetsuo, the director of the general office at the FTC, pointed out in 1958, the Japanese view of cartels resembled the German theory of cartels after World War I. It held that cartels could sustain rationalization, promote productivity, and support economic growth. More important, cartels could help balance demand and supply during recession. Without cartels, the excessive competition might lead to product dumping, and Japanese companies would lose their international markets (Sakane 1958).

The role of the FTC was complicated. On the one hand, it often made efforts to enforce the Antimonopoly Law even though it was not always successful. On the other hand, its view on many antimonopoly-related issues was often similar to that of MITI. In the 1953 amendment of the Antimonopoly Law, as MITI's official history of industrial policy points out, all of FTC's proposals, except in one matter, were adopted as the final version. Although the FTC strongly resisted MITI's proposal on the scope of relaxation, especially the definition of competition in the 1953 amendment, its proposals on issues such as joint action, international agreement, holding companies, reciprocal shareholding, the limit of reciprocal shareholding by financial institutions, the exchange of personnel, and exemptions from antimonopoly were very similar or exactly the same as those of MITI (see Table 2.2.8 in Tsūsanshō

1989, Vol. 5:284–287). As long as MITI and other bureaucracies did not directly challenge the authority of the Antimonopoly Law, the FTC was willing to make compromises, admitting temporary yet industry-specific exemptions. These actions need to be understood in a bigger structural context. When the Japanese state did not have the resources to develop a government-sponsored unemployment assistance program, cartels became important in sustaining employment by preventing the medium-size and small companies from bankruptcy.

THE POLITICS OF PROTECTING THE WEAK

Students of the Japanese political economy often see two competing pictures. On the one hand, the pro–big corporation industrial policy adopted by the Japanese state demonstrated a strong orientation toward strategic resource allocation; on the other hand, however, cartels and other types of nonmarket governing mechanisms that were aimed at protecting the medium-size and small companies led to the persistence of inefficiency in the Japanese economy. In reality, the seemingly contradictory coexistence of these two phenomena represents two sides of the same coin, and under the special historical constraints outlined here, one could not exist without the other. This coexistence, however, was not the result of careful planning but rather was an outcome of political compromise after the state's pro–big corporation competition policy faced strong opposition from medium-size and small companies, consumer organizations, and interest groups in the agricultural sector in the failed attempt to pass the 1958 amendment of the Antimonopoly Law.

During much of the 1950s, the competition policy adopted by the Japanese state showed a strong pro–big corporation orientation. This encouraged the Keidanren, the main organization for big corporations, to aggressively push through another amendment in the late 1950s. The Keidanren asserted that although the Antimonopoly Law had served to break down the managed economy, encourage market competition, and sustain economic democratization, it had also become a barrier that prevented Japan from restraining excessive competition. The Antimonopoly Law had weakened the foundation of industries and had held back the promotion of exports and the development of independent coordination by the private sector. The Keidanren argued that joint actions such as cartels should not be limited to certain industries. It also wanted to nullify the practice of obtaining advance official approval for organizing cartels, replacing it with de facto registration. In the rationalization cartels, moreover, the Keidanren argued that joint purchases of raw materials should be added to the list of permissions for specialized production and concentrated production. The state should also allow private companies to take joint action to prevent overlapped investment and over-investment, and it should permit financial institutions to reach agreement on interest rates (Keidanren 1958, 35–36). The key issue underlying the Keidanren proposal was the freedom of big corporations to organize cartels in any industry.

Although MITI was a major ally of the Keidanren in the attempt to pass the 1958 amendment, MITI had its own interests and goals. MITI held that the enforcement of the Antimonopoly Law must serve the state's industrial policy. Driven by competition in technological innovation, rapidly increasing investment in heavy-chemical industries had overheated the economy. MITI tried to coordinate private investments through its industrial policy. It had become clear to MITI that its control over the quotas of foreign exchange would soon lose effectiveness when the liberalization of trade started. MITI planned to place cartels under its own control and to use them as its new weapon. Urging a further relaxation of restrictions on recession cartels, exports promotion cartels, and rationalization cartels, MITI argued that cartels should also be used to maintain the long-term stability of basic production materials and materials that relied on international markets. (In both cases, the price fluctuation would have a negative impact on related industries.) Joint actions of private companies were especially needed in iron-steel, chemical, non-iron metal, and machine tool industries. MITI argued that its minister should have the power to restrain production, technology, production capacity and price, and trading partners. Private companies that intended to take joint action should apply for approval from MITI. More-over, when outsiders became a barrier to joint action, MITI's minister should have the power to order them to obey the agreement made by insiders. MITI would also have the power to supervise or even issue orders to the agencies established for the purpose of joint action. MITI tried to pass a comprehensive cartel exemption law that would virtually open the door to all kinds of cartels. This law would have eliminated all articles in the then-current Antimonopoly Law regarding the prevention of business concentration (Tsūsanshō 1989, Vol. 5, 379–382).

MITI and the Keidanren were strongly supported by the Prime Minister Kishi Nobusuke. Kishi, who had served as the Minister of Commerce and Industry during World War II, considered giving MITI sole authority for approving cartels and merging the FTC with the Economic Planning Agency. To ensure the success of the amendment of the Antimonopoly Law, Kishi appointed one of his political followers as commissioner of the FTC. In October 1957, an advisory committee was organized. Among 15 committee members, 8 represented big companies. Also among the members were scholars who supported the amendment, but as a critic of the amendment pointed out, this committee consisted entirely of "friends of cartels" (Tsūsanshō 1989, Vol. 5, 396).

MITI's proposal, however, encountered strong opposition. As the FTC saw it, MITI had successfully enacted many industry-based exemption laws. If this comprehensive exemption law were enacted, the Antimonopoly Law would be seriously undermined. Nor did big corporations support MITI's effort, but for different reasons. The Keidanren and several other business organizations criticized MITI for shying away from directly amending the Antimonopoly Law and trying to sidestep it by enacting a comprehensive exemption law. Business leaders also believed that the proposed expansion of licensing would increase bureaucratic control. If cartels were widely allowed in strategic industries, moreover, they would spread to all industries. Furthermore, if MITI had the power to issue orders to outsiders, the power of big companies would be strengthened. As a result of tensions between various state bureaucracies and strong opposition from the private sector, MITI's second attempt at enacting a comprehensive exemption law failed (Tsūsanshō 1989, Vol. 5, 365–376).

Before we assess the reaction to the failure of this amendment, let's look at the reasons for its failure. The strongest opposition came from consumer organizations, medium and small-size businesses, and the Farmer Association. Consumer organizations feared joint actions by big producers. They pointed out that when big businesses produced too much merchandise they did not want to sell it at lower prices. Instead, they tended to control consumers' incentives by reducing the amount of production and providing limited amounts and varieties of goods through joint actions in marketing, sales, prices, and services. As a result, consumers lost the freedom of selection in many products (Haruno 1958, 19). Medium and small-size companies feared that a further relaxation of the Antimonopoly Law would create a crisis for them. As they saw it, the major problem in the Japanese economy was its dual structure, whereby big businesses occupied the industries of basic materials, and economic resources were overconcentrated in oligopolies. In contrast, medium and small-size companies, whose manufacturing and sales depended heavily on the materials produced by big businesses, engaged in excessive competition. The keiretsu made medium and small-size companies more dependent on big companies and were forced to take all the risks in the marketplace. Medium and small-size companies asserted that the provision for reducing the gap in business capacity, which was eliminated in the 1953 amendment, should be revived, and that giant companies should be divided or restrained; cartels should be prohibited in principle; joint action by oligopolies should be prohibited; and both big corporations and the bureaucracies that practiced a joint action through administrative guidance, such as the advised reduction of production, should be subject to criminal investigation. Furthermore, articles should be added to the Antimonopoly Law to prevent unfair trade by the privileged economic power (Makino 1958; Nagai 1958). The Farmer Association had two major concerns. First, the proposed amendment would allow joint action by buyers of agricultural products, something that would weaken the position of farmers. Second, the proposal would also allow joint action by producers of fertilizers, agricultural machinery, and other materials and equipment (Fukuda 1958). Even the Shipbuilding Association opposed the amendment because raw materials constituted a large share of the price of its products, and any cartel of big producers of iron-steel would weaken its competitiveness.

The opposition movement quickly reached a national level. The central committee of the Farmer Association, the Japan Commerce Association, which represented the medium and small-size companies, the National Committee of Consumer Association, and the Housewife Association all issued statements, expressing strong resentment to the MITI proposal. The Farmer Association's position directly influenced the agricultural camp within the Liberal Democratic Party (LDP), which created a negative attitude of the party toward the amendment.

The proposed amendment to the Antimonopoly Law was also affected by a contemporary political event, the passage of the famous Police Responsibility Implementation Law. This bill, designed to smooth the process of the renewal of the U.S.-Japan security treaty by the Kishi Nobusuke cabinet, caused intense conflicts between the conservatives and the progressives in the Diet. Not only was the LDP involved in this political struggle with opposition parties, but also its leaders did not want to take the additional political risk of changing the division of labor among state bureaucracies, something that would also cause strong reaction in the Diet. It was to avoid confrontation that the LDP decided to delay sending the bill of amendment of the Antimonopoly Law to the Diet. Both MITI and the Keidanren had recognized that it was not a good time to push this issue further.

The failure of the bill of amendment to the Antimonopoly Law shows that when MITI and big corporations pushed the strategic resource allocation issue to the extent that would have a negative impact on the total employment strategy and political stability, they encountered serious resistance in distributive politics. The impact of this failure on Japanese distributive politics was decisive. Since then, neither MITI nor big corporations have again tried to amend the Antimonopoly Law comprehensively. The failure of the 1958 amendment shows that big corporations in the exports-related sector became efficient partly because they were forced to compete. Although big corporations enjoyed special treatment in state industrial policy, they had to remain competitive. In contrast, even though the medium-size and small companies did not enjoy equal treatment with big corporations in state industrial policy, they did enjoy more protection by virtue of their cartels, a privilege big corporations wished to share but could not.

JAPANESE WOMEN IN THE LABOR MARKET

Although the measures just discussed helped Japan sustain its total employment strategy, there were major gaps in the distribution of income among big corporations, medium-size and small companies, and family-owned mini shops. Why, then, did Japan also achieve a high level of egalitarian income distribution? According to Nomura Masami, Japanese women played an important role in reducing the income gaps in the Japanese household.

In 1992, 27 million Japanese women had jobs. Among them, 26 percent had never married, 10 percent were either divorced or widowed, and 64 percent were married. Among the latter, 28 percent had full-time jobs and 30 percent worked as part-timers. In other words, family shop owners, part-time employees, and full-time employees constituted approximately equal proportions of the female workforce. For those who worked as full-time employees, there is no doubt that their incomes contributed to egalitarian distribution (Nomura 1998, 66–67).

Part-time female workers, however, contributed to the egalitarian distribution differently. Nomura Masami argues that the strategy of total employment was sustained in part by the use of women as a marginal labor force, and it is the differences in the job patterns among the three employer categories – big corporations, medium-size and small companies, and family-owned mini shops – that partly explain egalitarian distribution in Japan. In big corporations, male employees are protected by the permanent employment system. They earn a wage that takes the family situation into consideration. The wives of these employees tend to be full-time housewives. In the medium-size and small companies, male employees are not part of the permanent employment system. Their wage is based in part on the family situation. Because of the gap in income distribution between big corporations and these medium-size and small companies, the wives of these employees tend to work part-time. In the family-owned mini shops, the issue of employment does not exist. Whether or not the family can make a living depends on their willingness to operate the business. In this group, there is not a wage system; instead, the family's income depends on the income of the business. The wives in this group work as family labor on a flexible schedule. Because of their varying levels of involvement in the labor market, the various roles played by married Japanese women among these three groups serves to proportionately equalize income distribution. Wives of male employees who have a big salary do not work. Wives of male employees who make less income in the medium-size and small companies supplement their household income with income from part-time jobs. As a result, the gap in income distribution measured by the Gini index, which is based on household income, is reduced (Nomura 1998).

It is necessary to point out here that Nomura's argument is not supported by sophisticated statistical data because of the absence of information on their husbands' incomes and occupations at the time women marry or quit work. Nevertheless, it is reasonable to expect that those Japanese women who marry better-educated Japanese men, who are more likely to work for big corporations and to have higher incomes, are more likely to quit work because they can afford to, and their husbands' earning power also affects whether they eventually leave the labor force, staying at home for a long time as full-time housewives (Brinton 1993, 171).

One thing is certain, however: Japanese tax law encourages women to work part-time. According to Japanese tax law, a dependent whose annual income is more than 1.3 million yen is subject to income tax. Meanwhile, many private companies provide a dependent allowance only to those whose annual income is less than 1 million yen. Economically, it does not make sense for a Japanese woman to work part-time to make more than 1 million yen because in that case her husband will not receive a dependent allowance for her. Moreover, because of a change in Japan's national pension system in 1985, full-time housewives and those who work part-time but make less than 1.3 million yen annually became eligible to receive the basic coverage of the pension for the elderly without paying any premium. Under such an incentive structure, many Japanese women try to limit their annual income to around 1 million yen (Nomura 1998, 114–115).

During the high growth period, a major controversy emerged concerning the trend of Japanese women continuing to work after marriage and even after childbirth. At issue was whether the primary role of Japanese women should be that of wife and mother or whether they should have the right to pursue a career and, if so, whether the welfare function should be carried by the family or the state. The leading ideology at the time rejected "arguments favoring women's rights to place career over family and sided with the proponents of a more conservative, neo-traditionalist argument for the priority of motherhood" (Buckley 1993, 350). In the early 1960s, even the Japanese government and various industrial commissions lent their voices to this debate. The Japanese government worried about the serious imbalance between the ratio of the number of unemployed persons to the number of active job openings. As an easy strategy, one might think that the state should encourage women to work to fill the labor shortage. The state, however, became increasingly concerned about the reduced birthrate, which in the long run would lead to the decline of the available labor pool (Buckley 1993, 351).

High growth in the 1960s further encouraged Japanese women to exit the labor market. Rapid economic expansion brought Japanese households a variety of home electronics products, salaries continued to rise, and disposable incomes grew in a climate of minimal unemployment and contained inflation. As a result, a mass consumption culture emerged that had a profound impact on the ideologies of the women's movement in Japan. In the 1960s, so-called my home-ism promoted an ideal lifestyle in which the stay-at-home housewife enjoyed state of the art electric appliances in spacious, Western-style kitchens. As a result, these women's lives were focused on the "interior spaces of the urban nuclear unit" (Buckley 1993, 352). To be sure, Japanese women in general suffered serious discrimination in the workplace and in the mainstream of society. "They have not occupied positions of significance in policy-making and business and their existence and voices have been pretty much ignored by men in formal arenas" (Iwao 1993, 7).

For Japanese women whose husbands worked for big corporations, the economic pressure to work gradually ceased to be an issue. In big corporations, the seniority-based wage was based on the assumption that the employee's family life should be ensured, fully taking into consideration the impact of the wage on the course of the family's life. The seniority-based wage increases along with the employee's age and tenure, but this does not mean that all employees of the same age and tenure receive the same wage. Instead, private companies conduct an annual review and rank their employees' performance. Those who are ranked high receive higher pay increases.

This wage system originated in 1946 in the electric industry when the industrywide labor union proposed a new system to the management of 10 companies. In this system, an employee's base salary consisted of three components: the years of service in the company, performance, and the daily needs of the employee and the members of his family (Kawanishi 1999, 109). When this proposal was accepted, it had a great impact on other industries, and the seniority-based wage system played an important role in sustaining Japan's high growth. Because young employees received the lowest pay, this system enabled Japanese corporations to reduce labor costs when they had to hire many employees to adapt to a rapid business expansion. In addition, this system was suited to the special historical environment of technological innovation. The pace of innovation in the high growth period was too fast for companies to adapt a post-specific wage system – that is, one in which wages are based on job function. The definition and review required by such a wage system would not only cost the company great energy but also would create tension and conflict between labor unions and management. This had been a major source of tension in labor relations in Germany as German companies adopted this system in the midst of rapid technological innovation (Nomura 1998, 6–77).

Under such circumstances, the issue of gender equality in the family began to be perceived differently by this group of women. For them, social status was only one of the many criteria for evaluating a housewife's status vis-à-vis that of her husband. The "available economic resources, freedom to determine disposal of time and money, and the degree of personal fulfillment" all mattered (Iwao 1993, 14). When a Japanese woman

> valued free time more than the professional challenges of a full-time job, she might opt to be economically dependent on her husband for income (in which case she would control the purse strings, thereby securing a solid source of self-esteem), but this does not mean her role in the family would be any less important. [This group of Japanese] women handle family relations in the community, affairs related to their children's education, and home management, enriching the family also through their cultural pursuits of one sort or another. (Iwao 1993, 14)

The changes in Japanese feminist ideologies exerted a great impact on the pattern of women's participation in the labor market and the fate of the total employment strategy during the high growth period.

THE TRADEOFFS OF THE TOTAL EMPLOYMENT STRATEGY

The total employment strategy involved major tradeoffs. The core of the tradeoffs was that the Japanese economy, for the sake of maintaining political stability, had to maintain many inefficient elements that in a liberal economy would be subject to periodic upgrading and replacement. Although cartels, government protections, and gender-based discrimination in the workplace had already begun to generate controversies even in the 1960s, the Japanese failed to take any major action. By creating and maintaining inefficiency, total employment had serious implications for the Japanese economy in the long run. It meant that to strengthen its international competitiveness, Japan had to constantly add new, sunrise industries to its existing economic structure because it could not replace the sunset industries.

In light of the liberalization of trade in the early 1960s, the negative impact of cartels and the protection of medium-size and small companies regarding concentration of production and economy of scale had already attracted Japanese attention. It became clear that the total employment strategy had served to prolong the existence of the dual structure of the Japanese economy. In the late 1950s, 30 percent of the labor force worked in family-owned mini shops. Compared with the British figure (0.2 percent), the Japanese percentage was very high. At the time, modern corporations employed only 46 percent of the total labor force in Japan, compared with 90 percent in Britain and 80 percent in the United States. The dual structure of employment resulted in a big gap in income distribution. Taking the salary paid by big corporations as 100, the salary of those who worked in small companies (10 to 30 employees) was only 50. In contrast, the same ratio in other industrialized countries was about 100 versus 90 (Nomura 1998, 32). The total employment strategy also created surplus employment in the agriculture and service industries. *Surplus employment* occurs in an industry when its marginal productivity, a measurement of the increase in output against the increase per unit of production factor, is lower than that of other industries. Surplus employment produces inefficiency. When more workers than are needed are employed by one industry, its total output does not increase proportionately (see Nomura 1998, 34–35).

Although the work pattern of Japanese women enhanced the egalitarian distribution of household income measured by the Gini index, the rise of gender-based discrimination also generated great controversy. The dualistic structure of the Japanese economy existed not only between big corporations and the medium-size and small companies but also between the permanently employed "haves" and the temporarily employed "have-nots." Japanese women tended to be the have-nots in the workplace (Brinton 1993, 130). The Japanese state and the conservatives intended to push Japanese women back into the family structure because they were worried about the potential negative impact of the declining birthrate on the labor supply, but the strategy they adopted only made the situation worse. Because Japanese women were often forced to return to the family when they married or had their first baby, those who wanted to pursue a career often chose either not to marry or not to have children. In the long run, the consequence of the conservative strategy accelerated, rather than stopped, the declining birthrate.

Gender-based discrimination also increased the percentage of *discouraged workers*, a term that refers especially to Japanese women who lost their interest in finding jobs. In general, the percentage of discouraged workers in Japan was higher than that of other developed countries. Compared with 0.2 in France, 0.6 in Britain, and 0.9 in the United States, the percentage of discouraged workers in Japan in 1993 was as high as 2.2 percent. This phenomenon is especially distinctive among Japanese women. In both Britain and the United States, the difference between men and women in the percentage of discouraged workers is about 0.2. In Japan, however, 0.9 percent of men and 4.0 percent of women were discouraged workers. If a person is unemployed, the government is obligated to provide social assistance. Discouraged workers, in contrast, are regarded as the "potential unemployed" – a category that, in the last analysis, does not create an immediate policy issue (Nomura 1998, 20–22).

As Japan witnessed a rapid revival of cartels, the gap in the dual structure of the economy did not show any sign of decreasing even when the economy experienced rapid expansion. The impact of the cartels on this dual structure can be seen in a comparison between Japan and Germany.

In the 1950s, the German antimonopoly policy took a direction opposite to that of Japan. West Germany failed to enact the competition law during the occupation period. In 1947, the same year Japan enacted its Antimonopoly Law, the German government rejected a proposal for a competition law because of strong resistance from private companies. The battle between the liberals and the industries over a competition law lasted for a decade, generating more than 20 legislative proposals. The key issue was whether cartels should be absolutely prohibited. In 1956, the two sides reached a compromise. The most important compromise included cartel exemptions (similar to Japanese legislation) that permitted so-called crisis cartels, standardization agreements, and a variety of other horizontal agreements. The ordo-liberals, however, also gained some advantages. The Law Against Restraints on Competition included a variety of measures aimed at preventing the abuse of economic power, including a variant of the quintessentially ordo-liberal "as if" standard of conduct. Compared with the Japanese case, the most important achievement was that the German competition law created a relatively autonomous office – the Federal Cartel Office (FCO) – to enforce the law. The FCO, David Gerber (1998) reports, became "an active and highly-respected institution, attracting and retaining many highly-qualified lawyers and economists and maintaining a high degree of autonomy. As a result, businesses, particularly larger firms, would have to pay close attention to the rules enforced by the FCO, and the competition law would become an important legal subject in practice as well as in law faculties."

Both Germany and Japan achieved rapid economic growth during the 1950s. However, the organizational structures of the two economies looked quite different (see Table 5.1). In Germany, high growth resulted in a decline of both the number of small businesses and the number of their employees. At the same time, there was a rapid increase in the number of big corporations. Between 1952 and 1957, the number of big corporations hiring 1,000 or more employees increased 37.8%, resulting in nearly one million

Table 5.1 *Changes in the Numbers of Companies in Germany and Japan 1952–1957*

Germany

Size of Company (Number of Employees) — Number of Companies

	1952	1957	% Change
Total	91,825	92,208	0.42%
1 to 9	42,285	41,261	−2.42%
10 to 49	31,315	21,211	−32.27%
50 to 99	8,313	9,179	10.42%
100 to 999	9,120	11,436	25.34%
1,000+	792	1,091	37.80%

Number of Employees

	1952	1957	% Change
Total	5,848	7,438	27.19%
1 to 9	172	169	−1.74%
10 to 49	729	711	−2.47%
50 to 99	583	645	10.63%
100 to 999	2,370	3,086	30.21%
1,000+	1,996	2,928	46.69%

Japan

Size of Company (Number of employees) — Number of Companies (thousand)

	1951	1957	% Change
Total	3,187	3,535	10.92%
1 to 4	2,640	2,739	3.75%
5 to 19	435	649	49.42%
20 to 99	101	131	29.70%
100 to 999	10.3	15.4	49.51%
1,000+	0.62	0.72	16.13%

Number of Employees (thousand)

	1951	1957	% Change
Total	16,154	20,815	28.85%
1 to 4	4,835	5,447	12.66%
5 to 19	3,862	5,528	43.14%
20 to 99	3,596	4,838	34.54%
100 to 999	2,398	3,499	45.91%
1,000+	1,463	1,504	2.80%

Source: Adopted from Imai, 1962, p. 31 with modification of categories.

new jobs. There was a clear trend toward production concentration in West Germany. In Japan, in contrast, the number of both big corporations and small businesses increased, but the pace of development of small businesses far surpassed that of big corporations. Between 1951 and 1957, the number of big corporations hiring 1,000 or more employees increased only 16.17%, creating only 40,000 new jobs. Thus, the concentration of Japanese companies was realized more in the form of "keiretsu-ization." The organizational structure of the Japanese economy was characterized by two distinct factors. One was the coexistence of a strong capital concentration in big corporations and the extreme capital dispersion among small businesses. The other was the structure of oligopolies in which none of the big corporations had achieved a dominant position in the market. In other words, few Japanese companies had achieved the dominant power and organizational capacity of trusts (in the United States) or *Contsuzne* (in West Germany) (Imai 1962).

How do we account for the differences between West Germany and Japan? According to Imai Tadayoshi (1962, 30–32), they were the result of three factors. First, Japanese companies relied heavily on a low-wage policy to sustain capital accumulation during the postwar economic reconstruction. Because big corporations had a significant advantage in raising capital in an environment in which capital was scarce, low wages were the only competitive weapon for small businesses. The low-wage policy, however, constrained the expansion of small businesses. Second, prices in Japan's domestic markets increased rapidly through several economic booms, and they were sustained at a high level. High prices reflected a high potential for making profits. This continued to keep marginal companies in business, and that in turn stimulated the development of small businesses. Third, stratification among big corporations was curtailed by the practice of indirect financing. In the 1950s, Japanese corporations borrowed others' capital aggressively, and Japanese banks often practiced overlending, a practice sustained by credit from the Bank of Japan. Under such a financial system, big corporations held equal capacities in raising capital, and it was difficult for any individual company to establish a superior status over oligopolies in the market. These three factors resulted in the delay of production concentration and excessive competition.

The Japanese pattern of adaptation to the postwar international economic order by adopting a practice of privatized social protection to address the issues related to employment had serious limits because it relied on three contingent conditions. First, the Japanese economy had to keep expanding so that it could absorb the inefficiency created by cartels and government protection. As long as the gains of the prevention of serious political breakdown by ensuring fast economic growth outweighed the inefficiency this strategy generated, its continued practice seemed rational. As soon as economic growth slowed, however, the costs of continuing to permit cartels and continuing to ensure government protection soon exceeded the gains. By that time, it was more difficult to pursue radical reform because the vested interests created by this strategy strongly opposed it.

Second, Japan's domestic markets had to be kept closed so that the inefficiency created by cartels and government protection could be treated as an issue of domestic income distribution. As long as corporations and individuals did not want to pay the taxes to support a government-sponsored social assistance program, they had to tolerate the cartels and government protection. As soon as the domestic markets were opened to international competition, the industries and sectors protected by cartels and government regulations faced significant challenges.

Third, the technological revolution had to enable Japan to keep adding sunrise industries. When these new industries were created by a wave of the technological revolution, the resulting increase in productivity helped the economy to absorb the loss due to the inefficiency created by cartels and government protection. When the technological revolution slowed, however, there were not enough frontier industries to provide sufficient boosts in productivity.

CONCLUSION

In the high growth period, the Japanese model of the welfare society, characterized by privatized social protection sustained by the total employment strategy, gradually evolved as an alternative to the welfare state. After a decade-long confrontation, major distributional coalitions made important political compromises. Big corporations gained the benefits of a state policy that nurtured competitive oligopoly. In return, they institutionalized the permanent employment system and a seniority-based wage, providing job security to their employees. Rather than fight for consumer interests through enforcement of the Antimonopoly Law and through price competition, employees of big corporations emphasized a sustained income and job security. Instead of demanding equal treatment under state industrial policy, medium-size and small companies enjoyed the privilege of organizing cartels.

These factors had a profound impact on the politics of the antimonopoly policy. The labor unions' position on the battle over mergers among big corporations became ambiguous at the end of the decade. After a major battle between postwar democratic reforms, the Miike dispute, and the anti-U.S.-Japan security treaty movement in 1960, the Japanese economic system began to reemphasize the encompassing nature that had first appeared in the compulsory equalization of the fascist movement of the 1930s. This time, however, this emphasis was driven, not by compulsory pressure from the state but rather by a compromise among major distributional coalitions.

Indeed, the total employment strategy helped Japan maintain political stability by sustaining employment and realizing egalitarian income distribution. Responding to the specific historical conditions of the deflationary fiscal policy under the Bretton Woods system and the asymmetric cooperation with the United States within the GATT system, the Japanese model of the welfare society served to promote the general theme of social protection in a cost-efficient manner. In other words, Japan was able to achieve the same goal with many fewer resources, and meanwhile the total employment strategy also enabled the country to concentrate its resources in economic growth rather than distribution.

The success of the Japanese model of the welfare society during the high growth period, however, relied heavily on three contingent conditions. First and foremost was Japan's asymmetric cooperation with the United States, which enabled Japan to keep its domestic markets closed. With the absence of international competition, the major distributional coalitions in Japanese domestic politics were able to compromise on the issues of cartels and government protection, because those who were efficient did not directly compete for the same markets against those who were not. With a closed market, the Japanese state could offer big corporations favors that differed from those it offered to the medium-size and small companies and maintain employment through both groups. The second contingent condition was the continuing high-speed economic expansion. Japan's high growth made it possible for the gains to outperform the losses. For example, high growth allowed one group of Japanese women – those who were married to men who worked at big corporations – to leave the labor market. It was also high growth that provided job opportunities for those Japanese women who wanted to work part-time. The former factor served to reduce the total household incomes of employees of big corporations. In contrast, the latter served to increase the household incomes of those who worked at the medium-size and small companies. The third contingent condition was the existence of many sunrise industries in the 1950s and 1960s (Katz 1998). The rapid improvement of productivity by big corporations through aggressive investment in production capacity and technological transfers in these sunrise industries easily outweighed the loss of efficiency resulting from maintaining privatized social protection. Because political stability – the reason for maintaining cartels and government protection – was extremely important to the development of the sunrise industries, the price of inefficiency generated by privatized social protection was worth paying.

CHAPTER 6

THE ROADS TO THE BUBBLE

In 1950–1970, sustained by the Bretton Woods system and the GATT system, the Japanese economic system was reconfigured to strengthen coordination between the state and the private sector, between banks and manufacturers, between trading partners, and between management and labor unions. The insurance mechanisms devised for supporting coordination, however, induced moral hazard – that is, Japanese corporations overborrowed and Japanese banks overlent. Although strong coordination weakened both shareholder control of management and bank monitoring of corporate borrowers, two mechanisms served to control and monitor Japan's payment problems: periodic tightening of the money supply by the Bank of Japan, and tight government regulation of the finance industry. Under these contingent conditions, excessive competition triggered rapid economic growth, which in turn helped absorb overbuilt production capacity.

Then in the early 1970s, the contingent conditions that had enabled the economy to tolerate excessive competition began to disappear. After the collapse of the Bretton Woods system, the risks of foreign exchange were privatized. The long-term movement of capitalist economies began to shift gears from the expansion of trade and production of 1950–1973 to a new stage in the expansion of finance and monetary activity. The need to hedge against the risks and the desire to pursue higher profits, both resulting from the fluctuation of exchange rates, led to the liberalization of finance. As a result of the liberalization of finance, the volume of daily foreign exchange trading, a measurement of international capital flows, grew between $10 billion and $20 billion per day in 1973 (with a ratio of foreign exchange trade to world trade that did not exceed 2 : 1), to $80 billion in 1980 (with a ratio of foreign exchange trade to world trade being about 10 : 1), to $800 billion in 1992 (with a ratio to world trade of 50 : 1), and then to $1,260 billion in 1995 (with a ratio to world trade of nearly 70 : 1, equal to the entire world's official gold and foreign exchange reserves) (Eatwell and Taylor 2000, 5).

After the breakdown of national barriers between financial markets, all segments of the global capitalist economy were tightly interdependent, both nationally and internationally. "This new source of huge risks is poorly understood and certainly not fully captured by internal monitoring" (Eatwell and Taylor 2000, 45). Operating in a completely new international monetary regime characterized by a floating exchange rate and the globalization of finance, the Japanese economic system, which was experiencing an intrinsic dilemma between strong coordination but weak control and monitoring in its corporate governance, began to malfunction, and, in the end, the Japanese economy headed toward a major crisis. Drawing on the strength of the institutional perspective, I highlight in this chapter how the shift of global capitalism toward the expansion of finance and monetary activity caused the malfunction of Japanese domestic economic institutions. I also demonstrate how the causal mechanism of excessive competition induced by the dilemma of strong coordination but weak control and monitoring in Japanese corporate governance, which formerly sustained high growth, contributed to the rise of the bubble in the 1980s. The floating exchange rates and the increasing free flow of international capital substantially increased the risks for the Japanese economic system at several levels, some due to factors that were shared by the advanced industrialized countries and others due to factors that were specific in the Japanese case.

At the macro level, Japan's international financial policy, as with that of other major advanced industrialized countries, began to face the serious challenge of the Mundell-Flemming trilemma. Because of its heavy dependence on U.S. markets for exports and because of the rise of Reaganomics in the United States, the Mundell-Flemming trilemma in Japan appeared to be closely related to tense international trade disputes with the United States and subsequent policy measures adopted by both countries. After the Bretton Woods system collapsed, the goals of Japanese public policy – to balance payments (this time in the form of reducing its huge trade surplus) and to maintain a stable exchange rate between the dollar and the yen – began to conflict with the goals of sustaining economic growth and avoiding a painful structural adjustment. The Bank of Japan's intervention in the foreign currency market, which aimed to maintain a desirable exchange rate level, often led to a money oversupply. The Japanese state adopted an expansionary fiscal policy to balance payments, maintain economic growth, and avoid political instability in the structural adjustment. Because the expansionary fiscal policy aimed to create domestic demand by adopting new urban development plans, it often served to boost stock and real estate prices, and substantially increased the self-capitalization of Japanese corporations. All these factors created a favorable environment for a bubble.

At the micro level, the excessive competition in corporate investment induced by weak control and monitoring in corporate governance now became a vital problem to Japanese corporations. In the new environment of the globalization of finance, not only could Japanese corporations easily make mistakes under the flood of capital, but their investment behavior could also be significantly affected by the changing incentive structure shaped by public policy under the impact of the Mundell-Flemming trilemma. After the First Oil Shock ended the high growth, moreover, the overbuilt production capacity could no longer be absorbed easily. As a result, the risks of excessive competition in corporate investments and bank lending increased rapidly. In addition, the liberalization of finance gave more freedom to Japanese corporations to raise capital in overseas financial markets. This freedom, moreover, coincided with the process of Japan's becoming the largest creditor country in the world, and this meant that the cash flow of Japanese corporations increased substantially. Influenced by all these factors, it was easier than ever for Japanese corporations to engage in speculative investments.

Although these changes strongly demanded that Japanese corporations establish mechanisms for tighter control and monitoring, the Japanese response was the opposite. Under the pressures of the rapid appreciation of the yen and the First Oil Shock, Japanese corporations began to reduce both their bank loans and their interest payments. Although this action served to improve the financial health of individual corporations, it also had a significant negative impact on the banks' capacity to monitor corporate investment behavior. As banks lost their leverage with corporations, they could not exercise effective control or monitoring. When banks lost their corporate customers, they were forced to make collateral loans to the medium-size and small companies and even to individuals, and this helped build the foundation for the bad loans that appeared in the 1990s. Because corporations no longer depended on indirect financing, the former monitoring function exercised by the Bank of Japan for the entire economic system was also weakened.

Against this background, a bubble occurred in the Japanese economy in the second half of the 1980s.

EXCESSIVE COMPETITION AND THE TWO BUBBLES

Although the Japanese bubble of the late 1980s is well known, another bubble, the one that occurred in the early 1970s, has often been neglected. Recent discussions on the Japanese economic crisis focus on the contrast between the success of the Japanese economy in the high growth period and its crisis in the 1990s; few analyses have paid serious attention to the identical pattern and similar triggers of these two bubbles and the similarities in corporate investments and bank lending between these two bubbles and the high growth period. Both the 1970s bubble and the 1980s bubble were sustained by aggressive corporate investments and bank lending. The role played by excessive competition was very similar to that in the high growth period except that the magnitude of the second bubble was much greater. There were some differences. In contrast to the high growth, which was financed by bank loans, the two bubbles were financed primarily by corporations' self-capital. In addition, the two bubbles' targets of investment shifted away from production capacity and technological transfers and toward the real estate and stock markets and service industries. In my view, the fact that the same Japanese economic institutions led to different outcomes during the high growth and the bubble has important theoretical implications in the discussion of globalization.

In both bubbles, Japanese corporations had plenty of capital for investment. In Japanese corporate accounting, the term *capital* includes both capital for business operation, such as investments in production capacity (including land for business operation) and in inventory, and capital for discretionary use (including cash, short-term securities, loans to subordinate companies, and stocks of subordinate companies). After the Nixon Shock in 1971, Japanese corporations' discretionary capital increased rapidly. During the high growth period, it remained at roughly 25 percent of the total capital. Its proportion, however, jumped to 40.6 percent in the first half of 1971, 40.8 percent in the second half of 1971, 31.4 percent in the first half of 1972, and 45.0 percent in the second half of 1972. In a further breakdown, the total amount of capital for discretionary use doubled – from 992.8 billion yen to 2,017 billion yen – between the second half of 1970 and the first half of 1971; cash held by Japanese corporations almost doubled, from 478.4 billion yen to 939.6 billion yen; short-term security increased about six times, from 64.1 billion yen to 431.6 billion yen; and investments and loans to subordinate companies increased 40 percent, from 450.0 billion yen to 649.2 billion yen. Between 1956 and 1970, internal capital, including both retained profits and depreciation of production equipment, accounted for 48.6 percent at most. In the second half of 1971, internal capital jumped to 70 percent, and by the second half of 1972, it reached 93.7 percent (Miyazaki 1985).

According to the White Paper on the Economy of 1987, whereas corporate investments in production capacity and inventory increased slowly between 1985 and 1986, corporate finance increased disproportionately between 1985 and 1987, reaching 30 trillion yen. The ratio of the increase of financial assets against the increase of liability was about 40 percent in the second half of the 1970s. In 1985, it reached 87 percent. By 1986, it exceeded

100 percent. This indicated that Japanese corporations no longer needed the capital for their actual business operations. Instead, all the capital raised was used in financial speculation through zai'tech (see Chapter 2). To avoid paying interest, in the late 1970s Japanese corporations tried to reduce the amount of money they borrowed. After the 1970s, in contrast, they no longer restrained the increase in their liabilities and financial assets. Rather, they concentrated on manipulating borrowed money and financial assets to make profits (Keizai Kikakuchō 1987, 267).

In both bubbles, Japanese corporations aggressively engaged in financial speculation, which directly triggered a rise in stock prices. In December 1970, the Nikkei Index was at 1,987 yen. By January 1973, it had jumped to 5,256 yen (Katsumata 1995, 170). Between January 1972 and November 1972, Japanese corporations, including banks, life insurance companies, trust banks, and other nonfinancial institutions, spent a total of 1,200 billion yen on stocks. In January 1972, the average capital return among 225 Japanese corporations listed in the First Department of the Tokyo Stock Exchange was 15.41 percent. By December of the same year, it had jumped to 28.28 percent. At the time, the average capital return rate in the major stock exchange markets in the world was between 13 and 18 percent. Japan topped the world in this measure in 1972 (Miyazaki 1985, 237–238).

The same pattern of stock price movement was observed in the second bubble in the late 1980s. On September 24, 1985, right after the Plaza Accord was announced, the Nikkei stood at 12,755 yen. By the end of January 1987, the Nikkei Index broke 20,000 yen. On the eve of Black Monday, the Nikkei Index had doubled in the two years since the Plaza Accord. During this period, the number of stock transactions in the Tokyo Stock Exchange also increased rapidly. In 1985, on average, 414 million shares were traded per day. In contrast, in 1987, that number jumped to 946 million shares. Furthermore, at the end of 1987, the market cap of Japanese stocks had reached 346 trillion yen, which was about the same size as Japan's GNP and 30 percent larger than the U.S. stock market. The Tokyo Stock Exchange at the time was the largest stock market in the world (Mitsuhashi and Uchida 1994, 194–195).

In both bubbles, Japanese corporations invested a huge amount of money in the real estate markets. In 1973, Japanese corporations spent 9 trillion yen in real estate speculation. Land prices for residential use in the Tokyo metropolitan area increased 19.9 percent in 1971, 15.1 percent in 1972, 35.9 percent in 1973, and 35.4 percent in 1974. During the same period, the prices of business use land in the Tokyo metropolitan area increased by 8.0 percent, 7.4 percent, 28.0 percent, and 23.7 percent, respectively. The national average price for residential land increased 33.3 percent in 1973 and

34.7 percent in 1974, and the national average price for business land increased 23.7 percent in 1973 and 23.6 percent in 1974. According to an investigation published in May 1972, among 100 Japanese citizens who had the highest incomes that year, 95 made their fortune through real estate speculation (Mitsuhashi and Uchida 1994, 34–35, 199).

The same pattern of land price increase occurred in the second bubble in the late 1980s. By the end of 1987, the market value of the entire land area of Japan reached 1,673 trillion yen, 2.9 times that of the United States. A popular Japanese saying was that "using Japan's land can buy the United States twice" (Mitsuhashi and Uchida 1994, 197). In the 1980s, Japanese land policy faced a major dilemma. On the one hand, the Japanese recognized the problem of overpopulation in Tokyo. On the other hand, the Japanese had a dream of turning Tokyo into an international center for finance and information. The huge surplus in the current accounts brought Japan not only capital but also ambition. The image of an overpopulated Tokyo conflicted with the city's image of itself as a major world financial center, representing Japan as a rising power (Imōkawa 1986, 90–91; Sassen 1991).

What caused these two bubbles? What kind of role did the institutions and mechanisms that had sustained the high growth play in the rise of the bubble? Why did excessive competition in corporate investments and bank lending not create any problem in the high growth period but result in the two bubbles in the early 1970s and the late 1980s? In the following sections, I discuss the profound changes in the international economic order that created a new environment in which strong coordination but weak control caused the Japanese economic system to malfunction.

THE COLLAPSE OF THE BRETTON WOODS SYSTEM

As mentioned earlier, the first profound change in the international economic order was the collapse of the Bretton Woods system. This system had functioned to promote prosperity by sustaining fixed exchange rates and controlling the free flow of capital across national borders. It enabled the industrialized countries to both maintain stable exchange rates and pursue domestic economic growth and full employment.

This international monetary regime, however, contained an intrinsic dilemma, often called the Triffin dilemma after Robert Triffin, who first discovered it. The Triffin dilemma refers to the fundamental contradiction in the Bretton Woods system between, on the one hand, the mechanism of liquidity creation and, on the other hand, international confidence in the dollar (Triffin 1960). The Bretton Woods system relied on deficits in the American balance of payments to provide liquidity – chronic deficits that, over the long run, would undermine confidence in the dollar. Robert Gilpin (1987, 135) explains it this way:

> The growth of foreign dollar holdings that were not backed and redeemable by American-held gold at $35 per ounce would eventually destroy faith in the system, and this would lead, in turn, to financial speculation and ever-increasing monetary instability. Either America's balance-of-payments deficits had to stop (thereby decreasing the rate of liquidity creation and slowing world economic growth) or a new liquidity-creating mechanism had to be found.

During the Cold War, the United States followed a policy of asymmetric cooperation, whereby it allowed Japan and other ally countries to have easy access to its huge markets without reciprocal treatment. Japan enjoyed the benefits of an undervalued yen in international trade and accumulated a huge trade surplus, but it refused to adjust the exchange rate between the dollar and the yen to balance its trade surplus with the United States.

By adopting this free-rider position, Japan helped bring down the Bretton Woods system, which had contributed greatly to its postwar economic prosperity. Between 1963 and 1969, Japan's productivity increased nearly 40 percent, in contrast to a 10 percent increase in West Germany and a 10 percent decrease in the United States. When inflation in the United States and the Western European countries floated the prices of exported goods in that period, the prices of exported Japanese goods remained stable. As a result, the prices of Japanese heavy-chemical industrial products were about 20 percent lower than those of the United States. Between 1960 and 1968, Japan's foreign currency reserve remained around $2 billion. When the Japanese share of international markets expanded, Japan's foreign reserve increased rapidly to $3.5 billion in 1969, $4.4 billion in 1970, and $7.6 billion in 1971 (Arisawa 1976, 510–511).

Ironically, although the Japanese regarded the Bretton Woods system as the key factor in their postwar economic growth, they were not willing to do anything to save the system from collapse. Facing increasing U.S. pressure to adjust the exchange rate, West Germany appreciated the mark twice – once in 1961 and again in 1969. Japan, in contrast, refused to consider this option. The Japanese believed that the appreciation of the yen would lead to a slow-down in the rate of economic growth. The German economy grew on average 5.0 percent in 1960–1965 and 4.7 percent in 1965–1970. The Japanese economy, in contrast, grew on average 10.0 percent and 11.6 percent in the same periods. The Japanese believed that the major reason for the German economy's lower growth rate was the appreciation of the mark. In addition, they believed that a growing, inflationary economy would stabilize domestic politics, whereas a stable, deflationary economy would depress people and destabilize domestic politics (Katsumata 1995, 150–152). Since the late 1940s, the Japanese ideology of developmentalism had been dominated by the view that priority should be given to economic growth rather than to the stability of consumer prices (Gao 1997, 161–164).

The Triffin dilemma created by the asymmetric cooperation between the hegemonic country and its allies eventually broke the Bretton Woods system. In 1971 the United States closed the window of gold in order to maintain its policy autonomy (Gilpin 1987). Here is how it happened. In 1971, the United States had a trade deficit for the first time in 78 years. Although its payments, which include both the current account and the capital account, had been in the red for most of the postwar period, its international trade in the current account had been in the black. In response to domestic pressure, the U.S. government chose the priority of maintaining its autonomy in domestic policy objectives over maintaining the dollar's major currency status. On August 16, 1971, U.S. President Richard Nixon announced an emergency economic policy; he froze the U.S. dollar and foreign currencies exchange and enforced a 10 percent tax on imported goods, aiming at forcing foreign currencies to appreciate their values in order to reduce the trade deficits of the United States. This unexpected external event, called by the Japanese "the Nixon Shock," presented a difficult test for each national economic system in the capitalist world. On the day of that announcement, the number of transactions on the Tokyo foreign exchange market was 10 times higher than the usual number, and the total amount of the transactions reached 0.62 billion U.S. dollars. The Dow Jones Industrial Index in the Tokyo stock exchange declined 8 percent. A more profound impact of the collapse of the Bretton Woods system on the Japanese economy was the end of a stable exchange rate and the resulting privatization of the risks of foreign exchange. This set in motion some profound changes.

THE DILEMMA BETWEEN A STABLE EXCHANGE RATE AND
THE BALANCE OF DOMESTIC DEMAND AND SUPPLY

When exchange rates became unstable, the international financial policy of the Japanese state began to face a serious challenge from the Mundell-Flemming trilemma. The collapse of the Bretton Woods system launched an era in which it became difficult for the Japanese state to achieve multiple policy objectives simultaneously.

When the U.S. government closed the window of gold in 1971, all Western European countries immediately closed their foreign exchange markets to avoid damage. Japan, in contrast, kept its foreign exchange market open. The Bank of Japan held that the stable exchange rate of one dollar to 360 yen had been the most important factor in Japan's postwar economic growth. In the previous two decades, the entire economy had been organized around this fixed exchange rate. The proportion of the dollar in Japan's foreign currency settlement was as high as 92 percent. Japan intended to prevent any major change in the exchange rate.

The Bank of Japan supported the old exchange rate between the yen and the dollar for only 12 days, during which time big Japanese trading companies and banks, expecting the yen to be appreciated, sold 4 billion dollars. On the last day alone, 1.2 billion dollars were sold on the Tokyo foreign exchange market. Between July 1971 and February 1973, Japan's foreign reserve increased from $7.9 billion to $19 billion (Heiwa Keizai Kikaku Kaigi 1977, 158). Expecting an economic recession to follow the appreciation of the yen, in December 1971 the Bank of Japan also lowered its interest rate, from 5.25 percent to 4.75 percent, and again in June 1972, from 4.75 percent to 4.25 percent, then a record low in Japan's postwar history. The expansion of exports had already increased the incoming flow of foreign currency and the savings of financial institutions. As a result, city banks began to return their loans to the Bank of Japan, and the overloan phenomenon, which started in 1956, had disappeared by the end of 1971 (Katsumata 1995, 164). These facts show that without the Bretton Woods system, maintaining a stable exchange rate could easily have led to the oversupply of money.

In addition to its expansionary monetary policy, the Japanese state adopted an expansionary fiscal policy. After the Nixon Shock, the Japanese were overwhelmed and seriously underestimated the strength of the Japanese economy. To counter the recession caused by the appreciation of the yen (from one dollar equaling 360 yen to one dollar equaling 308 yen), the Satō administration expanded public spending in fiscal year 1972, with an increase of 21.8 percent in the general account, an increase of 31.6 percent in government investments, and an increase of 4.5 times in national debts (Katsumata 1995, 161, 164). The Japanese government failed to recognize that after the rapid increase in the capital held by private corporations, the old-style Keynesian fiscal policy would not only fail to generate increased investment in production capacity but would also channel the oversupplied money to the stock and real estate markets, creating a bubble (Miyazaki 1985). In addition, the Japanese state, under the Tanaka administration, adopted an industrial reallocation plan, which further led to a 24.6 percent increase in the general account and a 28.3 percent increase in government investments.

The goal of the Tanaka plan was to "shift the priority from production and exports to the social welfare of citizens – to build social capital and develop the social security system to the level of developed countries" (Tanaka 1972, 24). At the time, 73 percent of Japanese industries were concentrated in the Pacific belt, and more than 32 percent of the population lived in 1 percent of the territory. The high growth strategy had created many problems, such as the coexistence of overpopulated urban areas and underpopulated rural areas, pollution, traffic jams, shortages in the energy supply, a shortage of labor, a low number of city parks per capita, and high consumer and land prices in metropolitan areas. To deal with these problems, Tanaka formulated an aggressive plan. The major components of the plan included the following (Tanaka 1972):

· Solving the problems of both over- and underpopulated areas simultaneously and broadening Japan's industrial base from major metropolitan areas to the whole nation, especially to the cold areas
· Building 10,000 kilometers of highways and 9,000 kilometers of high-speed railways and integrating them into a national transportation network
· Developing small cities with a population of 250,000 nationwide
· Improving the living environment of big cities
· Using a taxation policy to drive factories out of big metropolitan areas
· Turning Japan into an "information island" by building communication networks based on telephone, cable TV, TV telephone, and computer networks that could link households with the workplace.

From a 1990s perspective, the Tanaka plan had certain merits. It tried to address the issue of income distribution in economic hard times, not by protecting the weak but rather by providing the weak with opportunities to become strong. It was aimed not only at increasing public spending but also at using this spending to launch major reforms. A growth-oriented plan that contains a major reform component is not necessarily worse than a stability-oriented plan that focuses on muddling through. The Tanaka plan tried to deal directly with the problems within the system, aiming at creating a new economy and balancing the conflicting interests in a dynamic process. Compared with later development, the Tanaka plan was energetic, and it demonstrated that the leading politician in Japan had a big vision. The *New York Times* described the Tanaka plan as "urging an economic and social revolution like Franklin D. Roosevelt's," and Henry Kissinger praised its author as "very forceful, very direct, very attractive, very blunt-spoken" (both cited by Schlesinger 1997, 68), words that were rarely used to describe Japanese political leaders in the 1990s.

The Tanaka plan, however, was destined to fail for two reasons. First, its adoption was ill-timed, occurring as it did in conjunction with the Nixon Shock and the First Oil Shock and thus bearing more responsibility than it deserved for triggering hyperinflation. Had the timing been better, the plan's chance for success might have been greater, the Japanese economy might have recovered from its stagnation much sooner in the 1990s, and the author of the plan would have been internationally praised. Second, the plan lacked a land policy. Tanaka held that because the Japanese land area was small, the rise in land prices was inevitable, and the banks that were profiting from increased land values would be more willing to make loans. Without their continuing supply of capital, Japan's economic growth could not be sustained. Thus, Tanaka saw a rise in land prices as a benefit. When Tanaka later realized that the lack of a land policy might indeed ruin his plan for industrial allocation, he sent a bill – The Law Concerning National Land Use Planning – to the Diet, aiming to control the rapid rise in land prices. Ironically, this bill was interpreted by the opposition parties as encouraging further development of inflation, and it was not passed until 1974, after the bubble had already been triggered (NHK 1995, Vol. 4, 347–349).

Driven by the money oversupply and an expansionary fiscal policy, Japanese corporate investments were channeled into real estate and stock markets. The first bubble occurred and quickly burst, thanks to the First Oil Shock.

THE FIRST OIL SHOCK AND THE DEPARTURE OF
CORPORATE FINANCE FROM THE MAIN BANKS

The second major change in the external environment of the 1970s was the First Oil Shock. The direct impact of the First Oil Shock on the Japanese economy was twofold. First, it ended the high growth, which in turn substantially increased the risks of excessive competition in corporate investments, because without rapid economic expansion, the Japanese economy could no longer easily absorb the overinvestment. Second, the prospect of low growth resulting from the oil shock forced Japanese corporations to reduce the scope of their indirect financing, which in turn further weakened the banks' capacity to monitor corporate finance.

When the Organization of Petroleum Exporting Countries (OPEC) announced on October 16, 1973, that it would raise the price of oil an average of 70 percent, the Japanese, completely unprepared, experienced a major crisis. In 1970, 73.5 percent of the energy used in Japan depended on oil, compared with 44.6 percent in the United States, 49.5 percent in Britain, 56 percent in West Germany, and 65 percent in France. Only Italy showed a higher dependency, at 77.3 percent. In addition, 99.7 percent of the oil consumed by Japan was imported. In 1972, 80.7 percent of imported oil came from the Middle East. However, the Japanese perception of this challenge was more serious than the challenge itself. During the First Oil Shock, the supply of oil from the OPEC countries was rather stable. The amount of oil imported by Japan even increased between October 1973 and March 1974 compared with previous periods. After March 1974, the amount of imported oil declined, but this decline was the result of increased oil prices rather than availability (Mitsuhashi and Uchida 1994, 24).

Under pressure to improve efficiency, cost reduction became a focus of Japanese corporate strategy. It involved reduction of production and distribution costs, reduction of energy and labor costs by introducing automatic machine tools, increases in the economy of scale, reduction of new hires and a freeze in the replacement of retirees, increases in job transfers and temporary transfers, and reduction of subcontracting (Rekishigaku Kenkyōkai 1991, Vol. 5, 15). One chief component of cost reduction among big corporations after the First Oil Shock was to reduce the amount of their bank loans to avoid interest payments. This action had a profound impact on the relationship between the main banks and big corporations.

After the collapse of the Bretton Woods system and the First Oil Shock, according to Miyazaki Yoshikazu, three major transitions took place in corporate behavior and the role of the government in corporate finance. First, during the high growth period, Japanese corporations relied heavily on indirect financing. After the First Oil Shock, indirect financing was replaced by direct financing, especially in the growth industries in the exports-related sector. Second, during the high growth period, the keiretsu engaged in excessive competition, aggressively investing in new frontier industries in the form of the one-set strategy. After the First Oil Shock, however, the keiretsu tended to rely on raising prices. Third, during the high growth period, the Bank of Japan focused on providing equal opportunities to big corporations and to all major business groups in the private sector through its distribution of credit. After the First Oil Shock, in contrast, the Bank of Japan began to issue bonds for both central and local governments, aiming at raising capital for the public sector (Miyazaki 1985, 426–427).

How did the corporate strategy of reducing bank loans change the relationship between the main banks and corporations? The proportion of stocks and bonds within externally raised capital increased, as did the proportion of internal capital in corporate finance. Between the periods 1970–1974 and

1975–1979, the proportion of bank loans declined from an average of 83.9 percent to 63.8 percent, the proportion of corporate bonds increased from 5.9 percent to 17.7 percent, and that of stocks increased from 10.2 percent to 17.9 percent. The proportion of externally raised capital in the financial markets increased from 16.1 percent to 36.2 percent (Miyazaki 1985, 452). Meanwhile, the ratio of internal capital – measured by the retaining of profits plus the depreciation of equipment subscribed by investments in production capacity – also increased. A higher ratio means lower dependence on bank loans. In 1956–1960, that ratio was 0.48. It increased to 0.68 in 1965, 0.70 in 1970, and 0.99 in 1972. The First Oil Shock reduced it to 0.61 in 1974, but it began to increase again in 1975 (Miyazaki 1985, 409). The importance of internal capital increased more rapidly in manufacturing industries than in other industries. Between 1974 and 1977, the proportion of internal capital in all industries increased, on average, from 42.6 to 53.3. In contrast, that of manufacturing industries increased from 49.2 to 70.8 in the same period (Miyazaki 1985, 414).

After the First Oil Shock, the amount of capital for discretionary use held by Japanese corporations declined as the Japanese government tightened the money supply. After 1975, however, it began to increase again. Moreover, it took the form of short-term securities. By the end of 1976, the proportion of short-term securities in the total amount of discretionary capital was as high as 24.2 percent. This was sustained by a new development: the bond market. In theory, when corporations have plenty of self-capital but borrowed bank loans, they should pay back their bank loans. But to continue realizing profits from loan interest, Japanese banks often refused to allow corporations to pay back their loans faster. Because these corporations still relied on banks as their main financiers in the 1970s, they could not overrule the banks' position. In comparison with bank deposits, therefore, short-term securities became more profitable. Short-term security transactions also helped corporations to hide their profits. Before the end of their fiscal year, they could sell their bonds at a price much lower than the market price. Then they would buy them back after completion of the accounting procedure. In spring 1974, the annual rate of interest for short-term bonds was as high as 20 percent. When corporations actively engaged in short-term security transactions, however, their traditional links with banks were significantly weakened because such transactions basically took place between corporations and security companies, which had nothing to do with banks.

When the capital returns for short-term bonds transactions declined, they lost their role as a financial instrument for Japanese corporations. As a result, big corporations, relying on their business power, forced smaller banks to accept repayments of their loans. For example, Nissan paid back loans of 20 billion yen in both 1975 and 1976 to 30 of the 50 banks that had supplied capital. Hitachi returned 39.8 billion yen in 1975. Toshiba returned 4.2 billion yen in the second half of 1975 and returned 20 billion yen in the first half of 1976. Companies that had not made money sold their land, equipment, and stocks at below-market prices and used the money to pay their bank loans and thereby reduce the interest burden (Miyazaki 1985, 400–407). Corporate liabilities in Japan fell sharply, from 182 trillion yen in fiscal 1975 to only 8 trillion yen in fiscal 1985 (Calder 1997).

During the high growth period, indirect financing through bank loans weakened the individual shareholders' control over management. Inasmuch as the individual shareholders represented less than one-third of the total corporate ownership, bank loans lessened as part of the total capital of Japanese corporations, leading to an increasing role of institutional shareholders as major players in the stock and bond markets. With the continuation of reciprocal shareholding, this further strengthened the autonomy of managers. When corporations could use their own money without intervention from institutional shareholders, no one could effectively check the managers' behavior. What happened in the 1970s further challenges the effectiveness of the main banks' policy of delegated monitoring. To exercise monitoring, the main banks needed a certain leverage over their borrowers. When indirect financing was the dominant form of industrial capital supply, the main banks had comparatively greater power in exercising this monitoring. Yet, as I discuss in Chapter 4, during the high growth period the main banks failed to monitor corporations, driven by excessive competition among the main banks in making loans to big corporations. In the 1970s they exercised even less monitoring because the corporations no longer depended on their loans as the major source of industrial capital.

THE LIBERALIZATION OF FINANCE

The most profound change that resulted from the collapse of the Bretton Woods system, however, was the liberalization of finance. This marked a major shift in the long-term movement of capitalist economies. After a two-decade expansion of trade and production, global capitalism saw the beginning of an era of expansion in finance and monetary activity, and the rules of the game of international competition changed dramatically.

Japan's liberalization of finance in the early 1980s was driven by a combination of both U.S. pressure and the ambition of the Japanese elites. The U.S. government pushed the liberalization of finance in Japan for two reasons. First, it held that the huge and increasing U.S. trade deficit with Japan could be attributed to the low value of the yen, which in turn was caused by the closed Japanese monetary and financial markets. Whereas Japanese money could flow freely to other countries, other countries' money could not flow to Japan. This had resulted in a strong demand for the dollar but a weak demand for the yen (Rosenbluth 1989, 68–78; Vogel 1996, 174–175). Second, the U.S. government also believed that if Japan liberalized its monetary and financial markets, American financial institutions would obtain a significant share of the Japanese market. Although American corporations were on the defensive in manufacturing industries such as automobiles and home electronics, they were strongly competitive in the finance and service industries. Competing under the same conditions, American financial institutions could be highly successful (Mitsuhashi and Uchida 1994, 213).

At the Japan-U.S. summit between Prime Minister Nakasone Yasukiko and President Ronald Reagan in November 1983, the U.S. participants called for the internationalization of the yen and the liberalization of finance in Japan. U.S. Treasury Secretary Donald Regan, formerly a Merrill Lynch CEO, believed that a strong dollar was synonymous with a strong America. He also held that the weak yen was the major reason for Japan's trade surplus because the yen had not become an international currency and there was a weak demand for it. Regan insisted that Japan needed to take bold action (Burstein 1988, 128–130). After the summit, a special joint Japan-U.S. Ad Hoc Group on Yen/Dollar Exchange Rate and Financial and Capital Market Issues was established under the leadership of both countries' finance ministers (for detailed documentation on this group's activities, see Rosenbluth 1989, Chapter 3). This committee played a key role in speeding the liberalization of financial policy in Japan.

Within a year after the summit, two important state regulations on foreign currency exchange were abandoned. The first was the "actual need principle" in the trade of currency futures. Previously, the only foreign currency futures that could be traded were those that covered the foreign currency needed for international trade. This regulation aimed at preventing speculation in the foreign exchange market. Under the new rule, anyone could engage in trading foreign currency futures. The second state regulation was the "converting foreign currency to yen principle." Previously, private corporations that raised capital from overseas markets faced government control when they converted foreign currency to yen. Under the new rule, they were free to make the conversions. Japanese corporations were also allowed to bring back all the capital they raised through the Euro yen markets.

With these two measures, the Japanese monetary market was directly linked to the international monetary markets (Mitsuhashi and Uchida 1994, 215). By April 1988, the minimum requirement for certificate deposits had decreased to 50 million yen, and all the limits on the ratio between the certificate deposits and self-capital had been abolished. The original time scope of certificate deposits – from three to six months – was also expanded from two weeks to two years. Large deposits, with interest rates completely free, were introduced in October 1985, with a minimum deposit of 1 billion yen and a time scope of three months to two years. In October 1987, the time scope's lowest limit was relaxed to one month. In October 1989, the minimum requirement for a deposit was lowered to 10 million yen. By October 1989, the money market certificate (MMC) merged with the large deposit. Beginning in 1985, the interest rates of bank deposits began to reflect the market situation. The percentage of bank deposits that had free interest rates increased from only 15 percent at the end of 1985 to 65.6 percent at the end of 1990 (Mitsuhashi and Uchida 1994, 216–217).

In any explanation of the dynamics behind the liberalization of finance, however, the Japanese elites' ambition to became major players in international finance was as important as the U.S. pressure (Burstein 1988, 132). As Japan became the largest creditor country in the world, domestic concerns about the vulnerability of its balance of payments disappeared; such concerns had been a key factor in the tight control over capital mobility following the war. Now, the Japanese developed a strong desire for their country to play a more important role in international affairs. In the ruling LDP, Prime Minister Nakasone stood – with President Reagan of the United States and Prime Minister Thatcher of Britain – as one of the three major players in the neoliberal revolution. Within the Ministry of Finance, internationalists were able to win on a number of policy issues. For the first time in postwar history, the ministry announced in July 1980 that international banking would be classified as one of Japan's predominant industries. In the finance industry, business leaders as far back as the late 1960s had begun calling for the development of Tokyo as an international financial center. As Japanese banks became increasingly prominent in international financial markets in the late 1970s, they began to be more in favor of liberalization (Helleiner 1994, 152–156). Pressure from the United States helped Japanese banks and other financial institutions in the political struggle against those seeking to preserve the status quo.

ZAI'TECH

Against the background of the collapse of the Bretton Woods system and the liberalization of finance, what happened to corporate investments, which used to be characterized by excessive competition in investing in production capacity and technological transfer, at the micro level? The answer is that Japanese corporations engaged actively in so-called *zai'tech*, or financial technology. Zai'tech is the process whereby companies generate profits by investing in stocks and bonds.

Zai'tech became a major strategy for Japanese corporations in adjusting to the new economic environments. Because they could not downsize their labor force or sell their subordinate companies, it was difficult for Japanese corporations to restructure as quickly as did their American and European counterparts. In Japan, restructuring tended to take the form of nurturing new growth segments and reducing depressed segments within a company. Whereas the appreciation of the yen and the First Oil Shock restrained opportunities for Japanese corporations to invest in production capacity, they tried to improve profitability by investing in financial assets. In the early 1980s, 7 percent of Japanese corporations reduced their bank loans to zero, and 18 percent of them reduced the loans to less than 20 percent of their total capital. Debt reduction was especially prevalent in depressed industries, such as marine transportation (Iga 1987, 63). As Makino Noboru pointed out, in 1981 Japanese corporations had an invested production capacity of 7.4 trillion yen, but they had only 6.7 trillion yen of self-capital. By 1985, however, Japanese corporations had a 1.2 trillion yen surplus in self-capital. Some medium-size and small steel makers had deficits in their steel business but reported profits of several billion yen through zai'tech (Makino 1987, 25).

Zai'tech was sustained by the use of Special Monetary Trust (SMT) (*tokutei kinsen shintaku*), a practice by which corporations used trust banks to invest their money but with special guidance regarding which stocks, how many shares, and at what prices to buy and sell. In 1980, a change in the government regulation regarding corporate accounting provided an incentive structure for the growth of SMT. In the past, a corporation that owned stock of another company and bought more shares of the same company at a higher price had to report the adjusted price (adding the two prices and dividing by 2) to the regulatory authority. According to the new 1980 regulation, however, such corporations were allowed to report both prices separately in their accounting, thereby reducing taxes. For example, suppose that company A owned 10,000 shares of company B, shares that had been bought for 100 yen per share. Then company A decided to purchase another 10,000 shares of company B for 300 yen per share. When the market value of company B's stocks rose further to 400 yen per share, company A sold 10,000 shares. Before the new regulation was enacted, company A would have to use the price of 200 yen per share for accounting purposes (100 + 300 / 2 = 200). Under the new regulation, however, company A could report a purchase price of 300 yen per share for the 10,000 shares it sold, and the realized gain would become 1 million yen (400 yen − 300 yen × 10,000) rather than 2 million yen. Consequently, it would pay 50 percent less tax in this new system than it would have had to pay in the old system (Taketa 1985, 88–89).

The use of SMT grew rapidly in Japan during the early 1980s. Between March 1983 and June 1985, the assets in SMT accounts increased from 900 billion yen to 4 trillion yen. Stocks, bonds, and foreign bonds were the three major assets Japanese corporations transacted through SMT. The money used to buy stocks through SMT increased 3.7 times, from 300 billion yen in March 1984 to 1.1 trillion yen in March 1985, surpassing the growth rate of the total SMT. In both 1984 and 1985, many SMT accounts realized a capital return of 20 percent to 30 percent. Some of them even reported a 50 percent return on their investments. The proportion of transactions by institutional investors at the Tokyo Security Exchange increased from 23.0 percent in 1975 to 36.5 percent in 1985; that of individual investors declined from 58.0 percent to 41.4 percent (Taketa 1985, 90). The rapid development of SMT indicates that, sustained by the liberalization of finance, Japanese corporations began to shift away from their real businesses to financial speculation. Ironically, when the world praised Japanese corporations for their long-term thinking in business strategy in the 1980s, Japanese corporations had begun to turn to short-term profits earned at a rapid rate.

Another enabling factor for the growth of SMT was the weak control by shareholders over corporate management. Facing the uncertainty that followed the two oil shocks and the liberalization of finance, Japanese corporations tended to play the high risk/high return money game. In contrast, American corporations became more conservative in their corporate financing.

Statistical data between 1975 and 1985 show that in nonfinancial Japanese corporations, cash in corporate assets declined from 38.3 percent in 1975 to 29.0 percent in 1984. During this period, the amount of money deposited in saving accounts, whose interest rates were still regulated, did not change much. Trust funds, except for a temporary decline in 1982–1983, rose from 4.2 percent in 1975 to 6.8 percent in 1985. Before certificates of deposit became available in 1979, Japanese corporations tended to shift their assets from cash to savings accounts and from stocks to bonds. When the certificate of deposit was created as a financial instrument, its interest rate was deregulated and banks were allowed to compete by offering higher interest rates. Consequently, Japanese corporations tended to shift their assets from cash to certificates of deposit and bonds, and from stocks to certificates of deposit. In short, Japanese corporations tended to shift their assets to the financial instruments whose interest rates were deregulated because that could generate greater returns. Between 1983 and 1985, moreover, the flow of Japanese corporate assets was from cash to certificates of deposit and trust funds, and from stocks to certificates of deposit and trust funds. The expansion of trust funds was sustained primarily by SMT. SMT did not offer any insurance on investment return, and it was often used in the form of investments in stocks. This indicates that increasing numbers of Japanese corporations began to follow the high risk/high return principle in their corporate financing, a business strategy that was the opposite of the orthodox image they had of following long-term thinking (*Shūkan Tōyō Keizai* 1986/12/6, 22–24).

After the First Oil Shock, investing in financial assets was expected to generate a higher return than investing in material assets such as production capacity. Big American corporations, defined as those having more than $250 million in assets, tried to cover their losses in business operations by manipulating financial instruments in a much more conservative way. Between 1975 and 1981, when interest rates were high, American corporations tended to shift their money from treasury bonds, state and local government bonds, and commercial paper to overseas savings accounts in Eurodollars because the Eurodollar offered higher interest rates. Many corporations tried to make profits by gaining a higher rate in the Eurodollar market, meanwhile issuing commercial paper with a lower interest rate. The gap between the Eurodollar interest rate and that of commercial paper could be as high as 3 percent. Even after deducting all costs of issuing commercial paper, corporations could still make between 1 percent and 2 percent profit. When interest rates fell in 1983–1985, American corporations shifted their financial assets from certificates of deposit and overseas savings accounts back to U.S. treasury bonds because the latter were considered the safest financial instrument. This shift indicated that American corporations were being more conservative in corporate finance because the boards of trustees in American corporations were worried about possible failures in financial operations (*Shūkan Tōyō Keizai* 1986/12/6, 24–25). Because American corporations were under relatively more effective shareholder control through boards of trustees, they were more reluctant than Japanese corporations to engage in financial speculation.

Both Japanese and American corporations faced the same pressure to improve efficiency after the collapse of the Bretton Woods system and the two oil shocks, but each responded differently because of the different patterns of corporate governance. Even before the bubble formally appeared, there were many signs that Japanese corporations would face greater risks in the era of financial globalization because of weak shareholder control over management. Although American corporations engaged in short-term profit-seeking, they did so as part of their primary business operations. In dealing with financial instruments, American corporations were more conservative. In contrast, Japanese corporations focused on short-term profits, not in primary business operations but rather in corporate finance through zai'tech. They totally neglected the huge risks associated with the increasing amount of free flow of capital. In American corporations, boards of trustees exercised relatively strong shareholder control over management, prohibiting managers from engaging in speculation in the stock and real estate markets. Sustained by strong management autonomy and strong growth orientation, in contrast, Japanese corporations could easily engage in financial speculation. Japanese corporations' long-term orientation during the high growth period was actually compatible with their short-term orientation in the 1980s; both practices were sustained by a system of corporate governance characterized by weak shareholder control over management and weak monitoring of corporate borrowers by banks.

MULTILATERAL POLICY COOPERATION
AND THE PLAZA ACCORD

In the Japanese context, the liberalization of finance occurred in conjunction with the end of asymmetric cooperation with the United States. In the bilateral economic relations between Japan and the United States in the 1980s, monetary issues were often closely related to trade issues. As a result of its overdependence on the U.S. markets for its exports, Japan faced strong pressure from the United States to reduce its huge trade imbalance. The policy measures adopted by Japan, however, drove the Japanese economy into the Mundell-Flemming trilemma.

If the collapse of the Bretton Woods system, the First Oil Shock, and the liberalization of finance provided the necessary basic conditions for the Japanese bubble to take place, the 1985 Plaza Accord provided the necessary specific condition, in the sense that the Japanese mishandling of the rapid appreciation of the yen led directly to the bubble. Kikkawa Mototada (1998) maintains that the Plaza Accord was an American conspiracy to destroy Japan. This argument does not hold, however, for a number of reasons. First, as the U.S. government made clear from the beginning, this multilateral policy cooperation was aimed precisely at addressing U.S. trade deficits with its major partners by lowering the value of the dollar. Second, Japan had the option of not participating in this multilateral policy cooperation. Driven by the goal of becoming the dominant financial power in the world, however, Japan actively co-initiated the accord from the beginning. Third, even from the perspective of international competition, the monetary policy adopted by the U.S. government was at best a double-edged sword. It not only led to pressure on Japan but also helped Japan become the largest creditor country in the world. If Japan had not depended heavily on the U.S. markets, the increase in the trade surplus resulting from the U.S. policy of high interest rates would not have been as great as it was. As a result, Japan would not have been able to accumulate such a huge amount of wealth within such a short period of time.

According to Tsuruta Toshimasa, the imbalances of payments between the United States and Japan were sustained by the mismatch of policies between the two countries. The U.S. economy was an overspending economy; the Reagan administration had simultaneously enacted a tax cut and increased public spending. The subsequent increase in the country's budget deficit led to an increase in interest rates, which in turn induced an inflow of dollars. The high value of the dollar further lowered the prices of imported goods, something that led to trade deficits. As Table 6.1 indicates, driven by the high value of the dollar, the United States increased its trade deficits not only with Japan but also with many other countries, even those that had not been criticized as having trade barriers. In contrast, the Japanese economy was an oversaving economy. In such an economy, the government should have increased public spending to adjust its trade surplus. Instead, until 1987 it worked hard to reduce public spending. This policy contributed to a further increase in the trade surplus. In the 1980s, Japan's national saving, after taking budget deficits into account, was still higher than its national investments. The passive fiscal policy adopted by the Japanese government was an important reason for the rising trade surplus. In theory, the United States, facing trade deficits, should have reduced budget deficits; and Japan, facing trade surpluses, should have increased government investments. In reality, however, both countries were moving in the opposite directions. This was a major reason for the fluctuation of the exchange rate (Tsuruta 1987, 38–41).

In early 1985, a group of American economists produced a series of analyses asserting that the current levels of exchange rates and current accounts were unsustainable. In the scenario presented in these reports, the United States would not be able to pay the debts it was amassing, and the dollar was overvalued by at least 10 percent to 20 percent. Any unexpected incident that caused a loss of confidence could trigger a crash of the dollar. When investors eventually realized this situation, the economists predicted, they would flee dollar-denominated assets, leading to a hard landing. Facing rapidly increasing trade deficits, unprecedented domestic political pressures were growing on the U.S. government to adopt measures to address the issue. In 1985 alone, about 400 protectionist bills were submitted to the U.S. Congress (Grimes 1995).

Table 6.1 *U.S. Trade Balance with Selected Countries*

Country	1975	1980	1982	1983	1984	1985	1986
Canada	−407	−6,064	−12,757	−13,886	−19.954	−21,755	−22,920
Mexico	2,075	2,565	−3,749	−7,694	−6,028	−5,497	−4,910
France	867	2,220	1,565	−64	−2,076	−3,386	−2,913
Italy	410	1,186	−685	−1,547	−3,560	−3,386	−2,913
West Germany	−216	−733	−2,684	−3,958	−7,912	−11,189	−14,563
Sweden	38	150	−304	−848	−1,702	−2,199	−2,549
Hong Kong	−765	−2.053	−3,087	−3,830	−5,204	−5,610	−5,861
Taiwan	−287	−2,517	−4,526	−6,537	−9,765	−11,696	−14,267
Singapore	460	1,112	1,019	891	−304	−784	−1,345
South Korea	320	538	−108	−1,223	−3,370	−4,057	−6,374
Japan	−1,862	−9,924	−16,778	−19,289	−33,560	−46,152	−55,029

Source: Statistical Abstract of the United States, 1986, pp. 810–813, 1988, pp. 770–773.

When trade became the top policy issue, elites in the United States and Japan found that the exchange rate was a good alternative for adjusting payment imbalances. Under the Bretton Woods system, there had been little activity from domestic interest groups in the United States. Acting autonomously, the Federal Reserve Board made decisions on monetary matters. This fact has been attributed to, on the one hand, "the esoteric nature of the subject of international monetary policy and ignorance on the part of group leaders" (Odell 1982, 347) or, on the other hand, the free-rider problem contained in collective action in that "there was no conceivable excludability for groups adversely affected by the overvaluation of the dollar" (Gowa 1983, 26). In the early 1980s, however, the situation began to change. "Between 1979 and 1985, an annual average of 65 bills, resolutions, and proposals concerning monetary policy were introduced into Congress" (Frieden 1996). In 1983, Republican Senator Charles Percy introduced a resolution calling on the administration to negotiate a coordinated reduction in the value of the dollar. It passed the U.S. Senate unanimously. The Reagan administration did not respond to this call because "the Treasury disagreed on the notion of the overvalued dollar, claiming that U.S. high interest rates had not been a major determinant of exchange rate movements" (Kojo 1993, 200). The Senate passed another bill in May 1985 calling for any measures necessary to address the trade deficit issue, including unilateral intervention in the exchange market. "By late 1985, there were seven bills before Congress that included specific reference to exchange rate issues" (Frieden 1996, 129).

On the surface, monetary policy coordination was aimed at controlling currency stability. However, the real purpose was to achieve a desired exchange rate. An export surplus meant an increase in output and economies of scale so as to facilitate a faster rate of technological development (Schmit, cited by Gilpin 1987, 163), and rapid appreciation of a currency can result in a major depreciation of that country's overseas investments. "The purpose of policy coordination in the eyes of each of the leading economic powers," according to Robert Gilpin, "is to get its economic partners to do what it wants done but without its doing what the partners want done" (1987, 154). If Japan had not wanted to participate in the coordination, it could have firmly said no to the United States, just as it had done in the bilateral trade negotiations, regardless of U.S. government pressure.

Why, then, did Japan agree to participate in this multilateral policy coordination? The reason is that Japan's ambition was to become the dominant financial power in the world. The 1985 multilateral policy coordination of exchange rate policy was supported by the leading politicians in the Liberal Democratic Party and by bureaucrats in the Ministry of Finance. The Plaza

Accord was a result of close cooperation, which had been kept top secret until the last minute, between government officials of the United States and Japan. U.S. Assistant Secretary of the Treasury David Mulford and senior Japanese bureaucrat Ōta Tomomitsu at the Ministry of Finance began to talk about a strategy of lowering the value of the dollar in spring 1985. In June, Ōta approached Finance Minister Takeshita about the issue of coordinated intervention. Takeshita discussed it with U.S. Secretary of the Treasury James Baker in June 1985. They agreed to leave it to Mulford and Ōta to draft a detailed plan. Mulford and Ōta agreed to create a bilateral plan first and then extend the plan to the Europeans. To minimize the threats that leaks might pose to the exercise, they also agreed that the proposal should be kept secret and that no one else in their governments or central banks should be informed (Grimes 1995). As William Grimes (1995, 330) points out,

> The circle of people with foreknowledge of the Plaza plans was extremely small. In Japan, only Ōta [Zaimukan at the Ministry of Finance, who was in charge of drafting the plan], Takeshita [the finance minister], and Nakasone [the prime minister] knew about them until a little over a week before the meeting was to occur, when the Bank of Japan Governor Sumita Satoshi was finally informed. In the United States, the circle was just as small, comprising Baker, Undersecretary Richard Darman, and Mulford. Baker finally informed the President, and received his approval, the Tuesday before the meeting. Volcker [the chairman of the Federal Reserve] was brought in the next day.

In the negotiations, the United States pressed for more comprehensive policy coordination, which would include macroeconomic and structural policies. Japan, however, strongly insisted that it wanted to discuss only exchange rate policy. In the end, the Japanese approach prevailed.

In early September 1985, the U.S. government announced that the United States had become a debtor country after 71 years. In May of the same year, Japanese Finance Minister Takeshita predicted that Japan would become the largest lender country in the world within a year. This raised the expectation of a rapid decline in the value of the dollar, and that became the major reason for the policy coordination agreement (Katsumata 1995, 208). On September 22, 1985, the group of five (G-5) finance ministers and central bankers met at the Plaza Hotel in New York City and signed the famous accord. Officially, the Plaza Accord stated that "recent shifts in fundamental economic conditions . . . together with policy commitments for the future . . . [had] not been reflected fully in exchange markets and that economic fundamentals presented a disparate picture, albeit the international economic disparities at the time of accord were slowly giving way to a relatively more convergent performance" (Das 1993, 6). Unofficially, "the G-5 action can in fact be seen as an attempt by the Americans and the Europeans to pressure the Japanese to revalue the yen, to shift from an export-led to a domestic growth strategy, and to cut their massive trade surplus" (Gilpin 1987, 164).

Although some American economists, business leaders, and government officials knew at the time that a coordinated intervention in the currency market could reduce the U.S. trade deficits, no one really knew what the end results of such coordination would be. On the contrary, no one could have predicted that this policy intervention would lead to a chain of events that would trigger the rise and burst of the bubble in the Japanese economy. One indicator might have been that throughout the 1980s, much of the English-language literature on the Japanese political economy still concentrated on trade and the strength of the Japanese competition regime in coordination. But few would have believed that the Japanese economy was heading into a major crisis.

THE OVERSUPPLY OF MONEY

The Plaza Accord of 1985 did not set or even discuss target rates (Grimes 1995, 332). When the Japanese signed the accord, they overestimated their ability to control the movement of exchange rates. The Japanese government expected that the value of the dollar would go down 10 percent within a short time. Right before the Plaza Accord, the exchange rate was one dollar equaling 243 yen. The initial target of the Japanese government was about 220 yen. When the yen's value remained at one dollar equaling 200 yen at the end of 1985, the Japanese still felt comfortable. At the end of January 1986, Finance Minister Takeshita stated that Japan could accept one dollar equaling 190 yen. As the rate fell to one dollar equaling 180 yen, however, Japanese government officials began to believe that the value of the yen had become too high (Katsumata 1995, 210–211).

Then the pressures of adjustment, responding to the rapid appreciation of the yen, surfaced quickly. A government survey published in May 1986 indicated that corporate investments in production capacity had become a minus quantity for the first time in three years. A MITI survey showed that the situations of medium-size and small companies were continuing to deteriorate. The June 1986 survey on national income reported a drop in growth of 0.5 percent, the first negative growth in 11 years (Katsumata 1995, 215–216). According to a Ministry of Finance survey, the profits of all Japanese corporations increased 5.7 percent in 1985, but those of exports-related sectors declined 4.8 percent. Among them, electronic machinery declined 15.9 percent and iron-steel declined 24.9 percent. Hitachi reported its first negative return since the First Oil Shock. In 1986, corporate profits declined an average of 3.1 percent in all industries, 22.2 percent in the manufacturing industry, 42.9 percent in exports-related sectors, and 48.5 percent in electronic machinery. Iron-steel even reported a loss (Mitsuhashi and Uchida 1994, 182–183). There was panic in Japan. Centered on the manufacturing industries, various business associations, MITI bureaucrats, and a group of economists strongly demanded that the government adopt countermeasures.

Thus, it was the panic of the yen-appreciation recession that led to the adoption of an expansionary monetary policy. Beginning in January 1986, the Bank of Japan lowered interest rates. By February 1987, it had lowered interest rates five times, reducing the rate from 5 percent to 2.5 percent, the lowest rate in Japanese history. Low interest rates meant that corporations were able to get loans more easily. Banks had strong incentives and were also under pressure to make loans. Between March 1986 and January 1988, the Bank of Japan also intervened in the international currency markets; to lower the value of the yen, it reversed its practice of selling dollars and buying yen and began selling yen and buying dollars. This practice, as shown in Figure 6.1, increased the domestic money supply because the Bank of Japan had to use yen to purchase dollars. The intervention contributed to an additional money supply of 1.4 percent in 1986 and 1 percent in 1987 (Mitsuhashi and Uchida 1994, 182–183).

Under the Bretton Woods system, because Japan's major problem was a deficit in payments, the Japanese state had relied on a policy mix of an expansionary monetary policy and a deflationary fiscal policy. After the international monetary order changed to a floating exchange rate and Japan's payments changed to a surplus, Japan should have used a new policy mix of an expansionary fiscal policy (to boost the economy during recession) and a tight money policy (to prevent inflation). At the time, the Ministry of Finance was overly committed to the goal of rebuilding finance. As a result, Japan used an expansionary monetary policy to boost the economy. If Japan had responded to the pressure of the yen's appreciation by conducting structural reforms and improving efficiency, Japan's trade conditions would have improved and economic growth could have resumed after a painful adjustment. But constrained by the dual goals of promoting growth and stability, Japanese corporations were not able to use layoffs as a tool for adjustment. As a result, they demanded government intervention. Unfortunately, the adoption of an expansionary monetary policy led to an oversupply of money, which, although it would stimulate growth, would leave the efficiency issue unsolved and also would lead to inflation. Inflation, however, was considered in Japan to be inevitable when the economy grew.

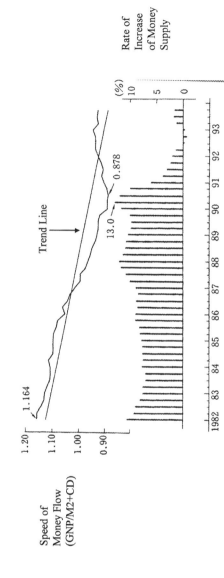

Figure 6.1. *Money supply and economic activity.*

Source: Mitsuhashi and Uchida, 1994, p. 200.

THE MAEKAWA REPORT

In the 1980s, the brain trust of Prime Minister Nakasone envisioned a drastic structural adjustment, but it was never really carried out. The appreciation of the yen after the Plaza Accord had slowed the Japanese economy, but Japan's trade surplus continued to increase. In 1985, Japan's trade surplus rose by 35 percent, reaching $61.6 billion. It jumped to $101.6 billion in 1986. The ratio of current account surplus to total GNP reached 4.5 percent, the highest in the postwar period among all major industrialized countries (the United States reached 3.8 percent in 1947, and West Germany reached 3.6 percent in 1986). Calculating statistics based on the yen, the surplus in Japan's overseas current account began to decrease beginning in July 1985 and continued to decrease for the next three years. Nevertheless, calculating the numbers based on the dollar, the surplus in Japan's overseas current account kept growing.

The G-7 summit was to be held in Tokyo in May 1987. Prime Minister Nakasone, anticipating criticism from Western countries, appointed Maekawa Haruo, the former president of the Bank of Japan, to head a private brain trust to draft a policy proposal addressing Japan's trade surplus problem. The committee published a report in April 1986, one month before the Tokyo G-7 summit.

The Maekawa report maintained that the continuing imbalances in Japan's current account not only were unhealthy for the Japanese economy but also would breed a crisis for the global economy. Japan had arrived at a turning point, and it needed to make a rapid transition. The report suggested that Japan take as a mid-term goal for its public policy the reduction of the current account surplus. The report held that the surplus was basically created by the structure of the Japanese economy, which had a strong export orientation. To realize the goal of a payments balance, the report suggested that the Japanese government create domestic demand by emphasizing housing policies, urban redevelopment, increases in income, decreased in the number of work hours, and promotion of domestic consumption. The report also maintained that Japan should change its industrial structure by encouraging foreign investments, reforming agriculture, and helping depressed industries shift their business operations to new fields of production. It regarded access to Japanese markets as a very important measure and argued that Japan should encourage imports of foreign products. The report called for stabilization of exchange rates and the liberalization of finance and advocated that Japan make more contributions to official development aid. Finally, the report asserted that Japan should end the policy of giving tax breaks to postal savings (Mitsuhashi and Uchida 1995, 185–187).

The publication of this report caused a heated debate in Japan. Among several contending issues were the questions of the real cause of the trade surplus and whether the adoption of a domestic-demand-driven economic policy was a good strategy. In 1986, some leading Japanese economists, such as Komiya Ryūtarō and Shimomura Osamu, maintained that the huge surplus in Japan's current account was created by U.S. economic policy and argued that Japan should not be responsible for reducing its trade surplus. Pressing Japan to take action without changing U.S. macroeconomic policy would lead only to bigger Japanese trade surpluses. On the issue of a domestic-demand-driven economic policy, it was widely agreed among Japanese economists that such a policy would lead to inflation. They pointed out the danger contained in the strategy of reducing the trade surplus by increasing domestic demand. To bring down the 1985 level of the current account surplus, according to their calculation, domestic demand had to be strong enough to sustain growth at 33 percent per year. As soon as the annual growth rate reached 7 percent, however, the efforts to increase domestic demand would inevitably create inflation (Katō 1986, 62–66).

THE ADOPTION OF AN EXPANSIONARY FISCAL POLICY

Various interest groups, however, did not want to suffer the painful structural adjustment envisioned by the Maekawa report. As the yen started to appreciate again in January 1987, a consensus emerged that called for the adoption of a stimulus package. The government economic estimate published at the end of 1986 predicted that the economy would grow at the rate of 3.5 percent for 1987. Most estimates conducted by the private sector held that the rate would not exceed 2 percent. Moreover, the unemployment rate published in May reached 3.1 percent, the highest since such surveys had been conducted. This number had an important symbolic implication in Japan. In postwar Britain, the welfare state, whose major goal was to realize full employment, had regarded 3 percent unemployment as inevitable. But to the Japanese, 3.1 percent unemployment was real unemployment (Katsumata 1995, 216). At the G-5 Louvre meeting on February 21, 1987, the participants agreed that "further substantial exchange rate shifts could damage growth and adjustment prospects, and the desirability of stabilizing the exchange rates around present levels was acknowledged . . . . [but the] exchange rate should not be relied on as the sole policy instrument of correcting the current account and trade imbalance" (Kojo 1993, 224–225). In April 1987, critical business organizations united in pressing the Japanese government to adopt a substantial fiscal stimulus package. The opposition parties asserted that the government should also introduce an income tax cut, increase public spending in welfare and public works, and pay attention to small business issues and unemployment.

In the LDP, supporters of a fiscal stimulus package gained strength in the battle with those who supported a reduction in budget deficits in the administrative reform. Before the Plaza Accord, the mainstream factions within the LDP, represented by Prime Minister Nakasone and Finance Minister Takeshita, made the reduction of government budget deficits their major policy agenda. In contrast, the nonmainstream factions – who represented the interests of the construction industry – supported an expansionary fiscal policy. By 1987, public spending had been restrained for six years, a policy that had generated a great deal of anger within the LDP. Aiming at winning the next prime ministerial election, these nonmainstream politicians began to attack Nakasone (Tomabechi 1985, 24–25). Faced with strong political pressures, Nakasone accepted fiscal stimulus measures.

Earlier, in 1979, the Japanese government had adopted the *minus ceiling* principle for its annual budget in order to rebuild finance after the surge of budget deficits emerged in the wake of the First Oil Shock. According to this principle, each year the general account expenditure in the government budget should be reduced by 10 percent, and government investment should be reduced by 5 percent. In July 1987, the Ministry of Finance changed the budget ceiling from minus 10 percent and minus 5 percent to 0 percent. In late May 1987, the Japanese government adopted a comprehensive fiscal expansion program of 6 trillion yen, equivalent to 1.8 percent of GNP (Kojo 1993, 227–228). As part of this stimulus package, local governments adopted three large-scale urban development plans in the greater Tokyo metropolitan area. These plans not only stimulated a rise in land prices but also triggered increases in the stock prices of companies that owned land.

This expansionary fiscal policy was adopted after the Bank of Japan lowered its interest rates, having seriously overestimated the economic situation. As early as October 1987, a survey taken by the Bank of Japan showed that the number of corporations reporting their business situation as "good" had begun to rise. In the first quarter of 1986, corporate profits had declined in all industries. Although the manufacturing industry suffered the most in the rapid appreciation of the yen after the Plaza Accord, the decline of its profits lasted for only two quarters. In 1987, the average corporate profits in all industries increased 31.7 percent, and those of manufacturing increased 34.5 percent; both numbers were the highest level ever (Mitsuhashi and Uchida 1995, 189–190). After the Plaza Accord, the financial assets of private corporations increased rapidly. Under such circumstances, a record low interest rate was already problematic. Such an expansionary monetary policy should have been enough to boost the economy. On top of the expansionary monetary policy, however, the Japanese government adopted an expansionary fiscal policy. This meant that Japan was using two similarly directed policy instruments. Because an increase in public spending was closely related to the construction industry and the real estate market, Japan's policy mix not only led to an oversupply of money but also channeled private investments into financial speculation.

Japan was repeating the mistake it had made after the Nixon Shock. In both cases, the Japanese government used a policy mix of both an expansionary monetary policy and an expansionary fiscal policy after the yen had appreciated rapidly. In both cases, moreover, the Bank of Japan first lowered the interest rate, an action that, along with its intervention in the foreign exchange market, led to an oversupply of money. When the effect of these actions became obvious, the state added an expansionary fiscal policy. In 1972–1973, Japan kept the currency market open after the United States closed the window of gold. This, too, led to a rapid increase in the money supply as private corporations sold dollars and purchased yen before the anticipated appreciation of the yen. Then the Satō cabinet adopted an expansionary fiscal policy, and it was further enhanced by Tanaka's plan for industrial reallocation. In 1985–1987, the Bank of Japan increased the money supply by buying dollars and selling yen after the Plaza Accord caused a temporary economic slowdown. The Bank of Japan also lowered interest rates to the lowest level in history. Both measures had already served to stimulate the economy. At the moment the economy was just beginning to recover, however, the government adopted a large expansionary fiscal policy package. In both cases, this combination of an expansionary fiscal policy and an expansionary monetary policy was the major factor leading to the bubble. In contrast, in 1978–1979, when the yen appreciated rapidly and the government also adopted an expansionary fiscal policy, the Bank of Japan kept raising interest rates, tightening the money supply. The bubble did not appear.

Critics of this policy pointed out that the government could not rely on a macroeconomic policy alone to respond to the appreciation of the yen after the Plaza Accord, because a low dollar would push Japanese corporations to shift production overseas; as a result, the benefits of low dollar and high yen might not be returned domestically. Low interest rates would further increase the oversupply of money, leading to speculation in the land and stock markets. Critics argued that the government should pursue aggressive structural reform rather than simply an expansionary fiscal policy. Otherwise, the Japanese economy might end up with deindustrialization, in which domestic demand would decline while imbalances of payments would continue (Ōuchi 1987). In addition, they maintained that intervention by the central banks in Japan and European countries – an action aimed at stabilizing exchange rates – had increased the money supply and created the danger of inflation. When the growth rate of the money supply doubled that of the GNP and increased more than 10 percent per year, the Japanese monetary authority could no longer simply formulate its policy according to the single consideration of stabilizing the exchange rate (Tsuruta 1987).

Against this macroeconomic policy environment, Japanese corporate governance began to yield different outcomes in micro-level corporate behavior. In what Saskia Sassen (1991, 70) calls the "secularization of finance," Japanese corporations began to rely more heavily on equity finance by issuing convertible bonds in domestic markets and warrant bonds in overseas markets to raise capital. "Convertible bonds" refers to bonds that could be converted to stocks under certain conditions. As a financial instrument, convertible bonds combined both capital gains and a guaranteed interest payment. Warrant bonds worked similarly. Attached to these was the right to buy newly issued stocks within a certain percentage of the amount of the bonds. Until 1986, the total annual amount of equity finance issued by Japanese corporations was about 4 trillion yen. During the peak of the bubble, that figure jumped to 12 trillion yen in 1987, 18 trillion yen in 1988, and 26 trillion yen in 1989. The total amount of equity finance in 1989 alone had gone beyond that of the seven years 1980–1986 combined (Miyazaki 1992, 135).

In the second half of the 1980s, two trends took place simultaneously. On the one hand, big corporations increasingly relied on self-capital. On the other hand, the medium-size and small companies increasingly relied on bank loans. Bank loans as a percentage of the total corporate finance of big corporations remained at 30 percent after 1987. In contrast, that of medium-size and small companies increased from 30.7 percent in 1985 to 39.8 percent in 1990. Between 1975 and 1989, the proportion of self-capital in big corporations increased from 17.0 percent to 36.4 percent. Before 1986, whereas self-capital increased, the total financial assets held by corporations increased very slowly. In other words, the increase in self-capital was driven primarily by the increase in reserved profits. Between 1986 and 1989, self-capital increased more rapidly. This time, however, it was driven primarily by equity finance through the financial markets. The pattern of corporate finance in Japan changed during the 1970s from indirect financing based on bank loans to internal financing based on reservation of profits, and again in the 1980s on direct financing sustained by equity finance (Miyazaki 1992, 162–163).

These changes had profound implications for corporate governance. As discussed in Chapter 4, institutional shareholders could not control management, and Japanese managers had a great degree of autonomy. In the high growth period, however, the main banks had some degree of leverage over corporations, and the Bank of Japan's monetary policy served to monitor the investment behavior of Japanese corporations because tightening the money supply would immediately reduce the availability of investment capital. As Japanese corporations began to raise capital through the financial markets, the main banks completely lost their leverage. In addition, the effectiveness of the Bank of Japan's monetary policy as the ultimate monitoring function was also weakened because corporations no longer depended on bank loans to the same degree. By engaging in equity finance, corporations rapidly increased their investment risks because of the system's weak control and monitoring.

In the 1980s, Japanese corporations were able to move quickly toward equity finance because of certain mechanisms and institutions, especially business groups that were devised to strengthen coordination in the high growth period. Between 1983 and 1989, Japanese stock shares increased three times. According to Miyazaki Yoshikazu's analysis of equity finance by the six major keiretsu in Japan during the 1980s (1992, 168–169), between 1987 and 1989 alone, more than 20 billion new shares of stock were issued. In comparison with the number of new shares issued between 1980 and 1985, the number of new shares issued between 1985 and 1990 was greater in all six major keiretsu. Between 1980 and 1985, the number of shares of stock increased 22.2 percent in the Mitsui group, 20.1 percent in the Sumitomo group, 15.0 percent in the Mitsubishi group, 17.7 percent in the Fuyo group, 16.9 percent in the Miwa group, and 18.1 percent in the Daiichi group. Between 1985 and 1990, however, the shares issued increased 27.6 percent in the Mitsui group, 21.2 percent in the Sumitomo group, 26.9 percent in the Mitsubishi group, 23.4 percent in the Fuyo group, 23.3 percent in the Miwa group, and 21.1 percent in the Daiichi group.

Who bought these stocks? Given that Japanese corporations focused on the stabilization of shareholders in the early 1950s and the late 1960s, how did they prevent hostile takeovers when the entire country was obsessed with financial speculation? The major strategy was reciprocal shareholding. Between 1980 and 1990, the proportion of reciprocal shareholding within the groups had declined slightly in all six groups, with the Mitsui group declining from 17.62 percent to 16.54 percent, the Sumitomo group from 26.74 percent to 24.06 percent, the Mitsubishi group from 29.26 percent to 26.89 percent, the Fuji group from 16.26 percent to 15.44 percent, the Miwa group from 16.78 percent to 16.64 percent, and the Daiichi group from 14.12 percent to 12.06 percent (Miyazaki 1992, 167). Given the rapid increase in the number of new shares and the relatively small decline in the proportion of reciprocal shareholding within the business groups, research done by NHK concludes, "It cannot be denied that the unique Japanese practice of reciprocal shareholding among corporations made the huge amount of equity finance, 60 trillion yen in three years, possible" (cited by Miyazaki 1992, 166). Without the practice of reciprocal shareholding, Japanese corporations could hardly have carried that huge amount (Miyazaki 1992, 169).

The active role played by business groups in the equity financing of big Japanese corporations shows that the strength of the Japanese economic system in coordination had become a weakness in the new era of the globalization of finance. In the 1950s and 1960s, the strength of business groups in coordination was represented by their strong growth orientation. The one-set investment strategy pushed Japanese keiretsu to compete vigorously with one another to invest in production capacity and technological transfer in new frontier industries. Despite the weak monitoring by banks of their corporate borrowers and the weak control by shareholders over management, aggressive corporate investment was limited mainly to the field of production. In the 1980s, however, that had changed. As the Japanese government relied on an expansionary fiscal policy to adjust Japan's trade surplus, more business opportunities were created in large-scale construction projects than in production. The strength of coordination implemented by Japanese corporations, originally devised to promote production, now was being used to play the money game through equity finance.

BANKS DURING THE BUBBLE

The liberalization of finance exerted a profound impact on Japanese banks. Before the liberalization, the regulated yet low interest rate created a strong demand for capital. This situation provided banks with a good opportunity to make profits by producing and processing information. After the liberalization, however, banks had to compete vigorously for borrowers by lowering their interest rates. As a result, their profits also declined. In addition, the liberalization of finance also meant deregulation of corporate bonds, something that provided more alternatives for corporations to raise capital. Big corporations, which had accumulated enormous amounts of capital, obtained greater power in their relationship with the main banks (Keizai Kikakuchō 1996, 297–298).

The pattern of banks' aggressive lending continued during the bubble in the 1980s. Figure 6.2 shows that between 1980 and 1989, whereas the total loans to all industries increased about 120 percent, loans to the real estate industry increased more than 300 percent. Most of the loans to nonbanking industries went to real estate speculation, which increased more than 700 percent. Figure 4.1 and Figure 6.2 show that the pattern of aggressive investments and the pattern of aggressive capital supply during the high growth period remained unchanged during the bubble. Just as Japanese corporations used financial tools to compete intensively with one another in covering losses in their real business operations, Japanese banks also entered into fierce competition. In the past, big corporations had been the major customers of big city banks. As these customers became financially independent, city banks turned to medium-size and small companies as their new borrowers. The trust banks, which had been the major financiers of these medium-size and small companies, then shifted their capital to stocks. In 1986, about 400 trillion yen in Japanese corporate assets were involved in zai'tech. Of this number, 90 percent was invested in relatively safe assets, and 10 percent demonstrated a high-risk and high-return orientation. In other words, about 40 trillion yen was invested in the special trust fund market (Naitō 1986, 19).

Let's look at the situation in more detail. When big corporations rushed to equity finance, banks were under strong pressure to find new borrowers, and banks increased their loans to medium-size and small companies dramatically. According to official statistics, among the total loans provided by Japanese banks in 1975, the share held by companies with capital less than 100 million yen was 33.3 percent; the share held by companies that had capital of between 100 million yen and 1 billion yen was 25.5 percent; and the share held by companies with capital of more than 1 billion yen was 41.2 percent. As big corporations began to leave the main banks, the shares of each of these groups changed. In 1980, the share of the first group (capital less than 100 million yen) increased to 39.7 percent; that of the second and the third groups (capital of 100 million to 1 billion yen and capital of more than 1 billion yen) changed to 27.0 percent and 33.3 percent, respectively. The practice of zai'tech by big corporations in the early 1980s accelerated the trend. By 1985, the share of the first group further increased to 44.7 percent and that of the second and the third groups dropped to 25.2 and 30.0 percent, respectively. As big corporations began to rely on equity finance, Japanese banks lent more to the medium-size and small companies (capital less than 100 million yen). In 1990, the proportion of total Japanese bank loans held by such companies increased to an astonishing 65.1 percent, almost two-thirds. That of companies whose capital was 100 million yen to 1 billion yen declined to 12.5 percent, and that of companies whose capital was more than 1 billion yen declined to 21.7 percent (Keizai Kikakuchō 1996, 300).

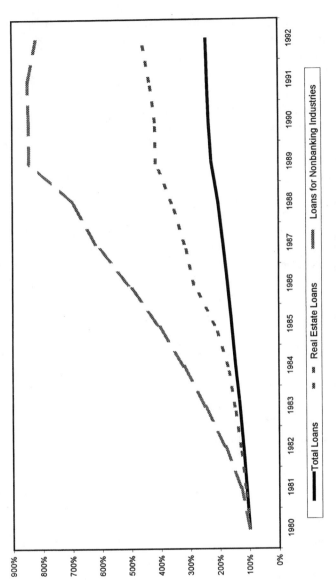

Figure 6.2. *The changes in real estate-related loans (by percentage).*

Source: Based on the data in Mitsuhashi and Uchida, 1994, p. 201.

Total Loans   Real Estate Loans   Loans for Nonbanking Industries

During the 1980s, banks emphasized loans to medium-size and small companies that used land or stocks as collateral. Of total bank loans, the proportion of bank loans with land as collateral increased from 17 percent in 1984 to more than 20 percent after 1987. The proportion of bank loans with stocks as collateral increased from 1.5 percent to more than 2.5 percent. Because both land prices and stock prices increased rapidly in 1986, the borrowing capacity measured by the values of land and stocks as collateral also increased accordingly. This increase enabled these companies to borrow more money and then to use the money in new financial speculation. Between 1986 and 1989, both equity finance and bank loans increased more than 20 percent each year. These loans served to increase credits and became an important contributing factor to the rise of the bubble (Miyazaki 1992, 139–141). More importantly, among the medium-size and small companies that borrowed from banks using land or stock as collateral, there was a clear pattern of variation among different industries. Distribution, service, construction, real estate, finance, insurance, leasing – all these industries borrowed huge amounts of money. Between December 1985 and December 1989, medium-size and small companies borrowed 37.7 trillion yen from city banks, 8.0 trillion yen from the Long-Term Trust Bank, and 10.3 trillion yen from trust banks. Among these, the distribution and service industries received 16.3 trillion yen, the construction and real estate industries received 17.7 trillion yen, and the finance, insurance, and leasing industries received 17.0 trillion yen. These industries were directly related to the sectors that were the first to collapse when the bubble burst (Miyazaki 1992, 170).

The expansionary fiscal policy triggered rises in stock prices by providing good investment opportunities. At that time, the orthodox price/earning ratio was no longer able to legitimize stock prices. The Japanese financial industry created a new criterion, evaluating stocks by their "potential value." According to this criterion, if a company held land and the price of land tended to rise, then the company had high potential value, and its stock should go up. The situation looked similar to that of Internet stocks in the United States in the late 1990s. When the money supply increased rapidly, these new urban development plans provided new opportunities for speculation in real estate and the stock market. As a result, both land prices and stock prices jumped and then collapsed. According to Mitsuhashi and Uchida (1994, 209), there were three mechanisms that caused the rise in stock prices. The first was the rise of stocks in general, which increased the use of equity finance. Then the increase in equity finance pumped more money into stock market speculation, which in turn raised stock prices. The second mechanism was the price increases of individual stocks. The rise in the price of land owned by a company and the rise of the value of its stock increased the "potential value" of the company. This in turn further raised the price of its stocks. In the third mechanism, stocks and land held by banks as collateral increased the potential value of banks, which could then make more loans. This in turn raised the price of the bank's stocks (Mitsuhashi and Uchida 1994, 209).

After the First Oil Shock, Japanese corporations ceased to use the main banks for their capital supply. Driven by the need to improve efficiency, corporations tried to reduce their interest payments by paying loans held by the main banks and reducing their investments in production capacity. Although the main banks continued to be the center of business groups, their leverage with corporations was weakened significantly. The monitoring of corporations by the main banks was never effective in postwar Japan. Compared with the period after the Nixon Shock and the First Oil Shock, however, the banks' monitoring was relatively better in the period of the 1950s and 1960s because as long as Japanese corporations faced a shortage of capital, banks had a bigger say in their internal affairs.

THE TWIST OF TECHNOLOGICAL INNOVATION

Facing the challenge posed by the Nixon Shock and the First Oil Shock, Japan reexamined its long-standing belief in the strength of coordination and evaluated whether it should continue to rely on it to improve efficiency via technological innovation. The oil shock changed the Japanese perception that heavy-chemical industries constituted the optimal industrial structure. These industries' oil dependency threatened the Japanese economy because of its potential for making Japan more vulnerable to outside forces. At the time, moreover, a transition of the industrial structure was critical to Japanese economic survival. MITI started two important projects aimed at reducing the Japanese economy's dependence on oil. In 1974, MITI's Sunshine Plan focused on developing substitute energy sources; then in 1978, MITI introduced its Moonlight Plan, which emphasized energy-saving technology. Meanwhile, the Japanese also quickly shifted the emphasis of their industrial structure to high-tech industries. As a result, Japan was able to reduce its dependence on oil for energy from 77 percent in 1973 to 56 percent in 1985 (Hara 1995, 101). Sustained by competitiveness in energy saving, pollution control, high performance, and technologies with a high information density, Japanese automobiles and home electronics dominated the international markets in the 1980s (Mitsuhashi and Uchida 1994, 87).

Japanese industrial policy has promoted the development of knowledge-intensive industries since the 1970s. In 1973, the Long-Term Vision of Industrial Structure, published by MITI, singled out automobiles, industrial machinery, electronics, and materials as its four major focuses. MITI main-tained that from that time forward, state industrial policy should shift from a traditional emphasis on the distribution of resources in production to the prediction of the needs of civilian products and the promotion of research and development. MITI also asserted that in the future the state would play the role of a third party, operating between consumers and producers and between industries and companies in the same industry. The government not only would provide assistance to private companies through its fiscal and taxation policies but also would provide money directly to sponsor research in impor-tant industrial projects.

In the past, even though Japanese corporations had performed well in international markets, few products they offered were based on new tech-nologies Japan could claim as its own. Corporations imported technologies, and even the products themselves, in order to remain competitive in the inter-national marketplace. By the late 1970s, however, Japanese corporations started mass production of new products based on new technologies – their own. In two areas – automobile and home electronics – Japanese corporations had sizable successes in the international markets. Japanese compact cars, which were highly energy-efficient, increased their market share in the United States from 440,000 in 1970 to 2,470,000 in 1980. In home elec-tronics, Japanese corporations invented VCRs, compact discs, big-screen tele-visions, word processors, and fax machines. They were also highly competitive in making electronic watches, digital watches, headphone stereos, video cameras, computer games, digital notebooks, and computer-assisted lenses (Harada 1998, 34–35). In spite of these successes, however, the Japanese economy had a negative growth of 0.2 percent in 1974 as a result of the decline of private investment in production capacity and housing and gov-ernment investment in infrastructure. Only exports continued to grow, with an annual increase of 23.2 percent. Until 1977, the growth rate of exports continued to be higher than that of total national investments, both private and public. Measured by the U.S. dollar, Japanese exports jumped from $36.9 billion in 1973 to $103 billion in 1979. Among the major exported Japa-nese products, the automobile had a rapid increase, replacing oil tanks as the core export. During the 1970s, North America, Western Europe, and South-east Asia became three major export destinations, absorbing massive numbers of Japanese exports. The share of these three counties of total Japanese exports increased from 59 percent in 1975 to 66 percent in 1980 (Rekishigaku Kenkyūkai 1991, Vol. 5, 10–11).

The emphasis on technological innovation led Japan to great success in improving productivity in the exports-related sector. In comparison with Western European countries, the Japanese success was related to its reliance on a major component: technological innovation. This was not a purely distributional strategy. As Linda Weiss (1998, 114) points out in her comparative studies,

> The critical problem in the Swedish system is not so much the fact of distribution (what Peter Katzenstein has called "domestic compensation") as the absence of a developmental complement to balance distributive goals. In short the one-sidedness of the formula, particularly marked in Sweden, produced an institutional complex promoting a strategy of employment and distribution without a corresponding focus on stimulating industrial growth.

Japan introduced the strategy of relying on technological innovation to improve efficiency after the collapse of the Bretton Woods system and the First Oil Shock. In a typical Anglo-Saxon business, an efficiency strategy means reducing the production cost per unit. The first cut is often the labor force. In Japanese business, an efficiency strategy also means reducing production costs. But instead of reducing the number of employees, the company achieves the reduction in costs by adopting advanced production technology and strengthening coordination among all those involved in production.

After the Plaza Accord and the appreciation of the yen, Japan failed to identify new strategic industries and to conduct significant structural reforms. Instead, Japanese corporations attempted to improve profitability by engaging in financial speculation. By moving toward the service industry, Japanese corporations began to lose one of their traditional strengths.

This presents a puzzle concerning the Japanese economy in the 1990s. We know that between 1988 and 1990, Japanese corporations aggressively increased their investment in production capacity. The level of investment even exceeded the level during the high growth period. Why, then, after spending so much money in research and development, did Japanese corporations fail to strengthen their competitiveness in the 1990s? The answer is that much of the investment by major manufacturing industries, such as those in precise machinery and electronics, was aimed at further enlarging production capacity rather than creating new, revolutionary products. New products indeed kept coming to the market, but they were driven more by what is called "bubble technology" than by innovation. *Bubble technology* refers to technology that adds an insignificant new feature that is appealing but does not add any new substantial function (Uchihashi and Yakushiji 1993). During the bubble, capital index – a measure of capital cost per unit of added value – increased rapidly. This was misinterpreted by the Japanese White Paper on the Economy as an indicator of technological innovation.

According to Katsumata Hisayoshi (1995, 251), however, it should have been interpreted as a decline in profits and capital productivity.

Ironically, although Japan has often been called "the information society" and Japanese corporations have been well known for their capacity for collecting information, they were left far behind in their competition with the United States in the information revolution. Between 1985 and 1993, the amount of investment by American corporations in information technology, as a proportion of total private capital formation, increased from about 20 percent to 35 percent. During that same time, the proportion of the same investments by Japanese corporations increased only from 13 percent to 18 percent. According to a Nakatani study, by the mid 1990s, only 9.9 percent of Japanese offices were using personal computers, in contrast to 41.7 percent of American offices. The market cap for databases in Japan was only about 220 billion yen; that in the United States was six times higher (Nakatani 1996). In January 1997, the Internet had 16,146 host addresses. Among them, the United States occupied 10,113. In contrast, Japan had only 734, constituting only 7.3 percent as many as those of the United States.

According to Nakatani Iwao (1996, 285–286), the difference between Japan and the United States in coping with the information revolution lay in the difference in corporate strength in the two countries. Japanese corporations had formerly been strong in coordination, especially horizontal coordination. In contrast, American corporations had a clearly defined system of responsibility in which each individual employee was given room for creativity while the executive decision maker allocated resources strategically. Nevertheless, U.S. workers were weak in horizontal coordination. As a result, in all industries whose production required a high level of horizontal coordination, such as automobiles, home electronics, and machine tools, Japanese corporations were able to compete effectively. In contrast, American corporations, sustained by their strength in individual creativity and control of resource allocation, were able to maintain their competitiveness in the medical, petrochemical, aerospace, and computer software industries. In the 1990s, the information revolution helped American corporations overcome their traditional weakness in horizontal coordination and increase their productivity. The information technologies, moreover, broke various boundaries among individuals, departments, companies, and even nation-states. American corporations have obtained enormous strength in this regard. Japanese corporations had achieved strong coordination and were able to share information in a closed system, but when the information revolution brought about an open system, Japanese corporations confronted a significant challenge.

In his recent analysis of the reverse course of the Japanese economy, Richard Katz emphasized that the Japanese economy matured after the 1970s. Katz held that there were many infant industries in the 1950s; government protection was needed and made sense. As the Japanese economy matured, however, the continuation of such protection became self-defeating. Citing Dale Jorgenson, Katz pointed out that between 1960 and 1979, only one-third of the increase of Japanese productivity could be attributed to improvement in efficiency, and two-thirds came simply from shifting capital, labor, and output from the farm to the factory and, within manufacturing, from sectors such as textiles to industries such as machinery. As the Japanese economy grew, productivity gaps lessened and the pace of structural shifts slowed (Katz 1998, 138). In the 1970s, both the state and private corporations could still identify a new direction, moving away from the heavy-chemical toward the automobile and home electronics industries. The problem was that these two industries in the end provided only 12 percent of Japanese employment (Harada 1998, 36). The failure to occupy a leading position in the emerging information revolution and the shift toward the service industry during the bubble became part of the reason for the stagnation of the Japanese economy in the 1990s.

FROM PRODUCTION TO SERVICE

Under the pressure of the high yen, the focus of the multidimensional integration of the keiretsu shifted toward the service industry, which aimed at maintaining profitability by entering new business fields. Facing the appreciation of the yen, few companies had a strong incentive to invest in production capacity despite low interest rates. The reason was that when wholesale prices declined about 11 percent in 1986 compared with those of 1985, interest rates became very high. If Japanese corporations had invested in production capacity, they would have ended up losing money. Instead, they tried to reduce inventory (Naitō 1986, 17). As an alternative, they adopted the strategy of entering new business fields. In 1986, among 1,888 public companies listed on the Tokyo Stock Exchange, 371 had added new businesses. On average, each company added 3.9 new businesses. For example, New Japan Steel published a long-term business plan in which it indicated its intention to involve itself in new materials, electronic information systems, and health care. Automobile maker Mazda also extended its business operations to information processing, telecommunications, leisure, publishing, finance, leasing, personnel supply, education, and transportation. A number of big corporations even established their own colleges and universities (Niwa 1988). Some commentators pointed out that previously,

Table 6.2 *Financial Profits at Major Japanese Manufacturing Firms*

Manufacturing Firm	Financial Profits	Percentage of pre-tax
	(billions of yen)	
Toyota Motor	149.6	37.6
Matsushita Electric	109.2	58.8
Nissan Motor	89.4	65.3
Sharp Electric	28.0	73.2
SONY	27.2	62.8
Honda Motor	22.7	26.1
Sanyo Electric	21.5	134.2
Isuzu Motors	16.4	1,962.4

Source: Calder 1997, p. 20. Permission located on p. xi, this volume.

American management had been criticized for paying too much attention to short-term investments and Japanese management had been praised for making long-term investments. But now, in the boom of zai'tech, Japanese entrepreneurship had begun to decline (Itō 1985, 42–43).

As Table 6.2 shows, during the bubble the gains of Japanese corporations, including some household names in the West, through financial speculation became an important source of profits.

Resort development and luxury apartment complexes were the two popular investment choices. In the late 1980s, all types of industrial corporations engaged in the resort development boom. By 1988, there were 75 development plans covering about one-third of the total Japanese territory. Companies that had invested in golf courses financed their projects by selling advance memberships. In the 1980s, Japan witnessed a second boom in corporations investing in leisure industries; the first leisure boom had occurred during the 1972–1973 bubble. Back in the 1960s, most leisure businesses were operated by the electric railway companies and concentrated on golf clubs and hotels. After the Nixon Shock, even textile companies, trading companies, and food companies entered the game. In the bowling alley industry, 17 companies entered in 1970, 46 in 1971, and 30 in 1972. By 1973, Japan had 3,515 bowling alleys. These investments, however, took heavy losses during the First Oil Shock. The number of bowling alleys in 1976 was drastically reduced to 879 (Okano 1988, 51–52). In the second leisure boom in the 1980s, the Tokyo Disneyland theme park, a 150 billion yen investment, exerted a great impact. Before it opened in 1983, few Japanese had believed that it could generate 10 million visitors per year; at that time,

Tokyo's population was only 10 million. Later, the Tokyo Disneyland indeed succeeded in generating 10 million visitors every year. Its success was attractive to Japanese corporations, especially those in depressed industries. Because the appreciation of the yen had intensified competition in these industries, investing in the leisure industry became a survival strategy. By building high-value-added leisure resorts, many companies in depressed industries aimed at pursuing high growth (Okano 1988).

Golf club memberships became an investment instrument. Before the 1980s bubble, Japan had twice experienced golf club membership booms – once in 1961–1963 and again in 1972–1973. In the 1972–1973 boom, more than 100 golf clubs were built within one year. These clubs suffered greatly during the First Oil Shock. The 1987 boom was similar to the earlier one inasmuch as both were driven by surplus money. The difference was that in the 1987 boom many people who did not play golf bought golf club memberships purely for speculation. After they made money by buying and selling one membership, they would shift to a new one. By contrast, in the 1972–1973 boom, those who bought memberships tended to hold them, using them as collateral to borrow money to buy new memberships. The interest rate for membership loans in 1985 was as high as 17 percent. During the bubble, the market value of one membership in the most expensive club reached 350 million yen. A British Broadcasting Corporation journalist noted that 300 million yen, the fee for a single membership in Japan, would build an entire new course in Britain (*Shūkan Tōyō Keizai* 1987).

Luxury apartment complexes were another target of corporate investment. Because land prices increased quickly, many Japanese chose to buy these housing units rather than detached houses. During the bubble, the price of luxury apartments in the Tokyo metropolitan area increased rapidly. Until 1985, between 10,000 and 20,000 new luxury apartments were waiting for buyers. In 1987, that number declined to 2,000, the lowest in history. The smaller supply was driven by the pressure of demand and rising land prices. In one case, when a real estate company opened a new 252-unit luxury apartment complex for sale, 8,500 buyers rushed in. The entire complex was sold within one day. Because the construction companies could not meet the high demand, they sometimes resorted to lotteries to assign buying rights. Some lottery winners even made fortunes by selling their buying rights.

Other commodities, including pension insurance, diamonds, and famous paintings, also became financial instruments for both corporate and individual investors. Pension insurance (*yōrō hoken*) refers to a financial instrument in which buyers make a one-time payment (instead of making incremental monthly payments); after the period specified in the contract, the investor receives the amount of the payment plus interest. Between 1982 and 1986, new contracts for pension insurance increased fivefold. Between April 1986 and December 1986, life insurance companies collected 2.9 trillion yen from sales. Before the tax reform of 1987, pension insurance was allowed to generate a higher return. According to Japanese tax law, annual interest income of less than 500,000 yen was not subject to taxation. For this reason, the most popular pension insurance during the bubble was the one for which consumers paid 1.2 million yen and received 1.69 million yen in five years (*Shūkan Tōyō Keizai* 1987).

Of course, not all the money went into outside investments. Japanese corporations also invested a lot of money in production capacity. Corporate investments in production capacity increased 8.6 percent in 1987 and 16.6 percent in 1988, breaking the record set during the high growth period. It remained high at 14.1 percent in 1989 and 11.2 percent in 1990. The ratio between production capacity investment and the GNP was 18.7 percent in 1988, 20.5 percent in 1989, and 21.5 percent in 1990 (Mitsuhashi and Uchida 1994, 191). Overinvestment in production capacity in the late 1980s was one of the important reasons that the Japanese economic recovery was slow in the 1990s. The bubble was created by corporate speculation in real estate and stocks. At this late stage, it also began to be sustained by aggressive investment in production capacity. After the bubble burst, it took a long time for Japan to absorb its overbuilt production capacity.

Even local governments engaged in financial speculation. In the 1980s bubble, there was also a boom in the establishment of trusts for publicly owned lands. By late 1986, according to one statistic, 4 prefecture governments had already adopted such trusts. An additional 8 prefecture governments and 35 city governments were in the process of examining them. The number of land trusts increased rapidly. At the end of March 1984, there was one case. By the end of March 1985, the number had increased to 75. Another year later, it had jumped to 305. At the end of September 1986, there were 504 land trusts. Among these, 282 were from individuals; 190 cases involved the management of office buildings; 149 cases involved luxury apartments and apartment complexes; 142 cases concerned multiple-use buildings. Tokyo occupied 235 cases. Many of these trusts were indeed a successful application of zai'tech. For example, the Tokyo city government established a trust for a piece of land it owned. It received proposals for a multiple-use office building complex from eight trust banks. It selected three of the eight. Together, the trust dividends it received from these banks were 2.4 times higher than it originally estimated (*Shūkan Tōyō Keizai* 1986a, 131–132).

Land trusts were regarded as having many merits. The trust owner could enjoy the benefits of development of the land in the form of trust dividends. Although still the owner of the land, meanwhile, the trust owner did not have to take care of the land, thereby reducing the financial as well as personnel burden and relying on private sector know-how for planning, management, and business operation. By doing so, the trust could carry out public policy regarding the land and promote an exchange between the government and the private sector. These dividends could be used as further construction capital (*Shūkan Tōyō Keizai* 1986a, 133).

THE BEGINNING OF DEINDUSTRIALIZATION

The appreciation of the yen rapidly increased the assets both of Japanese banks and of corporations. Rising production costs pushed Japanese banks and corporations into overseas markets for new investment opportunities, and the Japanese became major players in international expansion.

The overseas investments of Japanese financial institutions increased from $380 million in 1980 to $3.81 billion in 1985, and to $7.24 billion in 1986. The proportion of financial institutions in the total Japanese overseas investment increased from 8.1 percent to 32.4 percent in 1986. Not only did the financial institutions establish overseas branch offices and engage in mergers and acquisitions, but they also bought many real estate assets (Keizai Kikakuchō 1987, 270).

Driven by the high yen, Japanese corporations also rushed into overseas investing. *The Economist* reported that, surprisingly, Japanese investments in overseas markets in 1986 were not concentrated in automobile or other manufacturing fields but rather in finance, insurance, and real estate. Among the total Japanese investments in the United States in 1986, only 17 percent were in manufacturing (most of these were made by auto parts makers, who had followed the automakers overseas). In contrast, 32.4 percent of Japanese overseas investments in 1986 went to finance and insurance, 17.9 percent went to real estate, 8.3 percent went to commerce, 8.6 percent went to transportation, and 8.7 percent went to other service industries (*The Economist* 1988/7/4). Japanese real estate companies also invested heavily in overseas markets. Because land prices in Japanese urban areas rose sharply in 1985–1987, the real estate industry had made huge profits, which substantially increased its investment capital. Because the interest rate was very low in Japan, real estate companies could borrow even more money and then invest it overseas. Before 1985 the accumulated Japanese investments in U.S. real estate were only between $2 billion and $3 billion. In contrast, in 1986 alone, the Japanese invested between $5 billion and $6 billion in U.S. real estate markets. More than 70 corporations engaged in real estate investments, doubling or tripling the Japanese investments in the United States within one year (Hashimoto 1987).

Among the Japanese investments in overseas real estate markets, the United States was the top destination. New York, Hawaii, and Los Angeles were the three most desired locations (*Shūkan Tōyō Keizai* 1986a). At that time, the United States reformed its tax laws, increasing taxes on capital gains in 1987, raising taxes from 20 percent to 28 percent for individuals and from 28 percent to 34 percent for corporations. Therefore, many owners of real estate tried to sell their assets before the laws became effective (Hashimoto 1987, 79). Corporations were the chief players in overseas real estate investments. In the New York market, 90 percent of the purchases made by Japanese corporations were aimed at profit-making. In Hawaii, in contrast, between 30 percent and 40 percent of such investments were aimed at using the property as corporate resorts. In contrast to Hawaii, where 80 percent of Japanese buyers signed contracts after one visit, in New York many Japanese corporations bought buildings without seeing them. Individual investors also increased rapidly in the mid-1980s rush to invest in overseas real estate. Whereas in the past, most Japanese individual buyers of foreign real estate had been either doctors or owners of medium-size and small companies, in the 1986 rush, even salaried men joined the game. Buying a condominium on Fifth Avenue in New York City or a cottage-style house on Kauai Island in Hawaii became a symbol of both financial and cultural capital (*Shūkan Tōyō Keizai* 1986a).

Of course, Japanese corporations also invested in overseas production capacity. Such investments, however, also reflected the deindustrialization that was occurring at home. Under the pressure of the high yen, many high-tech industries that had helped Japan survive the external challenges of the Nixon Shock and the two oil shocks in the 1970s began to move their production bases to overseas locations. By 1985, for example, Matsushita, the largest home electronics maker in Japan, had shifted 42 percent of its production overseas. When the exchange rate reached the level of one dollar equaling 180 yen, more corporations shifted their production bases overseas, leaving only their research and development operations in Japan. The Japanese then shifted their exports from goods to information and technology (Ōuchi 1987). Moving production bases to Asian countries was also popular among big Japanese manufacturers. After the yen appreciated quickly, Japanese imports from the newly industrialized economies (NIEs) of Asia increased. Many Japanese corporations were also concerned that companies in the NIEs would become their major competitors in the U.S. markets. To meet this challenge, Japanese corporations considered establishing subordinate companies in Southeast Asian countries. They perceived themselves as playing the role of a headquarters specializing in management and planning. Japanese corporations realized that even if they refused to transfer their technologies to Southeast Asia, American or European corporations would do it because they were all under pressure to improve efficiency. Rather than lose the competition on this front, Japanese corporations argued, they should take action to establish production bases in Southeast Asia (Narita 1986).

After the Plaza Accord, medium-size and small companies were under strong pressure. As increasing numbers of big corporations moved their production bases overseas, medium-size and small companies began to lose their contracts. By the 1970s, Japanese home electronics already had production bases in Southeast Asia. Some makers of color televisions and VCRs also established their production bases in North America and Western Europe while retaining the production of high-value-added products and of research and development of high-tech products in Japan. In the 1980s, all major Japanese automobile makers started establishing production bases in the United States. Then in the late 1980s, the internationalizing of production began to exert a great impact on the business environment of the medium-size and small companies. As more big corporations began overseas production, they increased their orders of raw materials and parts from host country companies because these companies could supply materials at much lower production costs. As a result, medium-size and small Japanese companies received fewer orders for raw materials and parts for exports-oriented products (Ishiro 1988).

Driven by the pressure of the high yen, Japanese manufacturers in the exports-related sector bought parts from Asian countries. This practice put direct pressure on prices for parts in Japan. In the late 1980s, some big corporations used the Asian market prices of parts, which were about 50 to 60 percent lower than those in Japan, to negotiate prices in the Japanese markets. In exchange for the continuation of parts orders from big corporations, medium-size and small companies in Japan had to bring costs down drastically. In many cases, it became a war of survival for these companies, allowing them no profits and merely keeping them busy. Thus, for these companies, the appreciation of the yen after the Plaza Accord began a new era – one of competition with other Asian countries. According to research by the Economic Research Institute of the Machinery Promotion Association in 1988, the percentage of Asian companies in the NIEs that could not compete with the medium-size and small Japanese companies ranged from 34 to 54 percent in different production fields. Three years later, however, this number had declined to between 12 percent and 21 percent. At the time, only between 18 percent and 32 percent of Asian companies in the NIEs could manufacture products with a given design. Three years later, however, the percentage had increased to between 36 percent and 45 percent (Ishiro 1988, 26).

CONCLUSION

With the disappearance of the contingent conditions in the international economic order that had sustained the high growth period, the roads taken by the Japanese economy since the early 1970s caused the country's economic system to malfunction. The intrinsic dilemma between coordination and control took the system by storm.

The rise and subsequent burst of the two bubbles in the early 1970s and the late 1980s prove the reverse of the Bretton Woods system: that the depression-preventing nature of this system lay in its control over the free flow of capital and a fixed exchange rate. With these two measures, a national government could pursue the goals of promoting domestic growth and at the same time maintaining a stable exchange rate. Beginning in the early 1970s, however, global capitalism entered the stage, countering the depression-preventing regime and moving toward the release of market forces. In two decades, liberalization of finance, deregulation, and privatization became the leading policies adopted by many industrialized countries. Without the two Bretton Woods protection measures, however, the goal of maintaining stable exchange rates directly conflicted with the objectives of domestic policies. The Bank of Japan's intervention in the foreign exchange market, aimed at countering the rapid appreciation of the yen, often led to an oversupply of money. The oversupply of money, in turn, contributed directly to the imbalance of domestic demand and supply because it created too much pressure on the supply side to spend money, and it easily led to inflation and the bubble.

Another factor that profoundly changed the environment of Japanese public policy was the discontinuance by the United States of its asymmetric cooperation with Japan in international trade. Japan's unwillingness to address the trade surplus issue not only contributed in part to the collapse of the Bretton Woods system but also invoked a set of issues in which mistakes in Japanese responses to U.S. pressures caused the situation to deteriorate further. Despite its huge trade surplus, Japan was not willing to open its domestic markets. As an alternative, its elites were willing to liberalize the finance industry, participate in multilateral integration of monetary policy, and adopt an expansionary fiscal policy to create domestic demand; such demand not only fit the Japanese ambition to become a leading economic power but also was closely tied to powerful domestic interest groups such as the construction industry. What the policy makers failed to recognize, however, was that these measures would further weaken shareholders' control and banks' monitoring of private corporations and that the resulting unmanaged freedom of the corporations would inevitably increase risks for investments.

Two major structural changes were also critical in the rise of the bubbles. First, the balance of Japanese payments changed from deficit to surplus. Second, the high growth period ended with the First Oil Shock. As a result of successful promotion of exports, the self-capital of Japanese corporations increased rapidly, and their dependence on the main banks declined. Under pressure to improve efficiency, the corporations reduced the scope of indirect financing with the main banks. As the liberalization of finance provided them with freedom to raise capital in overseas markets, they began to engage in direct financing or equity financing, profiting from financial speculation in the stock and real estate markets. The expansionary fiscal policy adopted by the state further channeled private investment into the stock and real estate markets. The intrinsic dilemma between coordination and control, formerly under control, now became a significant challenge for the Japanese economy.

Even in the 1980s, some Japanese observers had already argued that the globalization of finance was creating a major challenge to the macroeconomic aggregates of the Japanese economy. The Japanese financial industry had formerly been protected by the state, which controlled the free flow of capital. When capital was scarce in the 1950s, centralized management of capital through the Bank of Japan's credit to the main banks worked relatively well. After Japanese corporations began to raise capital through equity finance, however, the main banks' monitoring virtually disappeared (Iga 1987, 64). To some analysts, Japan's economic situation in the 1980s resembled that of the United States on the eve of the Great Depression. First, the 1980s Tokyo Exchange movement of the Nikkei Index looked similar to that of the 1920s Dow Jones Index. Second, in both periods, no one was willing to invest in production capacity while there was plenty of surplus capital. Third, in both periods, there was a serious imbalance of trade. After World War I, the United States became a major exports power, while Britain lost its international competitiveness. Many observers, looking at the situation with regard to U.S.-Japanese relations in the late 1980s, saw similarities between the two periods. Fourth, in both periods, there was a significant increase in debts. After World War I, Germany had a huge debt because of war compensation penalties. In the late 1980s, a number of countries in Central and South America and in Asia suffered a similar debt problem. In the late 1980s, the average price/earning ratio of Japanese corporations reached 60, a number that was 25 times higher than the international average. The total stock cap listed in the Tokyo Exchange had reached 340 trillion yen and was on the same level as in the United States. Given the size of the population, the size of the GNP, and the sales of these corporations, Japanese stock prices were about three times higher than they should have been (Makino 1987, 25–26). To these analysts, Japan was at the cliff's edge. They believed that if Japanese investors did not pull out of their stock and real estate investments by the end of 1987, they would suffer a great loss. One economist even predicted that in one to three years, the global economy would have a major recession, triggered either by the debt problem in Central America or the deficit problem in the United States (Uno 1987, 22–23).

This chapter shows that the globalization of finance provides a new angle to reexamine the issue of the competitiveness of the Japanese economy of the 1980s. When U.S. analysts of the time discussed Japanese competitiveness, an important measurement of Japan's strength in international competition was its trade surplus with the United States. The trade surplus was often attributed either to the trade barriers in Japan's domestic markets or to the strength of the Japanese economic system in production. To be sure, both factors mattered. Revisiting this issue today in light of the globalization of finance, however, we must also factor in the impact of the strong dollar policy adopted in the first term of the Reagan administration in the early 1980s on the rapid increase of the Japanese trade surplus with the United States. Seen this way, Japanese companies were competitive, but less competitive than was indicated by the trade surplus with the United States in the 1980s.

CHAPTER 7

THE STRUGGLE OF
THE WELFARE SOCIETY

In the early 1970s, triggered by two important structural changes, the long-term movement of the capitalist economies shifted gears from social protection to the release of market forces. As the First Oil Shock ended the era of high-speed economic growth in all advanced industrialized countries, various models created for social protection came under mounting pressure. In Western Europe, the welfare state began to face serious fiscal challenges in the 1970s as government spending, which functioned as a counter-cyclical tool, increased substantially. Meanwhile, two factors – the need to hedge against the risks of foreign exchange and the desire to pursue higher profits from the opportunities provided by the floating exchange rates after the collapse of the Bretton Woods system – led to the liberalization of finance. Efforts to remove the barriers to market forces soon spread over various industries and sectors, and this resulted in a neoliberal revolution represented by the widespread adoption of programs of deregulation, liberalization, and privatization in advanced industrialized countries. Against such a background, did the institutions and mechanisms established for social protection since the Great Depression and World War II survive? If they did, at what cost?

Since the 1970s, the conventional wisdom has predicted the decline of the welfare state. Because social provision accounted for an increasing share of gross national product, rates of expenditure growth that were well in excess of overall economic expansion could not possibly be sustained after the First Oil Shock. Yet a number of recent studies have argued that "the impact of electoral politics has not been dwarfed by market dynamics. Globalized markets have not rendered immutable the efficiency-equality tradeoff" (Garrett 1998, 2). Social democratic corporatism survived the 1980s more or less unscathed by the forces of market integration (Garrett 1998). Even in the United States and Britain, the two countries that are usually considered the leaders in the neoliberal revolution, "the success of direct attacks on social programs generally has been limited. Despite fluctuations that have largely echoed the business cycle, social expenditure has roughly maintained its share of economic output in both countries" (Pierson 1994, 4).

During this process, two conditions on which the Japanese economy was contingent – asymmetric cooperation with the United States in the GATT system and the high speed of economic growth, which sustained the success of the total employment strategy in the high growth period – disappeared. Formerly, the policy of asymmetric cooperation had allowed Japan to export aggressively while keeping its own domestic markets closed. In addition, the high speed of economic growth had made it possible for Japan's gain in maintaining political stability to outweigh its losses in the practices of cartels and of government protection of weak sectors and industries. After the early 1970s, however, the collapse of the Bretton Woods system and increasing trade friction between the United States and Japan resulted in strong international pressures on Japan to open its domestic markets.

Facing these challenges in the early 1970s, Japan, under the leadership of Prime Minister Tanaka Kakuei, tried two new alternatives. First, as discussed in Chapter 6, the Japanese state promoted the industrial reallocation plan, which was aimed at dispersing development opportunities to the rural areas and addressing income distribution issues by providing the weak with opportunities to grow. Because of bad timing and the absence of a land policy, however, this action stimulated inflation and financial speculation in real estate and stocks. Second, Japan also explored the possibility of building a welfare state right before the First Oil Shock. The strong preference for production and capital accumulation during the high growth period had generated many social problems, such as pollution and the dual structure of the economy. Social resentment stimulated the environmental movement and resulted in strong demands for increased attention to social welfare. In response, the conservative LDP, state bureaucrats, and business leaders considered addressing social welfare issues, but the First Oil Shock resulted in a political environment that would not support a welfare state. Instead, attention was refocused on the idea of the welfare society.

After the high growth period ended, pressure to improve efficiency increased, and market selection served to intensify distributive politics. During the high growth period, it had been easier for each major distributional coalition to share a piece of the pie because the pie was constantly growing. When economic growth slowed, however, it became more difficult to distribute the pie fairly. Without alternative ways of social protection, the demand grew for government protection, and the LDP faced a major crisis in maintaining its dominance in the election (Pempel 1998).

With the failure of Tanaka's two proposed alternatives, the system returned to its old institutional logic of total employment sustained by privatized social protection, this time with a significant extension. Although the practice of permanent employment had been questioned briefly during the First Oil Shock, strong demands from labor unions for job security and higher wages, together with the hyperinflation associated with the confrontational strategies of both sides, soon brought all parties to the negotiation table. In exchange for labor's cooperation in slowing the growth of wages, big corporations were forced to continue the practice of permanent employment. By the time the rapid appreciation of the yen's value after the 1985 Plaza Accord created new pressures on Japanese corporations to adjust labor costs, permanent employment had become a deeply institutionalized ideology in corporate governance, enforced in part by the world's widespread praise of the practice. Although the opportunistic behavior of cartels organized by the oil industry awakened public consciousness of consumer rights – eventually leading to the 1977 amendment of the Antimonopoly Law – government protection of the weak sectors and the sunset industries increased substantially. This protection is represented by the passage of the Large Scale Retail Store Law in 1973 and the Depressed Industry Stabilization Law in 1978. So even though the preconditions for practicing the total employment strategy had disappeared beginning in the early 1970s, the Japanese economic system nevertheless continued to practice it on an unprecedented level.

In the 1971–1989 period, the Japanese economic system showed two seemingly contradictory trends. On the surface, the system continued to rely on the total employment strategy to maintain political stability, and at first it worked well. Throughout the 1970s and 1980s, Japan's response to the two oil shocks was regarded as a model for the advanced industrialized countries. Meanwhile, however, Japan's participation in the neoliberal revolution and the rise of the bubble in the 1980s significantly weakened economic equality as the ownership of real estate and stocks became an important factor in social stratification. More fundamentally, the costs of continuing the total employment strategy increased substantially until they outweighed the gains of maintaining political stability. This has generated strong criticisms (Katz 1998; Pempel 1998). These two contradictory trends were like a double-edged sword. Although they generated short-term success, they also laid the foundation of a major crisis in the long run. Moreover, the absence of an effective unemployment program during this period of Japan's structural adjustment always produced strong domestic political opposition to any proposed policy of opening the country's domestic markets. This opposition induced Japan to give in to other types of international pressures, including liberalizing the banking industry, adopting an expansionary fiscal policy, and engaging in multilateral monetary policy coordination. These endeavors in turn contributed to the rise of the bubble.

THE END OF ASYMMETRIC COOPERATION

Keeping its domestic markets closed, a policy enabled by asymmetric cooperation with the United States under the GATT, had been a cornerstone supporting Japan's total employment strategy. But then the United States began to push the agenda of liberalization and deregulation in its international economic policy because "a world order in which the flow of goods and capital is determined largely by market forces will maximize the advantages for the country with the highest level of technical development and with the most enterprising and strongest firms" (Block 1977, 3). To lead the transition of the international trade regime, the United States discontinued its asymmetric cooperation with Japan in the early 1970s, making strong demands for reciprocal treatment of U.S. corporations in Japanese markets.

In comparison with the high growth period, the 1971–1989 period was characterized by a series of trade frictions between Japan and the United States. Japan responded to the challenges of the collapse of the Bretton Woods system and the two oil crises by shifting its industrial structure from heavy chemicals to automobile and home electronics. As the Japanese trade surplus with the United States increased from $1.7 billion in 1975 to $11.6 billion in 1978, the U.S. Congress threatened to pass retaliatory legislation, including a surcharge on imported Japanese television sets. Under this pressure, Japan agreed in 1977 to limit its TV exports to the U.S. market. In 1978, Japan agreed to provide the United States with reciprocal market access to Japanese domestic markets, to increase imports of manufactured goods, and to increase its strict quotas for agricultural products. In response, the U.S. Congress dropped its retaliatory legislation. Then, during the Second Oil Shock, Japanese automobiles, which were more energy-efficient than American ones, flooded the U.S. market, causing unemployment and financial losses in the U.S. automobile industry. The U.S. Congress again threatened to limit Japanese automobile imports. On May 1, 1981, the Japanese government announced that it would voluntarily restrain its exports of automobiles to the U.S. market for the next two years. Nevertheless, as the U.S. trade deficits with Japan increased rapidly, there was a growing belief throughout the United States that Japanese trade practices were unfair (Prestowitz 1988, 418–422). Trade negotiations between Japan and the United States involved telecommunication, electronics, medicines and medical equipment, semiconductors, wood products, automobile parts, supercomputers, tobacco, oranges, soda, fish, beef, and the granting of permission for foreign lawyers to practice in Japan (Fukushima 1992).

As early as 1981, on a trip to Japan, Etienne Davidson, the commissioner for trade of the European Economic Community, called on the Japanese to establish an overall target for imports of manufactured goods. Davidson pointed out that Japan's imports of manufactured goods were about the same as those of Switzerland, a country with about 5 percent of Japan's population. Japanese trade was following a strange pattern, Davidson said. The other industrialized countries were at the same time large importers and exporters of machine tools, automobiles, and other machinery. Japan was the only exception. To correct this problem, Japan needed to pursue a structural solution. Although this view was endorsed by some U.S. government officials, it was dismissed by the mainstream bureaucrats, who favored the alternative of attacking specific, identifiable barriers to trade (Prestowitz 1988, 449–450).

According to Glen Fukushima, the bilateral agreements produced by trade negotiations between the two countries often failed to achieve their goals. The trouble usually started with pressure brought to bear on the executive branch of the U.S. government by American corporations and Congress. After a series of internal adjustments among various bureaucracies, the U.S. government would present its demands to the Japanese government. The Japanese government usually would reject the allegation that there were trade barriers in Japan but would offer "explanations." As internal pressures increased, the U.S. government would tell the Japanese government that certain areas needed further investigation or that Japan should make certain procedures more transparent. After a long process of negotiation, the Japanese government would pick some areas to "give in." Then when an agreement was signed, the U.S. government would present it as a major achievement to American corporations and Congress, whereas the Japanese government would downplay the implications of the agreement, minimizing criticisms from domestic interest groups. About a year after these agreements had been made, either American corporations or the U.S. Congress would again complain that access to the Japanese markets was still not improved and would demand bilateral agreements that included a target percentage of the American share of the Japanese market. The U.S. government, with several exceptions, tended to oppose this kind of outcome orientation in bilateral trade negotiations. It held that if the procedure of materials and parts purchases by Japanese corporations were only made more transparent, American products should be able to penetrate Japanese markets. Thus, the U.S. government put further pressure on the Japanese government to change

Japanese procedures of corporate purchasing and examination (Fukushima 1992, 62–64).

In January 1989, the U.S. government under the Bush administration began to emphasize the Structural Impediments Initiative (SII). Driven by criticism of seemingly ever-increasing trade deficits with Japan and by pressure from Congress to apply to Japan the Super 301[1] provision of the 1988 Trade Act, the U.S. Treasury Department held that there must be important structural barriers in the Japanese economy, because the trade imbalance between the United States and Japan had still not been narrowed even after the rapid appreciation of the yen following the Plaza Accord. Unlike the Commerce Department and the Office of the U.S. Trade Representative (USTR), which supported an outcome-oriented approach focused on an actual target, the Treasury Department supported a process-oriented approach and therefore highlighted what it saw as structural barriers (Fukushima 1992, 198). Japan experts in the U.S. government warned that if Japan were listed under Super 301, the two countries' political and military ties would be seriously damaged. The Bush administration tried to please Congress by listing Japan under Super 301 but identifying only those problems in those fields for which Japan could offer easy solutions. Some members of Congress and the Senate had meant for the Japanese distribution system, the keiretsu, and the Antimonopoly Law to be identified under Super 301. Instead, the Bush administration chose to identify only supercomputer, satellite, and wood products. To divert the attention of Congress, the Bush administration decided to pursue SII (Fukushima 1992, 199–200).

The Japanese government agreed to talk about SII under three conditions. First, the nature of the talk was to be a consultation rather than a negotiation. Negotiations would yield binding agreements, but consultations would not. Second, SII would need to be mutual. In other words, Japan could also identify structural problems in the U.S. economy. And third, any outcome from the talks would not be interpreted as an "agreement." This meant that the United States could not retaliate against Japan after the talks for

---

1 Super 301 refers to Section 301 of the Trade Act of 1974, as amended by section 1302 of the Omnibus Trade and Competitiveness Act of 1988. It required the U.S. Trade Representative (USTR), within 30 days following the National Trade Estimates (foreign trade barriers) Report to Congress in 1989 and 1990, to identify U.S. trade liberalization priorities. This identification included priority trade barriers as well as priority countries and estimates of the amount by which U.S. exports would be increased if the barriers did not exist. USTR was required to initiate (regular) section 301 investigations on all priority practices within 21 days after submitting the report to the House Ways and Means and Senate Finance Committees. USTR was required to negotiate agreements that provided for the elimination of, or compensation for, the priority trade barriers within three years after the initiation of the investigation. This authority expired in 1990. However, since 1994, Super 301 has been implemented by USTR under an executive order of the president. Legislation introduced in the 106th Congress (S. 19 and S. 101) would establish a Super 301 for agriculture. Source: http://agriculture.house.gov/glossary/super_301.htm.

violating an agreement. The U.S. government accepted all three conditions (Fukushima 1992, 205–207).

In the final report, the U.S. participants emphasized the imbalance of over-saving and underinvestment; land policy; the income distribution system; the gaps in consumer prices between the Japanese market and international markets; the keiretsu; and the exclusionary trade pattern of Japanese compa-nies. In contrast, the Japanese side focused on the imbalance of undersaving and overspending caused by budget deficits, corporate investments, and pro-motion of productivity; reform of the antitrust law; corporate behavior (especially the lack of a long-term perspective by management); deregulation of imports and exports; research and development; promotion of exports; and education and training of the labor force (Fukushima 1992, 209–210). Japan agreed to go further in using an expansionary fiscal policy to adjust Japan's trade surplus by spending 430 trillion yen on public investments over the next 10 years; this practice, it was estimated, would increase Japanese spend-ing from 7.2 percent to 8.4 percent of total GNP. It agreed to revise the Large Scale Retail Stores Law, reducing from 10 years to 1 year the time limit in which established stores could delay new large store openings. Japan also agreed to reform its land tax policy to encourage landowners to sell or develop their land. Meanwhile, however, the Japanese strongly resisted the proposals calling for more enforcement of the Antimonopoly Law and restraining the keiretsu (Schoppa 1997, 12).

The passage of the Super 301 provision in the 1980s signaled a significant transition of the Pax Americana. After the United States replaced Britain as the world's chief hegemonic power, the U.S. government first opened its own markets to other countries, at the same time explaining to the domestic audi-ence that this was a gesture in support of its demand for reciprocal treatment of U.S. exports in these countries. The United States was the hegemonic leader in the international order, and its relationships with its allies were not horizontal but vertical. For this reason, the United States not only lent weapons to Britain during World War II but also tried to establish interna-tional economic order through the Marshall plan, the GATT, and the IMF. Beginning in the 1970s, however, the vertical yet asymmetric relationships between the United States and other countries faced new challenges because Europe and Japan began to demonstrate strong international competitive-ness. That is why the United States gave up asymmetric cooperation in inter-national trade. Reciprocity was no longer simply a gesture to satisfy domestic politics but rather had become a major principle in U.S. international economic policy (Yakushiji 1988).

The Japanese strategy of total employment, however, depended heavily on having closed domestic markets. In the absence of international competition, the Japanese state could achieve a political balance by adopting a pro–big corporation policy in an effort to promote exports, meanwhile allowing medium-size and small companies to organize cartels and protecting the weak sector by heavy government regulations. If Japan had completely opened its domestic markets, strong foreign competition could easily have driven many medium-size and small companies out of business. Because Japan had not developed a strong government-sponsored unemployment assistance program, widespread bankruptcies would have led to political instability. Thus, no one in Japan would give in on this matter. Having a huge trade surplus while reluctantly opening its own domestic markets, however, Japan was under strong international pressure. As an alternative to opening domestic markets, as discussed in Chapter 6, Japan acceded to the demands from the United States on the liberalization of finance, creating domestic demand by adopting an expansionary fiscal policy, and multilateral monetary policy coordination. While doing so, Japan was able to avoid potential unemployment by keeping its domestic markets relatively closed. But this policy mix led to the bubble, whose bursting would eventually increase the pressure of unemployment on a much greater scale.

THE END OF THE HIGH GROWTH AND BEGINNING OF DECLINING PROFITABILITY

The First Oil Shock brought an end to the high-speed economic growth, completely changing the environment for Japan's total employment strategy. The profit rate of capital in the current accounts of all Japanese corporations reached its peak of 5.6 percent in 1973. In the next two years, it declined to 1.9 percent, the lowest by far in the country's postwar history. In the first half of 1975, one-fourth of the companies listed in the Tokyo Stock Exchange suffered from negative earnings, and the rate of profit on sales for the major manufacturing corporations fell to 0.9 percent, much lower than the 4.26 percent recorded during the 1965 recession and the 3.64 percent recorded during the Nixon Shock (Mitsuhashi and Uchida 1994, 79–80). Even by 1979, Robert Brenner (1998, 166) reports, "manufacturing profitability had failed to recover much, remaining considerably lower than it had been in 1974, only about 12 percent higher than it had been at the depths of the oil crisis in 1975, and 40 percent below its level in 1973, when it had already fallen 22 percent below its 1969–70 peak."

Western analysts in the 1970s and 1980s tended to pay exclusive attention to two major factors. One was the rapidly increasing number of Japanese exports, and the other was Japan's political stability during the structural adjustment after the First Oil Shock. These factors, however, had been achieved at a heavy cost of inefficiency. As Robert Brenner (1998, 165–166) argues,

> Up against a suddenly stagnant world market and intensified international competition, but needing to sell at just about any price in order to make use of the capital stock that they had only recently so vastly expanded and a labor force that they could not easily lay off, Japanese manufacturers simply had no choice but to keep a lid on the prices of their mostly tradable goods to maintain output and sales. Whereas in the non-manufacturing private sector, firms raised prices at an average annual rate of 18.3 percent, in manufacturing they could raise prices at an average annual rate of just 7.5 percent. Even so, firms in the manufacturing sector could not prevent capacity utilization from dropping a staggering 22 percent over the two years, compared to only 4.6 percent in the non-manufacturing private business sector. With capacity utilization and price increases so much reduced, profits had to plummet.

Under such circumstances, the continuing practice of permanent employment delayed the structural adjustment Japanese corporations had to make after the First Oil Shock. When the profit level declined but corporations continued to keep surplus workers, sooner or later these corporations were going to have to lose competitiveness. In the 1970s and 1980s, two things helped Japanese corporations to maintain their surplus workers: the rapid expansion of exports and the bubble economy. However, as discussed in Chapter 6, both of these were sustained by many contingent conditions. The quality of Japanese products certainly contributed to Japanese competitiveness. Meanwhile, however, the impact of the strong dollar and the weak yen influenced by Reaganomics was as important as the quality of Japanese products in promoting Japanese exports to the United States. When these contingent conditions disappeared, those Japanese corporations that had kept their surplus workers would face significant financial burdens.

TWO ATTEMPTED DEPARTURES FROM THE PAST

Confronting drastic changes in the international environment of the early 1970s, Japan briefly experimented with two new strategies to sustain economic growth and employment: One was the plan for industrial reallocation, and the other was the attempted development of a social welfare program. The failures of these two attempts led the Japanese economic system to return to its old institutional logic of keeping everyone in business to maintain political stability in the new environment.

It is instructive to examine the industrial reallocation plan in more detail. This plan represented a new logic in the Japanese economic system because it was aimed at addressing the issue of the distribution of economic welfare, not by protecting the weak but rather by providing the weak with opportunities to become strong. This plan was envisioned by Tanaka Kakuei, the youngest prime minister and also the only prime minister in postwar Japan who had never received a college education. Tanaka was the first Japanese politician who intended to conduct a drastic reform of the Japanese economy. When the Nixon Shock took place in 1971, the consensus was that the Japanese government should increase public spending to counter the recession resulting from the appreciation of the yen. What was special about the Tanaka plan was that it was aimed not only at increasing public spending but also at using this spending to address many problems accumulated during the high growth period and to "shift the priority from production and exports to social welfare of citizens, build social capital and develop the social security system to the level of developed countries" (Tanaka 1972, 24). At the time, 73 percent of Japanese industries were concentrated in the Pacific belt. More than 32 percent of the Japanese population lived in 1 percent of the Japanese territory. Moreover, the high growth strategy had created many problems, such as the coexistence of overpopulated urban areas and underpopulated rural areas, pollution, traffic jams, a shortage of energy supplies, a shortage of labor, a low number of parks per capita in metropolitan areas, and high consumer and land prices in metropolitan areas. Tanaka's aggressive plan was designed to deal with these problems. Its major components included the following (Tanaka 1972).

· Solve the problems of both over- and underpopulated areas simultaneously and shift Japan's industrial base from major metropolitan areas to nationwide areas, especially the cold-weather areas.
· Build 10,000 kilometers of highways and 9,000 kilometers of high-speed railways and integrate them into a national transportation network.
· Develop small cities nationwide with populations of 250,000.
· Improve the living environment of big cities.
· Use tax policy to drive factories out of large metropolitan areas.
· Turn Japan into an "information island" by building communication networks based on telephone, cable TV, TVs, telephones, and computer networks that could link households with the workplace.

Two main factors doomed this plan to failure. The first was that although the government adopted an expansion policy that was aimed at stimulating demand, the supply side was still restrained by the recession cartels organized in 1971 after the Nixon Shock. Among 13 such cartels, 8 were still in effect at the end of 1972. As Katsumata Hisayoshi points out, the contradictory policies adopted by the Japanese government were the major driving force behind the rise of wholesale prices (1995, 166). Later, the rising oil prices during the First Oil Shock triggered hyperinflation, and that made the Tanaka plan more untenable. The second major factor was the lack of a land policy. The Tanaka policy held that because the Japanese land area was small, the rise of land prices was inevitable. With banks profiting from increased land values, they would be more willing to offer loans. Without their continuing supply of capital, Japan's economic growth could not be sustained. In this sense, a stable rise in land prices would not be a problem but rather would be a benefit for the Japanese economy (NHK 1995, Vol. 4, 347–349).

The failure of Tanaka's industrial reallocation plan closed the door to significant reform of Japan's economic structure. Meanwhile, the pressure of distributional politics led to the adoption of increasing numbers of government protections, and that in turn seriously restrained the dynamics of the economy. In the early 1970s, Tanaka and Fukuda were the two chief contenders for power within the Satō faction of the LDP. Both held strong philosophical stands. Tanaka believed in economic growth, whereas Fukuda believed in stability. These two ideological stances reflected a major division in postwar Japanese economic policy. One cannot easily judge the value of each of them without a specific historical context. In the early 1970s, Japan faced a serious dilemma. On the one hand, the international environment had changed profoundly, and continued high growth had become impossible. On the other hand, the problems that had accumulated during the high growth of the 1960s could not easily be addressed without a high growth environment.

After Tanaka's plan failed, Fukuda's stable growth strategy dominated the policy paradigm. Indeed, Fukuda succeeded in calming inflation. Nevertheless, the adoption of a stable growth environment also significantly reduced the options of Japanese public policy in addressing the issues of income distribution. As a result, the Japanese economic system took the direction of relying on rigid government protection of the weak rather than providing them with opportunities to improve their competitive position in the market. Reexamining the 1970s from a 1990s perspective, and taking into account the fact that both the Tanaka and the Fukuda plans needed to address the issue of distribution in economic hard times, one may feel that a growth-oriented plan with a major reform component might not necessarily have been worse than a stability-oriented plan that did not have a reform component.

In an effort to sustain economic growth, another attempt was made to develop the welfare state. By the end of the 1960s, Japan's production orientation and strong preference for capital accumulation had generated a great deal of resentment. Pollution and environmental damage created by high growth led to social protests. The dual structure of income distribution also attracted major attention. Taking as 100 the 1971 wage and benefit level of big corporations (those with more than 5,000 employees), that of companies with 100 to 299 employees was only 65.9, and that of companies with 30 to 99 employees was only 63.8. Although company-based benefit programs had supplemented the country's poorly developed program of public welfare, these private programs had no redistributive function, nor could they replace public welfare. Indeed, between big corporations and medium-size and small companies, gaps in company-based benefit programs were much bigger than gaps in salary. Taking as 100 the 1971 company-based benefit level of big corporations (those with more than 5,000 employees), that of companies with 100 to 299 employees was 45.3, and that of companies with 30 to 99 employees was only 47.2. Gaps also existed in pension programs. Although corporate pension programs had been widely institutionalized by the early 1970s, the gaps in payments varied greatly. The one sum retirement allowance paid at big corporations (those with more than 1,000 employees) was equivalent to 50.4 months' salary. That in companies with 100 to 299 employees was only 39.8 months, and that in companies with 30 to 99 employees was only 29.5 months (Shinkawa 1993, 92–93).

These problems associated with distribution had been neglected, creating, by the early 1970s, a crisis for the conservatives. This crisis was reflected in the rise of social movements, progressive political parties, and left-wing labor unions. In 1970, the progressive forces had been elected to the post of governor at all three major local governments, including Tokyo, Osaka, and Kyoto. Progressive politicians had taken 6 of the 9 big cities and 138 of 643 small cities. In addition, the mass media began to dwell on welfare-related issues. Various magazines published special editions on Japan's backwardness in social welfare, attracting widespread attention from the general public (Shinkawa 1993, 110–111).

Under the leadership of Tanaka Kakuei, the Japanese government declared 1973 as the "First Year of the Welfare Era." Although the Ministry of Finance showed resistance, Tanaka pushed through a pension plan that would provide the elderly with 50,000 yen monthly income. Pempel (1998, 187) describes the efforts this way:

> Free medical care for the elderly, initially offered by progressive local governments, was introduced at the national level. The proportion of total national medical expenses paid by the two public insurance programs was increased

from 17.2 percent (1966–1972) to 27.3 percent (1973–1975). Payout levels in both the Employee Pension System and the National Pension System were also substantially enhanced. The employee benefit was nearly doubled to about 45 percent of the average income; the national pension was increased proportionately. More important still, indexing to the cost of living was introduced into both systems.

The effort to develop the welfare state, however, ran up against bad timing. As the First Oil Shock ended the high growth period, the welfare state initiative faced a drastically changing political environment. The recession after the First Oil Shock led to a shortage of 3.8 trillion yen in the state tax revenue in fiscal 1975. The Japanese government had to issue 3.48 trillion yen in national debts. As a result, the dependence of the government budget on deficit financing increased from 11.3 percent in 1974 to 26.3 percent in 1975, 29.9 in 1976, more than 30 percent in 1977, and 32 percent in 1978. The Ministry of Finance attributed the rapid rise in the national debt to the increase in welfare spending. According to its statistical data, the average annual increase in welfare spending in 1971–1974 was 26.2 percent. Although the Ministry of Finance tried to control the speed of this increase, it was still maintained at 21.4 percent in 1975–1978. Only in 1979 was the Ministry of Finance able to bring down the annual increase to 12.5 percent. In 1980, it was a single digit (Shinkawa 1993, 146–147).

Fukuda Takeo, who replaced Tanaka as Japanese prime minister, took a conservative stand because his first priority was to control inflation. In 1975, the LDP published its "Life-time Welfare Plan," which asserted the importance of self-reliance and criticized the expansion of public spending on welfare. A group of conservative intellectuals further provided a theoretical foundation for the LDP's political stand by asserting that in the last analysis welfare should be a national minimum. Japan should not create weak human beings who would rely heavily on the state, as reflected in the British and Scandinavian types of welfare states; instead, Japan should depart from the European model. In other words, the assertion of the welfare society in the Japanese context was a direct rejection of the European model of the welfare state.

Another, more conservative group named Group 1984 regarded the effort to develop the welfare state as an attempt at "suicide." Group 1984 argued that the fall of civilizations often originated within. The fall of the Roman Empire, it held, was induced by the indulgence resulting from a concentration of wealth and prosperity. The Roman expansion of welfare led to inflation, economic stagnation, and then a reduction in productivity. The country was dominated by a quasi-democracy that emphasized ultra-egalitarianism.

In short, when the civil society emerged and citizens began to demand limitless rights, Rome started its journey toward the welfare state. Soon, it experienced stagnation and decline (Shinkawa 1993, 116–117). Group 1984 correctly predicted that the Japanese economic slowdown in 1974 might not be temporary, but permanent. Under such circumstances, it maintained, the constraints of natural resources and energy, the increasing cost of environmental protection, the shortage of labor, and the rapid increase in wages would directly threaten economic growth. As long as the Japanese exercised self-discipline, these problems were solvable. However, also according to Group 1984, the internal enemy was becoming increasingly powerful because of the emergence of the civil society represented by the collapse of the traditional family and community, the rise of individualism and ultra-egalitarianism, and increasing public spending, all of which were eroding Japanese social dynamics and leading the Japanese to lose self-discipline (Shinkawa 1993, 117–119).

THE CHALLENGE TO CARTELS AND THE STATE-LED NONMARKET GOVERNING MECHANISMS

Cartels, especially those organized for medium-size and small companies, had been an important cornerstone in sustaining the total employment strategy (see Chapter 5). The end of the high growth period, however, significantly increased the cost of cartels to the economy as a whole. This cost arose not only from the inefficiency of the cartels but also from the "black" cartels organized by the oil industry during the First Oil Shock, which created a snowball effect in deepening the crisis. As a result, the legitimacy of cartels was profoundly brought into question and the institutional foundation of the total employment strategy was weakened, if only indirectly.

In the high growth period, cartels and other types of state-led nonmarket governing mechanisms served to prevent bankruptcies of the medium-size and small companies and thus to sustain employment during economic recessions. Although these practices had resulted in inefficiency, they had never encountered a major political challenge. (The only exception was the attempted but failed 1958 amendment of the Antimonopoly Law, which implied an expansion of cartels to big corporations in all industries.) When economic growth slowed, the number of cartels exempted from enforcement of the Antimonopoly Law increased from 845 in 1970 to 979 in 1972. After the First Oil Shock, however, the total number of cartel exemptions decreased instead of increased. By 1976, the total number of such exemptions declined to 528 (Kōsei Torihiki Iinkai 1977, 769). Why did the number of exemptions decline? The reason is that the black cartels organized by the oil industry during the First Oil Shock generated strong resentment by the general public. The cartels, together with the administrative guidance of the state, began to be seriously questioned. In 1977, the Antimonopoly Law was amended. For the first time in postwar Japan, an amendment of the Antimonopoly Law did not aim at promoting but rather at restraining cartels. As a result, cartels, one of the cornerstones of the total employment strategy, began to face a new political environment.

A look at the history of cartel behavior explains why. Big corporations had regarded the First Oil Shock as a golden opportunity for making profits, and they organized various cartels to raise prices simultaneously. Between November 1972 and October 1973, 12 oil companies, which shared 95 percent of the Japanese oil markets, secretly met five times, taking common action to raise oil prices (Kōsei Torihiki Iinkai 1977, 320–321). On February 6, 1974, a document written by a marketing director at the General Oil Company, one of the two leading oil companies, was discovered at the Budgeting Committee of the Upper House and was brought to light. This document called the oil shock "the chance of a lifetime" and ordered a significant increase in the retail price of the company's oil. It also gave detailed instructions on how to deal with MITI, the mass media, and individual consumers. For example, it asked the company's retail chain stores to raise the price of lamp oil 1,000 yen per kiloliter but explained that the order should be issued orally rather than in writing to prevent the company's being caught. Meanwhile, the document instructed the company's retail chain stores to use deferred data to show to MITI and the mass media. If any retail store dared to report to the government that the company had raised its lamp oil price, the company would discontinue wholesale dealings with that store. The document also said that when consumers asked why the price had gone up, the retail store was to attribute the rise to increases in wage and delivery costs (Mitsuhashi and Uchida 1994, 28–29).

Increasing concentration of production created a favorable environment for big corporations to use nonmarket governing mechanisms to make profits. In 1973, in 10 industries – including beer, whiskey, film, glass, watches, and several other products – the top company's market share had reached 50 percent and the combination of the top two companies' shares had become as high as 75 percent. As a result of significantly reduced competition, the leading companies were able to raise the prices of their products more freely, and, through implicit cooperation, dominant companies were able to adopt a so-called price leadership strategy.

Another factor in the rise of prices was the new economic environment that found its beginnings in the early 1970s, when the Japanese economy shifted from high growth to slow growth. In the high growth period, big corporations, having high expectations of economic expansion, had attempted to gain market share by aggressively lowering prices. After the collapse of the Bretton Woods system, however, the yen's value appreciated rapidly and the future of economic growth in Japan became uncertain. Responding to this new environment, big corporations began to raise prices to ensure profits rather than make new investments in production capacity. Against such a background, consumer prices rose 20 percent, and wholesale prices rose 30 percent, soon after the First Oil Shock started (Minosō 1977, 136–137). Oil products and petrochemical industries constituted more than 22 percent of the existing cartels at the time.

In short, during the high growth period, oligopoly in Japan served to maintain the dynamics of market competition, but when growth slowed, it began to restrain market competition. This change had a profound impact on the Japanese economy. Rising oil prices, for example, had a snowball effect on consumer prices. Housewives staged a "run" on products such as toilet paper, salt, and washing detergent. Meanwhile, the FTC conducted on-the-spot inspections for possible violations of the Antimonopoly Law in industries such as aluminum refining, aluminum compression, manufacture of aluminum sashes, raw concrete, painting materials, tires, and oxygen. The FTC also advised many industries to abolish their cartel practices, including those in oil, agricultural machinery, manufacture of refrigerators, toilet paper, instant noodles, and milk.

The opportunistic behavior of black cartels violated the norm in Japan. According to the norm, when Japan faced a major external challenge, the public interest and the national interest were expected to prevail over private interests. In the 1950s and 1960s, big corporations could justify their desire for pro–producer competition policy as being helpful in promoting exports, achieving Japan's economic independence, protecting Japanese domestic markets, and sustaining employment in the liberalization of trade and foreign investment. Back then, cartels and other anticompetition measures could be presented as serving to maintain employment. Although big corporations obtained enormous economic benefits from the state's pro–producer competition policy, they also had to provide job security for their employees through the permanent employment system and provide business opportunities to the medium-size and small businesses. Any selfish move by big corporations without compensation would trigger a strong political reaction. During the Great Depression, for example, opportunistic gold transactions by the Mitsui Bank led to radical retaliation, which in turn led to the assassination of its president by right-wing activists. In 1958, big corporations also encountered a major failure in pushing the amendment of the Antimonopoly Law at the expense of the medium-size and small companies in the agriculture and service sectors. Although the Japanese tended to tolerate cartels, the opportunistic behavior of black cartels during a national crisis could in no way be justified.

MITI's administrative guidance also became a target for criticism. Both MITI and the private sector preferred administrative guidance rather than direct control of corporations. To MITI, administrative guidance was much more convenient than the licensing of cartels because licensing did not affect companies outside the cartels; administrative guidance, on the other hand, could be applied to all companies. In addition, as the liberalization of trade eliminated MITI's control over foreign currency exchange in the 1960s, its leverage over private companies was significantly weakened and administrative guidance became MITI's major means of manipulating the private sector and ensuring its policy objectives. Private companies also preferred MITI's administrative guidance. Although the 1953 amendment of the Antimonopoly Law opened the door for cartels, the FTC still enforced a relatively rigid standard in approving cartels and also required a great deal of paperwork and numerous bureaucratic procedures. It was much easier for private companies to negotiate with MITI about the substance of administrative guidance than to deal with the FTC concerning legal matters (Heiwa Keizai Keikaku Kaigi 1977, 127–128).

The control mechanisms used to respond to the First Oil Shock were perceived as being directly responsible for the rise of black cartels. On November 19, 1973, at the meeting of deputy ministers, the Japanese state adopted the Outline of Administrative Guidance Concerning the Reduction of Civilian Consumption of Oil and Energy. This policy was carried out beginning the next day by various ministries in their administrative domains. According to these guidelines, the commercial use of energy was to be substantially reduced. Evening business hours were reduced, and gasoline stations had to close on Sundays. More important were two laws enacted by the Japanese state: the Oil Demand-Supply Adjustment Law (drafted by MITI) and the Emergency Measures Concerning Civilian Life Stabilization (drafted by the Economic Planning Agency). The Oil Demand-Supply Adjustment Law gave the MITI minister the authority to advise private companies to take common action in the market, determine the standard retail price of oil products, and advise private companies to reduce their prices. Although the FTC and the LDP raised the issue of whether these measures had violated the Antimonopoly Law, MITI was able to get it through the Diet in the name of the national interest (Tsūsanshō 1991, Vol. 12, 23–24).

Another factor in the rise of black cartels in the oil industry was the attempt by the Japanese state to rely on the price stabilization cartels to control rapidly rising prices. On November 20, 1973, MITI formally applied to the FTC to exempt the price stabilization cartels from enforcement of the Antimonopoly Law. On November 30, MITI and the FTC agreed that any common action taken by private companies under the state's administrative guidance would not be treated as a cartel and thus its actions would not violate the Antimonopoly Law. As Tsuruta Toshimasa (1982, 236–239) points out, this policy directly sustained the rise of black cartels. Assuming that the state was going to exercise price control and organize price stabilization cartels, private companies hastened to raise the prices of their products as high as possible. The prices were thus frozen by the state at a high level, allowing private companies to take big profits. The typical intervention by the state industrial policy, in other words, created a bonanza for black cartels.

Facing strong resentment from the general public, MITI and a group of politicians within the LDP tried to revive the Price Control Ordinance. This legislation had been enacted in March 1946 under the order of the GHQ in an effort to control hyperinflation. According to this ordinance, most prices were determined by the public authority. Any violation of this ordinance would lead to a term of 10 years in jail or a 100,000 yen fine. Although the Japanese state did not revive this proposal, it used the threat of it to induce cooperation from the private sector. Prime Minister Tanaka Kakuei called a special conference on consumer prices on February 4, 1974; attendees included all cabinet members, 85 business leaders, and bureaucrats of various ministries. At this conference, Tanaka pointed out to the business leaders that between June and December 1973, real consumer prices had gone up far beyond the prices estimated by MITI. Opportunistic speculation in the market by private companies had been widely reported by the mass media. If this situation continued, Tanaka told the group, the government would launch investigations and might seize the profits obtained through such speculation. Tanaka asserted that to stabilize market prices, business circles should actively cooperate with the government (Mitsuhashi and Uchida 1994, 25–26).

The negative impact of the oil industry's black cartels on the Japanese economy quickly changed the political environment, and Japanese consumers became more sensitive to cartel-related issues. This in turn made it more difficult to justify the cartel exemptions. All this explains why the total number of cartels exempted from enforcement of the Antimonopoly Law declined in the 1970s.

THE EXPANSION OF GOVERNMENT PROTECTION OF INEFFICIENT SECTORS AND SUNSET INDUSTRIES

The total employment strategy relied heavily on government protection of companies in inefficient sectors and sunset industries. When economic growth slowed, many such companies faced the danger of bankruptcy, and they strongly demanded more government protection. Concerned about the negative impact of bankruptcies on employment, the Japanese state expanded such protection in an effort to maintain political stability. A series of laws gave these weak sectors and industries the right to organize cartels. When the high growth period ended, however, the losses from the inefficiency created by these cartels increased very rapidly compared with the gains of political stability. Although these cartels served to prevent massive corporate bankruptcies in the short run, they simply postponed the solution of the problem rather than solving it. In the long run, this only increased the social cost of the inevitable adjustment.

The enactment of the Large Scale Retail Store Law in 1973 marked the beginning of a shift from what Richard Katz (1998, 165) calls "accelerationism" to "preservationalism." The Japanese retail industry consisted of more than 1.6 million retail stores and provided 5.6 million jobs. It was characterized by numerous small-scale, family-owned mini stores and multiple levels. A comparison is instructive. In the United States, for every 1,000 people there were 1.6 wholesale stores and 6.1 retail stores. The respective numbers for Germany were 1.9 and 6.6. In contrast, the Japanese numbers were 3.4 and 12. In the late 1940s and throughout the 1950s, the Japanese retail industry had absorbed a major portion of the surplus labor force. In the 1960s, large retail stores developed rapidly as a result of the shortage of labor. In addition, by 1965, more than half the Japanese households owned refrigerators. By the early 1970s, for every 1,000 households, 652 in the countryside and 344 in metropolitan areas owned cars. These changes had sustained the increase in the number of supermarkets (Harada 1998, 74). As Frank Upham points out, "One major factor was demographic. Suburbs grew in previously rural areas where there had been little commercial activity. Increased discretionary income and heightened interest in consumer protection led to a change in consumer behavior that made changes in the industry structure possible" (1993, 269). During the high growth period, the retail industry was basically governed by state licensing and taxation policies. Another important factor in the survival of small shops was consumer demand. When growth slowed, the market slack emerged, and one of the cornerstones that supported the retail industry collapsed. As a result, medium-size and small retailers organized a powerful political campaign, forcing the state to enact the Large Scale Retail Stores Law.

The Large Scale Retail Stores Law was "aimed at ensuring business opportunities for the medium-size and small retailers around large scale retail stores, and promoted normal development of the retail industry" (Tsūsanshō 1993a, Vol. 13, 507). By emphasizing protection of small retailers, this statement implies that large-scale retail stores, whose competitive efficiency is sustained by their economies of scale, had begun to enter an area dominated by a large number of small shops. Restrained by the law, retail stores with a size greater than 1,500 square meters (or 3,000 square meters in designated areas in major cities), were subject to government regulation with regard to their size, days of business operation, closing time, and number of holidays. Large-scale retail stores were required to register with MITI. According to this law, when MITI received such a registration, it would pass to the local chamber of commerce this information as well as the types of goods the store sold. The opinions of the local chamber of commerce would be sent to the Examination Committee of Large Scale Retail Stores, which in turn would send its opinion back to MITI. This procedure simply politicized the process of business operation and made it very difficult for large-scale retail stores to expand.

The enactment of this law intensified the conflicts between large-scale and small retailers. Before the law went into effect in 1974, registrations by large-scale retail stores at various local bureaus of MITI had doubled compared with those of the preceding year. The enactment of the law did not stop the development of large-scale retail stores. Before 1974, there were about 1,700 large-scale retail stores in Japan. Between 1974 and 1978, 1,504 new stores registered with MITI. As competition in the retail industry intensified, the number of cases that involved conflicts and adjustments also increased rapidly. Between 1974 and 1977, a total of 461 cases were reported. Some of them even went to court (Tsūsanshō 1993a, Vol. 13, 517). In 1977, the amendment of the Special Measures Law Concerning Adjustment of Retail Industry established a new adjustment procedure whereby various trade associations of medium-size and small companies could request that the governor of the prefecture inspect the business expansion plan of large-scale retail stores. The governor could then advise the large scale retailers to delay their opening date or reduce the size of their operation, or even stop the implementation of the plan for six months, which could be extended to one year if necessary. The governor was empowered to issue an order to enforce this advice and could fine the store officials for not following it. The governor also had the power to report to MITI, and MITI could adopt the same procedure against those who did not follow its advice (Tsūsanshō 1993a, Vol. 13, 519–520). Conflicts regarding the enforcement of these regulations led to an amendment of the Large Scale Retail Store Law in 1979. The amendment made the regulations more rigid. The size of retail store subject to government regulation was lowered to 500 square meters. The adjustment procedure for retail stores with a size of 1,500 square meters and greater would continue to be managed by MITI, but stores of 500 to 1,500 square meters would now be controlled by local governments.

In his comparative analysis of government regulation of the retail industry, Tanaka Masanori points out four major differences between the Japanese policy and those of three major European countries. First, the laws regulating retail industry in the European countries did not prohibit the opening of large-scale retail stores. Only Japan basically froze such expansion, with the central government controlling the size of such proposed stores. Second, only Japan treated retail stores between 500 square meters and 1,500 square meters as large-scale retail stores. Third, Japanese state regulation of the retail industry was very similar to its regulation of the manufacturing industry; MITI placed explicit constraints on retail stores. Fourth, in Europe, only France regulated large-scale retail stores. The structure of the retail industry in France was similar to that of Japan, but the enforcement of the law was much more rigid in Japan than in France (1986, 100–101). Under heavy government protection, the Japanese retail industry became very inefficient. According to the official government estimate, 40 percent of the retail prices of domestic goods and 59 percent of the retail prices of imported goods were attributable to distribution costs. In Japan, according to Frank Upham (1993, 266),

> Stores with only one or two employees accounted for 60 percent of all stores, yet generated less than 14 percent of all sales. Conversely, the 1,754 largest stores, with less than four hundred thousand employees, sold 40 percent as much as the almost 1.5 million smallest stores and their more than three million employees. The annual sales per employee in the largest stores was more than four times that of those in the smallest.

The Depressed Industry Stabilization Law of 1978 was another major effort by the Japanese state to maintain employment in the sunset industries. The most contentious issue was what kind of cartel should be used to coordinate the response in the depressed industries. MITI's initial proposal identified the "instructed cartels" (*shiji karuteru*) – that is, cartels to be included for regulation. MITI maintained that its minister should be given the power, after consultation with the Committee on Industrial Structure, to instruct private companies to establish mandatory cartels, reducing production capacity by taking common action. MITI also wanted the power to prohibit those outside the instructed cartels from adding new production capacity and to exempt the mergers and transfers of business among companies in these industries from Antimonopoly Law enforcement (Tsūsanshō 1993b, Vol. 14, 23).

The FTC, however, strongly opposed the MITI proposal for instructed cartels. The FTC maintained that the Antimonopoly Law's defining of cartels as recession cartels should be sufficient to deal with common actions to reduce production capacity. The FTC argued that it would not be enough for MITI to designate the cartels to be regulated before allowing the industries themselves to make efforts in that direction. If MITI forced those outside the instructed cartels to reduce production capacity, it would mean that efficient companies would also be regulated by the law, which was designed for inefficient companies. In addition, the FTC did not agree with the Antimonopoly Law exemptions because they would contradict the Antimonopoly Law's existing regulations and also would work against the international trend in competition policy (Tsūsanshō 1993b, Vol. 14, 24).

MITI's proposal, received a cold reception. The *Japan Economic News* pointed out that after the First Oil Shock changed the structures of both domestic and international demand and raised the cost of Japanese products, any enforcement of adjustments in both industrial and corporate structure would hamper Japanese companies' ability to compete with those in the developing countries. In this sense, instead of emphasizing fiscal policy along with creating demand, Japanese companies needed to reorganize their structures, reduce production capacity, and change their fields of business. To sustain these efforts, it was necessary for the government to assist with employment and financing. But MITI's proposal, the newspaper maintained, was aimed at protecting private companies without letting them take responsibility for themselves. MITI's proposal was also criticized by the New Freedom Club and the Japanese Socialist Party, and even the Keidanren was divided on this issue. To demonstrate the flaw in MITI's logic, economist Ueno Yudaka used the example of pupil equalizing. He said that MITI's proposal was like organizing a special class for dropout students and then treating all students at the achievement level of these dropouts. We should remember, he maintained, that normal students were not dropouts; the purpose of helping dropouts was to enable them to return to the normal class rather than keeping then always as dropouts (Tsūsanshō 1993b, Vol. 14, 27).

MITI countered these arguments by insisting that Japan could not rely on independent cartels controlled by private companies or instructed cartels initiated by the state without the power of enforcement. It cited two reasons. First, the reduction of production capacity and the improvement of industrial structure were precisely the goals of industrial policy, for which the MITI minister should be responsible. Second, it would be difficult for companies in the depressed industries to adhere to the terms for independent cartels.

Eventually, each side made compromises. The law gave MITI the power to organize instructed cartels, but these cartels had to be approved by the

FTC before they became effective (Tsūsanshō 1993b, Vol. 14, 28). According to Michael Beeman, this law blended the approaches promoted by both the FTC and MITI. "The FTC succeeded in putting forward its view that the law would first and foremost emphasize the self-help efforts of industry to make necessary adjustments in a competitive economic environment, while MITI succeeded in ensuring that the state could intervene with legal measures to ensure the effectiveness of these efforts should they break down or prove unattainable" (Beeman 1997, 178–179).

After the law went into effect, however, MITI found itself overburdened. It organized instructed cartels in eight of the fourteen designated depressed industries. As Mark Tilton points out (1996, 9),

Japan's basic materials were affected by internationally high costs. With the exception of aluminum, the industries have been able to maintain high domestic prices without seeing any significant increase in net imports. Three of the four core industries covered under cartels have commanded high prices for standardized goods, ranging from an average of 60 percent above import prices for petrochemicals (1982–92), to 48 percent for most blast-furnace steel plate (1984–92), to 57 percent for cement (1980–92).

While the Japanese surplus production capacity declined, Japan remained a net exporter. "In none of these high-cost and high-price sectors (except primary aluminum) did a shift to net imports force Japan to cut back its domestic production" (Tilton 1996, 11).

Why did the Japanese fail to make a structural transition in the industrial basic material sectors? A report published by the Committee on Industrial Structure in 1982 provided some answers. The industrial basic material sectors constituted a big chunk of the Japanese economy. They provided 17.5 percent of the employment, 32.8 percent of production output, and 43.8 percent of total fixed assets in the manufacturing industries. In addition, their operations were closely related to the quality of Japanese automobiles, electronics, and machine tools. If there was to be a decline in industrial basic materials, a decline in these industries would follow. At the time, the foundation of future technology was believed to be centered on fine ceramics and biotechnology, and these, too, were related to industrial basic materials. If this sector declined, Japan would lose the technological foundation of its future technologies. Another serious concern was the national security implications. Because Japan relied heavily on imports of industrial basic materials, if its trading partners reduced supplies or imposed high prices, a weak industrial basic material sector would leave Japan unable to make a counterattack. In addition, the supply side of the Japanese economy would encounter strong uncertainty, and Japanese companies might be forced to accept unfavorable terms in international trade. Finally, this sector provided 10 percent to 50 percent of the employment and 10 percent to 70 percent of the production output to the medium-size and small companies in local communities. Therefore, it was considered critical to the maintenance of political stability (Tsūsanshō 1993b, Vol. 14, 46–47).

THE TRADEOFFS BETWEEN JOB SECURITY AND WAGES

The permanent employment system practiced by big corporations, one of the major cornerstones of the total employment strategy, played a crucial role in maintaining Japan's political stability during the structural adjustment after the First Oil Shock. Meanwhile, however, this practice also began to impose increasing financial burdens on big corporations. Under the great pressures of the structural adjustment, this system forced Japanese corporations to maintain surplus workers. Although big corporations in the exports-related sector were able to aggressively export their products to international markets, they could do so – constrained as they were by the high cost of maintaining surplus labor – only by accepting low profitability. The labor unions were successful in ensuring job security, but it came at the cost of lower wages (Brenner 1998; Dore 1986, 1987). Although in the short run the Japanese economy as a whole managed to maintain political stability, in the long run it also seriously weakened its position in international competition.

As Fred Block points out, "The more open an economy, the greater the likelihood that painful adjustments will be necessary, and these painful adjustments create a risk of intense social conflict" (1977, 3). The permanent employment system encountered a difficult test during the First Oil Shock. Driven by pressure to improve efficiency, many Japanese corporations in fact adjusted their employment policies. According to official statistics from a Ministry of Labor survey conducted between April and June 1975, in manufacturing industries 71 percent of Japanese companies had adjusted their employment policies; 54 percent of them had restrained overtime hours (thereby reducing the burden of financial compensation); 16 percent had stopped renewing (or had even fired) temporary workers and part-time workers; 50 percent had reduced or stopped mid-career recruitment; 23 percent had transferred workers to alternative job posts; 20 percent had asked workers to take temporary leave; and 5 percent had solicited voluntary early retirement and had cut back recruitment. Only 29 percent of Japanese companies had not adopted any measure (*Ekonomisuto* 1994, 55). An historical comparison shows that the numbers in all these categories during the First

Oil Shock were significantly higher than the numbers in the same categories during the recession caused by the yen appreciation after the 1985 Plaza Accord and the early stage of the economic crisis in the 1990s.

Inasmuch as big Japanese corporations were ready to adjust their employment policies during the First Oil Shock, why did the permanent employment system survive? It survived because it became a struggle not only between management and labor but also between the state and labor unions. There were some clear signs indicating that privatized social protection was no longer enough for the structural adjustments after the high growth ended. Responding to the challenge of employment adjustment, labor unions began to fight for their interests, "not just by demanding employment security from management, but also by demanding an employment security policy from the government" (Kume 1998, 169). In contrast to the high growth period – when job and wage issues could be settled at the company level and management had an incentive to maintain its highly skilled workers – it had become more difficult for labor unions to achieve their goals strictly by negotiating. After the early 1970s, labor unions became more actively involved in public policy-making. Labor unions in depressed industries, such as open-hearth and electric-furnace steel, openly urged the Japanese state to allow these industries to organize recession cartels and to reduce overbuilt production capacity. They also demanded legislation to ensure job transfers for redundant workers. These actions led to a significant revision of the Employment Insurance Law in 1974. "This law prescribed that company management in consultation with the union set up a plan to retrain laid-off workers for new jobs. The government would also provide the laid-off workers with various allowances for job hunting as well as an extended unemployment allowance. Furthermore, the government would subsidize employers who hired the targeted laid-off workers" (Kume 1998, 172–173).

In 1974, the Japanese labor movement reached its postwar peak; labor unions had more than 12.5 million members, and, at 34 percent, its highest proportion of the labor force in history. There were 10,000 labor disputes; those involving more than a half-day strike increased from 45 percent of disputes in 1973 to 68 percent in 1974, with a total participation of more than 14.3 million workers (Rekishigaku Kenkyūkai 1991, Vol. 5, 78). In the 1974 spring strike, organized labor combined the institutionalized format of wage negotiation with a new set of political demands: control of inflation, protection of the weak, and the right to strike for workers in the public sector (*Ekonomisuto* 1974, April 30, 6).

The lack of a government-sponsored social assistance program directly contributed to the rapid increase of wages in 1974 and 1975, something that further stimulated inflation. Facing inflation triggered by the yen's appreciation and Tanaka's industrial reallocation plan, labor unions demanded significant salary raises to maintain the standard of living. At the time, business leaders complained that if the Japanese wage kept increasing at an annual rate of 20 or 30 percent, it would exceed that of West Germany in 1975 and that of the United States in 1978, and Japan would have the highest wages in the world. Because Japan depended heavily on trade, competitive wages would be vital to the international competitiveness of Japanese products. A rapid increase in salaries was like committing suicide. The Japanese state also warned that a rapid increase in wages would further stimulate inflation. By 1974, the state was already trying to control inflation. Because expenditures by individual households constituted more than half of the total demand in the economy, a sizable salary increase would counter the state's policy of restraining demand (*Ekonomisuto* 1974, April 30, 7).

Nevertheless, labor unions emphasized the lack of social welfare in Japan and their needs for wage increases. They maintained that the major causes of inflation were the state's plan for industrial reallocation and corporations' opportunistic speculation during the First Oil Shock (Rekishigaku Kenkyūkai 1991, Vol. 5, 78). Even though the annual growth rate of Japanese productivity was −0.4 percent in 1974 and −3.9 percent in 1975, average salaries rose 26.1 percent and 11.5 percent in those two years, respectively, resulting in an increase in consumer prices of 24.4 percent in 1974 and 11.8 percent in 1975 (Mitsuhashi and Uchida 1994, 44). Some companies, such as Toyota and Nissan, even raised workers' salaries more than 30 percent. Using a strike without defined duration, workers at a transportation company gained a 41.5 percent salary increase (*Ekonomisuto* 1974, April 30, 6).

After seeing the negative interactions among the employment adjustment, labor unions' demand for higher wages, and inflation, management and the labor unions compromised. In 1975, newly elected Prime Minister Migi Takeo made a commitment to control the rise of consumer prices within 15 percent. As a result, both the number of labor disputes and the number of participants in the Spring Strike decreased nearly 30 percent, and the number of strikes that involved more than half a day declined 50 percent. The Japanese government made a great effort to control wholesale prices and the prices of food and vegetables, asking the labor unions to soften their demands for annual salary raises. In response, the labor unions reduced their demand to a 3 percent wage increase. Private corporations then used this opportunity to push for rationalization measures. The Japanese state, business leaders, and labor unions had learned a great lesson from the First Oil Shock. When the Second Oil Shock took place in the late 1970s, the Japanese economic system coped with it effectively. Japanese corporations avoided layoffs, and labor unions restrained their wage demands. As a result, the Japanese economy achieved a growth rate higher than that of any other major industrialized country.

By the time the yen's value appreciated rapidly after the 1985 Plaza Accord, the permanent employment system had become a ritual, sustained not only by widespread international approval but also by the self-reinforcing ideology of employee sovereignty. In the manufacturing industry, only 40 percent of Japanese corporations adjusted their employment policies, compared with 71 percent that did so in 1975; only 26 percent restrained overtime hours, compared with 54 percent in 1975; only 6 percent stopped contract renewals or laid off temporary or part-time workers, compared with 16 percent in 1975; only 12 percent reduced or stopped mid-career recruitment, compared with 50 percent in 1975; only 11 percent reallocated workers, compared with 23 percent in 1975; only 3 percent asked workers to go on call, compared with 20 percent in 1975; only 3 percent asked employees to accept early retirement or actually laid off workers, compared with 5 percent in 1975; and 60 percent of Japanese corporations in the manufacturing industries did not adopt any adjustment policy, compared with 29 percent in 1975 (*Ekonomisuto* 1994, 55).

Although the permanent employment system was widely praised, it required two major tradeoffs. One was declining profitability because of the surplus labor force. In 1975, among big corporations in the manufacturing industry (those having more than 1,000 employees), the surplus labor force was 18 percent in management, technical, and professional positions, 23 percent in clerk positions, 22 percent in skilled worker positions, and 26 percent in unskilled worker positions. In 1986, the surplus labor was 15 percent in management positions, 17 percent in clerk positions, 23 percent in skilled worker positions, and 22 percent in unskilled worker positions (*Ekonomisuto* 1994, 55).[2] Maintaining surplus labor led to lower corporate profits. As Robert Brenner (1998, 172) points out,

By 1978–1979, the rate of profit in [Japanese] manufacturing remained no less than 35–40 percent below its level of 1973. In contrast, profitability outside had risen by around 13 percent above its 1973 level. The average annual growth of unit labor costs in non-manufacturing was actually 25 percent higher over the period than in manufacturing, but, being largely immune to the downward pressure on prices that plagued manufacturing, it could translate the very sharp reduction in the growth of wages into higher

2 In the 1975 statistics, management, technical, and professional positions constituted one category. In the 1986 statistics, management was separated from technical and professional positions, which showed a 13 percent shortage in the labor force.

profits. With its better profitability recovery, the non-manufacturing sector was able to attract investment so as to increase its capital stock at an average annual rate of growth almost 25 percent higher than in manufacturing, and this despite the fact that any given increase in capital stock in non-manufacturing was much less effective in raising labor productivity than in manufacturing. While the manufacturing labor force (in terms of the number employed) fell by 7.8 percent between 1973 and 1979, the non-manufacturing industrial labor force grew slightly and service sector employment grew by a striking 15 percent.

The second tradeoff resulting from the permanent employment system was stagnant growth in wages. According to a study done by OECD, Japan had high wage flexibility when it came to a tradeoff with unemployment or consumer prices. In the tradeoff with consumer prices, the Japanese wage parameter was 0.93 in contrast with 0.22 in the United States, 0.44 in West Germany, 0.47 in France, and 0.33 in Italy. In the tradeoff with unemployment, the Japanese wage parameter was −3.31 in contrast with −0.33 in the United States, −0.25 in West Germany, −0.31 in France, and −0.17 in Italy. This means that when 3 percent wage increases created 1 percent unemployment, Japanese labor unions would choose to give up the wage increases in exchange for job security. In this regard, company-based labor unions played an important role. Unlike industry-based or profession-based labor unions, company-based labor unions were more sensitive to a company's profitability and performance. Because their interests were closely tied to those of the company, in wage negotiations they tended to sacrifice wage increases for job security (Okazuka 1987, 29).

COMPETITION POLICY IN A WELFARE SOCIETY

In the 1970s, Japanese competition policy faced a serious dilemma. On the one hand, the negative economic impact of the black cartels during the First Oil Shock had generated strong resentment. There was a strong demand for a tougher competition policy against cartels. On the other hand, cartels had been a major cornerstone sustaining the total employment strategy. After the high growth period ended, the pressures on employment increased rapidly. It was difficult to conduct a radical reform that would create massive unemployment. This dilemma was reflected in the political struggle centered on the 1977 amendment of the Antimonopoly Law.

In fall 1973, amid the crisis caused by the First Oil Shock and the public resentment against the black cartels, the FTC proposed to the Diet an amendment of the Antimonopoly Law. At the end of the same year, the Special Committee on Price Measures of the Upper House attached a resolution to the bill concerning the Emergency Measures on Stabilizing Civilian Life. It demanded that the government enforce the Antimonopoly Law and endow the FTC with the authority to divide monopolies and dismantle cartels. The FTC published the Outline of the Bill Concerning the Amendment of the Antimonopoly Law on September 18, 1974.

This proposal emphasized four policy areas. With regard to cartels, the FTC proposed granting itself the authority to order companies that had raised prices through cartels to return their prices to their original level. It also proposed the introduction of penalties on profits made by cartel-sustained prices. With regard to oligopoly, the FTC proposed a system in which oligopolies that had raised their prices would have to make public their original price breakdown. With regard to monopoly, the FTC proposed a deconcentration program in which any company that held a monopoly position would be divided into several companies. With regard to the overconcentration of economic power, the FTC proposed to control the amount of reciprocal shareholding among big corporations, and a limit on reciprocal shareholding by financial institutions. Thus, the FTC's proposal asserted a radical change in the Japanese competition policy. It enjoyed the enthusiastic support of consumer groups, the opposition parties, and many scholars and opinion leaders, but it encountered strong opposition from business communities, MITI bureaucrats, and many conservative politicians in the LDP.

When Migi Takeo became prime minister in December 1974, he made a public commitment to the amendment of the Antimonopoly Law. How did that come about? Throughout the postwar period, the LDP had adopted a pro–big corporation competition policy. In the first half of the 1970s, however, the LDP was hit with an unprecedented crisis: It was criticized for corruption, as exemplified by the Rockweed scandal. The hyperinflation of the early 1970s, exacerbated by the opportunistic behavior of big corporations, caused a strong reaction from the general public. As the leading party, the LDP was criticized for supporting speculation by big corporations. In the election for the Upper House in July 1974, in addition to the Rockweed scandal, the opposition parties criticized the LDP's entanglement with big corporations and the impact of money politics. According to a survey conducted on November 21, 1974, support for the Tanaka Kakuei cabinet had declined to only 12 percent, the lowest number for any administration in Japan's postwar political history. Eventually, Tanaka was forced to resign. Migi, a leader of a minority faction in the LDP, became prime minister because his image as a clean politician provided a way for LDP to rebuild its political support. It was under these circumstances that the Migi cabinet made its public commitment to amend the Antimonopoly Law (Shibagaki 1977, 180).

The battle over the amendment geared up. Because the prime minister had made a public statement on this issue, MITI and the Keidanren could not oppose the idea directly. Instead, they adopted a strategy of forestalling the FTC proposal by formulating a government proposal. On December 17, the Prime Minister's Office established the Forum on the Amendment of the Antimonopoly Law, whose membership consisted of representatives from academia, consumer groups, business circles, and labor unions. On December 29 of the same year, the LDP also established its Special Investigation Committee on the Amendment of the Antimonopoly Law.

The strategy adopted by the LDP was to agree with the FTC in general but to oppose any substantial measures. On February 25, 1975, the Prime Minister's Office made its position public. On deconcentration, it established a precondition: Before the FTC could order a monopoly to transfer part of its business, it would have to confer with the minister who governed that industry. In other words, the FTC would be required to obtain MITI's agreement in order to divide a monopoly. The LDP rejected the FTC's proposal of asking private companies to make public their price breakdown when they raised prices in concert. Instead, the LDP proposed that private companies simply report to the FTC and the Diet their reasons for raising prices. The LDP also rejected the FTC's proposal of asking private companies to return to their original level any prices raised through the cartel. As an alternative, the LDP proposed that private companies should report to the FTC about what they planned to do after the cartel was dissolved. On the limit on reciprocal shareholding, the LDP proposed that exceptions should be allowed (Shibagaki 1977, 183). Legal scholars strongly criticized the government's proposal and supported the FTC's position. In the hearing process in the Lower House, five political parties together revised the government proposal. After this revision was sent to the Upper House, however, it failed because of strong opposition from the LDP members.

The trend among major advanced industrialized countries toward a tougher competition policy at the time encouraged the FTC to enforce the Antimonopoly Law. In 1975, Takehashi Toshihide, the commissioner of the FTC, traveled to the United States, West Germany, Britain, France, and Italy. He also exchanged opinions with the officials in charge of competition policies in various industrialized countries during a conference on restrictive business customs held by the OECD in Paris. At a press conference after returning from Europe, Takehashi maintained that "the more liberal economies all have a strong antimonopoly policy. Countries that have a strong competition policy operate their economies more efficiently. Conversely, when the economy is under strong government control, there is little room for the competition policy and the economy does not operate smoothly"(Mainichi Shinbunsha Keizaibu 1975, 31). Takehashi said that he had observed that in both West Germany and Britain, companies were being asked to lower the prices they had raised through cartels. In West Germany, although the cartel bureau belonged to the Ministry of Economy, the bureau director had the authority to reject the economic minister's order. In contrast, in France, prices were determined by a contract between the government and private companies. Because the government's control was strong, there was not much room for competition. In Italy, half of the important industries were nationalized, and private companies coexisted with nationalized companies. No Antimonopoly Law existed. Where state intervention was strong, the economy was not efficient at all. Takehashi concluded that only through competition would an economy be dynamic (Mainichi Shinbunsha Keizaibu 1975, 32).

In April 1976, for the third time, the Japanese government sent to the Diet its proposal as an alternative to that drafted by the FTC on the amendment of the Antimonopoly Law. On May 8, the Lower House held a hearing. Although the opposition parties presented their own proposal, their intent was to revise rather than reject the government proposal because they were afraid that strong opposition to the government proposal might further discourage the limited incentive of the LDP to amend the law. After a compromise, the opposition parties reached an agreement with the LDP and gained the approval of the Lower House on June 25. Because of opposition from MITI and the LDP, however, this bill was not discussed by the Upper House. The central issue of the Diet's 75th regular session was the reform of election laws, so the bill had no chance of being examined, and the Diet session was extended from May 25 to July 4. Meanwhile, a revised bill endorsed by five opposition parties was also sent to the Diet. Neither of these two bills had a chance to be discussed, and both died.

After this failure, 26 Japanese consumer groups published a joint statement. They held that although the proposal drafted by the five opposition parties in 1975 represented a setback from their original demands, it was acceptable, given that the story of the Antimonopoly Law itself was a history of setbacks. They wanted to hold the government and the LDP responsible for the failed effort and strongly demanded that the amendment be passed (Shōhisha Dantai 1976, 46). Consumer groups argued that because Japan could no longer rely on a bureaucrat-led managed economy, the Antimonopoly Law had become indispensable to the maintenance of order in the market. Inflation was not a result of the shortage of materials and merchandise, they argued, but instead had been created by the cartels' common action in consumer pricing. They complained, however, that the FTC's proposal did not touch the issue of how to ensure consumers' rights. They especially demanded the right to initiate antimonopoly lawsuits (Takeuchi 1974, 18).

In December 1976, Fukuda Takeo became prime minister. At the time, the LDP was under increasing pressure to push the amendment of the Antimonopoly Law. In the election for the House of Representatives, the LDP was nearly defeated and held a narrow majority in both houses of the Diet. As a result, some standing committee chairmanships were controlled by the opposition parties for the first time in 18 years (Beeman 1997, 159). Under these circumstances, Fukuda made a public commitment to push the agenda of the amendment. After a series of internal negotiations within the LDP and external negotiations with the opposition parties and related bureaucracies, a bill was formulated. It was stronger than the one proposed by the government in July 1976, but it was still considered weaker than the one endorsed by the five opposition parties (Beeman 1997, 160–164). After four years, the amendment of the Antimonopoly Law was passed.

The total employment strategy exerted a great impact on this 1977 amendment of the Antimonopoly Law. First, labor unions at big corporations were not very active. The bigger the corporation, the greater the job security of its employees. A tougher competition policy, in contrast, means less monopoly profit for big corporations, and thus less capacity to continue the practice of permanent employment. Because Japanese employees identified themselves more strongly with the companies they worked for than as individual consumers, the proposal to strengthen consumer interests did not generate enough political support from labor unions. Under the permanent employment system, labor unions' real concern was not how much more purchasing power they could gain as consumers from a more rigid Antimonopoly Law; rather, their concern was how much more job security and income they could gain. As long as these two conditions were satisfied, they usually did not have much political incentive to participate in the social movement against big corporations.

Second, the response by medium-size and small companies to the FTC's proposal was also ambiguous. In theory, the medium-size and small companies should have supported the amendment because they would be better off with a strengthened Antimonopoly Law that ensured equal opportunities in market competition. In reality, however, the majority of the business done by medium-size and small companies was tied up with big corporations through the keiretsu. Companies in this category were also sensitive to any reform that would prohibit them from organizing cartels, which had been their major means of avoiding bankruptcies. On February 18, 1975, the Central Committee of the National Association of Medium-Size and Small Businesses issued a public statement. It asserted that only the cartels organized by big corporations would dominate the market and make monopoly

profits. The ones organized by medium-size and small companies had functioned only to prevent disorder in the market and to maintain proper standards of business operation. When the FTC decided to divide any monopoly,
the statement said, it should consult with the ministry that governed the
industry and should pay special attention to the potential negative impact
of such action on medium-size and small companies. The group strongly
opposed the FTC's proposal to publish the original price breakdown explaining why they had raised prices simultaneously. It also strongly opposed the
FTC's proposal to order cartels to lower their prices to the original levels. It
stressed that the state should supervise the actions of big corporations to make
sure they paid their subcontractors on time, but it opposed the idea of dividing the monopolies, because that might jeopardize their businesses. In other
words, the group wanted the FTC to oppose any proposal that might hurt
the medium-size and small companies, even if these companies might be hurt
much less than big corporations and in the end might gain more (Zenkoku
Chūshō Kigyō Dantai Chūō-kai 1975, 30–31).

Clearly, the keiretsu significantly changed the relationship between big
corporations and the medium-size and small companies. Instead of competing with big corporations at a horizontal level, these medium-size and small
companies acted as subordinates at a vertical level. As a member of a keiretsu,
the medium-size and small companies no longer regarded big corporations
as a major threat but instead saw them as a source of business contracts. Constrained by such an institutional environment, the medium-size and small
companies did not take a position opposing the big corporations. Instead,
they tended to believe that they would be in trouble if big corporations were
in trouble. It is also clear that Japanese cartels organized by medium-size and
small companies had performed an important role in income distribution.
This distribution, however, was not achieved in the form of government assistance to those who had lost in market competition; instead, it took the form
of a government policy that tried to keep everyone in business. As far as the
medium-size and small companies were concerned, the government policy on
cartels was as much a competition policy as a social policy.

Shaped by such complicated circumstances, efforts to strengthen market
competition encountered enormous resistance. Business leaders also used this
relationship between big corporations and medium-size and small companies
to justify the pro–big corporation competition policy adopted by the state.

THE RISE OF INEQUALITY

The Japanese economic system tried hard to sustain the total employment
strategy after the First Oil Shock. As a result, Japanese unemployment
remained relatively low. In conjunction with its success in exports, the

Japanese model of social protection – in particular, the practice of permanent employment by big corporations – attracted widespread attention in the 1980s. It was perceived as successful because it achieved the goal of simultaneously sustaining economic growth and improving economic equality. Even after the bubble collapsed, the image of Japan as a highly egalitarian society remained intact. According to the latest studies by Japanese scholars, however, this idealistic image may have neglected some important changes. When the long-term movement of capitalist economies shifted from social protection to the release of market forces, Japan was no exception, but it was influenced by the neoliberal movement. As a result, although equality in income distribution remained stable throughout the 1970s, it deteriorated significantly in the 1980s, especially in the second half of the 1980s amid the rise of the bubble. This suggests that the two structural shifts in the long-term movement of capitalism in fact reinforced each other, and the expansion of finance and monetary activity served to undermine the institutional foundation of economic equality.

Income inequality between employees of big corporations and employees of medium-size and small companies further increased in the 1980s. Taking the national average wage as the base of comparison, the wage of those who worked at giant corporations (those with 5,000 or more employees) was 28.6 percent higher in 1978 but 32.1 percent higher in 1988. The wage of those who worked at big corporations (those with 1,000 or more employees) was 20.5 percent higher in 1978 but 21.8 percent higher in 1988. In contrast, the wage for those who worked at companies with 300 employees was 1 percent higher than the national average wage in 1978, but it fell to 1.6 percent lower in 1988. The wage of those who worked at companies with 100 employees was 7.4 percent lower than the national average in 1978 but 11.9 percent lower in 1988. The wage of those who worked at companies with 30 employees was 15.7 percent lower than the national average in 1978 but fell to 20.3 percent lower in 1988. In the same period, the wage of those who worked at companies with 10 employees was 21.2 percent lower in 1978 but 25.3 percent lower in 1988. If we discount the effect of the quality of the employees and the companies, emphasizing only the effect of the companies' sizes on wages, the gap between the wage at giant corporations and the national average wage was narrowed to 23.1 percent in 1978 and 27.2 percent in 1988. The gap between the wage at companies with 100 employees and the national average wage, however, further deepened from 7.5 percent lower to 12.1 percent lower in 1978, and from 11.9 percent lower to 15.4 percent lower in 1988 (Tachibanaki 1998, 100–101).

In measuring equality in distribution, both income and assets are major factors. During the bubble, the greatest loss in equality occurred in that

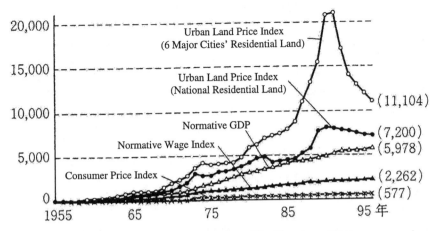

Figure 7.1. *The changes of land (residential land) prices, GDP, wages, and consumer prices.*
Source: The Prime Minister Office's "Household Survey." Cited in: Tachibanaki 1998, p. 135.

measured by assets. As Figure 7.1 shows, the bubble economy brought a rapid increase in land and stock prices. As the Japanese government adopted an expansionary fiscal policy in 1987, the upper classes derived their income from speculation in real estate and stock markets; the result was conspicuous consumption among this group but a widening gap between the rich and the poor (Itō Makoto 1988). A survey taken by the Economic Planning Agency measures this gap between the assets of those who owned one or more houses and the assets of those who did not. When the survey sample was limited to those who owned one or more houses, the Gini index of assets increased from 0.467 in 1983 to 0.535 in 1988 and then fell slightly to 0.520 in 1989. When the survey sample included both homeowners and nonhomeowners, the Gini index of assets increased from 0.668 in 1983 to 0.734 in 1988 and then fell to 0.726 in 1989 (cited in Tachibanaki 1998, 14). As a further breakdown, among the 9,574,000 yen, which was the averaged total annual household income in Japan in 1990, wages contributed 7,012,000 yen in the total income, but 54.3 percent in the total inequality; income from house(s) and land contributed 1,776,000 yen, but 32.8 percent, and stocks contributed 786,000 yen, but 12.9 percent. It is clear that rental income generated from the ownership of a house or land played an important role in Japanese distribution, constituting roughly one-third of the total household income (Tachibanaki 1998, 63).

The ownership of stocks and bonds also became a major factor in social stratification in Japan. As discussed earlier, individual shareholders owned only about 30 percent of the total stocks in the 1970s. During the bubble in the 1980s, stock prices rose rapidly; between October 1986 and April 1987, for example, the Nikkei index jumped 46 percent. This rapid rise exerted a great impact on the distribution of assets. At the same time, the Japanese government also abolished its policy of tax exemption for interest earned by small bank savings. In December 1986, individual savings in Japanese banks totaled as much as 545 trillion yen; 70 percent of these accounts were exempted from income tax. When account holders learned that the government planned to levy taxes on these individual bank deposits, many of them shifted their money to the stock market. As a result, in 1988 total bank deposits and certified deposits decreased 7.5 percent from the 1987 level. Deposits whose interest rates were regulated declined 6.9 trillion yen, the first large-scale decline since Japan began to conduct such surveys in 1954. In that same year (1987), the total amount of money spent on stocks increased 5.45 trillion yen. Thus, this phenomenon, known as zai'tech (see Chapter 6), had become an important instrument not only for corporations but also for individuals (Miyazaki 1992, 130–131).

Suppose that we divide the Japanese population into five groups according to income levels, with each representing 20 percent of the general population. In 1984, the first group (those with the lowest income) held only 6.3 percent of the total stocks held by individual households; the second group held 8.0 percent, the third, 12.4 percent, the fourth, 18.3 percent, and the fifth (those with the highest income), 55.0 percent. In 1987, after stock prices jumped, the increase in asset values witnessed major variations among these five income groups. Total assets increased 2.8 trillion yen in the first group (those with the lowest income), 5.5 trillion in the second group, 5.1 trillion in the third group, 8.3 trillion in the fourth group, and 24.4 trillion in the fifth group (those with the highest income). If we take as a sample only those households that held stocks, the Gini index of asset distribution in 1985 was 0.622. When we include in the sample those households that did not own any stocks, the Gini index of asset distribution was as high as 0.924, very close to 1, which indicates complete inequality (Tachibanaki 1998, 139–141).

Gender-based inequality also increased. Although the bubble economy of the second half of the 1980s created more job opportunities for Japanese women and more Japanese women entered the labor market, the majority of these workers became "office ladies," and many married women tried to work only part-time.

In the Japanese model of the welfare society, various institutional barriers discouraged women from working full-time. Among Japanese corporations with 30 or more employees, 81 percent had established a spouse allowance system by the early 1990s. The amount of the spouse allowance was often 1 million yen, which was the limit of income that was not subject to tax. Among the corporations that had a spouse allowance system, 58 percent limited the allowance when the employee's spouse had an independent income (Higuchi 1995, 192).

Taxation policy in the 1980s also served to discourage Japanese women from having full-time jobs. In 1987, the Japanese state established the spouse special tax deduction system, providing benefits to those households in which the wives did not work (in Japanese, they were called "professional housewives"). To put this into perspective, let's briefly review the history of exemptions under the Japanese system of taxation. Beginning in 1949, a spouse who did not work had been counted simply as one dependent of the breadwinner; the tax deduction was the same for the spouse as for other dependents such as children. In 1961, to balance the treatment of married women whose households ran family businesses, professional housewives began to receive a special higher tax deduction. However, from that point on, the ordinary dependent tax deduction increased rapidly. By 1975, the difference between the dependent tax deduction and the spouse deduction had disappeared. Formerly, a married woman lost her tax deduction of 350,000 yen when her income reached more than 1 million yen. In the spouse special tax deduction system established in 1987, the tax deduction became progressive. In this system, if a married woman's annual income was 700,000 yen, she would receive the traditional 350,000 yen deduction as a dependent and another 350,000 yen special deduction as a spouse. The amount of the deduction was doubled. As her income increased, for every 50,000 yen, her deduction decreased by 50,000 yen. Therefore, a married woman with an annual income of from 700,000 to 1 million yen could deduct more than the 350,000 yen she could in the past (Higuchi 1995, 187–189). As Higuchi Yoshio (1995, 216) points out, the special tax deduction system might have been designed to protect Japanese women who did not work full-time, but in reality it may have served the high-income group. Because the tax deduction was not based on income but instead was based on the status as a spouse, it was more favorable to the high-income group than a deduction would have been that was simply based on the total amount of a household's taxable income.

Such incentive structures were also reflected in pensions and health insurance. A married woman who did not work (or who worked but had an annual income of less than 1.3 million yen) did not have to pay any premium to get health insurance. When she made more than 1.3 million yen annually, however, she had to pay the premium. According to a 1986 amendment to the Pension Law, a married woman who did not work could also receive the basic pension for the elderly without her or her husband having to pay any premium. She could also receive three-fourths of her husband's pension upon his death (Higuchi 1995, 190–191).

According to a survey of part-time workers conducted in 1990 with a sample of 15,887 married women, 35.7 percent of female part-time workers tried to control their income; among them, 84.6 percent were concerned about their own income tax and with trying to keep their income within the nontaxable limit; 81.5 percent of these women were also concerned with their husbands' income tax, spouse allowance, and other welfare benefits (Higuchi 1995, 209–210). As a result of income adjustment, the total annual working time of those who tried to control their income was on average 24.8 percent less than those who did not exercise control. In 1990, the average annual working time for part-time workers was 1,454 hours. In the same year, there were 5.24 million married women working part-time. This means that as a result of these efforts to control income for taxation and welfare benefits, Japan lost a total of 679 million working hours (Higuchi 1995, 217).

CONCLUSION

Unlike the mechanism of excessive competition, which immediately began to malfunction after the collapse of the Bretton Woods system, the mechanism of total employment continued to work relatively well, and was even widely regarded as successful, for two more decades. In this process, however, the institutions of privatized social protection became rigid, preventing the Japanese economy from making structural changes to compete in a new era, and they began to show that the longer the time span, the more their costs outweighed their benefits.

To be sure, the continuing practice of the total employment strategy helped to maintain political stability. Nevertheless, the cost of doing so increased substantially. Under asymmetric cooperation with the United States and the high speed of economic growth in 1950–1970, the Japanese economy was able to absorb the inefficiency created by permanent employment, by cartels, and by government protection of the weak sectors and sunset industries. During that time, the economic gains of maintaining political stability were greater than the losses of protecting the inefficient sectors andindustries. One important reason was that the Japanese strategy for industrial upgrading was not to replace sunset industries with sunrise industries, but rather to add sunrise industries on top of sunset industries in the economic structure. In the 1950s and 1960s, there were many sunrise industries in the Japanese economy as a result of the technological revolution. Thus, the increase of productivity in these industries could easily counter the inefficiency resulting from cartels and government protection of the sunset industries. In contrast, since the 1970s, there were no longer many sunrise industries as the Japanese economy became mature. Under these circumstances, the cost of maintaining the privatized social protection increased substantially.

This chapter portrays the profound impact of the major shift in the long-term movement of capitalist economies from social protection to the release of market forces on established institutions that were aimed at addressing distribution-related issues through the total employment strategy. It shows that international trade directly influenced domestic distribution in Japan. With the support of asymmetric cooperation with the United States, Japan had been able to keep its domestic markets closed while also maintaining a small government that relied on private institutions to perform the welfare function. This made the Japanese model of social welfare very resource-efficient during the high growth period. But when Japan came under increasing pressure to open its domestic markets and when high growth ended, the Japanese model of social welfare began to consume resources at a rapid rate. By freezing the entitlements of a variety of vested interests, the total employment strategy had weakened the capacity of the Japanese economy to adjust to a more competitive international environment.

When asymmetric cooperation with the United States ended in the early 1970s, Japan faced increasing pressure to open its domestic markets. Meanwhile, many newly industrialized countries and developing countries entered international competition, and Japan no longer had the comparative advantage of cheap labor. Under such circumstances, the longer the Japanese economy delayed making a structural adjustment, the heavier the cost it would face when it was forced to do so. In the beginning, Tanaka Kakuei tried to search for new solutions to the problem of inequality in the distribution of economic welfare and the need to continue economic growth. When Tanaka's industrial reallocation plan collided with public demands for the development of the welfare state, the Japanese state chose to return to the institutional logic of total employment by keeping everyone in business in an effort to maintain political stability. As a result, the Japanese economy gradually lost its dynamics.

That being said, making a normative judgment about the Japanese model of social welfare is difficult because such a judgment must be associated with the time span of each assessment. Since the Great Depression, with the exception of a short period in the 1950s, the Japanese model has always preferred stability over efficiency. Over the years, the leading normative judgment about this choice has changed several times. In the 1950s and early 1960s, the permanent employment system was often considered a premodern system that would disappear in the process of industrialization. Throughout the 1970s and 1980s, Japan's political stability and economic success in exports further legitimized many of the institutions discussed in this book. Only after the bubble collapsed did it become clear that many of these practices had created major problems for the Japanese economy.

This chapter directly questions the adaptiveness of the Japanese economy since the First Oil Shock as it is portrayed by some analyses in the literature. I argue that the strategy of continuously maintaining total employment should be considered as much a successful adaptation to a new environment as a muddle-through behavior driven by institutional inertia. Although this strategy seemed to be working at the time, it greatly accelerated the internal tensions within the system between two competing goals: that of maintaining political stability and that of upgrading economic structure. This chapter also suggests that we need to discount the impact of the bubble on the persistence of privatized social protection in the second half of the 1980s. Although the rapid appreciation of the yen after the 1985 Plaza Accord posed a great challenge to the Japanese economy, the ensuing bubble dramatically improved the financial situation of Japanese corporations. That served to overshadow the urgency of structural adjustment and to create the illusion of the adaptiveness of the Japanese economy. Without the financial strength created by the bubble, the total employment strategy might have begun to lose its foundation a decade earlier.

CHAPTER 8

FIGHTING THE STAGNATION

My analysis of the reversion of the Japanese economy from prosperity to stagnation pays special attention to the rise of the bubble. As any bubble would eventually burst, I believe, the crisis of the Japanese economy in the 1990s was all but inevitable. In this chapter, I show that the deepening of the economic crisis was driven by a reversion of the institutional logic: when control and monitoring were suddenly strengthened in the big bang reform in 1996, the old growth engine of excessive competition lost its fuel; and, when the total employment strategy began to lose ground in the worst economic crisis since World War II, Japanese consumers, whose future incomes relied on their jobs, dared not spend money. As both corporate investments and consumer spending remained low, the Japanese economy continued to stagnate in spite of the budget deficits generated by government stimulation packages. I first analyze how the new developments in the dilemmas I have defined drove the Japanese economy into stagnation and economic crisis in the 1990s. Then I make some reflections on the theoretical implications of this study and discuss the future prospects of the Japanese economic system.

THE BURST OF THE BUBBLE

According to Miyazaki Yoshikazu (1992), the burst of the bubble spread its effects over the Japanese economy through three channels: corporations, banks, and individual households.

In the 1980s, Japanese corporate finance had experienced a rapid shift toward direct financing. Through equity financing, big corporations issued a total of 12.2 trillion yen in stocks, convertible bonds, and warranted bonds in 1988, and 22.9 trillion yen in 1989. Equity finance constituted 27.5 percent of the total capital supply in those two years. In 1990, however, the amount of equity finance fell to 12 trillion yen, or 18 percent of the total capital supply. In the same year, convertible bonds issued in the domestic market declined 60 percent, and warranted bonds issued in the international markets declined 68 percent. After stock prices declined rapidly, bond holders lost their incentive to convert the bonds into stocks. As a result, corporations had to repay the capital plus interest, a significant burden. Between 1990 and 1998, Japanese corporations had to raise 20 trillion yen for this purpose. To meet this challenge, they either sold their short-term securities to increase their cash flow, which led to still lower stock prices, or they issued nonconvertible bonds with higher interest rates, which forced them to reduce the amount they invested in production capacity (Miyazaki 1992, 239–242).

When stock prices fell rapidly, their value as collateral held by Japanese banks against their loans also declined. According to the agreement between Japan and other member countries at the Bank for International Settlements (BIS), 45 percent of the value of stocks owned by Japanese banks as collateral were calculated as their self-capital. If Japanese banks had sold the stocks to cover their losses in bad loans, that would have led to an even further decline in the banks' self-capital ratio. To increase the self-capital ratio to meet the requirement of the BIS, Japanese banks would have had to raise capital through either issuing stocks or borrowing money. Because Japanese banks suffered from low rankings after the bubble collapsed, however, the terms for borrowing were not favorable. Because the stock prices were low, it was also difficult to raise capital through equity financing. As a result, the only choice for Japanese banks was to reduce the amount of their loans, a practice that led to a shortage of credit. Because Japanese banks were having problems lending money, Japanese corporations suffered; they had neither access to the capital they needed nor the willingness to make new investments (Miyazaki 1992, 243–244).

The impact of the burst of the bubble on individual consumers further slowed the economy. According to one estimate, by late 1990, the collapse of the bubble had resulted in a loss of 270 trillion yen, and 22.6 percent of this loss, or about 61 trillion yen, belonged to individual investors. This loss led to lessened availability of consumer credit and reduced consumption of luxury merchandise. It also led to the decline of the prices of housing and golf club memberships. In comparison with the previous year, the sales of luxury apartments in 1991 declined 41.3 percent, returning to the 1978 level. Sales of resort housing declined 42.7 percent, and sales of automobiles declined for the first time since 1981. Toyota reported a 61.6 percent decline in profits in December 1991 – the largest one-year profit decline Toyota had experienced since 1974. Department stores in metropolitan areas began to experience sales declines that lasted until the end of the 1990s. The cause of weakened domestic demand was the loss of consumer confidence in the economy (Miyazaki 1992, 245–247).

THE DILEMMAS AMONG MULTIPLE POLICY OBJECTIVES
AND THE LIQUIDITY TRAP

In the 1990s, Japanese public policy continued to confront the Mundell-Flemming trilemma. This time, it was concentrated in the conflict between a stable exchange rate and domestic policy objectives. Between 1992 and 1995, the Japanese government spent 65 trillion yen, more than 10 percent of Japan's GDP, in efforts to counter the business cycle and to reduce the pain of its accompanying domestic disruptions. According to Adam Posen, however, the stimulus financial packages adopted by the Japanese state were not large enough; among the expansionary fiscal packages adopted since 1992 by the 12 largest OECD economies, 21 were larger than that of Japan for any single year (Posen 1998, 6). In the 1990s, the unemployment program in Japan was even less generous than that in the United States, let alone those in Europe. Japan's social welfare spending was at the bottom of the OECD in terms of the percentage of GDP. Facing strong uncertainty in economic hard times, individual consumers reduced spending. This served to diminish the automatic response of fiscal stabilizers to the business cycle (Posen 1998, 33).

The appreciation of the yen in the mid-1990s seriously undermined the effectiveness of Japan's expansionary fiscal policy. This policy was not able to effectively counter the recession caused by an overvalued yen, and a strong yen hurt domestic products in the international markets. Instead of appreciating the yen, the government should first have lowered it. In 1995, the exchange rate between the dollar and the yen reached one dollar equaling 80 yen. As the result of the yen's appreciation, half of the 65 trillion yen spent by the Japanese government was watered down. This action, accompanied by an expansionary fiscal policy, not only forced Japanese high-tech companies to move production offshore but also forced the Japanese economy to rely heavily on domestic sectors (Kikkawa 1998, 146–151). In the past, a rapidly improved demand in the international markets always enabled an expansionary fiscal policy to increase domestic demand and speed the recovery from a recession. Because of the highly valued yen in the mid-1990s, however, the international demand for Japanese products became relatively weak and could no longer play this role (Nemoto 1996, 57).

Another dilemma of Japanese public policy was the need to launch long-overdue structural reform at the same time the country was attempting to survive economic stagnation (for the debate on these competing goals, see

Gao 2000, 440–443). Between 1992 and 1996, the government adopted an expansionary fiscal policy, and the private sector chose to postpone the restructuring process. As a result, domestic demand, corporate profits, and the stability of financial institutions were maintained. The huge surplus in the country's current accounts and the unexhausted gains from the expansion of the 1980s softened pressures on the Japanese economy for radical structural reform. Although these factors made the structural adjustment relatively mild, they also delayed much-needed reform (Nemoto 1996, 59).

In 1996, the Hashimoto administration simultaneously carried out a deflationary fiscal policy and what was called the "big bang" policy for the banking industry. In its deflationary fiscal policy, the government limited the combined central and local government budget deficits to 3 percent of the GDP until 2003; in addition, it reduced the national debt by 4.3 trillion yen, raised the consumption tax from 3 percent to 4 percent, introduced local consumption taxes, and withdrew the personal income and property tax relief that had been in effect between 1994 and 1996. Meanwhile, the big bang program was designed to reform the banking industry. When banks' self-capital stood at less than 8 percent but more than 4 percent, the bank was required to make and implement a business improvement plan. When its self-capital stood at less than 4 percent, it was required to make plans to increase its self-capital; restrain or reduce total assets; refrain from entering new business operations and from opening new branch offices; reduce the number of existing branch offices; downsize the business operations of both domestic and overseas subordinate companies and refrain from establishing new ones; restrain or prohibit payments of dividends; restrain bonuses for senior managers; and restrain or prohibit high-interest deposit services. When banks had no self-capital, they were required to cease their business operations, with a few exceptions (*Shūkan Tōyō Keizai* 1997/1/18, 79). In its effect, the big bang was equivalent to or more powerful than a deflationary monetary policy.

This policy mix produced a liquidity trap in 1997–1998. In a *liquidity trap*, banks and consumers prefer holding safe, liquid cash to investing in risky, less-liquid bonds and stocks (Krugman 1999a, 66). The trap developed as follows. When banks refused to lend money to corporations, corporate bankruptcy increased rapidly. Until 1996, the annual number of corporate bankruptcies remained around 14,000 cases per year. In 1997, the number increased 12.5 percent to 16,365 cases. In 1998, the number jumped another 17.1 percent to 19,171 cases. This was the second highest number of bankruptcies in Japan's post–World War II history. Meanwhile, corporate debts rose to 14.2 trillion yen in 1997, and 14.3 trillion yen in 1998, continuing to break the record of corporate debts in the postwar history. As Adam Posen (1998, 5) points out,

> In the present Japanese and international economic environment, substituting structural reform for expansionary macroeconomic policy could be harmful, because the usual short-run effect of such reform is to add to unemployment and excess capacity. Such developments would further fuel Japanese investors' and savers' uncertainty and low expectations, even though sustainable higher growth remains attainable today without such reform. There is no pressing need to forgo stimulating aggregate demand and give up the benefits thereof while waiting for the benefits of further deregulation – the current rate of growth is not enough for Japan.

In many ways, the dilemma faced by the Japanese in the 1990s was similar to the one faced by the United States in the Great Depression. Both countries became a world economic superpower in a short period of time and experienced a bubble during that process. In both countries, the bubble burst after an unprecedented boom in the stock and real estate markets. Both countries were involved in a surge of internationalization and were forced to make a great transformation of their social and economic structures. In both cases, the transformation did not go smoothly; the countries suffered from deflation and experienced painful adjustments. In both countries, a return to fiscal contraction worsened the economic situation. In 1937, when the U.S. GDP was almost back to its 1929 level, President Roosevelt reduced the fiscal expenditures of the federal government, an action that aborted the economic recovery. Within one year, the U.S. GDP dropped one-third and stock prices fell 50 percent. It was a depression within the Depression. In 1937, the interest rate was lowered from 1.5 percent to 1 percent, and that rate continued for 11 years even though the U.S. GDP had returned to the 1929 level by 1940 (Yamada 1999). In 1996, when the Japanese economy began to improve after the burst of the bubble, Prime Minister Hashimoto also reduced fiscal spending and imposed the banking reforms of the big bang. These measures drove the economy into a deflation. The Bank of Japan's interest rate in 1999 was only 0.25 percent, much lower even than the U.S. rate of 1 percent during the Great Depression. In a major economic crisis, "accumulation of excess capacity and unemployment has eaten at the confidence of Japanese consumers and savers. The reluctant rise in fear and uncertainty can turn a recession into a depression if left unchecked by policy, even when those fears stem from the immediate situation and nothing more deeply forward looking" (Posen 1998, 4).

To save the economy from the deepening crisis, the Japanese government began to adopt an expansionary fiscal policy again in late 1998. Adopting a policy of fiscal stimulus to survive the economic stagnation, however, has created skyrocketing budget deficits. By March 31, 1999, the Japanese government had a debt of more than 9 trillion yen, which was roughly 18 times higher than the year's tax revenues (Katō 1999, 137). Even at the end of the 1990s, the Japanese government has not adopted double-entry accounting, in which it would have to report both its assets and its liabilities. It still relied on the nineteenth-century style of single-entry accounting, in which it reported only revenue and expenditures. In the post–World War II period, governments in most industrialized countries shifted to double-entry accounting. Japan was a major exception. Since the Meiji period, the Japanese state has held that double-entry accounting is for private corporations whose major goal is to make profits, whereas reporting income and expenditures should be sufficient in the government budget. When its revenue was not great enough to cover expenditures, the government simply issued national debts, and consequently the budget was always balanced on paper. This accounting method has sustained the Japanese style of distributional politics, in which politicians worked hard to deliver public projects to their constituencies. For example, because the government does not care much about the cost, it has often happened that the government has spent one billion yen to build a road on which fewer than 200 cars traveled per day (Katō 1999, 140).

If Japan continues to increase its budget deficits to save the economy, it may face a serious challenge in the near future. A growing number of economists think that the Japanese strategy of spending its way out of recession could backfire horribly in the coming years because the nation's savings have begun to trickle away. According to a 1999 Reuters news report, it may take many years before the surplus in the country's current accounts actually falls to zero, but it may take no more than two years before the financial markets start to speculate on that possibility.

Meanwhile, in the next 20 years Japan will become a society of the aged. The proportion of its population aged 65 or older will reach more than 20 percent by 2010 and 25 percent by 2020. The increasing pressure of an aging society will require increases in public spending, and the resulting huge budget deficits will inflict significant constraints on the future policy choices of the Japanese state.

A similar dilemma, although of a different cause, is shared by many Asian countries. The International Monetary Fund (IMF) held that the Asian financial crisis was created by the failure to control large payment deficits, the explosion in property and financial markets, mismanaged exchange rate regimes, rapidly expanding and poorly regulated financial systems, and an unwillingness to act decisively when confidence was lost. Thus, a radical reform of the economic system was needed. The IMF attached a wide range of conditions to each of its rescue packages to Asian countries (see Kapur 1999). The opponents of this approach assert that structural reform, no matter how desirable, can wait. It is far more urgent to make sure that deflation does not accelerate into a full-blown depression. When Asian governments undertake expansionary monetary and fiscal policies to counter the slump, they must worry that without control on outflows of capital, they may face a further currency collapse as investors, fearing inflation or lower interest rates, again rush for the exits (Krugman, 1999a; Wade, 1999).

STRENGTHENING BANK MONITORING

The strong coordination that is the hallmark of the Japanese economic system was built at the cost of weakening the banks' monitoring over corporate finance, a factor that contributed to Japan's high growth as well as the bubble. After the bubble collapsed, what happened to the relationship between Japanese banks and corporations? Did the main banks rescue the troubled corporations, as predicted by the delegated monitoring argument? An empirical analysis shows that the Japanese economic system has reversed its institutional logic, with banks radically tightening their monitoring over corporate borrowers. This action contributed to the liquidity trap in 1997–1998.

According to the rule of the Bank of International Settlements, banks that practice international business must maintain 8 percent of self-capital. If Japanese banks could not generate an 8 percent return from loans, their self-capital ratio would decline. In the 1990s, Japanese banks could seldom find corporations that were still willing to pay 8 percent interest. Consequently, banks were forced to enter other business fields and chose to downsize their financial assets to meet the BIS self-capital rule. To compete with foreign banks, Japanese banks also wanted to stop doing business with high-risk corporations. Ironically, although the BIS was created to prevent recession, by creating a credit crunch and liquidity trap it may have helped worsen the recession in Japan in the late 1990s (Konishi 1999, 274). The Japanese government was well aware of the implications to Japanese finance when it decided to sign an agreement with the BIS during the 1980s. At that time, however, it held that the requirement of 8 percent of self-capital would not be a major problem for Japan because Japanese stock prices kept rising, and 45 percent of the value of stocks owned by Japanese banks could be counted as self-capital (Kikkawa 1998, 96).

When Japanese banks began to be subject to the BIS self-capital requirement in October 1997, the Japanese economy was experiencing its longest
stagnation since the end of World War II. Within a month after Japanese
city banks cut bank loans by 15 trillion yen, Yamaichi Securities Company
and Hokkaido Bank declared bankruptcy. The restructuring action taken by
individual Japanese banks was correct at the micro level, but when all banks
took the same action at the same time, it led to the liquidity trap mentioned
earlier. Banking is an industry in which the first runner wins. When one bank
stopped lending and tried collecting its loans, everyone soon followed. The
effect of these actions at the macro level was gigantic, but the Japanese state
failed to take countermeasures to balance the effect of the banking reform.
This inaction triggered a vicious circle. As a result of the reduction in bank
lending, the economy further deteriorated, and bankruptcies and bad loans
increased rapidly. Accordingly, stock prices and the value of the yen declined
further, in turn further reducing bank lending (Koo 1999, 57–58).

Contrary to the conventional belief that big corporations would have less
trouble getting loans than would smaller ones, 56.6 percent of the giant corporations (those with capital greater than 10 billion yen) experienced a credit
crunch, compared with 42.9 percent of big corporations (those with capital
between 1 billion and 10 billion yen) and 27.2 percent of medium-size corporations (those with capital between 100 million and 1 billion yen). According to the same survey, the following types of companies had a difficult time
finding capital: trading companies, retailers, leasing companies, credit card
companies, automobile dealers, golf courses, and companies working in
iron-steel, oil refining, automobile, fiber, housing, paper, coal, and other ore
mining. In February 1999, 30.5 percent of companies in manufacturing, 38.2
percent in the service industry, 38.8 percent in the wholesale and retail
industries, 42.6 percent in the construction industry, and 43.8 percent in the
real estate industry reported that it was more difficult to borrow money
from banks compared with December 1998. Among these corporations, 40.0
percent of the giant corporations, 45.3 percent of the big corporations, and
34.2 percent of the medium-size corporations said that the credit crunch had
worsened between December 1998 and February 1999. Only 1.1 percent of
big corporations and 1.4 percent of medium-size corporations reported
changes in a positive direction (Tsūsanshō 1999).

Moreover, among the banks that lent money to these corporations, 13.2
percent were their main banks and 36.8 percent were their quasi–main banks;
together, these banks constituted precisely 50 percent of the total banks.
Among the banks that raised their standard of lending, 65.3 percent were
city banks, 51.1 percent were trust banks, 43.2 percent were long-term trust

banks, and 40 percent were local banks. As for how banks raised their standard, 63.8 percent involved an increase in interest rates, 60.3 percent involved refusal to renew regular loans, 53.0 percent involved refusal of loans for new projects or for increases in standing loans, 19.3 percent involved demands for an increased return, 16.8 percent involved tougher conditions for review and collateral, and 15.3 percent involved an extension of the review time. Among the reasons given by the banks, 86.7 percent said that they had simply reduced all lending assets, and 40.7 percent stressed that market conditions had worsened because of rising interest rates. On average, more than 70 percent of these corporations reported that the credit crunch had influenced their capital supply, 12 percent had reduced their inventory, about 7 percent had reduced their investments, and about 6 percent had incurred difficulties in obtaining capital for investments in production capacity and daily business operation (Tsūsanshō 1999).

According to the delegated monitoring argument, the corporations that got into trouble would expect to be rescued by their main banks. In the unprecedented economic crisis of the 1990s, however, Japanese banks began to take a closer look at their corporate borrowers. The Economic Planning Agency (Keizai Kikakuchō) conducted a survey among those companies listed on the Second Department of the Tokyo Stock Exchange that reported losses for more than two quarters between 1990 and 1995. The agency found that although these companies did not change their main banks more often than companies that did not report losses, about 50 percent of them experienced loan reductions from their main banks in contrast to 37 percent of the companies that did not report losses. Among those companies hit hardest, defined as not being able to make sufficient profits to cover the interest on their loans, 60 percent reported a decline in the loans they received from their main banks and 20 percent were forced to change their main banks. This indicates that the main banks took the passive position of reducing their loans to troubled companies rather than providing them with active rescues. As the Economic Planning Agency pointed out, this means that the main banks had become more selective in making loans. A regression analysis in the same research also shows that the decline in lending by the main banks to those companies that twice reported losses was clearly associated with the risk of such investments, whereas increased lending by the main banks was associated with the growth potential of a company (Keizai Kikakuchō 1997, 305–307)

Recently, the Japanese government has recognized this problem. To boost the economy, it has begun to encourage banks to continue lending to private corporations. This action, however, has created a new dilemma: The goal of restructuring banks conflicts with the goal of maintaining lending to high-risk corporations. If the banks emphasize the former, the liquidity trap will not disappear, and the Japanese economy might encounter deflation. If the banks focus on the latter task, however, they cannot be expected to solve the problem of bad loans very quickly. The Japanese will continue to face this dilemma in the near future (Hara and Fukuda 1999, 13).

THE EFFORTS IN TIGHTENING SHAREHOLDERS' CONTROL OVER MANAGEMENT

Weak control by shareholders over management has strengthened the autonomy of managers. In addition, reciprocal shareholding has reduced the risk of bankruptcy and hostile takeover and has lowered transaction costs in the form of marketing costs (Keizai Kikakuchō 1996, 371–372). This mechanism played an important role in both the high growth period and the bubble.

After the collapse of the bubble, the Japanese were forced to rethink the problem of how to strengthen shareholders' control over management. This issue, however, is more complicated than the issue of bank monitoring of corporate borrowers. It is easier for Japanese banks to tighten their monitoring because many banks and their corporate borrowers do not belong to the same business groups, and the traditional ties between banks and corporations were weakened in the 1970s and 1980s. In contrast, in the 1980s the relationship between shareholders and management remained stable and managerial autonomy was rather strengthened by the ideology of employee sovereignty.

In the 1990s, the gap widened between attitudes toward reciprocal shareholding and the reality of this practice. Reciprocal shareholding remained popular; according to a 1994 survey, 96 percent of Japanese corporations engaged in this practice. Of these, 13 percent exchanged stocks only with banks; 1 percent exchanged stocks only with other corporations; and 82 percent exchanged stocks with banks and other corporations. In the same survey, 90 percent of the companies said that although they did not see any specific merit in reciprocal shareholding, they would continue this practice anyway (Keizai Kikakuchō 1996, 371, 374). Nevertheless, the proportion of stocks held by either banks or corporations declined rapidly. In the 1990s, Japanese corporations were under strong pressure to restructure. They could no longer afford to share risks, and the demerits of maintaining stable costs through reciprocal shareholding were rapidly increasing. As profound changes occurred in corporations' relationships with banks and in the permanent employment system, reciprocal shareholding began to lose the support of these institutions and mechanisms (Keizai Kikakuchō 1996, 376).

During the 1990s, efforts to strengthen control over management have taken several forms. First, the ban on holding companies was lifted. The 1947 Antimonopoly Law had outlawed holding companies because the rise of militarism in Japan was seen as the result in part of the prewar zaibatsu, which were organized around holding companies. During the liberalization of foreign investment in the late 1960s, there was discussion on lifting this ban, but the effort failed in the face of strong resistance. After the bubble collapsed, however, means were being sought to strengthen control of corporate actions, and lifting the ban on holding companies was regarded as a major way for Japanese corporations to strengthen their hand in international competition. Because the profits of holding companies relied on dividends from investments, holding companies would demand higher returns and would apply objective criteria, such as return on equity, to evaluate the performance of their subordinate companies. This approach would promote efficiency. At the same time, the subordinate companies could also be mobilized because their responsibilities and rights would be clarified and their performance would be evaluated according to objective criteria. Holding companies would also serve as venture capital, making investments in frontier industries (Shimotani 1996, 21–22).

Second, a new accounting method was introduced in the 1999 fiscal year. Under the former system, individual corporations were the unit used in the disclosure of corporate information. As a result, during times of recession big corporations were able to transfer pressure for efficiency to their subcontractors, while maintaining a good performance record for themselves. The new corporate accounting standard is much closer to the international standard. Under this new system, Japanese corporations must report not only their own performance but also that of their business partners in which they own more than 50 percent of the stock or have more than 50 percent membership in the board of directors. The new standard will make it more difficult for big corporations to transfer bad performance to subordinate companies.

In addition, beginning in fiscal year 1999 Japanese corporations also were expected to report their cash flows. Formerly, Japanese corporations did not report the performance of the securities they owned. Beginning in fiscal 2000, however, they must report the performance of the short-term securities they own, and any gains and losses must be calculated as transactions according to their market value. Beginning in fiscal 2001, Japanese corporations will also be required to report the performance of the securities they own, not for market transactions but for reciprocal shareholding. The gains and losses on this type of securities do not count as current gains and losses but rather count as changes in self-capital. The introduction of the market value accounting method means that the earnings and self-capital of private corporations will be directly subject to market fluctuation. As a result, corporations will be forced to strengthen their control over the market value of their financial instruments and also to make choices among investment alternatives in reciprocal shareholding (Yoshii 1999, 144).

Third, the implementation of a manual published by the Monetary Supervision Agency in December 1998 is expected to have a great impact on the governance structure of the Japanese economy. This manual, the Monetary Examination Manual, was aimed at establishing a monitoring function by banks over corporate borrowers. One major impact will be on boards of directors. According to this manual, a board of directors bears an important responsibility. Formerly, boards of directors of Japanese corporations were chosen by management rather than the other way around. As a result, management in many banks – for example, the Yamaichi Securities Company and the Hokkaido Bank – "kept everything" from the board of directors. If boards of directors are given more responsibilities, as suggested in the manual, the power of management will be curtailed. But only recently have Japanese corporations abandoned the ideology of employee sovereignty, so strengthening the power of boards of directors will create new conflicts (Hara and Fukuda 1999, 12).

Fourth, the grading of Japanese corporations by international agencies such as Moody has had great impact on the capacity of corporations to raise capital in the financial markets, and it forces Japanese corporations to pay attention to their performance. In August 1998, Moody downgraded Toyota. One of the reasons was that the permanent employment system had weakened Toyota's international competitiveness. Automobile production per employee at Toyota declined from 59 in 1989 to 49 in 1998. In 1995, each dealer in the Toyota sales network sold 6,600 vehicles; that number declined to 5,500 in 1998. Between 1989 and 1998, while Toyota's domestic production was decreasing because of an increase in its overseas production and a decline in domestic sales, the number of its employees nevertheless kept rising. In contrast, Honda was able to increase its automobile production per employee from 44 in 1989 to 47 in 1998. Although Honda's total production remained at the same level, it achieved this goal by reducing the number of employees. Under strong pressure to improve efficiency, Toyota's CEO began to talk about the possibility of cutting employees and dealerships (Yoshida 1999). With bank monitoring and shareholders' control being strengthened, the new challenge to Japanese corporations became how to maintain Japan's comparative advantage in low transaction costs to facilitate corporations' competitiveness.

LOSING THE FOUNDATION OF TOTAL EMPLOYMENT

Since the long-term movement of capitalism shifted gears from social protection to the release of market forces in the 1970s, three aspects of globalization – the global capital markets, the growth of trade and competition from low-wage countries, and the revolution in technology and communications – have produced a "global squeeze" on wages and jobs in advanced industrialized countries and have exerted strong pressures on the institutions established for social protection since the Great Depression and World War II (Longworth 1998). According to Richard Longworth, "Global capital markets and their insistence on 'best practice' and highest returns have been pushing companies for twenty years to lower their costs by moving jobs overseas, cutting jobs at home, increasing the use of labor-saving technology, and, if possible, reducing wages and benefits" (Longworth 1998, 92). This process has created a wage gap between managers and workers, and workers particularly have suffered from undercompensation (Gordon 1996). What has happened to total employment in Japan? After the burst of the bubble in the early 1990s, the internal tension between the goal of maintaining political stability and the goal of elevating the economic structure has worsened, and the very institutions that sustained the total employment strategy began to lose their foundations in the process of deregulation and increasing offshore production. Although Japan has tried very hard to maintain employment, the unemployment rate nevertheless reached its highest level since the early 1950s. As the same time, the economy is still struggling to recover from stagnation.

What to do about privatized social protection has been the center of public debate in Japan during the 1990s (Gao 2000, 447–451). Advocates for radical reform hold that equality in postwar Japan has gone too far. Because the Japanese have emphasized equal outcome rather than equal opportunity, these reformers argue, the state has enacted too many regulations that have seriously restrained competition. This style of social protection directly conflicts with the new environment of globalization, in which Japan faces intense competition from low-wage countries. Furthermore, these advocates maintain that the strong Japanese adherence to the principle of equal outcome not only has delayed badly needed reforms but also has contributed to the economic stagnation of the 1990s. To create incentives, Japanese companies should replace the seniority-based wage system with an ability-based wage system and should introduce the U.S. practice of offering stock options to managers (Nakatani 1996, 243–244). Their critics, in contrast, argue that the core of Japanese capitalism lies in its equal distribution of both economic wealth and economic hardship. Consumer prices are indeed high, they acknowledge, but high prices have supported domestic employment. In the postwar period, Japanese companies have been able to shift their workers from inefficient sectors to efficient sectors within the business groups, and the permanent employment system has survived several tests (Uchihashi and Gurupu 2001, 1995, 146). Although the opponents of radical reform agree that some sectors and industries in the Japanese economy are not efficient, they emphasize the role played by these sectors and industries in providing employment opportunities. Withdrawing protection in these sectors and industries would create massive unemployment in Japan.

Until recently, Japan has tried to maintain the foundation of total employment. Most big corporations have tried to avoid massive layoffs, instead relying on other forms of adjustments, such as freezing new hires, increasing part-time workers, and reducing personnel through early retirements. Meanwhile, Japan still tries to protect its domestic markets because its closed markets have been the precondition for the total employment strategy. The Japanese understand this precondition well, and even in the 1990s consumers in Japan still supported the protection of the agriculture sector. According to a 1997 survey, 83.4 percent of the respondents supported food self-sufficiency; 45.9 percent of them held that although domestically produced food is more expensive than foreign products, they would prefer that as much of the food as possible be produced in Japan. They added that, of course, the cost of domestic production should be reduced (Vogel 1999a). Despite the pressure to improve efficiency, the exports-related sector has not strongly demanded that the government withdraw its protection of domestic sectors (Vogel 1999b). As a result, the shares of foreign products in the Japanese markets have been increasing very slowly. The share of expenditures on imported consumer goods increased from 1.6 percent in 1985 to 4.0 percent in 1995. Throughout the 1990s, Japan continued to trade stability for a slow upgrading of the economic structure and relied on privatized social protection to maintain total employment. As a result, according to Richard Longworth, this Japanese model stands against its major Western counterparts. Unlike the American phenomenon (plentiful jobs at low wages) and the European phenomenon (scarce jobs at high wages), the Japanese phenomenon is characterized by stability plus stagnation (Longworth 1998, 12, 77).

Despite these efforts, however, several structural changes have undermined the institutional foundation of the total employment strategy.

First, increasing numbers of big manufactures joined the trend of moving production offshore. Under the pressure of a high yen and high production costs in Japan, the share of offshore production among Japanese manufacturers reached 11.6 percent in fiscal year 1996. This number is still very low compared with 28.7 percent in the United States in 1995 and 23.0 percent in Germany in 1994, but it is nearly four times that in Japan at the time of the Plaza Accord in 1985 (Foreign Press Center 1999, 44). More important, the transport machinery and electrical machinery industries – in which Japan had the strongest international competitiveness – also had the greatest shares of offshore production: 24.9 percent and 19.7 percent, respectively. The relocation of production bases to foreign countries also stimulated an increase of Japanese exports of high-value-added capital goods and components needed for overseas production, and that served to prevent the "hollowing out" (deindustrialization) of the Japanese economy to some extent (Foreign Press Center 1999, 44–45), but the continuing trend of offshore production has certainly served to reduce job opportunities in Japan.

Offshore production by big manufacturers has also created a more difficult situation for their former subcontractors. According to a survey by the Fair Trade Commission in 1995, the biggest impact of the bursting of the bubble on medium-sized and small companies was a reduction in the number of contracts from big corporations and pressure for subcontractors to lower their prices. This impact was especially serious for makers of automobiles, computers, and other types of durable goods, and for the textile industries. Compared with the situation in 1993, 70 percent of them experienced large reductions in contracts in 1995, and about 20 percent lost their contracts completely. Because the parent companies were concentrating on production, on improving the efficiency of their production capacity, and on reducing workers' salaries in the structural adjustment, the medium-size and small companies were forced to reduce the prices of their products in order to ensure their contracts. In the construction, automobile, textile, and computer industries, 70 percent reported that their parent companies either set prices themselves or had a major impact on the price level. The medium-sized and small companies did not have much leverage over big corporations in the negotiations (Keizai Kikakuchō 1996, 246–247). More importantly, 21.8 percent of the medium-size and small companies, compared with 9.0 percent of big corporations, were willing to give up the practice of relational contracting. Compared with 54.1 percent of big corporations, 48.3 percent of them continue to practice relational contracting but place greater emphasis on technology-based strength (Keizai Kikakuchō 1996, 508).

The second structural change that has undermined the institutional foundation of the total employment strategy is that the number of corporate bankruptcies increased rapidly after the burst of the bubble, and that in turn contributed to a higher unemployment rate. Here's how it happened. The economic downturn created a difficult situation for corporate survival. The number of corporate bankruptcies began to grow rapidly after the First

Oil Shock and reached a record high of 20,841 in 1984. The figure dropped sharply during the bubble in the second half of the 1980s to bottom out in 1990s at 6,468, the lowest number since 1972. When the bubble burst, however, the number began to rise again. In 1998, there were 19,171 corporate bankruptcies in Japan, the second worst figure after that of 1984. Liabilities totaled about 14.4 trillion yen, the record worst figure and about four times that of 1984 (Foreign Press Center 1999, 46). The inefficient industries, which used to be protected by cartels and government regulations, suffered most; 28.4 percent of the bankruptcy cases occurred among construction companies, wholesale, 20.2 percent, and retail, 14.9 percent. Even the manufacturing industry accounted for 17.3 percent of the total bankruptcies (Foreign Press Center 1999, 47).

As a result, in April 1999 the nation's jobless rate for men rose to 5 percent, the highest since the Japanese government started its employment surveys in 1953. The number of unemployed people reached 3.42 million, and 1.15 million of them were forced out of their jobs as a result of either corporate restructuring or bankruptcy. The number of involuntary jobless people exceeded that of voluntary jobless people for the first time since December 1987.

Because job security was under great pressure, the loyalty of Japanese employees to their companies changed profoundly. According to a survey in 1995, the number of participants who had a very strong affection for their companies equaled only 11.7 percent, compared with 56.7 percent of those having affection for their families, 28.7 percent for their personal hobbies, and 26.9 percent for their hometowns. Asked what the major barriers were that would prevent them from shifting jobs, 42.3 percent mentioned the seniority-based wage system, and 39.5 percent mentioned the one-sum retirement allowance Japanese workers receive when they retire. Only 20.6 percent of the participants believed that their companies would take care of them in the future, and only 17.8 percent held that if they quit they would betray the trust of their company or bosses (Keizai Kikakuchō 1997, 65–67).

On the surface, Japan still appears to be an egalitarian society, but that image has been losing substance in the 1990s. The Japanese used to believe widely that their society was neither a society of class, like Britain, nor a society of ethnicity, like the United States. Rather, Japan was an egalitarian society that did not have a super-rich class. Even the CEOs of big corporations did not receive the kind of extraordinarily high pay as did their Western counterparts. Since the early 1980s, however, Japan's Gini index has increased rapidly, from 0.3491 in 1981 to 0.3975 in 1989, 0.4049 in 1990, and 0.4394 in 1993. Reaching 0.4 is considered a high level of inequality, and Japan has had the highest Gini index among major industrialized countries (Itō 1999b, 188–189).

An important factor that contributed to the deterioration of equality in Japan after the burst of the bubble was that Japanese women were facing more difficulties in maintaining their jobs, especially those who worked as part-time or temporary employees. To maintain the permanent employment system, Japanese corporations tended to cut these workers first in an economic recession. As they lost their jobs, they could no longer provide supplementary income for their households. Of course, the collapse of stocks and real estate prices in the 1990s served to narrow the gap between the rich and the poor, but income has become the new center of social stratification. The gap in personal income between those who maintained their jobs and those who lost their jobs increased rapidly, as did the gap in household income between employees who worked for big corporations and those who worked for medium-size and small companies and whose wives had lost their part-time or temporary jobs.

SEARCHING FOR A STABLE
INTERNATIONAL ENVIRONMENT

Robert Keohane and Joseph Nye (1977, 83) once observed that "August 15, 1971 [when the U.S. government closed the window of gold], marked the end of an international monetary regime as clearly as did 1914 [the end of the gold standard] or 1931 [the collapse of the gold-exchange standard]." From a Polanyian perspective, 1914 and 1971 represent one complete cycle in the long-term movement of capitalism. The efforts to release market forces in the late nineteenth century and again in the early twentieth century led to the collapse of the international monetary regime represented by the gold standard, and these events foreshadowed the Great Depression and World War II.

Taking a lesson from this experience, the postwar international economic order sustained efforts for social protection in order to prevent depression. After the collapse of the Bretton Woods system, the three major mechanisms that were established by major industrialized countries after World War II to prevent depression also began to malfunction. First, the separation between banking and securities and the relief mechanism established to prevent financial speculation began to deteriorate in response to the globalization of finance. Second, pegged exchange rates and control of the free flow of capital were replaced by the floating exchange rate system and the rapid expansion of international finance. Third, the counter-cyclical function built into government finance created the need for structural adjustments financed by skyrocketing budget deficits, and these adjustments began to damage macro-economic stability (Shibata 1996, 72–74). Under the Bretton Woods system, the Bank of Japan subordinated domestic credit expansion to maintaining the fixed yen-dollar exchange rate. Since the 1970s, however, the relationship between exchange rates and monetary policy has reversed. Exchange rates in the floating system have become the independent variable, and the monetary policy of the Japanese state has been driven by the rising yen (McKinnon and Ohno 1997, 2).

Without the Bretton Woods system, could the Japanese economic crisis of the 1990s have been prevented? It may be. Taggart Murphy (1996, 162) argues as follows:

> If Japan had acted on a pure calculus of economic rationality, it might have insisted that the United States finance its purchases of Japanese exports in yen, that if the United States wanted to be so profligate, it would need to borrow in a currency the Japanese could control. . . . Had the Japanese forced the United States to finance and pay for its Japanese imports and its government deficit in yen, the internationalization of the yen would have greatly accelerated.

Kikkawa Mototada also points out that when Britain and the United States were the major creditor countries in the world, successively, in the late nineteenth century and early twentieth century and again from the end of World War II and up to the 1970s, the pound sterling and the dollar were the major currencies. Both the British and the U.S. hegemonies were sustained by a stable exchange rate through the gold standard and the Bretton Woods system. When these two countries lent money to other countries, they lent in their own currencies. In contrast, when Japan became the major creditor country, the dollar was still the major world currency and Japan faced a floating exchange rate system. Kikkawa holds that the major mistake by Japan was to lend its money through the dollar instead of the yen because it gave the United States a strong incentive to force the Japanese yen to appreciate, something that would serve to reduce U.S. debts to Japan (Kikkawa 1998, 32–34).

Should Japan remain in the U.S.-proposed global financial architecture, or should it take the lead either to internationalize the yen or to create a regional currency in Asia? This issue remains unresolved (for the debate on this issue, see Gao 2000, 437–440). There are two major competing views in Japan. The advocates of the big bang basically support the "crony capitalism" argument in the international debate on the Asian financial crisis. Because the distribution of capital in the Japanese economic system has been driven by the state policy's goal of economic growth, they argue, there has been no clear boundary between private banks and a government agency that monitors them. This was the major cause of the crisis in the housing loan industry. These observers call for a conversion of the Japanese banking industry to the American system (Takenaka, 1996). They contend that just as the deregulation in the early 1980s enabled both the United States and Britain to regain vitality, a big bang reform would help Japan revitalize its economy (Kanzaki, 1997). To this school of thought, the current economic crises in Asia, Latin America, and Russia are caused in large part by domestic factors, such as corrupt national banking systems. Accordingly, they propose a new financial system based on transparency, accountability, adherence to international standards, minimization of the scope of risk, and the free movement of capital.

Another view, however, holds that the Asian financial crisis had its roots in the radical financial liberalization undertaken by governments of the region during the 1990s. These changes induced speculation by foreign capital, much of it belonging to hedge funds. This latter school believes that a new global architecture would consist of several monetary zones, each with some degree of protection through government controls on the movement of capital (Wade 1999). As Paul Krugman points out (1999a, 71),

> The idea that economies are being punished for their weaknesses is ultimately unconvincing on at least two grounds. For one, the scale of the punishment seems wholly disproportionate to the crime. Why should bad investment decisions lead not merely to a slow-down in growth but to a massive collapse in output and employment? Furthermore, if the fault lies with the countries, why have so many of them gotten into trouble at the same time?

He further argues that

> The answer is that the world became vulnerable to its current travails not because economic policies had not been reformed, but because they had. Around the world, countries responded to the very real flaws in post-Depression policy regimes by moving back toward a regime with many of the virtues of pre-Depression free-market capitalism. However, in bringing back the virtues of old-fashioned capitalism, we also brought back some of its vices, most notably a vulnerability both to instability and sustained economic slumps.

The establishment of an Asian currency has recently attracted serious interest. Some Japanese maintain that although the establishment of such a currency system would require a long-term effort, Japan should exchange ideas intensively with the central banks of Asian countries. Such an exchange might start with a payment settlement mechanism and then provide credit. In the end, it would lead to the creation of a central Asian bank (Odawara 1999, 294). These observers argue that Japan should work toward establishing a regional currency by cooperating with Europe and Asia. The first step would be the establishment of a wide band reference exchange rate system, with a range of 10 percent between the Euro and the yen, and then narrowing the band to between 2.5 percent and 3 percent. When the yen and the Euro are able to establish a stable exchange rate, other Asian countries would be able to establish their own stable exchange rates with the Euro through the yen. In the end, these observers believe, Japan should follow the German model, pushing the establishment of a common Asian currency. During the Asian financial crisis, Asian countries were attacked by the hedge funds because their currencies were pegged to the dollar. With a common Asian currency maintaining a stable exchange rate with the Euro, Japan as well as other Asian countries would be able to escape the volatility of the dollar (Kikkawa 1999a, 1999b).

Back in the 1970s, Japan was invited to join the Asian regional payment settlement, an agreement that would have led to the establishment of an Asian monetary unit. If Japan had joined the agreement, Indonesia, Thailand, the Philippines, and South Korea would have followed, but Japan gave up this opportunity because of strong opposition by the Ministry of Finance. Eventually, only Bangladesh, Pakistan, India, Iran, Nepal, Sri Lanka, and Burma signed the agreement, which is still in effect. None of these countries has experienced a major financial crisis in the 1990s (Odawara 1999, 292).

The economic stagnation in the 1990s forced the Japanese to rethink the liberalization of finance that occurred in the 1980s and to recognize the importance of the stability of the banking industry in preventing depression under the Bretton Woods system (Gao 2000). The American financial system established during the first U.S. New Deal program between 1932 and 1935 separated the securities function from the banking function. It was aimed at preventing the banks, which served as the center of the economy, from speculation failures in the stock market. Banks were not allowed to provide capital for speculation (Itō 1999b, 14–15). In postwar Japan, government regulation of the finance industry had been the major mechanism for preventing crisis. Even after trade and foreign investment were liberalized in the 1960s, the finance industry continued to be coordinated through the regulation of interest rates. In the 1950s and 1960s, the Bank of Japan and the Ministry of Finance used international payments and foreign currency reserves as the signals for monetary policy. To adjust the economic cycle, the Bank of Japan would directly intervene through open operation in the monetary market and its window guidance (see Chapter 2) (Ōuchi 1987, 21, 23).

The liberalization of finance in the 1980s, however, eradicated these depression-preventing mechanisms. Interest rates were deregulated, and corporations were allowed to raise capital from overseas markets. Financial institutions extended their business operations – from making loans to corporations to transactions in stocks and foreign currency. Banks, which bore a great responsibility, abandoned the principle of maintaining stability and began to provide capital for speculation. City banks established subordinate companies and placed them in charge of investments. After the Japanese government withdrew many safeguarding regulations, commercial banks also lost their protection. As a result, the risks faced by the Japanese financial system increased significantly (Itō 1999b, 14–15; Ōuchi 1987, 21, 23).

The Japanese have already begun to make efforts toward internalizing the yen to ensure the stability of the external economic environment. In September 1997, during the Asian financial crisis, the Southeast Asian finance ministers discussed a proposal to establish an Asian monetary fund. They asked Japan for help, and the Japanese government proposed a $100 billion fund to which Japan would contribute $50 billion. Because of strong opposition from the United States and Europe, however, this idea was not implemented. Again in 1998, the Japanese government proposed to establish a $30 billion Asian monetary fund. In February 1998, Mohamad Marhatir, the Malaysian prime minister, proposed a Southeast Asian payment settlement. Japanese Prime Minister Keizō Obuchi visited Europe immediately after the Euro came into being in January 1999. He asserted that Japan would further urge the internationalization of the yen and that Japan would like to see a "triplet" monetary system, with the yen standing with the dollar and the Euro. At the Asia-Europe meeting, Finance Minister Miyazawa also proposed that Asian currencies should adopt a foreign reserve "basket" system consisting of the Euro, the dollar, and the yen.

The internalization of the yen, however, is not a free lunch. As the opponents to this effort in Japan point out, Japan cannot afford to be a key currency country. The reason is that the amount of yen in circulation in the international economy is far less than that of the dollar. When Latin American countries experienced a financial crisis, it influenced only about 1 percent of the total dollars in circulation. If Japan had been the key currency country when the Asian financial crisis occurred, between 10 percent and 20 percent of the total yen in circulation would have been influenced. That would have caused a significant damage to the Japanese economy. In addition, if Japan were to become a key currency country in Asia, its financial and monetary policies would be constrained by international factors because under such circumstances Japan would have to take the responsibility for Asian countries (Sakai and Tahara 2000, 78–79).

Establishing a stable currency will be a crucial long-term task for Japan. In the debate on the reform of the international monetary regime, even the proponents of more stable exchange rates are fully aware that the changes in economic and political environments have made a return to the Bretton Woods type of pegged rate system impossible (see Gilpin 2000, 126). Under today's circumstances, according to Barry Eichengreen, the international monetary system has only two options. One is flexible rates, and the other is for a group of countries to create single currency such as the Euro. He argues that regional monetary unity may be essential to counterbalance the negative impact of global market forces (cited by Gilpin 2000, 128).

At this moment, Japan seems to be moving in the direction of establishing a regional currency. A joint Southeast Asian summit held in late November 1999 was attended by the prime ministers of Japan, China, and South Korea. It made a clear statement that the possibility of establishing a tariff agreement, a common market, and a common currency is real. Japan, China, and South Korea agreed to establish a joint center for economic research to examine the possibility. On May 6, 2000, Japan, China, and South Korea joined the Southeast Asian countries in signing an unprecedented multilateral agreement on currency exchange, aimed at establishing an economic and monetary monitoring system in the Asian economy. According to this agreement, when one country's currency is under attack, other countries will help sustain that currency. Although many details remain to be decided, this agreement is perceived as the first important step toward establishing a regional framework to maintain stability in the Asian economy.

SOME REFLECTIONS

In this book, I have examined the impact of the international economic order on the performance of Japan's domestic economic institutions via the evolution of two intrinsic dilemmas in the Japanese economic system; I have made this examination in the context of globalization, which caused the reversion of the Japanese economy from prosperity to stagnation. I have articulated a twofold argument. First, an economic system that is strong in coordination but weak in control and monitoring tends to perform well when production is globalized. When globalization changes gears and shifts from production to finance, however, it is highly likely that this system will encounter a major failure because the aggressive pattern of corporate investments sustained by weak control and monitoring can easily lead to massive speculation in the stock and real estate markets. Second, an economic system that relies on privatized social protection to maintain political stability tends to work better in a closed economy. When globalization removes national barriers to international trade, however, maintaining political stability through private means tends to generate strong international criticism. More importantly, overburdened private institutions can seriously handicap the system's capacity to upgrade the economic structure in the long run.

This study suggests that the goals of sustaining coordination and strengthening control in corporate governance, on the one hand, and the goals of maintaining political stability and upgrading economic structure, on the other hand, are two pairs of intrinsic contradictions in capitalist economies. In theory, strong coordination combined with strong control, and high political stability combined with a high system capacity for upgrading the economic structure, are the two poles in a continuum, and each economy can work out an optimal place on this continuum depending on specific national conditions. In reality, however, few economic systems have simultaneously obtained both virtues at a high level in the continuum because "each nation has evolved a system that is at once highly developed along one particular dimension of these problems while underdeveloped along another" (Kester 1997, 108).[1]

For example, consider the Japanese and Swedish models of social protection. Facing the challenge of globalization, a Japanese production system and a Swedish social protection system seem to be an ideal combination for one national economy. If Japan had a strong unemployment assistance program sponsored by a welfare state, big corporations would be free from the burden of surplus employees and the medium-size and small companies would not have to rely on cartels and government protection to survive. Under such circumstances, the mechanism of excessive competition would enable Japan to quickly upgrade its economic structure and improve its competitiveness in international markets. In contrast, if Sweden were to acquire a Japanese-style production system, it would make the best use of the welfare state's strength in social provisions against unemployment, thereby elevating its national competitiveness to a new level. In reality, however, neither of these situations

---

1 Although Kester was the first person to treat coordination and control in corporate governance as a major contradiction, he still holds that these two objectives in corporate governance are not incompatible and believes that it is possible to build a model of best practice with strong coordination and strong control. From an institutional perspective, however, this is not likely to happen because the mechanisms that maximize the capacity of a particular corporate governance in achieving one goal tend to limit its capacity in achieving the other. When Japanese banks tried to strengthen their control in the 1990s, for example, Japanese corporations immediately suffered a credit crunch and were no longer able to make aggressive investments.

seems to be likely to take place (for criticism of the Swedish model for lacking the Japanese production orientation, see Weiss 1998, Chapter 4).

This study suggests that the globalization of production and the globalization of finance have very different impacts on national economic institutions. The expansion of trade and production in the 1950s and 1960s was sustained by the Bretton Woods system, under which the central banks bore the risk of foreign exchange for corporations, and, thanks to the control over the free flow of capital, governments of advanced industrialized countries could pursue their domestic policy objectives without being influenced by other countries' financial policies. In this kind of environment, a system characterized by strong coordination but weak control and monitoring – that is, the system prevailing in Japan – was able to do well because coordination was what mattered in the promotion of trade and production. In contrast, the expansion of finance and monetary activity since the 1970s was accompanied by a floating exchange rate and the free flow of capital across national borders. That not only privatized the risks of foreign exchange and substantially increased the investment risks for private corporations but also intensified the internal tensions, as indicated by the Mundell-Flemming trilemma, among the competing policy objectives of the Japanese government in sustaining stable exchange rates, maintaining currency convertibility, and pursuing domestic growth. In this new environment, strong control and monitoring in corporate governance was necessary to avoid a major failure.

This study also suggests that the performance of the same institutions and mechanisms designed for social protection varied substantially in the various stages of the long-term movement of capitalist economies. A system that maintains political stability through privatized social protection may do well when the economy is closed, the economy grows at a high speed, and many sunrise industries are created by a technological revolution; these factors help an economy tolerate the inefficiency created by cartels and government protections and absorb the overinvested production capacity. Such a system, however, will have great difficulties when the economy becomes open, the growth of the economy slows, and there are not enough sunrise industries and economic booms to outweigh inefficiency and absorb overinvestment.

What are the implications of this study to Japan's past success? After the burst of the bubble, the debate on the developmental state has lost its heat. Furthermore, reflections and reexaminations of Japan's past success seem to have become forgotten tasks because Japan's observers are preoccupied with the present failure and uncertain future of the Japanese economy. By contrasting the performance of the same institutions and mechanisms during the high growth and during the bubble, however, this study sheds light on three long-debated issues related to the role of the developmental state in the Japanese miracle by falsifying three popular but faulty assumptions adopted by some analyses in the existing literature.

The first is a basic assumption, from which the other two assumptions are derived. The basic assumption is that if the developmental state was really important, it must have *dominated* the policy-making process or must have held an *exclusive* relationship with private institutions. *In reality, however, the developmental state in Japan was neither a ruler nor a dictator but rather was an organizer, sponsor, and guarantor of private institutions.* As I have demonstrated in this book, without the convoy administration provided by the Ministry of Finance, ensured access to the Bank of Japan's credits, and MITI's oligopoly policy, many private institutions that sustained excessive competition either would not exist at all or at least would not have worked in the same way that they did. Without a state competition policy characterized by pro-big corporation, pro-cartel, and pro-government regulation, none of the private institutions that supported the total employment strategy would have survived. The developmental state in Japan never considered itself the only actor in Japan's economic growth, acting in the same way as does a socialist state in a planned economy. Rather, it organized, sponsored, and guaranteed a wide range of activities of the private sector that aimed to strengthen coordination and maintain stability – the two cornerstones of Japan's high-speed economic growth.

The second faulty assumption is that if the Japanese state was developmental, it must have always been *strategic* in policy-making and economic administration by picking the winners and losers. *In reality, however, the developmental state in Japan also played an extremely important role in providing a stable supply of industrial capital and reducing investment risks.* The Japanese economy was a market economy instead of a planned economy. High growth in such an economy required not only strategic resource allocation by the state industrial policy but also aggressive investment by the private sector. Although the practices of the convoy administration and the ensured access to the Bank of Japan's credits do not look as strategic as MITI's industrial policy, they were essential to the creation of a favorable environment that allowed private corporations to make aggressive investments in production capacity and technological transfer. The developmental state in Japan worked hard to mobilize the private sector to participate in its growth program in a market economy, and it did not abuse its autonomy by ruling or dictating the private sector. In short, the Japanese state was developmental not only because it practiced an industrial policy but also because it played an important role in providing a stable supply of industrial capital and reducing investment risks.

The third faulty assumption is that if the Japanese state was developmental, it must have rationalized all troubled industries or transferred resources to more optimal uses. *In reality, however, the developmental state in Japan tried hard to avoid major public spending for unemployment protection in order to concentrate national resources on economic growth, and to sustain this developmental goal it privatized its role in social protection by allowing the existence of inefficient industries and sectors.* Cartels and government protections in postwar Japan never simply meant a surrender of the Japanese state to social pressures (of course, societal groups would pressure the state to provide social protection); they were also a deliberate choice by the developmental state under the historical constraints of a deflationary fiscal policy defined by the Dodge plan and the need to sustain an expansionary monetary policy to promote economic growth in the policy mix under the Bretton Woods system. To avoid major political disruptions, the developmental Japanese state's strong orientation toward production and economic growth was also supplemented by a strong orientation toward political stability that in many cases involved tradeoffs between efficiency and stability. Lacking significant resources, the total employment strategy was perceived by the Japanese state as the only way to be developmental. In short, the Japanese state was developmental not only because it worked hard to promote economic growth but also because it tried to avoid using public resources to maintain stability.

The developmental state argument need not reflect a value judgment. By highlighting the intrinsic dilemmas between strong coordination and weak control and monitoring and between high stability and a low system capacity for upgrading the economic structure, I show that the institutions and mechanisms derived by the developmental state contributed both to Japan's past success and to its recent failure.

Where does Japan stand now at the dawn of the twenty-first century? Will the Japanese economy recover? From a structural perspective, one can be slightly more optimistic than in the past two years because there appears to be a trend of recovery since the second quarter of 2000. Although this trend weakened by the end of 2000, the Japanese government and many economists still believe that the economy is on its way toward recovery. From an institutional perspective, however, what is important for the Japanese economy in the long run is not whether it recovers (sooner or later it will pull out of the recession) but rather whether it can ensure long-term prosperity. In this regard, the problems that have confronted the Japanese economy in the past two or three decades are far from over, and a number of major challenges lie ahead.

If the long-term movement of capitalist economies observed by Arrighi (1994) and Polanyi (1957 [1944]) repeats the previous cycle of globalization in a simplistic manner, the expansion of finance and monetary activity since the early 1970s will sooner or later lead to a major crisis of capitalist economies on a global scale. Following are two possible scenarios.

First, the global expansion of the financial markets has further exacerbated the problems of overbuilt production capacity and the long-term decline of corporate profits in capitalist economies discussed by Brenner (1998), problems that were first created during the postwar expansion of trade and production. As capital markets demand ever-greater efficiencies, numerous big corporations in advanced industrialized countries have moved their production base overseas. The offshore production sustained by globalized capital has served to turn overproduction to a global scale. As Richard Longworth (1998, 55–56) points out,

> In industries after industries, from high-wage Europe to low-wage Asia, producers are making more than customers can buy. . . . All these nations plan to export the cars they don't buy themselves. But with ever more countries building their own auto plants, it's hard to see where these export markets will be. More likely, the law of supply and demand will take over. With too many goods chasing too few buyers, prices will fall. . . . As prices fall, so will corporate profits and, soon after, so will wages. Plants will close. Jobs will vanish. Bank loans will go unpaid. Bankruptcies will grow. Buyers will stop buying, making the overcapacity even worse.

This situation may eventually lead to a major crisis for capitalist economies.

Second, financial innovation during the globalization of finance has been combined with technological innovation, and the combination of these two forces has not only made economic booms bigger and longer but has also made their bursts deeper and more pervasive (Mandel 2000). According to Michael Mandel, that could create an "Internet depression" starting in the United States. Mandel argues that even though there are many differences, the current situation resembles that of the 1920s in a remarkable way: the combination of financial and technological innovations. Just as the railroads in the late nineteenth century triggered the development of modern stock and bond markets and the automobile brought about the invention and widespread acceptance of consumer installment credit in the United States, the recent economic boom driven by the Internet has led to the increase of venture capital to one-third of all money spent on R&D in the United States in first quarter of 2000. When the growth of productivity slows, however, investment growth will also slow: "When the virtuous cycle of innovation and profit turns vicious, there is no obvious counterbalancing mechanism to stop the slowdown" (Mandel 2000, 64). In the past several years, the U.S. economy has been the only engine of global economic growth. A downturn of the U.S. economy will have significant effects on other advanced industrialized economies.

Both scenarios are beyond Japan's control, and whatever Japan does probably cannot make a big difference.

Are we on the eve of a major crisis of capitalism, as indicated by the increasing financial instability in the world, or are we at the dawn of a great technological revolution, as exemplified by the rapid development of the Internet and e-commerce? Should we push the trend of globalization by further releasing market forces, or should we pay greater attention to the issue of social protection? Could the possible collapse of the dollar's value, as many analysts have warned, trigger a major crisis in the international economic order?

A global crisis may still seem to be remote for the time being. Nevertheless, no one can be sure that it will not happen. As Robert Gilpin (2000, 12) reminds us, "Th[e] belief in the secure victory of liberated capitalism may turn out to be valid, but it is important to recall that the world passed this way once before in the laissez-faire era prior to the outbreak of World War I and the subsequent collapse of that highly integrated world economy." Against a crisis scenario, however, whether the reforms adopted by Japan in the 1990s – reforms that were aimed at further releasing market forces – will save the country from the crisis or simply drive the Japanese economy faster toward it, and whether the Japanese efforts to maintain the already deteriorated safety net will prove a wise choice on the eve of a major crisis, remain to be seen. Many of the arguments for radical reforms were based on the assumption that globalization will progress in a linear direction. Few advocates of the reforms have discussed what will happen when that process reverses its course.

If the downturn of the Internet sector proves to be temporary and the trend of the globalization of finance continues, Japan must address the issue of how to find alternative corporate governance that can exercise appropriate control and monitoring while still sustaining Japanese corporations in investing aggressively in new industrial frontiers. After the old mechanism of excessive competition contributed to the rise of the bubble in the globalization of finance, many institutions that sustained this mechanism have become the targets of reform when Japanese corporations again need to make aggressive investments in a new economy dominated by information technology to close the gap with the United States in international competition. As I demonstrated in Chapter 4, Japan responded to the technological revolution of the 1950s and early 1960s by adopting a financial pattern of banks' overlending and corporations' overborrowing, sustained by strong coordination but weak control and monitoring in corporate governance. Inasmuch as banks began to tighten monitoring in the late 1990s, resulting in a credit crunch in 1997–1998, will Japanese corporations still be able to make aggressive investments in the new economy? To be sure, Japanese corporations did increase their investments in information technology in 1999–2000, and these investments were regarded as the driving force behind the trend of economic recovery. The question is whether the scope and aggressiveness of future corporate investments can repeat the pattern of the 1950s and 1960s, when Japanese corporations rapidly built up international competitiveness in production technology via excessive competition.

If the release of market forces continues to be the leading public policy in advanced industrialized countries, Japan must address the issue of how to strengthen the government's role in unemployment protection amid the rising budget deficits and the pressure of an aging society. Japan will have to replace its privatized social protection with an effective government-sponsored unemployment program. The reasons are simple: Unless private corporations are freed of the burden of maintaining surplus employees, big corporations will not be able to compete effectively. Unless cartels are dismantled, the sunset industries and sectors will continue to be the center of international criticism in an era of globalization. Unless government protections of the family-owned mini shops are removed, Japanese consumers will continue to suffer from high domestic prices. All these changes, however, require an effective government-sponsored unemployment program. The total employment strategy simply will not work in the era of free trade. The development of a government-sponsored social protection regime, however, may not be easy because it may run into a deadlock: The aging Japanese society will demand huge public spending at a time when the government budget deficit is already equivalent to about 13 percent of Japan's GDP.

AN INSTITUTIONAL DIAGNOSIS OF THE STAGNATION

The conventional wisdom holds that without major reform of its economic institutions, the Japanese economy cannot be expected to recover from its decade-long stagnation. From an institutional perspective, however, the cause of the stagnation is not that Japan has not reformed, but rather that the reforms Japan conducted in the 1990s have destroyed the old mechanisms of economic growth while the new ones are still being established and being reconfigured with the remaining components of the old system. This by no means suggests that Japan should not reform. Instead, it highlights the often conflicting nature of the relationship between radical reform undertaken during a crisis and a quick economic recovery. Major institutional reform may benefit the Japanese economy in the long run, but it may be naive to use radical reform as the recipe for a speedy economic recovery.

Let us start from the basics of economics. Any economic growth, or in this case economic recovery, will not take place without investment. Both high-speed growth and high-speed recovery are sustained by rapidly increased investment. Investment has three major sources: government fiscal expenditure, corporate investments, and consumer expenditure. But even though the Japanese government has adopted several big stimulation packages in an effort to induce private spending, neither corporations nor consumers have responded effectively. Why?

The answer can be found, in part, in the reforms Japan conducted in the 1990s.

As I have demonstrated in this book, economic growth in postwar Japan was sustained by two major mechanisms: that of excessive competition, in which strong coordination but weak control and monitoring ensured the supply of capital for corporate investments, and that of total employment, in which the practice of keeping everyone in business and providing everyone with a job ensured consumer spending by maintaining the confidence of consumers in their future income. As long as these two mechanisms remained intact, increased government spending during a recession should lead to an increase in both corporate investment and consumer spending, thus leading to an economic recovery.

What has happened in the 1990s reforms, however, has been a reversion of the institutional logic in both the mechanism of excessive competition and the mechanism of total employment.

First, the big bang reform in the banking industry carried out in 1996 has drastically tightened the monitoring by Japanese banks over corporate finance. Consequently, many corporations have had great difficulty in getting loans. When they run out of capital, they cannot make aggressive investments as they have done in the past. The advocates of the liberalization of finance maintain that an increased free flow of capital enables those who need capital to have immediate access to it. However, as Joseph Stiglitz points out, the banking principle speaks the opposite. Banks lend borrowers more money in an economic boom, when their financial situation is good. But when borrowers fall into a financial crisis and need money the most, no bank is willing to lend than money because it considers the investment to be highly risky.[1] For this reason, I further argue, the liberalization of finance has simply made

---

[1] Stiglitz made this comment during a talk at Duke University on March 27, 2001.

both an economic boom bigger and an economic crisis deeper because more capital flows in an economic boom and more capital flees in a crisis.

Second, the changes in the Japanese employment system have significantly weakened the confidence of Japanese consumers in their job security. When they face strong uncertainty about their future income, one cannot expect them to increase their spending. Some economists argue that the government should create inflation, forcing consumers to spend money. It may work, but there is another possibility: When the future remains strongly uncertain, artificially created inflation may drive consumers to save even more because inflation also significantly increases the amount of money needed for an uncertain future.

As a particular form of the dilemma between the need for stability and the need to upgrade the economic structure, the goal of economic recovery often directly conflicts with the goal of institutional reforms. It is relatively easier to see that economic recovery tends to delay needed reform after a major crisis. In the past two years, many economic commentators have expressed such a concern about the Asian economies, which seemed to be in a trend of recovery at the time. However, the opposite also happens quite often: Major institutional reform in an economic crisis may delay economic recovery. This has been evidenced by both the big bang reform in Russia and the reform in state-owned enterprises in China. In both cases, the reform has directly contributed to the deterioration of the economic situation. Only after a certain period of time did both economies begin to recover. Why? Major reform in economic institutions means a radical change in the rules of the game. When the rules of the game are changed in one part of the economic system, the economic system must be reconfigured to establish a working relationship between the newly established rules and the old components that have not been reformed. That, however, takes time. Before this reconfiguration is accomplished, economic actors face strong uncertainty in the environment and greater risk in their investments. Under such circumstances, they tend to be more conservative about their investments. As a result, one cannot expect that the government stimulation package can achieve the same effect as it did in the old system.

A significant problem with the Japanese economic situation at this moment is that the reforms have been sweeping enough to destroy the old mechanisms of economic growth by drying up corporate investments and preventing consumers from spending money. In the meantime, however, these reforms might be too limited to establish new mechanisms of economic growth and reconfigure the entire economic system around them. Until Japanese corporations find a new way to ensure their capital supply and until middle-aged employees find a new way to ensure their job stability, it is less likely that they will spend money aggressively. As long as the spending from these two sources remains low, the Japanese economy is less likely to have a speedy recovery from its decade-long stagnation.

The Japanese economic system cannot return to its pre-1990s stage. The reforms of the 1990s have significantly damaged the two former mechanisms of economic growth, and it will be very difficult to rebuild them to the original pattern. Eliminating this possibility, a realistic expectation of the Japanese economy probably contains only two scenarios under the leadership of newly elected Prime Minister Koizumi Junichirō. First, the Japanese could conduct a major yet systematic reform and reconfigure their entire economic system in the environment of globalization. After several years of contraction, the newly established mechanism of growth would begin to work. In the second scenario, the Koizumi administration would return to the muddle-through pattern of reform after the failure of initial reform and continuing stagnation. "Muddle-through" here does not mean that the Japanese would not change at all but rather they would change too little, too slowly, and only when under strong pressure and having no other choice. As a result, it would take a long time for the Japanese economic system to establish new mechanisms of economic growth and the economy would remain in stagnation.

This second scenario is not unlikely. If Koizumi indeed carries out what he proposed during the political campaign – namely, limiting government budget deficits and addressing the bad loan issue – it means a potential decline in all three major investment sources. When the government budget deficit faces a limit, the government will spend less; when banks are forced to clean up bad loans, corporations will have more difficulty borrowing capital and thus will make fewer investments; when this happens, more banks and corporations will go bankrupt, and consumers will face stronger uncertainty in their future income and thus will spend less. In some way, this situation could repeat what Hashimoto did in 1996. Given the vested political interests in the existing system, the lack of an effective government-sponsored unemployment assistance program, and the possibility of a global economic recession resulting from the slowdown in the U.S. economy, it remains a question as to what extent the Japanese are really prepared for a course of radical action. Only when these reforms run their course will they definitely benefit the Japanese economy in the long run. Before the Japanese see a positive future, however, the Japanese economy may have to brave a multiple-year contraction. Koizumi has warned Japanese voters about this possibility.

REFERENCES

Note: Japanese authors use surname-first order for Japanese-language publication. When their English-language publications are cited, however, their names appear surname-last.

Aoki, Masahiko. 1994. "Monitoring Characteristics of the Main Bank System: An Analytical and Developmental View." In Masahiko and Hugh Patrick, eds., *The Japanese Main Bank System*. Oxford: Oxford University Press, pp. 109–142.

Aoki, Masahiko, and Hugh Patrick, eds. 1994. *The Japanese Main Bank System: Its Relevance for Developing and Transforming Economies*. Oxford: Oxford University Press.

Aoki, Masahiko, and Okuno Masahiro, eds. 1997 [1996]. *Keizai shisutemu no hikaku seido bunseki* (A Comparative Institutional Analysis of Economic System). Tokyo: Tokyo Daigaku Shuppankai.

Arisawa Hiromi. 1937a. *Keizai tōseika no nihon* (Japan Under the Managed Economy). Tokyo: Kaizōsha.

Arisawa Hiromi. 1937b. *Sensō to keizai* (War and Economy). Tokyo: Nihon Hyōronsha.

Arisawa Hiromi. 1937c. *Nihon kōgyō tōsei-ron* (The Industrial Control in Japan). Tokyo: Arikai Kaku.

Arisawa Hiromi, ed. 1976. *Shōwa keizaishi* (The History of the Shōwa Economy). Tokyo: Nihon Keizai Shinbunsha.

Arisawa Hiromi and Tsuchiya Kiyoshi, supervised. 1967. *Shihon jiyūka, honshitsu to taisaku* (The Liberalization of Foreign Investment: Its Nature and Japan's Responding Strategies). Tokyo: Shakai Shisōsha. pp. 3–124.

Arrighi, Giovanni. 1994. *The Long Twentieth Century: Money, Power, and the Origins of Our Times*. London: Verso.

Arrighi, Giovanni, and Beverly J. Silver, eds. 1999. *Chaos and Governance in the Modern World System*. Minneapolis: University of Minnesota Press.

Asher, David L. 1996. "Economic Myths Explained: What Became of the Japanese 'Miracle.'" *Orbis*. Spring.

Asher, David. 1999. "The Evolution of American Japan Policy, 1914–22: The Washington Conference and the Advent of 'Golden Imperialism.'" Unpublished paper.

Beeman, Michael. 1997. *Public Policy and Economic Competition in Japan: The Rise of Antimonopoly Policy, 1973–1995*. Ph.D. Dissertation. Oxford University.

Berger, Suzanne, and Ronald Dore, eds. 1997. *National Diversity and Global Capitalism*. Ithaca, NY: Cornell University Press.

Berle, Adolph, and Garliner Means. 1932. *The Modern Corporation and Private Property*. New York: Macmillan.

Bisson, T. A. 1954. *Zaibatsu Dissolution in Japan*. Berkeley: University of California Press.

Block, Fred. 1977. *The Origins of International Economic Disorder: A Study of United States Internaitonal Monetary Policy from World War II to the Present*. Berkeley: University of California Press.

Block, Fred. 1990. *Postindustrial Possibilities*. Berkeley: University of California Press.

Borden, William S. 1984. *The Pacific Alliance: United States Foreign Economic Policy and Japanese Trade Recovery, 1947–1955*. Madison: The University of Wisconsin Press.

Brenner, Robert. 1998. "The Economics of Global Turbulence." *New Left Review* 229: 1–262.

Brinton, Mary C. 1993. *Women and the Economic Miracle: Gender and Work in Postwar Japan*. Berkeley: University of California Press.

Buckley, Sandra. 1993. "Altered States: The Body Politics of 'Being-Woman.'" In Andrew Gordon, ed., *Postwar Japan as History*. Berkeley: University of California Press, pp. 347–373.

Burstein, Daniel. 1988. *Yen! Japan's New Financial Empire and Its Threat to America*. New York: Simon and Schuster.

Calder, Kent E. 1988. *Crisis and Compensation*. Princeton, NJ: Princeton University Press.

Calder, Kent E. 1993. *Strategic Capitalism: Private Business and Public Purpose in Japanese Industrial Finance*. Princeton, NJ: Princeton University Press.

Calder, Kent E. 1997. "Assault on the Bankers' Kingdom: Politics, Markets, and the Liberalization of Japanese Industrial Finance." In Michael Loriaux, Meredith Woo-Cumings, Kent E. Calder, Sylvia Maxfield, and Sofia A. Perez, eds., *Capital Ungoverned: Liberalizing Finance in Interventionist States*, pp. 17–57.

Campbell, John C. 1977. *Contemporary Japanese Budget Politics*. Berkeley: University of California Press.

Chinesenewsnet.com. 1999. "Dongmeng fenghui chengren yazhou gongtong shichang kenengxing" (The ASEAN Summit Acknowledged the Possibility of Asian Common Market). *http://www.duoweinews.com/Mainnews/headline/Sun-Nov-28-15-43-44-1999.html*.

Coase, Ronald H. 1937. "The Nature of the Firm." *Economica* N. S., pp. 386–405.

Cohen, Stephen D. 1998. *An Ocean Apart: Explaining Three Decades of U.S.-Japanese Trade Frictions*. Westport, CT: Praeger.

Das, Dilip K. 1993. *The Yen Appreciation and the International Economy*. New York: New York University Press.

DiMaggio, Paul. 1988. "Interest and Agency in Institutional Theory." In Lynne G. Zucker, ed., *Institutional Patterns and Organizations*. Cambridge: Ballinger Publishing Company, pp. 3–21.

DiMaggio, Paul, and Walter R. Powell. 1983. "The Iron Cage Revisited: Institutional Isomorphism and Collective Rationality in Organizational Fields." *American Sociological Review* 83: 147–160.

DiMaggio, Paul J., and Walter W. Powell. 1991. "Introduction." In Paul J. DiMaggio and Walter W. Powell, eds., *The New Institutionalism in Organizational Analysis*. Chicago: The University of Chicago Press, pp. 1–38.

Dobbin, Frank. 1994. *Forging Industrial Cultures*. Cambridge: Cambridge University Press.

Dore, Ronald. 1973. *British Factory: Japanese Factory: The Origins of National Diversity in Industrial Relations*. Berkeley: University of California Press.

Dore, Ronald. 1983. "Goodwill and the Spirit of Market Capitalism." *British Journal of Sociology* 34: 459–482.

Dore, Ronald. 1986. *Flexible Rigidities*. Stanford, CA: Stanford University Press.

Dore, Ronald. 1987. *Taking Japan Seriously*. London: The Athlone Press.

Dore, Ronald. 1999. "Japan's Reform Debate: Patriotic Concern or Class Interest? Or Both." *Journal of Japanese Studies* 25(1): 65–89.

Eatwell, John, and Lance Taylor. 2000. *Global Finance at Risk: The Case for International Regulation*. New York: The New Press.

Economic Planning Agency. 1990. *The Japanese Economy, 1955–65*. Tokyo.

Economist, The. 1988. "Sekai ni risansuru nihonjin" (The Era of Japanese Disapora) 7(4): 69–79.

Ekonomisuto. 1966. "Gabbei no naibaku" (The Inside Story of Mergers). Special Edition 7(20): 16–22.

Ekonomisuto. 1974. "Ōhaba chinage jitsugenshita 74 shuntō" (The 1974 Spring Strike that Realized Big Raises in Wages) 4(30): 6–7.

Ekonomisuto. 1994. "Hado na koyō chōsei no kanōsei mo" (The Possibility of Hard Employment Adjustment) 5(9): 54–55.

Ekonomisuto. 1967. "Gaishi shingikai senmon iinkai hōkoku" (The Report of the Special Committee of the Advisory Council of Foreign Investments) 6(20): 62–64.

Fallows, James. 1994. *Looking at the Sun*. New York: Pantheon Books.

Fishlow, Albert, and Karen Parker, eds. 1999. *Growing Apart: The Causes and Consequences of Global Wage Inequality*. New York: Council on Foreign Relations Press.

Fligstein, Neil. 1998. "Is Globalization the Cause of the Crises of Welfare States?" Unpublished paper.

Foreign Press Center. 1999. *Facts and Figures of Japan*. Tokyo: Foreign Press Center.

Frieden, Jeffry A. 1987. *Banking on the World: The Politics of American International Finance*. New York: Harper & Row.

Frieden, Jeffry A. 1996. "Economic Integration and the Politics of Monetary Policy in the United States." In Robert O. Keohane and Helen V. Milner, eds., *Internationalization and Domestic Politics*. New York: Cambridge University Press, pp. 108–136.

Friedland, Roger, and Robert R. Alford. 1991. "Bringing Society Back In: Symbols, Practices, and Institutional Contradictions." In Walter Powell and Paul DiMaggio, eds., *The New Institutionalism in Organizational Analysis*. Chicago: University of Chicago Press, pp. 232–266.

Fukushima Glen. 1992. *Nichibei keizai masatsu no seijigaku* (The Political Science of Japan-U.S. Economic Fractions). Tokyo: Asahi Shinbunsha.

Fukuda Oboe. 1958. "Nōka keizai ni ichijirushii appaku" (The Explicit Pressures on the Farmers). *Kōsei Torihiki* 2: 33–36.

Funabashi, Yoichi. 1988. *From the Plaza to the Louvre*. Washington, D.C.: Institute for International Economics.

Gao, Bai. 1997. *Economic Ideology and Japanese Industrial Policy: Developmentalism From 1931 to 1965*. New York: Cambridge University Press.

Gao, Bai. 1994. "Arisawa Hiromi and His Theory for a Managed Economy." *Journal of Japanese Studies* 20(1): 115–153.

Gao, Bai. 1998a. "Efficiency, Culture, and Politics: The Transformation of Japanese Management in 1946–1966." In Michel Callon, ed., *The Laws of the Markets*. Oxford: Blackwell Publishers, pp. 86–115.

Gao, Bai. 1998b. "The Search for National Identity and Japanese Industrial Policy, 1950–1969." *Nations and Nationalism* 4(2): 227–245.

Gao, Bai. 2000. "Globalization and Ideology: The Competing Images of the Contemporary Japanese Economic System in the 1990s." *International Sociology* 15(3): 435–453.

Gao, Bai. Forthcoming. "The State and the Associational Order of the Economy: The Institutionalization of Cartels and Trade Associations in 1931–1945 Japan." *Sociological Forum*.

Gardner, Richard N. 1969 [1965]. *Sterling-Dollar Diplomacy*. New York: McGraw-Hill Book Company.

Garrett, Geoffrey. 1998. *Partisan Politics in the Global Economy*. New York: Cambridge University Press.

Gerber, David J. 1998. *Law and Competition in Twentieth Century Europe: Protecting Prometheus*. Oxford: Clarendon Press.

Gerlach, Micheal. 1992. *Allied Capitalism*. Berkeley: University of California Press.

GHQ and SCAP. 1950. History of the Nonmilitary Activities of the Occupation of Japan: 1945–1951. Tokyo: Nihon Tosho Senta. Vols. 28, 29, 30.

Gilpin, Robert. 1987. *The Political Economy of International Relations*. Princeton, NJ: Princeton University Press.

Gilpin, Robert. 2000. *The Challenge of Global Capitalism: The World Economy in the 21ˢᵗ Century*. Princeton, NJ: Princeton University Press.

Gordon, Andrew. 1985. *The Evolution of Labor Relations in Japan: Heavy Industry, 1853–1955*. Cambridge, MA: Council on East Asian Studies, Harvard University.

Gordon, David M. 1996. *Fat and Mean: The Corporate Squeeze of Working Americans and the Myth of Managerial "Downsizing."* New York: The Free Press.

Gotō Shin'ichi. 1973. "Zaisei kinyū seisaku no rekishiteki kyōkun" (The Lesson in History of the Finacial and Monetary Policies). *Ekonomisuto* 10(13): 46–55.

Gotō Shin'ichi. 1990. *Shōwa Kinyūshi-21 seiki e no tenbō* (The Showa History of Finance-Prospects of the 21st Century). Tokyo: Taihei Insatsusha.

Gourevitch, Peter. 1986. *Politics in Hard Times: Comparative Responses to International Economic Crises.* Ithaca, NY: Cornell University Press.

Gowa, Joanne. 1983. *Closing the Gold Window.* Ithaca, NY: Cornell University Press.

Grimes, William W. 1995. *From the Plaza to the Bubble: Japan's Response to International Economic Policy Coordination, 1985–1988.* Ph.D. dissertation. Princeton University.

Hadley, Eleaner. 1970. *Anti-Trust in Japan.* Princeton, NJ: Princeton University Press.

Haley, John O. 1991. *Authority Without Power: Law and the Japanese Paradox.* New York: Oxford University Press.

Hannan, Michael T., and John Freeman. 1989. *Organizational Ecology.* Cambridge, MA: Harvard University Press.

Hara Akira. 1995. "Sengo gojūnen to nihon keizai" (The Fifty Years in the Postwar Era and the Japanese Economy). In *Nenpō nihon gendaishi 1995-sengo gojūnen no shiteki kenshō.* Tokyo: Higashi Shuppan. pp. 79–111.

Hara Eijirō and Fukuta Jun. 1999. "Ginkō ni 'kirareru kaisha'" (Corporations Abandoned by Banks). *Shūkan tōyō keizai* 3(20): 10–13.

Harada Yutaka. 1998. *Senkyū hyaku nanajūnen taisei no Shūen* (The End of the 1970 System). Tokyo: Tōyō Keizai Shinpōsha.

Haruno Haruko. 1958. "Shōhisha no rieki o wasureta kaisei" (The Amendment that Forgot the Interest of Consumers). *Kōsei Torihiki* February: 19–20.

Hashimoto Mitsuharu. 1987. "Naze taibei fudōsan tōshi rasshiu nanoka" (Why Rush for Investments in the U.S. Real Estate?). *Ekonomisuto* 2(24): 76–81.

Heiwa Keizai Kikaku Kaigi. 1977. *Kokumin no dokusen hakusho* (The White Paper of the Antimonopoly Laws by the Japanese People). Tokyo: Ochanominzu Shobō.

Helleiner, Eric. 1994. *States and the Reemergence of Global Finance From Bretton Woods to the 1990s.* Ithaca, NY: Cornell University Press.

Hidaka Chikage and Kikkawa Takeo. 1998. "Sengo nihon no mein banku shisutemu to kōporeito gabanansu" (The Main Bank System and Corporate Governance in Postwar Japan). *Shakai kagaku kenkyū* 49(6): 1–29.

Higuchi Yoshio. 1995. "Sengyō shūfu hōgo seisaku no keizaiteki kiketsu" (The Economic Implications of the Professional Housewife Protection Policy). In Hatta Tatsuo and Yashiro Naohiro, eds., *Ryakusha hōgo seisaku no keizaiteki bunseki.* Tokyo: Nihon Keizai Shinbunsha, pp. 185–220.

Hirst, Paul, and Grahame Thompson. 1996. *Globalization in Question: The International Economy and the Possibilities of Governance.* Cambridge, UK: Polity Press.

Hollingsworth, J. Rogers, and Robert Boyer, eds. 1997a. *Contemporary Capitalism: The Embeddedness of Institutions.* New York: Cambridge University Press.

Hollingsworth, J. Rogers, and Robert Boyer. 1997b. "Coordination of Economic Actors and Social Systems of Production." In J. Rogers Hollingsworth and Robert Boyer, eds., *Contemporary Capitalism: The Embeddedness of Institutions,* pp. 1–49.

Iga Takashi. 1987. "Zaiteku yori kashikoi hōhō ga aru" (There are Wiser Alternatives Than Zai'tech). *Ekonomisuto* 10(6): 62–65.

Ikenberry, G. John. 1993. "Creating Yesterday's New World Order: Keynesian 'New Thinking' and the Anglo-American Postwar Settlement." In Judith Goldstein and Robert O. Keohane, eds., *Ideas and Foreign Policy: Beliefs, Institutions, and Political Change*. Ithaca, NY: Cornell University Press, pp. 57–87.

Imai Tadayoshi. 1962. "Kado kyōsō haijo no konhon mondai" (The Fundamental Problem of Preventing the Excessive Competition). *Shūkan tōyō keizai* (Summer Bessatsu): 28–35.

Imamura Shigekazu. 1970[1956]. *Shiteki dokusen kinshihō no kenkyū* (Studies on the Antimonopoly Law). Tokyo: Yūhikaku.

Imōkawa Tokutarō. 1986. "Tokyo shūchū to chihō bunsan no tsunahiki" (A Tug of War between the Centralization of Tokyo and the Decentralization of the Locality). *Shūkan tōyō keizai* 12(13): 90–91.

Inotani Zen'ichi. 1937. *Nihon keizai oyobi keizai seisaku* (The Japanese Economy and Economic Policies). Tokyo: Ichigensha.

Ishirō Katsuji. 1988. "'Rieki naki hanbōku' ka de bōsatsu suru chūshō kigyō" (The Busy Small and Medium Corporations are Striving Without Profits). *Ekonomisuto* 9(27): 22–27.

Itō Makoto. 1988. "Nihon wa posuto foodeizm he no chōsei o oeta ka" (Has Japan Finished its Adjustment Toward Post-Fordism?). *Ekonomisuto* 9(6): 26–31.

Itō Mitsuharu. 1999a. "Nihon keizai ushiwareta jūnen" (The Ten Years of the Depression of the Japanese Economy). *Yomiuri* 3: 188–205.

Itō Mitsuharu. 1999b. "Nijūichi seiki no nihon o shijō genri dake ni makasete oite iika" (Is It O.K. for 21st Century Japan to Leave Everything to Market Principles?). *Ekonomisuto* 4(5): 10–16.

Itō Nagamasa. 1959. "Kasen zaiakuron no konyū o tadasu" (Correct the Wrong Argument of Evil Oligopoly). Shūkan Tōyō Keizai (Fall Betsusatsu).

Itō Nagamasa. 1968. "Nihon-teki kigyō baitariti no gensen to genkai" (The Origin and Limits of the Vitality of the Japanese Corporations). *Shūkan tōyō keizai* (Rinji Sōkan) 7(3): 142.

Itō Osamu. 1995. *Nihon-gata kinyū no rekishiteki kōzō* (The Historical Structure of the Japanese Style Finance). Tokyo: Tokyo Daigaku Shuppankai.

Itō Yoshikazu. 1985. "Nihon kigyō wa kane to hito no tsukaikata o machigaeteiru" (The Japanese Corporations are Making Mistakes in Ways of Using Money and Personnel). *Ekonomisuto* 9(17): 42–45.

Iwao, Sumiko. 1993. *The Japanese Woman: Traditional Image and Changing Reality*. New York: The Free Press.

Jensen, Michael C., and William Meckling. 1976. "Theory of the Firm: Managerial Behavior, Agency Cost, and Capital Structure." *Journal of Financial Economics* 3: 305–360.

Johnson, Chalmers. 1982. *MITI and the Japanese Miracle*. Stanford, CA: Stanford University Press.

Johnson, Chalmers. 1998. "Economic Crisis in East Asia: The Clash of Capitalisms." *Cambridge Journal of Economics*, 22.

Kanzaki, Y. 1997. "Deregulation in Japan: Big Bang or Big Whimper?" Unpublished paper, presented at the Woodrow Wilson Center on March 7 1997. The text appeared in the news group fukuzawa@ucsd.edu on March 11, 1997.

Kapur, Devesh. 1998. "The IMF: A Cure or a Curse." *Foreign Policy* 111: 114–126.

Kasai Hiro. 1999. *Densangata chingin taikei no sekai* (The World of the Electricity Industry's Wage System). Tokyo: Waseda Daigaku Shuppankai.

Katō Hideki. 1999. "Nihon koku no 'baransu shiito' shoshisan" (The Trial Balance Sheet of Japan). *Bungei shunjū* 5: 134–144.

Katō Hiroshi. 1986. "Maekawa repoto he no hihan ni kotaeru" (Reply to the Criticisms to the Maekawa Report). *Shūkan tōyō keizai* September 6: 62–66.

Katsumata Hisayoshi. 1995. *Sengo gojūnen no nihon keizai* (The Japanese Economy During the Fifty Years After the War). Tokyo: Tōyō Keizai Shinpōsha.

Katsumata Hisayoshi. 1986. "Shōgyōchi kyūtō wa infure no zenchō nano ka" (Does the Sudden Rise of Commercial Land Prices Signal Inflation?). *Shūkan tōyō keizai* 11(1): 28–29.

Katz, Richard. 1998. *Japan: The System that Soured.* New York: M. E. Sharpe.

Kawanishi, Hirosuke. 1999. Densan-gata chingin taikei no sekai: sono keisei to rekishi-teki igi (The World of the Electric Power Industry Wage Pattern: Its Origin and Historical Significance). Tokyo: Waseda Daigaku Shuppanbu.

Keidanren. 1958. "Dokusen kenshihō shingikai no tetsumon ni taisuru keidanren no kaitoku" (Kendanren's Reply to the Queries from the Committee on the Antimonopoly Law). *Kōsei torihiki* 11: 35–36.

Keidanren. 1963. *Keizai dantai rengōkai jūnenshi (shita)* (A Ten Year History of the Federation of Economic Organization). Tokyo: Keidanren.

Keidanren. 1978. *Keizai dantai rengōkai sanjūnenshi* (A Thirty Year History of the Federation of Economic Organizations). Tokyo: Keidanren.

Keizai Kikakuchō. 1964. *Sengo keizai-shi: keizai antei honbu-shi* (The History of Postwar Economy: the History of the Economic Stabilization Board).

Keizai Kikakuchō. 1976. *Gendai nihon keizai no tenkai: keizai kikakuchō sanjūnenshi* (The Development of Modern Japanese Economy: A Thirty Year History of the Economic Planning Agency). Tokyo: Ōkurashō Insatsu-kyoku.

Keizai Kikakuchō. 1988. "Nenji keizai hōkoku" (Annual Economic Report). *Ekonomisuto* 8(15): 238–247.

Keizai Kikakuchō. 1987. *Keizai Hakusho: Susumu kōzō tenkan to kongo no kadai* (The White Paper of the Economy: Ongoing Structural Transformation and the Future's Issues). Tokyo: Ōkurashō Insatsu-kyoku.

Keizai Kikakuchō. 1996. *Kokumin seikatsu hakusho* (The White Paper on Japanese Life). Tokyo: Ōkurashō Insatsu-kyoku.

Keizai Kikakuchō. 1997. *Keizai hakusho* (The White Paper on the Economy). Tokyo: Keizai Kikakuchō.

Kenen, Peter B. 1989 [1985]. *The International Economy*. Englewood Cliffs, NJ: Prentice Hall.

Keohane, Robert O. 1984. *After Hegemony: Cooperation and Discord in the World Political Economy*. Princeton, NJ: Princeton University Press.

Keohane, Robert O., and Helen V. Milner, eds. 1996. *Internationalization and Domestic Politics*. New York: Cambridge University Press.

Keohane, Robert O., and Joseph S. Nye. 1977. *Power and Interdependence*. Boston. MA: Little, Brown and Company.

Kester, Carl W. 1997. "American and Japanese Corporate Governance: Convergence to Best Practice?" In Suzanne Berger and Ronald Dore, eds., *Naitonal Diversity and Global Capitalism*. Ithaca, NY: Cornell University Press. pp. 107–136.

Keynes, John Maynard. 1920. *The Economic Consequences of the Peace*. New York: Harcourt, Brace and Howe.

Kikkawa Mototada. 1998. *Mane- haisen* (The Defeat in the Money War). Tokyo: Bungei Shunjū.

Kikkawa Mototada. 1999a. "Naze nihon no keiki rongi wa meisō suru ka." *Ekonomisuto* 4(5): 21–24.

Kikkawa, Mototada. 1999b. "Nihon yo, yen o sutenasai" (Japan, Please Abandon the Yen). *Bungei Shunjū* 3: 104–116.

Kikuchi, Haruo. 1943. *Keizaihō nyūmon* (Introduction of Economic Law). Tokyo: Tōyō Shoten.

Kishi Nobusuke. 1942. *Senji nihon keizai no susumu michi* (The Road for the Wartime Japanese Economy). Tokyo: Kenshinsha.

Kitschelt, Herbert, Peter Lange, Cary Marks, and John D. Stephens, eds. 1999. *Continuity and Change in Contemporary Capitalism*. New York: Cambridge University Press.

Kobayashi Hideo, Okazaki Tetsuji, Yonekura Seiichirō, and NHK. 1995. *"Nihon kabushiki kaisha" no showashi* (The Showa History of the Japan Inc.). Osaka: Sōgensha.

Kodō Rikuzo. 1963. "Sangyō taiseiron: sangyōkai kara no teishō" (On Industrial System: A Suggestion From the Private Sector). In Morozumi Yoshihiko, Minosō Hitoshi, Kodō Rikuzō, Masada Tadashi, and Chiyu Yoshihito, eds., *Sangyō taisei no saihensei*. Tokyo: Shunjūsh, pp. 107–136.

Kojo, Yoshiko. 1993. *Domestic Sources of International Payments Adjustment: Japan's Policy Choices in the Postwar Period*. Ph.D. dissertation. Princeton University.

Konekura Seiichirō. 1993. "Gyōkai dantai no kinō" (The Function of Trade Association). In Okazaki Tetsuji and Okuno Masahiro, eds., *Gendai nihon keizai shisutemu no genryū*. Tokyo: Nihon Keizai Shibunsha.

Konishi Kazuo. 1999. "BIS kisei ga ginkō o gyanbura ni shita" (BIS Regulations Have Turned Banks into Gamblers). *Bungei shunjū* 5: 272–275.

Koo, Richard. 1999. "7.5 chō en nosuika tōnyū de kanzen kaishō o mezase" (Aiming at the Liquidation by Additional Public Spending of 7.5 Trillion Yen). *Shūkan tōyō keizaii* 3(27): 56–59.

Kōsei Torihiki. 1953a. "Shūgiin keizai antei iinkai okeru dokusenhō kaisei ni taisuru san sankōnin no iken" (The Opinions of the Three Referees on the Amendment of the Antimonopoly Law at the Economic Stabilization Committee of the Lower House). 3: 18–23.

Kōsei Torihiki. 1953b. "Keizai antei iinkai kōchō kai ni okeru kōjutsunin no kōjutsu" (The Public Testimony by the Testimonees at the Hearing of the Economic Stabilization Committee). 5: 5–11.

Kōsei Torihiki. 1975. "Dokukinhō kaisei hōan no kokkai shingi keika" (The Proceedings on the Congress Discussions of the Amendments of the Antimonopoly Laws). *Kōsei torihiki* 7(297): 18–27.

Kōsei Torihiki Iinkai. 1977. *Dokusen kinshi seisahu sanjūnenshi* (The Thirty Years' History of Antimonopoly Policy). Tokyo: Kōsei Torihiki Iinkai.

Krasner, Stephen D. 1984. "Approaches to the State: Alternative Conceptions and Historical Dynamics." *Comparative Politics* 16: 223–246.

Krugman, Paul. 1994. "The Myth of Asia's Miracle." *Foreign Affairs* 73(6): 62–79.

Krugman, Paul. 1999a. "The Return of Depression Economics." *Foreign Affairs* 78(1): 56–74.

Krugman, Paul. 1999b. *The Return of Depression Economics.* New York: W. W. Norton & Company.

Kume, Ikuo. 1998. *Disparaged Success: Labor Politics in Postwar Japan.* Ithaca, NY: Cornell University Press.

Kunihiro Kazuto. 1941. *Keizai dantai* (Economic Organization). Tokyo: Nihon Hyōronsha.

Lincoln, James R., Michael L. Gerlach, and Peggy Takahashi. 1992. "Keiretsu Networks in the Japanese Economy: A Dyad Analysis of Intercorporate Ties." *American Sociological Review* 57: 561–585.

Lindberg, Leon, and John Campbell. 1990. "The State and the Organization of Economic Activity." In John L. Campbell, J. Rogers Hillingsworth, and Leon N. Lindberg, eds., *Governance of the American Economy.* Cambridge: Cambridge University Press, pp. 356–395.

Longworth, Richard C. 1998. *Global Squeeze: The Coming Crisis for First-World Nations.* Chicago: Contemporary Books.

Loriaux, Michael. 1991. *France After Hegemony.* Ithaca, NY: Cornell University Press.

Loriaux, Michael, Meredith Woo-Cumings, Kent E. Calder, Sylvia Maxfield, and Sofia A. Perez. 1997. *Capital Ungoverned: Liberalizing Finance in Interventionist States.* Ithaca, NY: Cornell University Press.

Maeta Hikoyoshi. 1966. "Tsūsan seisaku ga mezasu mono" (The Goals of Industrial Policy). *Shūkan tōyō keizai* 7(20): 50–54.

Mainichi Shinbun Keizaibu. 1975. *Kōtori wa moeta* (The Burning of the Fair Trade Committee). Mainichi Shinbun.

Makino Asahiko. 1958. "Futō ni keishisareta chūshō kigyō" (Unfairly Neglected Medium-Size and Small Companies). *Kōsei Torihiki* 2: 25–29.

Makino Noboru. 1987. "Shinjinrui ga uri denhyō o kaku hi" (When the New Generation of Manager Issue the Sell Order). *Shūkan tōyō keizai* 3(14): 24–27.

Mandel, Michael J. 2000. *The Coming Internet Depression*. New York: Basic Books.

Maotani Tsutomu. 1978. "Wagakuni chūshō kigyō no chii to sono henka" (The Status and its Change of Japanese Medium-Size and Small Companies). In Kiyonari Tadao, Maotani Tsutomu, Shōya Kuniyuki, and Akiya Shigeo, eds., *Chūshō kigyō ron*. Tokyo: Yūhikaku.

Masamura Kimihiro. 1985. *Sengoshi* (Postwar History). Tokyo: Tsukuma Shobō, Vol. 1.

Matsui Haruo. 1938. *Nihon shigen seisaku* (The Japanese Policies of Resources). Tokyo: Chikura Shobō.

McKinnon, Ronald I., and Kenichi Ohno. 1997. *Dollar and Yen: Resolving Economic Conflict between the United States and Japan*. Cambridge, MA: The MIT Press.

Meyer, John W., and Brian Rowan. 1991 [1977]. "Institutionalized Organizations: Formal Structure as Myth and Ceremony." In Walter Powell and Paul DiMaggio, eds., *The New Institutionalism in Organizational Analysis*. Chicago: University of Chicago Press, pp. 41–62.

Minemura Teruo. 1940. *Hō to tōsei keizai* (Law and the Managed Economy). Tokyo: Tōyō Shoten.

Minemura Teruo. 1951. *Keizaihō* (Economic Law). Tokyo: Sanwa Shobō.

Minosō Hitoshi. 1963. "Sangyō taiseiron: dokusen seisaku no tachiba kara" (On Industrial System: From An Antimonopoly Policy Perspective). In Morozumi Yoshihiko, Minosō Hitoshi, Kodō Rikuzō, Masada Tadashi, and Chiyu Yoshihito, eds., *Sangyō taisei no saihensei*. Tokyo: Shunjōsha, pp. 75–106.

Minosō Hitoshi. 1977. "Nihon ni okeru dokusen seisaku no tenkai to sono mondaiten" (The Development of the Antimonopoly Policy in Japan and its Major Issues). In Heiwa Keizai Keikaku Kaigi, ed., *Kokumin no dokusen hakusho*. Tokyo: Ochanomizu shobō, pp. 119–153.

Mitsuhashi Tadahiro and Uchida Shigeo. 1994. *Showa keizaishi* (The Economic History of the Showa Era). Tokyo: Nihon Keizai Shinbunsha.

Miyazaki Yoshikazu. 1963. "'Kado kyōsō' no kōzai" (The Merits and Dismerits of "Excessive Competition"). In Kōsei Torihiki Kyōkai, ed., *Kokusai kyōsō to dokukinhō*. Tokyo: Nihon Keizai Shinbunsha, pp. 47–74.

Miyazaki Yoshikazu. 1966. *Sengo nihon no keizai kōzō* (The Structure of the Postwar Japanese Economy). Tokyo: Shin Hyōron.

Miyazaki Yoshikazu. 1985. *Nihon keizai no kōzō to kōdō* (The Structure and Behavior of the Japanese Economy). Tokyo: Chikuma Shobō. Vol. 1.

Miyazaki Yoshikazu. 1990 [1985]. *Riben Jingji de Jiegou he Yanbian* (The Structure and Behavior of the Japanese Economy). Beijing: Zhongguo Duiwai Jingji Maoyi Chubanshe.

Miyazaki Yoshikazu. 1992. *Fukugō fukyō* (The Mixed Recession). Tokyo: Chūō Kōronsha.

Miyazawa Toshiyoshi. 1940. "Gaikan narabi ni wagakuni" (Overview and Japan). *Kokkagaku kenkyū* 54(9): 1–39.

Morozumi Yoshihiko. 1962a. *Kyōsō to dokusen no hanashi* (The Story of Competition and Monopoly). Tokyo: Nikei Bunko.

Morozumi Yoshihiko. 1962b. "Furansu keizai ni okeru keikaku" (Planning in the French Economy). *Keizai Hyōron.*

Morozumi Yoshihiko. 1962c. "Sangyō seisaku no kyōchōteki tenkai" (The Cooperation for Carrying out the Industrial Policy). *Shūkan tōyō keizai* (Summer Betsusatsu).

Morozumi Yoshihiko. 1962d. "Furansu no kyōchō keizai taisei" (French Coordinated Economic System). *Nihon keizai to shinsangyō taisei.* Tokyo: Tōyō Keizai Shinpōsha, pp. 3–31.

Morozumi Yoshihiko. 1963a. "Sangyō taiseiron: tsūsanshōgawa no ichiteian" (A Proposal From MITI). In Morozumi Yoshihiko, Minosō Hitoshi, Kodō Rikuzō, Masada Tadashi, and Chiyu Yoshihito, eds., *Sangyō taisei no saihensei.* Tokyo: Shunjūsha, pp. 3–74.

Morozumi Yoshihiko. 1963b. "Keizai seichō to dokukin seisaku" (Economic Growth and the Antitrust Policy). In Kōsei Torihiki Kyōkai, ed., *Kokusai kyōsō to dokukinhō.* Tokyo: Nihon Keizai Shinbunsha, pp. 15–45.

Morozumi Yoshihiko. 1966. *Sangyō seisaku no riron* (The Theory of Industrial Policy). Tokyo: Nihon Keizai Shinbunsha.

Murakami Yasusuke. 1968. "Ōkata gōben ni taisuru gakusha seimei" (On Scholars' Declarations About Mergers Among Big Corporations). *Shūkan tōyō keizai* (Rinji Sōkan) 7(3): 42.

Murakami Yasusuke. 1992. *Hankoten no seiji keizaigaku* (Anticlassical Political Economy). Tokyo: Chūō Kōronsha, Vol. 1 and Vol. 2.

Murakami Yasusuke. 1994. *Hankoten no seiji keizaigaku yōkō* (An Outline for Anticlassical Political Economy). Tokyo: Chūō Kōronsha.

Murakami, Yasusuke. 1996. *An Anticlassical Political-Economic Analysis: A Vision for the Next Century.* Stanford, CA: Stanford University Press.

Murphy, R. Taggart. 1996. *The Weight of the Yen.* New York: W. W. Norton & Company.

Nagai Mamoru. 1958. "Karuteru kanwa no imisuru mono" (The Implication of Relaxing Cartels). *Kōsei Torihiki* 2: 29–32.

Naitō Tetsu. 1986. "Manei henchō!? shikin unyō no shinchōryū" (Irregularity of Money!? New Trends in Use of Funds). *Shūkan tōyō keizai* 12(6): 16–27.

Nakano Shirō. 1982. *Tanaka seiken 886-nichi* (The Eight Hundred and Eighty-Six Days of the Tanaka Administration). Tokyo: Kōsei Mondai Kenkyūjo.

Nakatani Iwao. 1996. *Nihon keizai no rekishiteki tenkan* (The Historical Transformation of the Japanese Economy). Tokyo: Tōyō Keizai Shinpōsha.

Nakayama Ichirō. 1972. "Sensansei no riron to jissai" (The Theory of Productivity and Reality). In Seisansei Honbu, ed., *Seisansei kōjō shirizu,* pp. 331–344.

Namiki Nobuyoshi. 1988. "Keiki hendō rongi ni aratana shiten o" (New Points of View in the Contraversy on the Fluctuation in the Economic Boom). *Ekonomisuto* 12(6): 64–69.

Narita Junji. 1986. "Sangyō no kūdōka wa osoreru ni tarazu" (No Need to Worry About Deindustrialization). *Shūkan tōyō keizai* 10(25): 102–106.

Nemoto Nobuya. 1996. "Fusai defure ga nihon keizai ni noshikakaru" (The Debt Deflation Lies Heavily on the Japan Economy). *Ekonomisuto* 12(17): 57–59.

NHK. 1995. *Sengo 50-nen sono toki nihon wa*. (Japan, 50 Years After the War). Tokyo: Nihon Hōsō Shuppan Kyōkai.

Nihon Keizai Renmeikai. 1940. *Kenkō sangyō tōsei no kekken jitsujō narabini kore ni taisuru gyōshūbetsu kaizen iken* (The Problems in Present Economic Control and the Proposal for Improvement From Each Industry). Tokyo: Nihon Keizai Renmeikai.

Nihon Seisansei Honbu. 1985. *Sensansei undō 30 nen shi* (A Thirty Year History of the Movement of Productivity).

Nishinarita Yutaka. 1994. "Sengo kiki to shihonshugi saiken katei no rōshi kankei: nihon to nishidoitsu no hikakushi" (The Postwar Crisis and Labor Relations in the Process of Capitalist Reconstruction: A Comparative History Between Japan and West Germany). In Yui Daizaburō, Nakamura Masanori, and Toyoshita Narahiko, eds., *Senryō kaikaku no kokusai hikaku: nihon, ajia, yōroppa*. Tokyo: Sanseitō.

Nishiyama Tadanori. 1975. *Shihai kōzōron* (On the Structure of Control). Tokyo: Bunshintō.

Niwa Tetsuo. 1988. "Daikigyō no shinki jigyō wa naze shihai ga tsuzuku no ka" (Why Do the New Businesses of the Big Corporations Continue to Fail?). *Ekonomisuto* 10(18): 68–73.

Noguchi Yukio. 1995. *1940nen taisei* (The 1940 System). Tokyo: Tōyō Keizai Shinpōsha.

Nomura Masami. 1998. *Koyō fuan* (The Unstable Employment). Tokyo: Iwanami Shoten.

Odawara Ken'ichi. 1999. "Mane- haisen a-kyū senhan no sekinin o tou" (Hold A-Class War Criminals Responsible for the Defeat in the Money War). *Bungei Shunjū* 5: 292–295.

Odell, John S. 1982. *U.S. International Monetary Policy: Markets, Power, and Ideas as Sources of Change*. Princeton, NJ: Princeton University Press.

Ogino, Fujio. 1988. *Tokkō keisatsu taiseishi* (The History of Special Police). Tokyo: Sekita Shobō.

Okano Hiroaki. 1988. "Rizōto būmu wa honmono nano ka" (Is the Resort Boom Real?). *Ekonomisuto* 9(6): 50–56.

Okazaki Tetsuji. 1993. "Kigyō shisutemu" (The Company System). In Okazaki Tetsuji and Okuno Masahiro, eds., *Gendai nihon keizai shisutemu no genryū*. Tokyo: Nihon Keizai Shibunsha, pp. 97–144.

Okazaki Tetsuji and Okuno Masahiro, eds. 1993. *Gendai nihon keizai shisutemu no genryū* (The Origin of the Contemporary Japanese Economic System). Tokyo: Nihon Keizai Shibunsha.

Okazuka Eiko. 1987. "Koyō chōsei ka no shuntō o kangaeru" (Examine the Spring Strike During the Employment Adjustment). *Shūkan tōyō keizai* 2: 28–33.

Okumura Hiroshi. 1975. *Hōjin shihonshugi no kōzō* (The Structure of Corporate Capitalism). Tokyo: Nihon Hyōronsha.

Okumura Hiroshi. 1994. *Nihon kabushiki kaisha daikaizō keikaku* (A Plan for the Broad Reform of the Corporation). Tokyo: Kabushiki-gaisha Tokukan Shoten.

Okumura Hiroshi. 1995a. *Nihon shihonshugi no unmei* (The Fate of the Japanese Capitalism). Tokyo: Tōyō Keizai Shinpōsha.

Okumura Hiroshi. 1995b. *Hōnin shihon shugi no unmei* (The Fate of Corporate Capitalism). Tokyo: Tōyō Keizai Shinpōsha.

Okumura Hiroshi, Shibagaki Kazuo, Takeuchi Hiroshi, Nakamura Hideichirō, and Masamura Kimihiro. 1970. "'Zaibatsu' wa futatabi nihon o shihai suru ka" (Will *Zaibatsu* Control Japan Again?). *Shūkan tōyō keizai* 11(24): 6–15.

Okuno Masahiro. 1993. "Gendai nihon no keizai shisutemu: sono kōzō to kaikaku no kanosei" (The Contemporary Japanese Economic System: Its Structure and the Possibility of Reform). In Okazaki Tetsuji and Okuno Masahiro, eds., *Gendai nihon keizai shisutemu no genryū*. Tokyo: Nihon Keizai Shibunsha. pp. 273–291.

Ōkurashō. 1987 (1982). *Shōwa zaiseishi: shūsen kara kōwa made* (The Fiscal History of the Showa Period: From the End of World War II to the Conclusion of the Peace Treaty). Tokyo: Tōyō Keizai Shinpōsha.

Ōkurashō. 1991. *Shōwa zaiseishi* (The Financial History of the Showa Period). Tokyo: Tōyō Keizai Shinpōsha.

Olson, Mancur. 1982. *The Rise and Decline of Nations: Economic Growth, Stagflation, and Social Rigidities*. New Haven, CT: Yale University Press.

Otaka Kōnosuke. 1993. "'Nihonteki' rōshi kankei" ("The Japanese–type" Labor Relations). In Okazaki Tetsuji and Okuno Masahiro, eds., *Gendai nihon keizai shisutemu no genryū*. Tokyo: Nihon Keizai Shibunsha, pp. 145–182.

Ōuchi Hideaki. 1987. "Hajimatta atarashii sangyō tenkan" (The New Industrial Turnabout Has Started). *Ekonomisuto* 1(6): 20–26.

Pempel, T. J. 1998. *Regime Shift: Comparative Dynamics of the Japanese Political Economy*. Ithaca, NY: Cornell University Press.

Pempel, T. J., and Keiichi Tsunekawa. 1979. "Corporatism without Labor? The Japanese Anomaly." In Philippe C. Schmitter and Gerhard Lehmbruch, eds., *Trends toward Corporatist Intermediation*. Beverly Hills, CA: SAGE Publications.

Pierson, Paul. 1994. *Dismantling the Welfare State? Reagan, Thatcher, and the Politics of Retrenchment*. New York: Cambridge University Press.

Polanyi, Karl. [1944] 1957. *The Great Transformation: The Political and Economic Origins of Our Time*. Boston, MA: Beacon Press.

Posen, Adam S. 1998. *Restoring Japan's Economic Growth*. Washington, D.C.: Institute for International Economics.

Prestowitz, Clyde V. 1988. *Trading Places: How We Are Giving Our Future to Japan and How to Reclaim It*. New York: Basic Books.

Rekishigaku Kenkyūkai. 1991. *Tenkanki no sekai to nihon* (Japan and the World in the Transitional Period). Tokyo: Aogi Shoten.

Rinji Sangyō Gōrikyoku. 1932. *Jūyō sangyō no tōsei ni kansuru hōritsu kaisetsu* (Introduction of the Important Industry Control Law). Tokyo: Shōkōshō.

Rodrik, Dani. 1997. "Sense and Nonsense in the Globalization Debate." *Foreign Policy* 49 (Summer): 19–36.

Rodrik, Dani. 1998. "The Debate over Globalization: How to Move Forward by Looking Backward." Unpublished Paper.

Rosenbluth, Frances McCall. 1989. *Financial Politics in Contemporary Japan*. Ithaca, NY: Cornell University Press.

Roy, William G. 1997. *Socializing Capital: The Rise of the Large Industrial Corporation in America*. Princeton, NJ: Princeton University Press.

Ruggie, John G. 1982. "International Regimes, Transactions, and Change: Embedded Liberalization in the Postwar Economic Order." *International Organization* 36: 379–415.

Sabel, Charles. 1994. "Learning by Monitoring: The Institutions of Economic Development." In Neil J. Smelser and Richard Swedberg, eds., *The Handbook of Economic Sociology*. Princeton, NJ: Princeton University Press, pp. 137–165.

Sakaiya Taichi and Tahara Sōichirō. 2000. "Tetteishita shōnin kokka de ike" (Be A Complete Merchant Country). Chūō Kōron. April: 72–81.

Sakakibara Eisuke and Noguchi Yukio. 1977. "Ōkurashō-nigin ōchō no bunseki" (An Analysis of the Dynasty of the Ministry of Finance and the Bank of Japan). *Chūō kōron* 8: 96–161.

Sakane Tetsuo. 1958. "Dokusen kinshihō no kaisei hōkō ni furete" (On the Direction of the Antimonopoly Law Amendment). *Kōsei Torihiki* 7: 2–7.

Sanekata Masao. 1944. Tōsei kikō to kigyō keitai (The Control Mechanism and the Corporate Pattern). Tokyo: Daiyamondosha.

Samuels, Richard J. 1987. *The Business of the Japanese State*. Ithaca, NY: Cornell University Press.

Sasaki Kazuyuki. 1999. "Tokushū, Shitsugyō ka tenshoku ka" (Special Issue, Unemployment Or Change of Job). *Ekonomisuto* 4(13): 95–101.

Sassen, Saskia. 1991. *The Global City*. Princeton: Princeton University Press.

Schlesinger, Jacob M. 1997. *Shadow Shoguns*. Stanford, CA: Stanford University Press.

Schoppa, Leonard J. 1997. *Bargaining With Japan: What American Pressure Can and Cannot Do*. New York: Columbia University Press.

Sheard, Paul. 1989. "The Japanese General Trading Company as an Aspect of Interfirm Risk-Sharing." *Journal of the Japanese and International Economics* 3: 308–322.

Shibagaki Kazuo. 1987. "Sono haikei to dokusen kaisei mondai no tenkai" (The Background and the Development of the Antimonopoly Law Amendtment). In Heiwa Keizai Keikaku Kaigi, ed., *Kokumen no dokusen hakusho*. Tokyo: Ochanomizu shobō, pp. 155–189.

Shibata Tokutarō. 1996. " 'Daikyōkō hōshi taisei' wa iki tsumatta" (The Prevention System of the Great Depression is in Deadlock). *Ekonomisuto* 12(10): 72–74.

Shimizu Kaneo. 1940. *Nihon keizai tōseihō* (Japan's Economic Law). Tokyo. Genshōtō Shoten.

Shimotani Masahiro. 1996. Mochikabu gaisha kaikin (Lifting the Ban on Holding Company). Tokyo: Chūō Kōronsha.

Shinkawa Toshimitsu. 1993. *Nihongata fukushi no seiji keizaigaku* (The Political Economy of the Japanese Model of Social Welfare). Tokyo: Sanichi Shobō.

Shinkawa, Toshimitsu, and T. J. Pempel. 1996. "Occupational Welfare and the Japanese Experience." In Michael Shalev, ed., *The Privatization of Social Policy? Occupational Welfare and the Welfare State in Amreica, Scandinavia and Japan.* New York: St. Martin's Press.

Shōhisha Dantai. 1976. "Dokusen kaisei seifuan ni taisuru seimei" (The Statement on the Government Proposal on the Amendment of the Antimonopoly Law). *Kōsei torihiki* 5: 46.

Shūkan tōyō keizai. 1968. "Kanatsu no tōron shinkō no tame no mondaiten no shiteki" (The Issues for a Smooth Discussion) 7(3): 6–14.

Shūkan tōyō keizai. 1970. "Takyuka to daigetsushū no 'daini seki'" (Diversification and Centralization in the Second Century). 11(24): 16–23.

Shūkan tōyō keizai. 1986a. "Suru kaigai fudōsan tōshi ni supotto" (The Rush of Investments in Overseas Real Estate) 12(6).

Shūkan Tōyō Keizai. 1986b. "Kigyō gapei, shikaisha kyūshū ga kyūzō, oya no shūekiryoku bōkyō to seiban ittai nerau" (Corporate Mergers: The Increasing Buying out Subordinates Aiming at Strengthening the Profits and Manufacturing/Marketing Capacity). 10(18): 86–87.

Shūkan tōyō keizai. 1987. "Hajimatta risuku manei dai idō" (The Big Transfer of Risk Money Has Started) 3(14): 17–23.

Shūkan tōyō keizai. 1997. "'Sōki zeisei sochi' no mōten" (The Blind Spot of the Early Correction Strategies). 1(18): 78–79.

Soros, George. 1999. "Capitalism's Last Chance?" *Foreign Policy* 113: 55–66.

Soskice, David. 1999. "Divergent Production Regimes: Coordinated and Uncoordinated Market Economies in the 1980s and 1990s." In Herbert Kitschelt, Peter Lange, Cary Marks, and John D. Stephens, eds., *Continuity and Change in Contemporary Capitalism.* New York: Cambridge University Press, pp. 101–135.

Strange, Susan. 1986. *Casino Capitalism.* Manchester: Manchester University Press.

Suzuki Yoshio. 1974. *Gendai nihon kinyūron* (Money and Banking in Contemporary Japan: Theoretical Setting and Its Application). Tokyo: Tōyō Keizai Shiupōsha.

Tachibanaki, Toshiaki. 1998. *Nihon no keizai kakusa* (The Economic Inequality in Japan). Tokyo: Iwanami Shoten.

Takahashi Kamekichi. 1933. *Nihon keizai tōseiron* (On the Japanese Managed Economy). Tokyo: Kaizōsha.

Takenaka Keizō. 1996. "Nihongata ru-ru haibokusu notareai no nihon kokka senryaku toshite no mikokugata ru-ru" (The Dismantling Japanese Rule: American Rule as an Alternative National Strategy for Japan). *Ekonomisuto* 20: 60–66.

Taketa Shinji. 1985. "Kabutochō o yurugasu roku daichōryū" (Six Trends that Shake the *Kabutochō*). *Ekonomisuto* 10(14): 88–100.

Takeuchi Naokazu. 1974. "Shōhisha kara mita dokukinhō kaisei mondai" (The Problems of the Amendments of Antimonopoly Laws Seen by Consumers). *Kōsei torihiki* 3: 18–29.

Tanaka Jirō. 1942. "Keizai tōseihō no nerai to sono kiso kōzō" (The Goal of Economic Control Law and its Basic Structure). *Kokkagaku kenkyū.* 56(6): 103–126.

Tanaka Kakuei. 1972. *Nihon Retto Kaizōron* (On the Reform of Japan). Tokyo: Nikkan Kōgyō Shinbunsha.

Tanaka Masanori. 1986. *Nihongata ryūtsū shisutemu* (The Japanese Model of Distribution System). Tokyo: Chikura Shobō.

Teranishi Jūrō. 1993. "Meinbanku shisutemu" (The Main Bank System). In Okazaki Tetsuji and Okuno Masahiro, eds., *Gendai nihon keizai shisutemu no genryū.* Tokyo: Nihon Keizai Shinbunsha.

Teranishi, Juro. 1994. "Loan Syndication in War-time Japan and the Origins of the Main Bank System." In Masahiko Aoki and Hugh Patrick, eds., *The Japanese Main Bank System.* Oxford: Oxford University Press.

Tilton, Mark. 1996. *Restricted Trade: Cartels in Japan's Basic Materials Industries.* Ithaca, NY: Cornell University Press.

Tokunaga Shōjirō. 1985. "Kinyū no 'shōkenka kakumei' to yen no kokusaika" (The Financial Revolution of Securities and the Internationalization of Yen). *Ekonomisuto* 6(3): 104–112.

Tomabechi Shigemichi. 1985. "Honban mukaeru jimintō no naiju kōdai ronsō" (The Face Off Within the Liberal Democratic Party on the Debate on Increasing Domestic Demand). *Ekonomisuto* 3(21): 24–25.

Triffin, Robert. 1960. *Gold and the Dollar Crisis: The Future of Convertibility.* New Haven, CT: Yale University Press.

Triffin, Robert. 1964. *The Evolution of the International Monetary System: Historical Reappraisal and Future Perspectives.* Princeton Studies in International Finance, No. 12. International Finance Section, Department of Economics, Princeton University.

Tsuji Kichihiko. 1969. "Wagakuni sangyō shuchū no genjō to sono ruikeika" (The Present Situation and Typology of Japan's Industrial Concentration). *Shūkan tōyō keizai* 6(10): 100–114.

Tsuruta Shiburu. 1962. "Keiretsu yūshi no kōzai to sangyō kinyū no arikata" (The Merits and Dismerits of *Keiretsu* Financing and the Situation of Industrial Finance). *Shūkan tōyō keizai* (Summer Bessatsu): 36–43.

Tsuruta Toshimasa. 1982. *Sengo nihon no sangyō seisaku* (The Postwar Japanese Industrial Policy). Tokyo: Nihon Keizai Shinbunsha.

Tsuruta Toshimara. 1987. "Nihon wa seichō seisaku no suikyū ga kyūmu" (Japan Should Take the Growth Policy as Priority). *Ekonomisuto* 9(29): 36–41.

Tsūsanshō. 1957. *Sangyō gōrika hakusho.* Tokyo: Nikan Kōgyō Shinbunsha.

Tsūsanshō. 1964. *Shōkō seisakushi, Vol. 11: Sangyō tōsei* (The History of Commercial and Industrial Policy, Vol. 11: Control of Industries). Tokyo: Shōkō Seisakushi Kankōkai.

Tsūsanshō. 1989. *Tsūshō sangyō seisakushi, Vol. 5: Jiritsu kiban kakuritsuki (1)* (The History of the Policies of Trade and Industry, Vol. 5: The Establishment of the Foundation of Economic Independence, 1). Tokyo: Tsūshō Sangyō Chōsakai.

Tsūsanshō. 1990. *Tsūshō sangyō seisakushi, Vol. 10: kōdo seichōki (3)* (The History of the Policy of Trade and Industry, Vol. 10: The Period of High Growth). Tokyo: Tsūshō Sangyō Chōsakai.

Tsūsanshō. 1991. *Tsūshō sangyō seisakushi, Vol. 12: tayōka jidai (1)* (The History of the Policy of Trade and Industry, Vol. 12: the Period of High Growth (1)). Tsūshō Sangyō Chōsakai.

Tsūsanshō. 1993a. *Tsūshō sangyō seisakushi, Vol. 13: tayōka jidai (2)* (The History of the Policy of Trade and Industry, Vol. 13: the Period of High Growth (2)). Tsūshō Sangyō Chōsakai.

Tsūsanshō. 1993b. *Tsūshō sangyō seisakushi, Vol. 14: tayōka jidai (3)* (The History of the Policy of Trade and Industry, Vol. 14: the Period of High Growth (3)). Tsūshō Sangyō Chōsakai.

Tsūsanshō. 1999. "Iwayuru kashishiburi no jitsutai to kigyō katsudō e no eikyōni tsuite" (On the Actual Situation of Lending Difficulty and its Impact on Corporations). Japan Document Center, Library of Congress, pp. 1–7.

Uchihashi Katsuto and Gurupu 2001. 1995. *Kisei kanwa to iu akuma* (The Nightmare of Deregulation). Tokyo: Bungei Shunjū.

Uchihashi Katsuto and Yakushiji Taizō. 1993. "Mono zukuri ni shimei to hokoru o torimodose" (Taking Back the Mission and the Pride in Making Things). *Economisuto* 11(16): 34–38.

Ueda Hirofumi. 1987. "Senji tōsei keizai to shitaukesei no tenkai" (Development of Subcontract System Under the Wartime Controlled Economy). In Nihon Kindaishi Kenkyūkai, ed., *Senji keizai*. Tokyo: Yamakawa Shuppansha.

Ueda Hirofumi. 1995. "Senji keizai ka no shitauke kyōryoku kōgyō seisaku no keisei" (The Subcontracting in the Wartime Economy – the Formation of Cooperative Industrial Policy). In Hara Akira, ed., *Nihon no senji keizai*. Tokyo: Tokyo Daigaku Shuppankai.

Ueda Kazuo. 1993. "Kin'yū shisutemu-kisei" (The Financial System – Regulations). In Okazaki Tetsuji and Okuno Masahiro, eds., *Gendai nihon keizai shisutemu no genryū*. Tokyo: Nihon Keizai Shibunsha. pp. 35–60.

Ueda, Kazuo. 1994. "Institutional and Regulatory Frameworks for the Main Bank System." In Masahiko Aoki and Hugh Patrick, eds., *The Japanese Main Bank System*. Oxford: Oxford University Press, pp. 89–108.

Upham, Frank. 1993. "Privatizing Regulation: The Implementation of the Large-Scale Retail Stores Law." In Gary Allinson and Yasunori Sone, eds., *Political Dynamics in Contemporary Japan*. Ithaca, NY: Cornell University Press, pp. 264–294.

Upham, Frank. 1997. "Retail Convergence: The Structural Impediments Initiative and the Regulation of the Japanese Retail Industry." In Suzanne Berger and Ronald Dore, eds., *Naitonal Diversity and Global Capitalism*. Ithaca, NY: Cornell University Press, pp. 263–97.

Uriu, Robert. 1996. *Troubled Industries: Confronting Economic Change in Japan*. Ithaca, NY: Cornell Univeristy Press.

Vogel, Ezra, ed. 1975. *Modern Japanese Organization and Decision-Making*. Berkeley: University of California Press.

Vogel, Ezra F. 1979. *Japan as Number One: Lessons for America*. Cambridge, MA: Harvard University Press.

Vogel, Steven K. 1996. *Freer Markets, More Rules*. Itacha, NY: Cornell University Press.

Vogel, Steven K. 1999a. "When Interests Are Not Preferences." *Comparative Politics*, January: 187–207.

Vogel, Steven K. 1999b. "Can Japan Disengage? Winners and Losers in Japan's Political Economy, and the Ties that Bind Them." *Social Science Japan Journal*, in press.

Wada Yukako. 1998. "Japan's Welfare State and the Paradox of Equality." *Social Science Japan*, November.

Wade, Robert. 1997. "Globalization and Its Limits: Reports of the Death of the National Economy Are Greatly Exaggerated." In Suzanne Berger and Ronald Dore, eds., *National Diversity and Global Capitalism*. Ithaca, NY: Cornell University Press, pp. 60–89.

Wade, Robert. 1999. "The Coming Fight over Capital Flows." *Foreign Policy* 113: 41–54.

Wagatsuma Sakae. 1948. *Keizai saiken to tōsei rihhō* (Economic Reconstruction and Legislation for Control). Tokyo: Yūhikaku.

Weiss, Linda. 1998. *The Myth of the Powerless State*. Ithaca, NY: Cornell University Press.

Weiss, Linda. 1999. "State Power and the Asian Crisis." Unpublished paper.

Werner, Richard A. 1999. "The Bank of Japan and the Creation of the 'Bubble' in Japan." Unpublished paper.

Williamson, Oliver E. 1975. *Markets and Hierarchies: Analysis and Antitrust Implication*. New York: The Free Press.

Williamson, Oliver E. 1985. *The Economic Institutions of Capitalism: Firms, Markets, Relational Contracting*. New York: Free Press.

Williamson, Oliver E. 1987. "The Economies of Organization: The Transaction Cost Approach." *American Journal of Sociology* 87(3).

Wolferen, van Karel. 1990a. "Naze nihon no chishikijin wa hitasura genryoku ni suiju suru ka" (Why Do Japanese Intellectuals Come After the Political Power so Earnestly?). *Chūō kōron* 1: 68–98.

Wolferen, van Karel. 1990b. *The Enigma of Japanese Power: People and Politics in a Stateless Nation*. New York: Vintage Books.

Yakushiji Taizō. 1988. "Shin tsūshōhō o yomu to america ga miete kuru" (America Seen from the New Trade Law). *Ekonomisuto* 8(30): 40–48.

Yamada Shin'ichi. 1996. "Kikikan naki kiki ni sarasareru nihon keizai ima koso beikoku 'daikyōkō' no kyōkun ni manabe" (Japan which is Depressed in a Crisis Without a sense of Crisis Should Learn from the Lesson of the United States During the Great Depression). *Ekonomisuto* 12(10): 75–77.

Yamada Yūichirō. 1999. "Kieta 'daiwa shōken,' hajime no mochikabu kaisha no seisan" (The Disappearance of "Daiwa Securities": The Hope of Success of the First Holding Company). *Shūkan tōyō keizai* 4(10): 152–155.

Yamanouchi Yasushi. 1995. "Hōhōteki joron: sōryokusen to shisutemu tōgō" (On the Methodology: The Total War and the Integration of the System). In Yamanouchi Yasushi, ed., *Sōryokusen to gendaika*. Tokyo: Kashiwa Shobō, pp. 9–56.

Yashida Masashi. 1999. "Jibun no shiro wa jibun de mamore: toyota no koyō mo magarikado" (Take Care of Yourself: The Employment of Toyota Is Also Forced to the Corner). *Shūkan tōyō keizai* (Sangyō Tokushū): 50–51.

Yomiuri Shinbunsha. 1972. *Shōwashi no tennō* (The Emperor in the Showa History). Tokyo: Yomiuri Shinbunsha, Vols. 17, 18, 19.

Yoshii Kazuhiro. 1999. "Guru-pu kigyō zentai no kachi o jūshishita keieiei" (Toward Management that Emphasizes the Value of Corporation as Part of the Business Group). *Ekonomisuto* 4(5): 144.

Zenkoku Chūshō Kigyō Dantai Chūō-kai. 1975. "Dokusen kinshihō no kaisei ni kansuru iken" (Some Opinions on the Amendment of the Antimonopoly Laws). *Kōsei torihiki* 4(294): 30.

Zysman, John. 1983. *Governments, Markets, and Growth: Financial Systems and the Politics of Industrial Change*. Ithaca, NY: Cornell University Press.

INDEX